PIECES
OF THE
GAME

*The Human Drama of Americans
Held Hostage in Iran*

Col. Charles W. Scott
(US Army, Ret.)

Peachtree Publishers Limited

Published by
PEACHTREE PUBLISHERS, LTD.
494 Armour Circle, N. E., Atlanta, Georgia 30324

Copyright © 1984 Charles W. Scott

Manufactured in the United States of America

Design by Cynthia McDaniel
Art by John Breakey

First edition

Library of Congress Cataloging in Publication Data
Scott, Charles W.
    Pieces of the game.

    1. Scott, Charles W.   2. Iran Hostage Crisis, 1979-
1981--Personal narratives.   I. Title.
E183.8.I55S36   1984   955'.054   84-1735
ISBN 0-931948-51-7

For Kathy

But helpless Pieces of the Game He plays
Upon his Checkerboard of Nights and Days;
  Hither and thither moves, and checks, and
  slays,
And one by one back in the Closet lays.

LXIX Quatrain, Fourth
Edition
of the translation of "The
Rubáiyát of Omar
Khayyám of
Naishápur" by Edward
Fitzgerald.

CHRONOLOGY OF THE HOSTAGE CRISIS

WEEK 1   NOVEMBER 4-10, 1979

Iranian "student" militants seize the U.S. Embassy in Tehran and take hostages. They demand that the U.S. return the deposed Shah, Mohammad Reza Pahlavi, who had been admitted to the U.S. for medical treatment. Washington refuses. Iranian Premier Mehdi Bazargan and his cabinet resign. The U.N. Security Council calls on the militants to free the hostages, and President Carter orders all Iranians who do not comply with student visa requirements out of the country.

WEEK 2   NOVEMBER 11 - 17

Carter halts oil imports from Iran and orders a freeze on Iranian assets in U.S. banks.

WEEK 3   NOVEMBER 18 - 24

Thirteen Americans, women and blacks, and five non-Americans are released.

WEEK 5   DECEMBER 2 - 8

Iranians ratify a new constitution, making the Ayatollah Khomeini leader for life.

WEEK 6   DECEMBER 9 - 15

The Shah leaves the U.S. for Panama. The U.S. State Department expels 183 Iranian diplomats.

WEEK 8   DECEMBER 23 - 29

The hostages spend their first Christmas in captivity. Three U.S. clergymen visit the embassy. Iranian Foreign Minister Ghotbzadeh threatens to try the hostages if economic sanctions are imposed.

WEEK 9   DECEMBER 30 - JANUARY 5, 1980

The U.N. Security Council gives Iran until January 7 to release hostages or face sanctions. Secretary General Kurt Waldheim visits Tehran, but Khomeini refuses to see him.

WEEK 13   JANUARY 27 - FEBRUARY 2

New Iranian President Bani-Sadr discusses the possibility of negotiations. Canadian Embassy officials announce that they've smuggled six Americans out of Iran.

WEEK 14   FEBRUARY 3 - 9

The Iranian government says a commission will be formed to review alleged crimes of the Shah.

WEEK 16   FEBRUARY 17 - 23

A U.N. commission on the hostage crisis is formed. Any decision on the hostages is reported delayed until after the parliamentary election in Iran.

WEEK 19   MARCH 9 - 15

The U.N. commission visits Iran but is denied access to the hostages. Voting in parliament begins. The Shah will undergo surgery for an enlarged spleen.

WEEK 22   MARCH 30 - APRIL 5

Easter. Bani-Sadr offers to take custody of the hostages but fails to strike a deal with the embassy militants.

WEEK 23   APRIL 6 - 12

Khomeini announces that the militants will retain control of the hostages. The U.S. severs diplomatic relations with Iran and imposes economic sanctions. The militants threaten to execute hostages if military action is taken.

WEEK 24   APRIL 13 - 19

Carter imposes additional economic sanctions, bans travel by American citizens to Iran, and says that military action may be necessary. Barbara Timm, mother of a U.S. Marine held hostage, defies Carter's travel ban and flies to Tehran.

WEEK 25   APRIL 20 - 26

A U.S. rescue mission fails. The White House announces that eight American servicemen died in the abortive commando mission. The hostages are moved to secret locations to foil further rescue attempts.

WEEK 26   APRIL 27 - MAY 3

End of the sixth month. Secretary of State Cyrus Vance resigns, protesting the rescue attempt. Edmund Muskie replaces him.

WEEK 30   MAY 25 - 31

Skirmishes take place on the Iran-Iraq border. A new parliament convenes in Iran but postpones debate on the hostages.

WEEK 31   JUNE 1 - 7

In defiance of the travel ban, former attorney general Ramsey Clark visits Iran to confer with the Iranians. The conference adopts a resolution which condemns the American actions in Iran.

WEEK 34   JUNE 22 - 28

Iranian officials intimate that hostages not guilty of spying may be freed, but Bani-Sadr later issues a denial. The Shah, now in Cairo, is reported seriously ill.

WEEK 36   JULY 6 - 12

Amid Tehran newspaper reports that the hostages will be tried for espionage, hostage Richard Queen is released because of a neurological illness later diagnosed as multiple sclerosis.

WEEK 39   JULY 27 - AUGUST 2
The Shah dies.

WEEK 40   AUGUST 3 - 9

Iran's parliament orders state prosecutors to prepare for hostage trials in retaliation for the detention of Iranians in the U.S. American immigration officials order the release of 191 Iranians from U.S. prisons.

WEEK 43   AUGUST 23 - 30

Iran's U.N. representative says the hostage release process would be speeded up if the U.S. abandoned its freeze on eight billion dollars in Iranian assets.

WEEK 45   SEPTEMBER 7 - 13

Khomeini presents four conditions for the release of the hostages: return of the Shah's personal wealth, cancellation of U.S. claims against Iran, unfreezing of Iranian funds, and assurances of no future American interference in Iran.

WEEK 46   SEPTEMBER 14 - 20

New fighting breaks out between Iran and Iraq. Carter indicates no prospect for an early resolution of the crisis.

WEEK 47   SEPTEMBER 21 - 27

Major clashes take place between Iran and Iraq. The Iranian parliament calls for a freeze on the hostage issue. Muskie says he has assurances of Soviet neutrality.

WEEK 50 OCTOBER 12 - 18

Iranian Prime Minister Rajai flies to the U.S. for a U.N. Security Council debate on the Iran-Iraq war and suggests that a hostage decision is forthcoming.

WEEK 52 OCTOBER 26 - NOVEMBER 1

The Iranian parliament debates the hostage issue, but no decision is reached. Radio Tehran proclaims Iran "victorious over the U.S.," and announces that a "just method" has been arrived at for the release of the hostages.

WEEK 53 NOVEMBER 2 - 8

End of year one. Reagan defeats Carter in U.S. elections. The Iranian parliament votes to free the hostages if the U.S. meets Khomeini's demands. The militants claim to have turned over responsibility for the captives to the Iranian government. The U.S. hails the move as a major breakthrough.

WEEK 54 NOVEMBER 9 - 15

Algeria enters negotiations as a go-between and carries the U.S. response to Iran's terms to Tehran.

WEEK 56 NOVEMBER 23 - 29

Second Thanksgiving in captivity. Carter meets with his aides to clarify the U.S. answer.

WEEK 59   DECEMBER 14 - 20

Rajai says the hostages may be home by Christmas if America will guarantee that financial demands will be met. Iran demands that twenty-four billion dollars be deposited with Algeria as a guarantee for the return of the Iranian assets.

WEEK 60   DECEMBER 21 - 27

Christmas, 1980. The hostages broadcast messages to home. Muskie calls the financial demand unreasonable, and Iran counters that the hostages will be tried if the money is not paid.

WEEK 61   DECEMBER 28 - JANUARY 3, 1981

Iranian radio accuses the U.S. of procrastinating. Commentators say the hostages should be tried and executed. Behzad Nabavi, Iran's negotiator, says Iran will consider U.S. proposals if they are approved by Algeria.

WEEK 62   JANUARY 4 - 10

Three U.S. diplomats are moved to a secret location after being held in Iran's Foreign Ministry since the seizure of the embassy. Deputy Secretary of State Warren Christopher flies to Algiers, and Iran suggests that acceptance may come within a week.

WEEK 63   JANUARY 11 - 17

Iran no longer demands the twenty-four-billion-dollar deposit in Algerian banks, and parliament votes to accept third-country arbitration of the conflict. On January 15, new proposals are sent to Washington. Optimism grows for a settlement before Carter leaves office. U.S. and British bankers join Christopher in Algiers.

WEEK 64   JANUARY 18 - 24

The U.S. and Iran agree on the terms for the hostages' release. On January 19, Christopher signs the accord at 3:35 E.S.T. On January 20, after last-minute delays over fund transfers, the hostages leave Tehran on the four hundred and forty-fourth day of their captivity, minutes after Carter leaves office. On January 21, citizen Carter greets the hostages at Wiesbaden, West Germany.

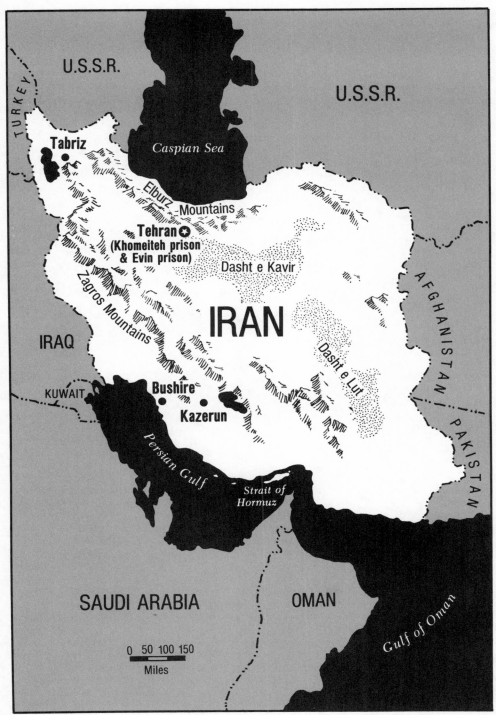

U.S.S.R.

U.S.S.R.

TURKEY

Tabriz

Caspian Sea

Elburz Mountains

Tehran ⊛
**(Khomeiteh prison
& Evin prison)**

Dasht e Kavir

IRAN

Zagros Mountains

IRAQ

Dasht e Lut

AFGHANISTAN

KUWAIT

Bushire

Kazerun

Persian Gulf

PAKISTAN

*Strait of
Hormuz*

SAUDI ARABIA

OMAN

Gulf of Oman

0 50 100 150
Miles

PROLOGUE

O East is East, and West is West, and never the
    twain shall meet,
Till Earth and Sky stand presently at God's great
    Judgment Seat;
But there is neither East or West, Border, nor
    Breed, nor Birth,
When two strong men stand face to face, though
    they come from the ends of earth!

> Rudyard Kipling,
> "The Ballad of East and
> West," 1889

This is a chronicle of a meeting of East and West as it was lived by two men, destined by fate to struggle as opposing pawns in an international chess game that held the world breathless for four hundred and forty-four days. At stake in this colossal contest were the lives of fifty-two American diplomats.

One of these men is a son of the East; the other is a product of Western culture and ethic. They are men with different, often diametrically opposed, views of the world in which they live. They are tossed together by a quirk of history — an "undiplomatic incident," a blatant, state-sponsored act of terrorism against an American embassy and its diplomatic staff. The name of the game is clearly blackmail. Or is it "justice" under the "eye-for-an-eye" code of the Islamic fundamentalists? There is no simple answer to this question. It depends on one's perception of history, beliefs, cultural background, politics, and, most importantly, one's allegiances.

1

One of these men is a radical, militant, Islamic fundamentalist; the other is a Christian who believes in democracy. One considers himself an Iranian patriot; the other is a loyal American. One is an aspiring professional revolutionary; the other is a professional soldier, essentially nonpolitical. One has been a political prisoner in the Shah's Iran; the other is a political hostage in the Ayatollah Khomeini's revolutionary Iran. One is the jailer; the other is his captive. One sincerely believes his militant actions are fully justified and will force the United States to return the deposed Shah to Iran for trial and execution; the other man believes none of this.

The Iranian has been taught and conditioned to loathe America. He considers the United States imperialistic, oppressive, amoral, scheming, and ungodly, with no redeeming attributes. The American has been a student of Persian history, language, literature, and poetry for half a lifetime. He has memorized all of the immortal — and most of the little-known — quatrains of the "Rubáiyát of Omar Khayyám," the Persian scientist and poet. He has a deep and abiding affinity for Iran and her people, which has been nurtured by his fluency in Farsi and his many close friendships with Iranians over a twenty-year period.

The only things the two have in common, at least in the beginning, are that both have a deep and abiding faith in God, both are romantics, and both have an insatiable curiosity, which leads them to listen for hours to each other's points of view. Through this dialogue they develop an unusual understanding, a mutual respect, and maybe even a glint of admiration for each other. Had the die of Providence which led their two countries to this confrontation been cast differently, they might even have become friends. But in their roles as combat adversaries, there never can be any genuine friendship, for one would execute his prisoner on a moment's notice, without remorse, if ordered to do so by his leader and idol, the Ayatollah Khomeini. And the other man would kill his captor equally as fast if it would enhance his chance of escape to freedom.

We in the Western world, especially in America, exert precious little time and intellectual energy in the pursuit of an understanding of "foreigners." We tend to view the world and analyze events only in our own terms of reference. We often fail to recognize that so-called foreigners also have hopes, aspirations, disappointments, frustrations, and sincere beliefs for which they are willing to lay their lives on the line.

We are, it is often said, the sum of our experiences. So, too, are foreigners. Whether or not we agree with other peoples' views, or they with ours, is not really relevant. What *is* important is understanding the motivations of other peoples while articulating our positions to them. Were we more successful in this endeavor, perhaps the polarization of millions against the United States would not be so easy to achieve for those who wish to see us fail. Many say this widespread antipathy toward the U.S. is the result of effective disinformation (or "black propaganda"), orchestrated by the Soviet Union and others who compete with us for the hearts and minds of men throughout the world. But all too often, it is a result of our insensitivity to the feelings of others. We do not seem to acknowledge the motivations, customs, and mores of foreigners. We often forget that to the rest of the world, *we* are the foreigners.

This book offers insights into the Iranian psyche, to the sincere beliefs of a large segment of the Iranian nation, which precipitated the attack on the American Embassy on November 4, 1979, the capture of sixty-six diplomats, and the imprisonment of fifty-two of these Americans for four hundred and forty-four days. It does not attempt to justify the Iranian rationale for this violation of customary international law, but only to explain it in the hope that an understanding of why it happened may reduce our vulnerability to a similar incident in the future.

This is also the story of one of the American hostages — his innermost fears, anxieties, hopes, reminiscences, mental excursions, and faith during four hundred and forty-four days of almost unbelievable stress and mental anguish. It is not *the* hostage story. No individual hostage is capable of telling *the* story. Because of the militants' practice of keeping all external information from the hostages and not permitting communication of any kind between them, there are fifty-two separate, distinct, and equally valid hostage stories. Each of us was, for varying reasons, not only a captive of the terrorists but also a prisoner of his own isolated fears and anxieties. There was, for example, the constant fear of trial and execution. And there was never any light at the end of our tunnel. When a man is sentenced to five years in prison, he can begin to count down from the beginning of his sentence. For the hostages, there was never any end in sight; we could only count the days we had survived. Our greatest fear was not knowing how or when the ordeal would end.

This is a story of endless months of darkness and constant terror, with its concomitant mental anguish. It is a story of thoughts of home, of God, of loved ones, and of one man's relentless faith in God and the United States of America. It is a story of a man finding peace with his God and, in an effort to retain his sanity, adopting a fatalistic attitude toward his destiny.

It is a story of singleness of purpose and striving to achieve goals in a crazy, totally unpredictable environment. It is also an account of Americans strengthening each other by maintaining their courage, their sense of humor, and the traditional American fighting spirit.

Finally, this book is the saga of an historic and stormy meeting of East and West, at the human level, by men and women who were "but helpless Pieces of the Game He plays."

4

Attack on
Fort Apache

1

AMERICAN EMBASSY, TEHRAN
SUNDAY, NOVEMBER 4, 1979

It is 5:30 in the morning, and, as usual, I'm awake before my alarm goes off. I'm a morning person, and even though it's still dark I'm wide awake and listening for sounds of Luigi, the ambassador's cook, in the kitchen directly below my room. When I hear him, I'll amble down the rear servants' stairs to the kitchen for my eye-opener cup of coffee and exchange of the latest gossip with my friend of twenty years, a man who knows the pulse of post-revolutionary Iran. Luigi speaks excellent Farsi and English, in addition to his native Italian. When I was here in the mid-sixties as an attaché, he was always good for a cup of coffee and a sandwich when I had time to drop by the kitchen of the Ambassador's residence.

But it is a very changed Iran I returned to seven weeks ago. The changes are obvious even in this spacious and elegant ambassadorial residence. In fact, I have come to view this grand house as a symbol of America's involvement in Iran — a revealing monument to the ebb and flow of our relations with this ancient people.

The ambassador's house, called simply "the residence," still has all of the diplomatic splendor one expects to find in an American mission abroad — priceless Persian carpets, a large staff of servants, expensive furnishings, and a big swimming pool. The stately building is surrounded by carefully manicured grounds, reminiscent of the finest estates in Beverly Hills. It has six bedrooms upstairs, each with a private bath. Mine is the "blue room," the second largest after the ambassador's suite, which is across the ornate hallway at the top of the main stairway. Bruce Laingen, the Chargé d'Affaires, occupies the ambassador's suite, since we do not have an accredited ambassador (the

Revolutionary government does not consider full diplomatic relations with the U.S. acceptable). My room has two large windows and double French doors leading to a private balcony overlooking the embassy grounds. From my balcony, I have a breathtaking view of the snow-capped mountains north of the city. But subtle shadows dull the glow of the omnipresent elegance.

Although damage from this year's Valentine's Day capture of the embassy by revolutionaries has been carefully repaired, the lingering odor of paint over the patched bullet holes in the informal dining room serves as an eerie reminder of the tenuousness of our position in the center of this city, populated by nearly four and half million embittered Iranians. All around there are reminders of better days, when lavish embassy parties and toasts to the Shah and our leaders were common. The Rosenthal crystal wine glasses, gathering dust in the magnificent china closets of the stately formal dining room, seem to cry out in the night, protesting their lack of use this past year. It's as though they sense the frustration of our degraded position here and miss the splendor of earlier days, when the Shah was King of Kings and America courted his good will and his favors — all, of course, in the national interest.

I can relate to the frustration many feel with our current position in Iran. I, too, am frustrated by it. I joined the Army at seventeen, spent six and half years as an enlisted man, then accepted a regular commission as an infantry officer. Although I have always loved the infantry, it was not enough to keep me busy and interested. The infantry clearly was my vocation, but I had a consuming interest in the Middle East, too. Fortunately, I was selected for the Army's Foreign Area Specialist Program. I studied the Middle East between tours of infantry duty, learned Farsi at the Defense Language Institute, and then served in Iran and in a series of intelligence-related assignments. For twenty years, I had the best of both worlds: I held all the necessary

8

infantry assignments to insure consecutive promotions, and I spent alternate tours serving in jobs concerned with U.S.-Iranian affairs. I studied the history, language, and culture of Iran, and spent considerable time here. Living in Iran and getting to know the people whetted my appetite for more study of this proud people, who had a great empire twenty-five centuries ago under Cyrus the Great. I studied the poems of Hafez, Ferdosi, and Omar Khayyám, memorizing most of the quatrains of Omar's "Rubáiyát" and developing an understanding of the Iranian psyche, customs, and mores. As an American, I have always sought to strengthen the ties between our two countries. That's why the vocally anti-American stance of the Iranian revolution has been such a disappointment for me personally.

Just last night, Master Sergeant Regis Ragan received a phone call from one of his Iranian friends, telling him that another demonstration against the embassy is planned for today. This is really nothing new; we've had more than our share of demonstrations since the Shah entered the United States for medical treatment thirteen days ago. But I'm uneasy nonetheless. I know the Iranian psyche and this revolution, and I'm not at all optimistic about our security and safety.

I have sensed from my first week here that the hard-line revolutionaries will not be satisfied until our embassy is closed and we all leave Iran. My first attempt to walk to the bazaar six weeks ago was a frightening and sobering experience. I always enjoyed rubbing shoulders with Iranians in the crowded marketplace before the revolution, but this time I was so intimidated by the glares and the caustic comments of the Iranians that I cut my walk short. Before I could make my way back to the embassy, however, a group of militant thugs approached me and asked if I was an American. I knew they were looking for trouble, so I told them, in German, that I was from West Germany and they let me go. But they made one point very clear: If I *were* an

9

American, they would be ready to rough me up a bit — or worse. One of the thugs advised me with a sneer that the Iranian revolution would not be over until "all foreigners and corrupters, especially Americans, are ousted!" He did not have to draw me a picture. What bothered me most was that he seemed to have the full support of the people in the street.

During supper with Bruce Laingen that night, our discussion had drifted to the revolution and the changes in Iran. Bruce is an articulate, distinguished professional diplomat who previously served as our Ambassador to Malta. He's in his late fifties, but clean living and a vigorous regimen of physical exercise have kept him not only boyish-looking, but youthful in his approach to life. Most of us on his staff consider him the ideal man to have in charge of a crisis situation. In a way, duty here is a constant series of crises, and we all know it.

Bruce had said he thought the worst was over, and that a gradual return to normal diplomatic relationships was on the horizon. After my fearful walk toward the bazaar that day, I didn't agree with Bruce's estimate at all. I told him of my encounter with the militant ruffians. "I hate to say it," I told him, "but the vibrations I'm getting indicate these radicals who persist in saying the revolution is not over may be more prophetic than we're willing to admit."

Bruce had called me a pessimist. I've been called many things over the years, but never a pessimist. On the contrary, because of my normal "can do" attitude, I've frequently been accused of being too optimistic. Recalling that conversation, I chuckle to myself. Oh, how I hope Bruce is right, and that I'm just being too cynical. But I have an intuitive feeling that he's wrong. Too often our diplomats lose contact with grass-roots movements because they deal almost exclusively with their counterparts in the host government who hold lofty positions and tell them what they think they want to hear. In spite of what the senior Iranian officials in the post-Revolutionary Government may be telling Bruce, I'm convinced that this revolution is not over. Perhaps for us, it's only the beginning.

Nonetheless, I have a job to do, and I find relief from the constant anxiety and uncertainty by keeping busy. And there is plenty to do. Master Sergeant Ragan and I have just finished an exacting mission that taxed our diplomatic ability and courage to the fullest. Ever since the revolution ousted the Shah — and the U.S. military assistance effort in Iran along with him — we had been trying to survey the garrison buildings previously occupied by advisory elements from the U.S. military. We finally got permission from both sides of the parallel Iranian governments and wasted no time. Ragan and I are the only Americans to set foot inside this installation since the revolution. We spent the weekend (Friday and Saturday in Iran) writing a report of the survey results to all interested government agencies in Washington. The message is detailed and complete. Ragan, who worked closely with the Iranian army for more than six years, did most of the work. He is an exceptionally competent noncommissioned officer, one of the best I've known in thirty years. Working with him during the survey was like watching a lioness returning to her lair after a long absence. He knew every room and storage vault in every building in the complex and what had been in it when the American evacuation was finally ordered.

Persuading the Iranians to allow us to do the survey, in spite of the tense political situation, was a coup of sorts. We are making *some* progress, I think to myself, in spite of the obstacles we're encountering from Washington. I recall how I had been told seven weeks earlier that there were no plans to admit the Shah to the U.S. His admittance, I was assured, would be out of line with our new strategy for Iran. We are trying to develop a new relationship based on respect, noninterference in Iran's internal affairs, and a recognition of the realities of the Iranian revolution. We believe we still need Iran and Iran still needs us, especially for military spare parts and as a check against Soviet expansion and subversion. The problem is in convincing the revolutionary government of these realities and overcoming their xenophobia. We know we're better off with Khomeini, even with his anti-American stance, than we would be with Iran in a state of total anarchy, which could be exploited by the Soviets. The U.S. government position is, essentially, better an anti-West government in Iran, as long as it's strong and independent, than a Communist or pro-Soviet government.

I'm convinced that this policy is in the best interest of the United States, and that's why I'm having trouble understanding the rationale for giving the Shah an American visa. To me, it is counterproductive to our government's goals and foreign-policy objectives for Iran. Admitting the Shah did not help what we're striving to achieve here in establishing this new relationship. In fact, it posed a major obstacle which may make our task impossible.

The aroma of freshly brewed coffee, carried up the back stairs by the soft morning breeze, breaks my pensive spell. Luigi is in the kitchen and it's time to join him for a leisurely cup before I shower and shave. Almost mechanically, I pick up my bathrobe and head down the service stairs. As usual, Luigi is sharp, friendly, and wide awake. He's a morning person, too, a pleasure to be with in these hours when most of the staff is still asleep. We always enjoy our early-morning exchange of gossip, facts, and ideas. It's obvious, as we greet each other, that Luigi is still very much concerned about the political intrigue generated by the Shah's admittance to the U.S. We both are puzzled by the fact that, at the last minute, the Islamic clergy ordered the big demonstration last Friday not to pass the embassy. Why the sudden change of plans? Were they concerned that the demonstration might get out of hand if it came here? Did they decide enough is enough, in light of earlier protests and demonstrations against the Shah's U.S. visit? Or are they trying to keep us off guard in preparation for a major action later? I ask Luigi if he has heard anything about a demonstration scheduled for today. He has heard nothing but says he would not be surprised; the streets are alive with rumors of a planned decisive action against the United States in retaliation for the Shah's U.S. hospitalization, and that clearly signals an action against us. We're the only target of opportunity. I remind Luigi of what happened on February 14, when militants stormed the embassy and held Ambassador William Sullivan and his staff hostage for the entire afternoon, until the Deputy Prime Minister, Dr. Ibrahim Yazdi, talked the militants into freeing their hostages. Luigi doesn't need to be reminded — he experienced it. Those who understand the revolutionaries know the embassy could be stormed again. Will the waving of this latest red flag before the revolutionary bull trigger a similar crisis? Luigi and I both fear it will, but we don't know when. We agree that the longer it takes the Iranians to play their hand, the more dangerous and dramatic it may be for us.

I glance at my watch and realize our talk has gone on longer than usual. There's much to discuss, and anything can happen — on this point, we both agree. I climb the long service stairs to my room to prepare for the day.

Breakfast in the informal dining room is always pleasant, well prepared, and elegantly served. Luigi takes great pride in presenting delicious, well-balanced meals. I'm struck this morning by the beautiful embassy china, with its gold border, shiny white background, and gold logo of the United States seal. I reflect for a moment on how proud I am to be here. It seems as if all my training as a foreign-area specialist on the Middle East and Iran was designed to prepare me for this position. I stare at the United States seal on my plate as I finish my scrambled eggs and bacon, and then I survey this beautiful room with its formal white dining set, well-tended house plants, and view of the terrace and pool area, and I'm proud to be here representing my country during these difficult days. I think for a moment how much I've progressed since my first tour in Iran in the early 1960s, when, as a junior assistant attaché, I was invited to the Ambassador's residence only for official parties. Now I'm living here. Things aren't all bad, I think, as I grab my suit coat and head out the back door for the two-hundred-and-fifty-yard walk down the tree-lined, manicured garden path to my office in the main Chancellery building.

It's a cool fall morning and there's a promise in the air of rain, always welcome in Tehran. I think of the beautiful fall mornings I have spent in this country during previous tours, and how our image has changed since then. No longer are we Americans the respected builders of modern institutions designed to bring Iran into the twentieth century. We have become the objects of Iranian hatred and resentment, forced to defend everything we've done here — and most of it has been for the good of those who make us the object of their ridicule and animosity.

Regis Ragan and Liz Montague, Bruce Laingen's secretary, are the only other early birds I see as I enter my office. The office is small, perhaps too small for the large mahogany executive desk, credenza, bookcases, and comfortable leather overstuffed chairs that adorn it. It's also dark and dismal. Most of the light which normally would bathe the room in the perpetual Tehran sunshine is shuttered out by a steel insert, filled with sand, that has been placed inside the window sill as a precaution against rocks, bottles, and small-arms fire. It serves as a constant reminder that we're in a very dangerous environment, and the days when this was a plush assignment are over. After the construction of these unusual steel "curtains" and the other security devices, installed in the wake of the revolution, our Marine guards dubbed the embassy complex "Fort Apache." An appropriate name, I think, considering the demonstra-

14

tions and riots that have interrupted the normalcy of this American outpost more than seven thousand miles from the U.S.

It is five minutes till nine as I stroll into the glass, sound-proof security cage in the room we use for staff meetings. Bruce Laingen enters at nine o'clock sharp, notebook and the latest embassy cables in hand. The meeting is low-key and uneventful. More discussion by Barry Rosen of the International Communications Agency on the violently anti-U.S. Iranian media releases. The introduction of Bob Blucker, a new arrival in the Economics section, resplendent in his gray tweed, three-piece business suit. Bob obviously was impressed by the visit he had with David Rockefeller in New York before coming to Iran, and he tells us all about it. He's a specialist on oil matters and is warmly welcomed by Bruce. This is his first tour in Iran, and he clearly is pumped up over his new position.

After the meeting, I question Bruce on the problem of diplomatic immunity for my six officers and noncommissioned officers in the Defense Liaison Office. This issue has become a sore point with me. Although we were sent to Iran with diplomatic passports, we have been denied diplomatic identification cards by the Iranian Ministry of Foreign Affairs. They contend it would be political suicide to grant diplomatic immunity to U.S. military personnel serving at the U.S. Embassy. The State Department personnel all have diplomatic immunity, and so do those working in the Defense Attaché Office. I've been disturbed by the cavalier attitude of those in the Political Section who contend that it really matters very little whether we have diplomatic immunity or not. They say I can always refuse to give my personnel driving privileges, thereby avoiding the risk of their being held in the event of a traffic accident. I maintain that in post-revolutionary Iran, we need all the protection we can get, and diplomatic immunity is absolutely essential. I have promised to notify the Department of Defense if this issue is not quickly resolved. Bruce tells me he's leaving immediately to meet with key officials of the Ministry of Foreign Affairs. He promises to discuss the immunity problem with them today. Mike Howland, from the security section, and Vic Tomseth, the senior political officer, leave with Bruce for the Ministry.

I return to my office still a bit frustrated over the immunity situation. After a short meeting with my staff, I resume my fight against the seemingly endless paper war. But my mind wanders, so I stop working for a minute and peer out over the steel-barred window of my office; all I can see is the sky because of the large steel box filled with sand, but I'm mesmerized by the puffy clouds.

My daydreaming is interrupted by the awesome chanting of a marching horde of demonstrators. The sound indicates they're about a block east of the embassy on Avenue Taleghani, about two hundred and fifty yards from my office window. The roar is more frightening as it increases in volume and intensity, rapidly closing in on the embassy. The mob is larger than usual and, from the sound, the demonstrators are marching in step and screaming anti-Shah, anti-America, and anti-Carter slogans. "Cheerleaders" with portable bullhorns prompt them. They have been conditioned to blurt out their hatred on cue. I hear what they're saying clearly as they move past my office window to the west: "Death to the Shah! Death to America! Death to Carter!" How many times have we heard these threatening chants in recent weeks? Don't these people ever tire of these haunting demonstrations? Is it really political activism or simply too much unemployment and too much revolution that keeps the mobs so volatile?

But this is not the usual demonstration in front of the embassy. About a minute after lead elements of the mob pass my office window, a Marine guard races through the second-floor hallway yelling, "They penetrated the motor pool gate!" I dash downstairs through the main lobby of the Chancellery to the glass-encased Marine guard post No. 1. I want a firsthand look at what's going on via the closed-circuit TV which monitors all entrances to the embassy complex. I'm appalled and frightened by what I see — Iranian militants scaling the embassy gates and quickly cutting the chainlocks with bolt cutters, admitting hordes of screaming and vengeful followers. This obviously is a well-planned and executed, militarylike operation. Their timing is perfect. Most are wearing cloth bibs with black and white stenciled silhouettes of Ayatollah Khomeini covering their chests — as though they're convinced that these images of their revolutionary idol will protect them from bullets. Or are they looking for a gun fight so they can air pictures of Khomeini's likeness bathed in revolutionary blood? Most of the attackers wear military field jackets, and some have a telltale bulge behind the shoulder — they're carrying concealed automatic weapons.

A uniformed Iranian National Policeman, posted to provide security for the embassy, is actually embracing and kissing the militants as they pour through the motor pool gate and run inside the embassy grounds.

There are no security forces in evidence from the Iranian government; they're doing nothing to repel our attackers. Embassy staff and locally hired Iranians scurry for safety. Most of them race upstairs to the second floor, which is protected by a heavy steel security door, designed to delay attackers so that sensitive communications equipment and classified documents can be destroyed. I watch all this on the closed-circuit monitors inside guard post No. 1, but suddenly the TV screen monitoring the main gate goes black, flashes, and then produces only an off-channel, snowy image. The swarming militants have knocked the camera off its perch, high up on the exterior wall of the Chancellery building. Marine guards around me load their

17

shotguns. One issues tear-gas grenades as his comrades hurriedly put on flak jackets. Gas masks also are being distributed.

I grab a gas mask, check it out quickly, and dash back through the maze of excited human traffic to my second-floor office. We purged our files and safes and destroyed sensitive documents as soon as the Shah arrived in the States, so there's no panic here. But tension and uncertainty are obvious. Master Sergeant Ragan, my oldest Iranian hand, knows irate Iranians are capable of doing almost anything when they're whipped into a frenzy, and he anticipates the worst. I'm also afraid. Our attackers want to force their way inside the building. Do they intend to kill us? Or will they try to burn the embassy and expel us all from Iran? How far will they go in their attempt to force the return of the Shah?

"The bastards are inside the Chancellery building!" screams a Marine guard shrilly as he Paul Reveres through the second-floor hallway. People are sitting along both sides of the wide hallway as they've been instructed to do by the security chief, Al Golacinski. It's like the final moments on the deck of the *Titanic* must have been. Disbelief and terror highlight the facial expressions of everyone, including the local Iranian employees who have been herded to the second floor for their protection. I stop a young Marine, Billy Gallegos, who's running down the hall. He is excited and scared, but he's more incredulous than anything else. "How'd they manage to get inside the Chancellery so damned fast?" I ask him. He's breathing hard and his huge chest is expanding and contracting rapidly. His eyes are dancing with fear as he pushes me, almost carefully, out of his way. "Sir, I've go to go. They came in through the only window in the basement that didn't have steel bars."

That window is on the west end of the building and was fortified only with a heavy steel mesh screen, which they cut through easily with the same bolt cutters used earlier to get inside the embassy gates.

I smell tear gas, which has been used to slow down the advance of the militants.

I sprint to the ambassador's office, where Ann Swift is trying to telephone the State Department Operations Center in Washington. John Limbert, who speaks fluent Farsi, also is on the phone talking to someone in the Iranian Ministry of Foreign Affairs. He's trying to get word of the attack to the Chargé, Bruce Laingen. He finally gets through to Bruce and the Iranian Chief of Protocol. The Protocol Chief assures him that Iranian security forces have been notified of the attack and are on the way. Protection of an embassy is the responsibility of the host government — in this case, the Iranians. It is *not* the responsibility of the United States Marine guards. They are armed too lightly and there aren't enough of them to conduct a deliberate defense. Their mission is to protect the ambassador and provide local security, not to defend in an "Alamo"-type defensive perimeter.

I relieve John Limbert on the phone and paint a picture to Bruce Laingen of what's happening. He is dismayed and puzzled as to why Iranian security forces have not already arrived. Navy commander Don Sharer rushes by and I draft him to survey the area and tell me what's going on so I can tell Bruce. There's no single vantage point where the entire situation can be observed, so Don darts from window to window assessing the situation and then passing his observations on to me. It's cumbersome and inefficient, but it's all we can do. Bruce is asking more questions than I can answer. "What do they want? Are they armed? How many are there? Have any security forces arrived yet?"

Ann finally gets through to the State Department desk officer. She is calm and appears to be low-keying the situation as much as possible. This is typical of the State

Department: Don't ever let the higher-ups know you've lost control of the situation at your embassy. Don is angry. Like me, he resents Ann's "don't rock the boat" remarks. The situation is bad, and if help doesn't arrive soon, it surely will get worse. There's no way to defend this embassy. We can only try to delay our attackers so documents can be destroyed. I ask Bruce's permission to destroy everything classified. He's reluctant to give the order for total destruction at this time. Nevertheless, destruction of highly sensitive papers already is in progress, despite the absence of a specific order.

Sergeant Paul Lewis of the Marine guards says the chief of security, Al Golacinski, is outside talking to the demonstrators. But from our window we see Al, his hands tied behind his back, being prodded around by the militants. He has been taken prisoner. We also see a number of off-duty personnel, who apparently have been brought here from the embassy apartments a couple of blocks away, being paraded blindfolded through the compound. Golacinski, surrounded by the terrorists, yells that the demonstrators only want to stage a sit-in to protest the Shah's visit to the U.S. If that's the case, why have they broken into apartments outside the compound and taken other Americans prisoner? I see terrorists with extra cloth blindfolds, handcuffs, and ropes cut into three-foot lengths — ideal for securing captives. A number of the militants are women, most of them in their early or mid-twenties, and all are wearing either the full-length black *chador* [a cape that covers the body from head to toe] or gray *babuska* [bandanna]. Although I see several automatic weapons brandished by the attackers, there still are no security forces in sight. Outside the Chancellery building, the militants are in complete control. I try to phone Luigi at the ambassador's house. An Iranian answers the phone shouting, "Death to the Shah! Death to America! Death to Carter!" I hang up and try to call the deputy chief of mission's house. Bill Keough, a giant of a man who was superintendent of schools in Tehran before the Shah's downfall, and who is here on a visit from Pakistan to reclaim books from the old U.S. High School library, has been a house guest at the residence. Again, a terrorist answers the phone and blurts out in English that the embassy "spy nest" has been taken over by the "people" and is closed. I hang up, fully aware of the gravity of our situation: they intend to take over the embassy and hold all of us prisoner.

Dick Morefield, the American Consul General, is on the phone from the Consulate, located inside the embassy compound one hundred and seventy-five yards west of the Chancellery. He asks for permission to destroy the visa plates, so they will not fall into the hands of the militants. He's talking to someone on the other phone in the Ambassador's office. He relays the message to me and I pass it to Bruce Laingen. Bruce asks about the situation at the consulate and I relay the question to whoever is talking to Dick on the phone. The militants are on the roof of the Consulate and threatening to burn the building if they're not admitted. I pass this to Bruce, and he orders me to tell Dick to destroy the visa plates if he's convinced the situation warrants. It obviously does.

It is more and more evident this is no spontaneous assault. Our attackers had good intelligence on the embassy. They hit all the critical gates and apartments, both inside and outside the complex, simultaneously, and they knew exactly which window in the Chancellery basement would be the easiest to penetrate.

Only one tear-gas grenade has been fired — the one I smelled minutes ago. I pass this information to Laingen. Bruce orders that no more grenades be fired and that we do nothing to raise the level of violence. At first, I disagree with his decison. I want to shoot it out with the militants. Indefensible though the embassy is, I still have a professional soldier's instincts — I prefer to go down fighting. But I realize more vividly than ever the urgency of our situation. After mentally racing over the limited options we have available, I'm convinced Laingen's decision is correct. Were we to get in a fire fight here, we all would be killed. This city's four million people are enraged at the United States. Knowing the volatility of Iranians in a mob, I'm convinced that if we shoot at them, we may kill a good many, but they will continue to attack and we won't have a chance. There's also the problem of the safety of other Americans in Iran. If we kill Iranians, I'm sure we will all be killed, but in addition, what reprisals will the mobs take against other Americans here?

After another carefully worded telephone "painting of the situation" for Bruce, he gives the order to destroy all sensitive materials, classified codes, and documents. The tempo of activity in the communications vault rises to fever pitch. Iranian female employees have been moved to the vault for their own safety. This is the last delay position available. Two of the older women are hysterical. They know their own people and what they're capable of doing when aroused. Just being near them is unnerving. I make my own survey of the second floor — all personnel not already captured have retreated to this final position. The second-floor hallway is crowded with distraught staffers. The senior Marine guard, Staff Sergeant Mike Moeller, and Colonel Lee Holland, the Army attaché and chief of embassy security during the earlier attack on the embassy, have told everyone to sit as low as possible in the corridor to avoid injury from objects thrown by the militants through the office windows on either side of the hallway. Lee looks almost comical in his flak jacket and combat gear. It really isn't funny, but for a moment I laugh at Lee and jibe him on his World War III apparel. He maintains his sense of humor but, as a Vietnam combat veteran and hostage during the earlier takeover, he also is very much aware of the danger we're in, and his concern penetrates our feeble attempts at

22

making light of the situation. Fear and uncertainty are etched on the faces of those cowering in the upstairs hallway. Our greatest terror is the unknown. What will they do to us after we're in their hands? It seems inevitable that soon we will be captured — it's only a matter of time — but we must do all we can, short of an actual shoot-out, to gain all the time possible to complete the destruction of documents and other sensitive items.

My feelings are more of frustration than of fear at this point. I feel helpless, no longer in control, and I mentally kick myself for accepting this assignment in the first place. God knows, I realized the risk involved, but I had been assured that the Shah was not going to be admitted to the States. I feel betrayed by my own government. Our officials in Washington don't seem to care: The Shah apparently is more important than a group of American diplomats. I'm angry, not only at our attackers, but at our government, too.

Al Golacinski is now outside the steel door which bars entry to the second floor. He pleads loudly with us to open the door. He says again that the militants "only want to stage a sit-in; they will not harm any of us." Al is under immense pressure and probably the threat of death if he doesn't cooperate with his captors.

All of a sudden, there's talk of surrender. I don't know where the idea got started, but certainly it had to be discussed sooner or later. I talk it over with Bruce and he asks about the progress in the destruction of documents. Bert Moore, the embassy administrative officer, says an additional forty-five minutes to an hour is needed to complete the destruction.

I smell smoke! I look at the safelike steel door from my position inside the Chargé's office, and I see smoke and flames rising menacingly from the crack underneath it. The Iranians have decided to burn us out. . . . But how much of this building will burn unless they use Molotov cocktails? The smoke gradually is getting more dense. I pass this information to Bruce, who again asks about the progress of the destruction. Bert Moore suggests that the communications vault door be locked and those involved in the destruction efforts continue with their work. The situation already is tense, and conflicting information on what's going on and what should be done adds to the confusion and chaos.

Sergeant Moeller, the senior Marine, orders his troops to break down their light weapons and lock them in the communications vault. The ammunition is to be locked in a safe to keep it out of the hands of the militants. Bruce suggests that John Limbert negotiate surrender terms with the militants, since he speaks fluent Farsi. Someone finds John and he agrees to talk to the "enemy."

The weapons have been locked in the communications vault as the dreaded moment of surrender inches closer.

Suddenly, without any specific order, I see the huge steel door open. Angry militants storm inside, grab the startled diplomats, tie their hands, and blindfold them. In less than a minute, at least two dozen militants are in the room. One is a skinny, loudmouth, hyperactive man in his late twenties with a wide space between his upper front teeth. He is livid and violent. He pummels one of the Marines and screams at him in flawless English, "Where are the guns?" The Marine and several other Americans tell him there are no guns. He's totally out of control with rage. "We know you have guns; we saw them. Give them to us or you will be killed!"

I'm still on the phone with Bruce, but I tell him it won't be long before I have to hang up. As three militants enter the room and charge toward me with fire in their eyes, Mike Howland, who is with Bruce at the Ministry of Foreign Affairs, picks up an extension phone and tells me to "surrender with my head held high in the Sullivan tradition." At the moment, I don't need that kind of bullshit heroics. I'm

angry, but I have no time to reply to Mike. My personal hell
is opening before my eyes.

The telephone is snatched from my hand and
I'm physically restrained by two terrorists. One asks, "Who
were you talking to?" I tell him I was talking to Ayatollah
Khomeini, and he said to let us go right away. The militant is
not in a mood for humor. He backhands me across the face
and repeats the question. This time I tell him I was talking to
President Carter. He doesn't like that answer, either, but one
of his comrades enjoins him not to hit me again. Two of the
terrorists are holding me as a third shouts in broken English,
"You are a CIA spy and you were sent here to destroy
Iranian revolution and put Shah back in power. You will not
speak. You are under arrest!"

"How the hell can I be under arrest?" I reply.
"You're not a cop and I, along with the rest of these Americans, am a diplomat. You have violated international law by
attacking this embassy." One of the heavies holding me
twists my arm and tells me to shut up. My hands are tied
quickly and very tightly behind my back, and I'm jostled out
into the hallway. The mob outside and in the stairwell is
screaming the usual death-to-everybody chants. We all have
our hands tied behind our backs, and our exodus from the
building begins. The militants order the Iranian local employees outside first. Then I'm pushed toward the steel door.
Unfriendly hands probe my pockets. Everything is ripped
from them, including my billfold. One of the militants spots
my military identification card. "You are colonel in American Army, huh? What are you doing here in embassy? You
are much in trouble. You are CIA, trying to overthrow
revolution. You will pay for your crimes against the Iranian
people." I say nothing; what's the use?

Suddenly, without warning, I enter a world of
total darkness and even greater uncertainty; I'm blindfolded. My blindfold, apparently made of heavy muslin, is
tied very tightly around my head, completely covering my

eyes and nose. Breathing is difficult from the first moment, and my quickened pulse seems to beat audibly inside my head as a result of the tourniquetlike blindfold. I'm led down the stairs and out through the shouting mob of militants, tripping and stumbling several times. The militant holding my right arm is mean, applying more force than necessary to push me through the mob toward some unannounced destination. Ironically, the militant holding my left arm and shoulder is soft-spoken and almost apologetic, telling me to be careful and advising me when we approach steps or other obstacles. He speaks to me in a whisper in broken English, "Do not worry; we will not hurt you. We only want the Shah for trial and execution. You will not be hurt at all. Please believe me." A Jekyll and Hyde act, I think, as I'm guided along the path I walked earlier this morning when I was still a free man.

I know the embassy grounds well enough to know where I am in spite of the blindfold, but I find the shouting and the whispering and the sneers of the militants we pass unnerving, to say the least. I'm shoved inside a building — apparently my home, the residence — up a few stairs and down a hall, then into a room which, judging from the echo, is very large. I guess it's the main living room. I'm pushed into a chair and my shoulders and feet are tied tightly to it. I hear others enter and receive similar treatment. In spite of our being admonished constantly not to speak, I hear an occasional voice speaking in English, either asking a question or complaining about our treatment. There are no answers, and in each case of a speaking infraction, the culprit is forcefully told to keep silent.

I hear weapons clanking in the next room. They're being either assembled or disassembled. A couple of militants pick up my chair, with me still tied to it, and turn it around. I'm aware that I'm now facing a wall. I hear Bob Ode, the eldest of the embassy staff employees, giving the militants hell. He's told to shut up, but he continues to tell

26

them he will not tolerate this outrage. Finally, he's quiet, too.

Time drags on and my mind plays tricks on me. I hear the whispers of our captors, who at times seem to be amused, elated, and then fearful. What are they going to do? How long is this to go on before they decide either to kill us or let us go? What do they expect to gain? A million questions race through my mind, partially as a result of fear and uncertainty, and partially as a result of the overly active mental process that accompanies the loss of one's sight. For the first time in my life, I'm being exposed to the frustration and fear of unbridled terror. I think of my family and home, and I have a gnawing feeling that I may never see either again. My head aches from the combination of tension and the tight blindfold. I ask aloud to have my blindfold loosened. Someone examines it and decides it's not tight enough. He unties it and pulls it even tighter. "Thanks a lot," I mutter.

As the afternoon drags on, I'm able to understand more of what my captors are saying — and I don't like what I hear at all. The militants are discussing the relative merits of leaving us where we are or moving us to some other area where there will be less danger of ricochet hitting one of them if they're ordered to shoot us. I feel my body trembling. I begin to pray. I pray for the safety and well-being of my family. Betty, my wife, knows only too well how Iranians can be riled up by political events, and she is keenly aware of the violence that is endemic to this society. I wonder if word of our capture has hit the news at home by now. What a terrible Sunday it must be for my family if it has. I also wonder what's going on in the Pentagon and the State Department. If things run true to form, they're going to be burning a lot of midnight oil. They probably will form a task force immediately to mull over various options to secure our release . . . or maybe they'll decide to take direct military action against Iran for this serious breach of international law and not worry about the embassy staff. My mind is racing through the options in high gear. I rationalize that they will not take military action, primarily because it won't resolve the situation and could provide an excuse for Soviet intervention into Iran. At least I hope that's the way they'll look at it. I also realize that I'm emotionally involved in this crisis, and my ideas and thoughts definitely are biased in favor of an option that will provide some degree of assurance of survival. But, given the mood of the Iranian people, I'm not convinced such an option exists. I pray for forgiveness of my sins, and I make a number of promises concerning the conduct of my life should God in His infinite mercy let me come out of this situation alive.

Prayer helps my mood, but it doesn't allay my fears. I'm too much a realist to think for one moment that this is going to end anytime soon in a way that we all want it to end. From the conversations I have overheard already, I'm convinced that our captors are willing to go for broke. They don't value our lives at all, and they place very little value on their own. They are radical Moslems bent on revenge for the perceived crimes of the Shah — and the United States government — against the people of Iran. We all work for this same United States government, so it follows, in their view, that we are criminals, too. Iranian revolutionary justice is a farce, from what we've seen of the wholesale summary executions that have taken place this year, and I wonder if we are going to become another statistic in the Iranian quest for blood and revenge.

The only thing I've been able to distinguish through my blindfold is that it's getting dark. I hear the click of switches shortly after one of the militants instructs another to turn on the lights.

I let out a yell in English that I have to go to the toilet. A militant rushes over and tells me to shut up. I ask him how I'm supposed to let them know when I have to relieve myself, and he replies that I'll be taken when it's my turn. Twenty minutes later, two guards untie my bonds, except for my hands (which are still tied behind me), and escort me to the bathroom. I count the steps and turns, trying to confirm our exact location. I'm led into a smaller room and my blindfold is removed and my hands untied. I was right — I'm in the powder room on the first floor of the residence, and judging by the turns and the distance from where my chair is located, I'm being held in the main living room of the residence. The bathroom is already a filthy mess. There's no toilet paper, and the presence of an Iranian water jug is ample proof that the militants are using the same bathroom.

After I'm retied to my chair, I hear an American moving about with the terrorists, assisting them in making a list of names of their prizes and the position each of us occupies. As the group approaches me, I recognize the American voice as that of Sergeant Joe Subic of the Defense Attaché Office. "This is Chuck Scott. He's a full colonel in the Army and speaks good Persian. He has been in Iran many times before and used to be an attaché."

Oh God, I say to myself, that kind of help I can do without. One of the Iranians grabs me by the chin and, almost spitting in my face, asks if I am CIA. I tell him I'm not, and he calls me a liar and moves to the next American. Staff Sergeant Joe Subic, U.S. Army, is actually helping them. I wonder what, if anything, they did to get him to cooperate.

Subic's nonchalance in giving information to the militants gives me a panicky feeling. As a professional soldier, he's supposed to know better. If he has caved in so soon, I'm afraid they may find out some things about my earlier associations with Iranians that will expose me to questioning and even more danger. I wish I'd had a chance to talk to Subic before the Iranians got to him, but it's too late now. Mainly, I wish they didn't know that I've been here before and that I speak the language.

It must be after nine in the evening when I'm approached by a guard who asks if I'm hungry. I tell him I am. He unties me and moves me to the kitchen, where my blindfold is removed. Several Iranians and three other Americans are seated at the kitchen table eating Iranian bread and white goat cheese. I join them and eat in silence. No discussion is allowed among the Americans, and when I look over at Colonel Tom Schaefer, I'm told not to look at the others — just hurry up and eat.

Later, after being tied to my chair again for about an hour, a militant asks if I want to sleep. I tell him yes, I'm tired, so he unties the bonds holding me to the chair and tells me to lie down on the marble floor. My feet are retied and my hands are still bound behind my back. It's cold on the floor, and I can hear every movement in the room. I'm uncomfortable, but I'm exhausted and emotionally drained. I decide to make the best of a bad situation and try to sleep.

It doesn't work, though. I'm too tense to sleep, as my tired and confused mind relives the events of the day. I'm also angry at our intelligence organizations for not uncovering the plan to attack us. Our failure to target and penetrate the Shah's opposition groups before the revolution has a direct bearing on our situation tonight. We relied too much on the Imperial Iranian Intelligence organizations, such as SAVAK, to provide intelligence on these organizations for two principal reasons: first, as an economy-of-force measure, since SAVAK was supposedly doing a good job of reporting; and second, because we didn't want to offend the Shah by conducting intelligence operations on his opposition right under his nose.

As a result, we got only the information on the opposition that the Shah wanted us to have. Therefore, we had no network of sources and informants on the ground and operational when the Shah was ousted. While I'm sure we're still getting information on the Khomeini government by sophisticated means, such as electronic intercepts, we are not getting the kind of day-to-day HUMINT (human intentions intelligence) we need on groups such as the one that staged the attack today. It would take a tremendous amount of money and personnel assets to penetrate all the political elements in Iran that have the capability to disrupt the operation of our embassy. But it would have been nice to know that this was going to happen. If nothing else, we could have deserted the embassy and let them have it, while we tried to exfiltrate or hide until we could arrange to get out of the country through one of the other embassies. But I realize it's wasted energy to dwell on what might have been.

I always thought I had a pretty good understanding of the Iranian people — their motivations, aspirations, likes, dislikes, and fears — but today's events make me wonder. How far will these militants go? If they're serious about holding us until the Shah is returned for trial, we're in for a long ordeal. In spite of the long list of friends I have made in the country — or, perhaps, because of this fact — I'm well aware of the Iranian people's hatred of the Shah and of our government for supporting him. I know from my own experience how difficult they can be in negotiating, and, as I try to find relief from my unknown hell in fitful sleep, I'm far from optimistic that this situation can be resolved without bloodshed.

2

AMERICAN EMBASSY, TEHRAN
NOVEMBER 4 - 25, 1979

I've been dozing only a short time when I'm jostled awake by a nasty-voiced Iranian militant.

"You are Colonel Scott of CIA. Get up! On your feet!"

I try to comply with his demand, but my feet are tied and my wrists are bound tightly behind my back. As I struggle to get up, the owner of the threatening voice kicks me in the ribs. The pain is sharp and searing; I gasp for breath as strong hands drag me to my feet. My blindfold is ripped off by the hate-filled terrorist. He spits in my face. As my eyes begin to focus, I see that he's even uglier and more livid-looking than his voice betrayed. His eyes are bulging and he reeks with body odor. He spits in my face again and sneers, "You are Colonel Scott of CIA. Do not try to lie. We know who you are."

With all the calm I can muster, I tell him, "I am Colonel Scott, United States Army. I am not with the CIA."

"You will come with us, Mister Colonel Scott. You are in much trouble!"

The ropes are removed from my ankles, and again I'm tightly blindfolded. The stiff cloth is much too snug, and I can feel my pulse fighting to circulate blood to my head. My temples are throbbing in protest, my head feels light, and my rib cage is flashing a message of pain to my brain, protesting against my captor's solid kick. I'm led out of the room and down the hallway. I stand and wait silently; guards on either side of me firmly grip my upper arms, as if I may race off into the night to freedom — with blindfold, tied hands, and aching ribs. I smell stale kitchen odors — the residual scent of the morning's bacon and the bread and goat cheese we were given earlier by our captors. I assume this is Luigi's kitchen. It seems like an eternity ago when I met with him earlier this morning. After about ten minutes, I'm escorted outside the building, down the three steps from the rear kitchen door, to the asphalt path leading to the Chancellery.

It's raining and the temperature has dropped. But after being tied up so long, it feels good. It reminds me of other nights at home in Stone Mountain, Georgia, when I would walk my dog Heidi and enjoy the serenity of my neighborhood, with its beautiful homes, well-tended lawns, and freedom. The gentle kiss of the fresh, cool air is reassuring. It seems to be God's way of soothing my anxiety and pain and telling me, "These things too shall pass."

Suddenly, I'm pushed forward and down the path by my guards in what I believe is the direction of the Chancellery. There's a demonstration going on some distance from where we started our oudoor walk; it gets louder as we get closer to the Chancellery and the main street in front of the embassy, Avenue Taleghani. A bullhorn incites the crowds to louder condemnation of the Shah, President Carter, and the United States government.

"Death to the Shah! Death to Carter! Death to America! Death to the hostages!"

I can't believe my ears. They're shouting, "Death to the *guerenganha*" — the *hostages*. They're calling for our execution. There's a sudden increase in my pulse rate and my breathing.

Outside the gates, the crowds are being whipped into a frenzy by the cheerleaders with their bullhorns. I completely forget the rain and the cool night air and concentrate on the desperation of my situation. I'm certain that I'll never leave this place alive. There seems to be no way this thing can end without all of us being killed.

The two-hundred-and-fifty-yard walk to the Chancellery seems like the proverbial last mile.

"E-stairs," warns the guard to my right, as I stumble on the bottom step and hear the heavy steel security door open with a creak. They lead me inside the Chancellery. One of the guards warns his comrades not to speak Farsi around me because I understand the language. I knew my speaking Farsi would be a liability once they discovered it, and I curse Joe Subic for giving our captors this information.

There are sounds of activity everywhere inside the Chancellery. As we move down the corridor, all the voices I hear are speaking guttural Farsi. I hear hammering and the noise of furniture and heavy steel safes being moved. An electric drill buzzes away against hard steel. They apparently are cutting the safes open. I also hear what sounds like an acetylene torch burning through steel, and I can smell the acidic odor of burning paint and acetylene.

I'm led into a room and forced to perch on what seems to be a high stool. My feet are tightly tied together with rough rope, and then my blindfold is checked to make sure I can't see anything. I can't.

I sense there are others in the room watching me, but there's not a sound except for the background noise of the hammering and cutting and the haunting chants of the demonstrators outside the embassy grounds. I can see enough light through the blindfold to tell that the room is well lighted. I try to stay as calm as possible. I'm sure they're watching, and I assume they're trying to frighten me. They have succeeded, but I don't want them to know it. Minutes are like hours, but I sit silently atop my stool and wait. It's very uncomfortable, and my back and shoulders begin to ache. My ribs hurt with each breath, and the tight ropes have cut off the circulation in my hands, which are alternately aching and numb. I'm afraid and physically exhausted, but I know I must prepare myself mentally for what is to come.

These people have a long and undistinguished history of torture and cruelty. They seem to take sadistic delight in inflicting physical pain and mental anguish on each other, as well as on their enemies. I have just become one of their enemies, and I know that I'm in for a long and grueling interrogation. I also know that every man has his breaking point, and I worry about how I'll react under great pressure or pain. I pray for strength to get through this ordeal, and pray that I will not do anything that will shame me or my country. In spite of fear and fatigue, my adrenalin is flowing.

As I pray, I'm distracted by thoughts of a book which I read years ago called *Brainwashing*. I'm amazed at how God seems to give us special strength when it's really needed. I recall pertinent paragraphs and ideas from the book almost verbatim. The writer postulated, based on a series of studies of brainwashing survivors, that those who had managed to retain their sanity and resist the brainwashing better than others had used similar techniques. He theorized that under severe physical and psychological stress, the human willpower can become a "floating line"; that is, one may rationalize and consent to do or say things he never would do or say under normal circumstances. Therefore, one must establish goals and objectives before the brainwashing and physical abuse begins, so that a standard is established and retained, and the line does not float, even under the most severe physical or psychological pressure. The theory makes good sense to me. I know I must establish realistic and achievable goals quickly, if I'm to withstand the rigors of interrogation which I know are coming. I try to analyze my situation logically in order to find appropriate goals. We are not at war with Iran — at least not yet. Does the military code of conduct apply? Do I give them only my name, rank, serial number, and date of birth? If they get physical right away, am I being foolish to persist in giving only this information? My job here is strictly an overt liaison mission, and I have been involved in nothing against their government.

But I know they'll be trying to find some excuse for having taken over our embassy. I'll have to be very careful what I say. I'm convinced that I'll never see home again, but if I do somehow get out of this alive, I must conduct myself so I can hold my head high for the rest of my life. My main objective must be to maintain my integrity. To do this, I'll have to achieve my goals. I quickly outline them:

(1.) No matter what they do to me, I will not write anything for them. I know they would love to flash some handwritten document before the news media. No matter what I wrote, it would be considered some sort of confession. Besides, if I consent to write something for them, it'll be interpreted as a sign of moral weakness on my part, which they will exploit. I vow I will not write anything for them, period.

(2.) I will not do or say anything that could prove embarrassing to my country. I'm sure they'll try to get me to condemn the Shah and ask (or plead) for his return to Iran for trial. I have an obligation as a soldier to remain loyal to my country, even in a messy situation like this. I was not a fan of the Shah, because I'm sure he was guilty of many violations of human rights. But that's all beside the point now — I know where my loyalty must be. I realize that my personal feelings about the Shah and our President's allowing him to come to the United States will make this goal difficult to achieve. However, it must be a goal and I must achieve it.

(3.) I will not do or say anything that could possibly bring added danger or pressure on my fellow hostages. I only wish I had had a chance to talk this one over with Joe Subic. His roll call, conducted for the benefit of our captors, is probably responsible for my being awakened from sleep and brought here, obviously for interrogation. Joe must have been scared to death to provide that kind of help to these characters. I hope he soon learns this is not the way an American fighting man conducts himself when he's taken prisoner. Maybe that's his problem. Perhaps Joe simply does not yet realize that these people *are* the enemy. And that leads to my final goal.

(4.) I will remember that I'm an American soldier and these militants are the "enemy" — in every sense of the word. We are being held hostage — a terrorist act and a clear violation of international law — and no matter what they claim their grievances to be, they are the *enemy*.

It dawns on me, as I go over the goals I've just set, that two of them are in the Military Code of Conduct, the written code that tells military men how they must act if they become prisoners of war. I try to remember the rest of the code. Have I omitted anything important? I can't think clearly, but I'm sure that I have covered all the bases. I must remember to stick to these goals no matter what happens to me. I vow to myself and to God that I will not be weak. In effect, I have psychologically written myself off, anyway. I would rather die than live knowing that I failed to measure up to my standard of conduct. I am resolved that my line will not float.

At least I know what to expect. My last assignment as a noncommissioned officer was as an instructor in interrogation techniques at the Army Intelligence School. I also have been trained in evasion and escape and counterinterrogation techniques. I have been an interrogator, but I've never been on the receiving end, except in an academic environment.

Suddenly my blindfold is removed, and I can see around the room — I'm in the office of Bert Moore, the embassy administrative officer. The office has been rearranged to facilitate interrogations. On either side of Bert's big executive desk, a table has been added. Behind the desk and each of the tables sits a mean-looking Iranian interrogator. The one in the middle, who appears to be the leader, is a tall, broad-shouldered man about thirty to thirty-five years old. He's wearing a dark gray ski sweater and blue, well-pressed, civilian slacks. He is clean-shaven and speaks in excellent Americanized English. He stares at me and says softly, "Hello, Mr. George Lambrikis; how are you? Do not waste time telling me you are Colonel Scott. We know who you are."

"My name is Charles W. Scott," I reply. "I'm a colonel in the United States Army. I'm not George what's-his-name." I instantly make a conscious decision not to say George's last name. I'm not going to let them beat me down by repetition.

"Search him!" commands the chief interrogator.

Three militants from the gallery of about ten spectators seated on the floor behind me come forward, untie my hands and feet, and pull me to a standing position. I notice my watch and billfold on the table in front of my interrogators, along with the rest of the contents of my pockets, which were taken from me as soon as I was captured.

The chief tells me to strip, except for my shorts.

"You can go to hell. I'm not going to undress for a bunch of terrorists," I respond.

"If you do not, we will undress you. We only want to search your clothes. Take them off!"

"Go to hell!"

The militants who are holding me look to the leader for instructions. They don't have to wait long — he tells them to remove my clothes. They hesitate for a moment, then ask for two others from the rear to help them. I realize there's no point in fighting them, so I untie my shoe laces and remove my shoes, socks, slacks, shirt, tie, and T-shirt. My kelly-green sports jacket, which I had left on the rack in my office, is dumped on the table in front of the chief.

"We will see what you are trying to hide," says the chief as he begins to check my clothing and personal items. My belt is cut apart along the seam with my own pocketknife. The heels are removed from my shoes and the innersoles are ripped out. The lining is torn out of my favorite sports jacket, and my billfold is ripped to pieces.

The chief interrogator examines my Rolex GMT Master. "This must have a radio or homing device in it. Take the back off and check it out." He hands my watch to one of the militants, who produces a pair of pliers, a screwdriver, and a large butcher knife. He trys to pry the back off my watch with the screwdriver but fails. Then he gives the butcher knife a try with the same result.

"How does the back come off this watch?" says the chief.

I tell him that a special tool is required to break the factory seal. He says that's a lie — it must be specially sealed by the CIA to hide a radio or some other spy device.

They continue to search the rest of my belongings, but my watch remains center stage. They're convinced there is something in it, but they're unable to get it open. I'm sure they're going to break it before they give up. One militant holds the watch on the table while another poises the screwdriver against the back, hitting it with the side of his steel pliers, which he uses as a substitute hammer. At first I cringe, not wanting them to destroy my twenty-year-old prized timepiece. Then I realize I probably never will get it back, even if we're released. I stand in my shorts, watching the ridiculous proceedings with a degree of detachment, on the verge of laughter. But it's not funny to them. They've seen too many spy movies, and they couldn't be more serious.

Finally they give up on my watch, my clothing is returned, and I'm told to dress quickly. My shoes and belt are not returned. Nor is my billfold or the other items from my pockets. After I dress, I am retied and seated again on my high stool.

The Iranian positioned behind the table to my left addresses the leader in Farsi. He calls the leader

Hossein, so I assume that's his name. They whisper to each other for a minute and then Hossein speaks directly to me in English. This time his tone is louder and more intimidating. "You are under arrest, and you are in big trouble! We know who you are and what you were doing in Iran. If you do not cooperate with us, tell the truth on all matters, and admit who you really are, you will be killed by the Iranian people. Your name is not Scott and you were not born in the United States. Your name is George Lambrikis, you were born in Greece, and you have worked for many years for CIA and the Shah's SAVAK to oppress, torture, imprison, and kill innocent Iranian people. We have proof of this from files in the embassy and from some of your friends who have already given us information. We do not want to have to hurt you, or to kill you, but that is up to you. You must first admit who you are. What is your name?"

"My name is Charles W. Scott."

Hossein is under control, but he's faking impatience. "That is a lie. You are George Lambrikis and you work for CIA! You must tell the truth; we do not have time to listen to your lies. Again, what is your name?"

"My name is *still* Charles W. Scott."

Hossein asks very calmly in a softer tone, "What are you doing in Iran this time, Mr. Lambrikis? Why did CIA send you here? Before you answer, let me tell you this: We already know who you are and what you were doing in Iran. George Lambrikis, you were sent here to set up a military coup to get the Shah back in power so more innocent Iranian people can be put in prison and tortured." Hossein's tone and the tempo of his speech rise as he begins to threaten me. "We will make it very hard for you if you do not stop with your lies and tell us all the truth!"

"Look, no matter what you say, my name *is* Scott. I was not sent here by the CIA, and I'm not employed by the CIA. If you want confirmation of my name and what I'm doing in Iran, ask your own government. I never even heard of the man you're talking about, George . . . whatever his name is."

A rotund, apelike figure sitting to Hossein's right interjects his two cents. He apparently does not speak English, and obviously is impatient with the delay. He's wearing a black sweater and a black ski mask so that I can't see his face. He sneers in guttural Farsi, "Look at this imperialist pig! He speaks only lies. He is playing with us, and he is trained to tell lies when he is asked questions. Let's save time and get his blood flowing *now*. It is useless to try to treat him nice. In a few minutes I can have him telling *only* the truth."

Hossein is playing the good guy. "George, did you understand what my friend said? We know you speak fluent Farsi, so you must have understood. I am being nice to you, but if you persist with only lies, I will let my friend talk to you in his own way. From now on, you will speak only Farsi!"

I decide not to give them any unnecessary advantage by speaking Farsi. Instead, I reply calmly in English, "That's right, I speak some Farsi, but not enough to answer your questions. You want to talk to me, but I don't want to talk to you, so I refuse to be placed at a disadvantage by speaking Persian to you."

There is a heated dialogue in Farsi between Hossein and the man in the ski mask who grunts like a pig — I mentally name him Pig Face — concerning the merits of getting right into some form of torture. I assume this is for my benefit — a pre-planned act, intended to intimidate and scare me into giving them information.

"Mr. Lambrikis," Hossein says, "your American friends have already told us you speak good Farsi, and we have your false records under the name of Scott which you were using as a cover to hide your real identity, so you could make contact with counterrevolutionaries and set up a coup. You might as well tell the truth and speak Farsi. It will save our time and yours, too. And it may even save you a lot of pain. Or even your life, which is in our hands."

Hossein pauses for several minutes, staring at me. The others are silent. Then he adds, "You have been to Iran before; you know how easy it is to get rid of a body in Tehran. Remember, right now your government does not even know we have arrested you. We can kill you, dump the body, and never admit we even saw you."

There's truth in what he says about hiding a body in Tehran. I know they can kill me, but I have no choice; I try again. "I'm telling the truth. I speak Farsi, but it's rusty. I haven't used it in years. I know you can kill me, but there is nothing I can do about that. I am not George what's-his-name; I am Charles W. Scott."

Finally, the third interrogator speaks in whispers to Hossein. He's a well-dressed, muscular man in his mid-twenties who speaks English with a slight British accent, such as one hears among Jordanian Arabs and residents of the West Bank. His Persian is far from fluent; he speaks only to Hossein, and he speaks in English. He must be an observer or advisor to the militants, I figure. He tries to stare me down for a full five minutes before he blurts out his threat directly to me in English. "Mr. Lambrikis, you are not cooperating. You must cooperate or you will die, slowly! We will treat you like the Jews treat our men who are fighting for the return of their homeland, and you will not like it. You must be polite and answer all the questions you are asked or you will be in bigger trouble. Do you understand, Mr. Lambrikis?"

He is shouting as he moves from behind the table, pointing his finger at me until he's directly in front of me. Then he grabs the front of my shirt and begins to shake me. "The Shah tortured and killed thousands of Iranians who were innocent of any crime! The same thing can happen to you if you do not stop your lies! Do you want to die? Are you not ashamed of your government's support of the Shah's regime? Your CIA brought all the latest techniques for torture to Iran and trained SAVAK in their use here and in the United States. You will pay for these crimes against the Iranian people! Now, no more lies; tell the truth! What is your name and what were you doing against the revolution?"

My mind is racing. I'm convinced I will not live through this interrogation, but I reason that each moment I can stall them with idle chatter is another moment of life. God, how tenuous it all seems at this moment. But in spite of my overwhelming sense of fear and uncertainty, I'm also angry. I will not give in. If I'm going to die anyway, I might as well go out like a soldier — loyal to my country to the end. If I were to do otherwise, I might as well be dead. The ghosts of thousands of American servicemen who suffered as prisoners of war without capitulating to their captors would haunt me forever. I'm on the front line, and I know my severest test as a soldier and as an American is taking place right here. I will not back down, but I have to be very careful about what I say.

I speak directly to the man with the British accent. "You speak of torture during the Shah's reign, and you threaten me with the same thing. You're brave, pushing me around when I'm tied and can't defend myself. How can you talk about torturing someone who is a diplomat in your country?" I tell him if he does this, he's just as bad as he claims the Shah was. I also tell him that the United States has been working hard to establish a new relationship with the revolutionary government, and that we wanted to build this new relationship on mutual respect, recognizing the new realities of post-revolutionary Iran. I tell him our government has supported the provisional government because we did not want to see Iran without a government, in a state of anarchy. We believe that if this were the case, his neighbor, the Soviet Union, would move in. Even though he resents America's support of the Shah, the Shah is gone and today is a new day. They do not speak when I pause, so I continue;

the more I talk, the longer I live. I explain that we still need each other. We don't want to see Iran and the Persian Gulf fall to the Soviets, and they, whether they know it or not, still need a pipeline from the U.S. for spare parts for their military equipment. In holding us now, they clearly and blatantly have violated international law. They have placed themselves and their revolution in a no-win situation. The United States government can't just pack up the Shah and send him here. That would be giving in to terrorism and surrendering to blackmail.

There's still no reply, so I keep talking like a politician at a Fourth of July picnic. It's my only chance. They had mentioned in their threat to me the way Israelis have treated Arabs in the occupied lands. "What does that have to do with me?" I ask. They also had accused the CIA of teaching SAVAK the latest methods of torture. But Iranians have been torturing each other for twenty-five hundred years, I tell them; they've never needed any help from anyone at that kind of thing. "I have read your history," I say. "Don't try to sell me that kind of crap!"

The third interrogator, walking back to his table, says he has seen villages in occupied Palestine and Lebanon bombed by American-made Israeli bombers. He has seen the kind of terrorism my government supports, and it is worse than anything he will do to me. He says he knows what our Air Force did to the poor oppressed people of Vietnam and what we've done all over the world to interfere in the internal affairs of oppressed millions. He asks what I know about Vietnam and Nicaragua and the role my CIA friends played in the oppression of the masses in these countries. Then he concludes by asking, "What is this word *crap*, what does it mean? I know it is not polite, and I have told you you must be polite."

I'm tired, but this is so far out in left field that I figure I may as well keep talking. It may not help, but it can't hurt. I tell him I'm a professional soldier, not a politician. I know very little about our relations with Nicaragua or Vietnam. "You're right about one thing, though: *Crap* is not a polite word, but it very well describes the line you're trying to sell me."

Hossein has been sitting impatiently, waiting for his chance to speak again. He apparently feels his position threatened by his fellow questioners. He goes over the George Lambrikis and CIA themes again, in depth; he's beginning to sound like a broken record. Then he says that even though the U.S. government pretends the Shah is very sick, his people know that the Shah is in America only to put together a coup, and that Carter and his henchmen are helping him to seize power again, just as our government did when the fascist, Eisenhower, was president. In 1953, he says, our government staged a coup to put the Shah back in power and to get rid of Prime Minister Mossadeq. All of the oppression in Iran since then, the killing of more than seventy thousand innocent Iranians, is the fault of our government. "You were here with your other spies in the embassy to do the same thing again," he says, "so that you could steal the resources of my country and corrupt our people with your imperialist and anti-Islamic ways. For years, your only interest in Iran has been to keep the Shah in power so you could use our land as a military base against your enemy, Russia, and at the same time exploit the poor people of Iran by stealing our oil and other natural resources."

I decide to be a bit surly, hoping this session will wind down soon. It's already been going on for several hours. "Do you have a specific question? Or do you want me to comment on what you have said?"

Pig Face is livid after Hossein translates for him. "This son of a pig is deliberately giving us a load of goat drippings," he says. "You are being too patient with him. He needs to have the brazenness beaten out of him. How long are we going to listen to his propaganda lies before we teach him to show some respect?"

Hossein speaks to me in an almost conciliatory tone. "Mr. Lambrikis, my friend speaks the truth. Did you understand what he said?"

I can't help wondering who really is in charge. If it's Pig Face, I'm not going to avoid the heavy hand much longer. So I weigh my words carefully as I reply, trying to be as calm and declarative as possible. "I didn't understand all of what your friend in the ski mask said, but enough to gather that he hates my guts. Tell him I already know you can torture me or even kill me, but that won't change anything. Killing me is not going to bring the Shah back or dampen your friend's hatred and frustration. And if you do kill me, or any of us, I'm sure you will pay dearly. I am not your enemy; I was here to help your government. But you will be my enemy if we are not released quickly."

I'm not sure that came out the way I intended. They're already the enemy, but there's no sense in driving that point home. They're hostile enough already. If they proceed to some form of torture, I know it's all over for me. If I'm badly beaten or disfigured, I know I'll never be released or seen alive again.

Hossein speaks, showing his anger for the first time. "You must be polite! You must not ask questions; you must only answer my questions! If you do not, you will be in even more trouble! I am trying to be very polite to you, but my friends are not as patient as me, and if you do not stop your lies and bad remarks, I will lose patience, too!"

The interrogator with the British accent and the poor Farsi chimes in as soon as Hossein finishes. He says again that I must first admit my real name and that I was sent to Iran to help organize a coup against the revolution. He again asks my name and my reason for being here.

Trying to be firm despite my fatigue, I tell them again who I am and deny being George Lambrikis.

Hossein speaks with a sneer as he points his finger at me. "His name is your name! You are George

Lambrikis, and you might as well admit it. It is getting late, and you must be getting tired. If you ever expect to sleep again, you must tell us you are Lambrikis!"

"My name is *still* Charles W. Scott."

Hossein grins slightly as though he knows a secret that will change my story. He speaks softly but with a definite threat in his voice. "I have other work I must do, but my friends will take you for a walk so you can have time to think about your situation. When we meet again back here in a little while, I hope you will have learned how important it is to admit who you are and what you were doing in the embassy spy nest."

Pig Face and several of the others who have been part of the gallery at my inquisition move on me immediately. I'm blindfolded and dragged from my stool. There must be at least four or five terrorists prodding and pushing me as I'm led out the door of the administrative office, down the hall, and outside into the chilly night air. I hear crowds chanting death slogans from a distance of about fifty yards. As soon as they spot me, they change their chant to "Kill the spy!" It's about as frightening as anything can possibly be, but I know intuitively that it's going to get worse. I'm told to walk faster, and the militants leading me on both sides suddenly release my arms and shoulders.

I'm stunned as I walk directly into a stationary object. It's a tree, and the damned thing doesn't give at all. I feel the trickle of blood flow from my nose to my upper lip, and I taste the salty red liquid. I hear Iranians laughing all around me, and I hear the chanters, who apparently are still outside the embassy fence, laughing and enjoying the show.

In spite of the pain, I'm more concerned by the fact that they've allowed me to be injured in the face. I'm plagued by the realization that if I'm seriously injured or disfigured, they will kill me and dispose of my body.

"You must walk faster!" comes the admonition from one of my tormentors. It sounds like Pig Face. I try to move without hitting any more immovable objects, but it's no use — I'm being steered so that I walk into every possible obstacle.

Within fifteen minutes, they become dissatisfied with the damage I'm inflicting on myself. I'm pushed and shoved until I fall down. I try to regain my footing, but with my hands tied behind my back, it's futile. Each time I try to stand, I'm kicked or punched again until I'm back on the ground.

I decide to act as though I'm more hurt than I really am by remaining on the ground, but that ploy doesn't work. I'm kicked repeatedly in the back and kidneys. The pain is excruciating. I try again to stand. This time Pig Face grabs me by the collar and spits in my face as he blurts out still another threat: "You will learn to cooperate or we will turn you over to the people outside the gates. They will tear out your eyes and cut off your penis . . . . You will wish you were back here with us, you pig!"

I figure this is how it's going to end for me, but I'm still not willing to roll over and play dead. I can't fight back, but in sheer frustration and anger I listen carefully for Pig Face to speak again. He does, this time choking me as he speaks. "I want to kill you, Colonel, for all you and your country have done. We are only wasting time talking to you inside."

I have his range, even with the blindfold, and I spit, aiming at the source of the hate-filled, threatening voice. I'm right on target, judging by the outraged yells and the volley of punches I get. He hits me in the face while holding my collar with his other hand.

One of the other terrorists apparently jumps on Pig Face and admonishes him in Farsi, "*Saresho-na-zan!*" [Don't hit him in the face!]

Pig Face is like a mad dog as he curses me in the most colloquial and abusive Farsi I've ever heard. My body is one concentrated source of pain. My back and groin hurt so much that I almost forget my difficulty in breathing — a result of the earlier solid kick to my rib cage. Suddenly I'm knocked to the ground again by a sickening kick to the groin. I know I'm going to throw up as I roll on the ground in anguish.

I must have passed out. As I begin to recover my senses, I'm aware that, for some reason, the beating has stopped. I also notice that it's still raining. I wasn't sure at first if the moisture was my own blood or rain; it's both. I can feel the soothing rain on my face as I lie semiconscious and motionless on the ground. I hear my tormentors whispering and I still hear the haunting mob outside the embassy walls chanting their messages of hate and revenge against America, President Carter, and the ex-Shah. But cries for my death have been dropped from the list of slogans.

For a few moments, I'm aware of nothing; I must have passed out again. As I regain consciousness, I am being hauled to my feet by unseen hands. Behind the hands, voices tell me to be "more careful." I'm led, this time without violence of any kind, back inside the Chancellery building, to what I believe to be the same room I was dragged from about an hour ago.

My blindfold is removed, and I see that I'm seated on the same stool I was on before my "walk." I hurt all over, and I'm having trouble thinking straight; but I'm also angry, and my adrenalin is still flowing. Hossein is seated at the big desk and still has the "I've-got-a-secret" smirk on his hateful face.

"I hope you enjoyed the fresh air and you are now ready to tell the truth," he says softly. "I am sorry if you fell, but that is not my fault. You must learn to go where the students lead you without resisting, or you may hurt yourself. Is your mind now clearer? Do you remember who you are?"

Oh, you son of a bitch, I think. How long can this continue before they get impatient and kill me? I'm scared, angry, and frustrated, Why doesn't Washington do something? Even if they were to bomb the embassy, it would at least get this thing over with and save me additional pain. I know I've got to be tough, but I don't feel tough at all. I'm just an American at the wrong place at the wrong time.

"Yeah, I still remember who I am; I'm Colonel Charles W. Scott, U.S. Army, and I've been beat up by your brave souls who get a kick out of working out on a man who is tied and blindfolded and can't defend himself. I'm not George what's-his-name, and I never will be. I don't like your little games, and you're just a mob of terrorists."

Hossein is still cool and soft-spoken. "You are still not being polite. You have learned nothing. Your government can do nothing to save you. Sooner or later you will admit that you are CIA. For now, I will ask you some other questions; then later, we will get back to your real name."

Hossein continues in a solicitous tone. He says he knows how angry the American people were with the war in Vietnam and that our government was forced to get out of the war because our people demonstrated their opposition. "We are not angry at the American people," he says, "because we think they will again take to the streets, forcing Carter to return the Shah. We do not hate the American people; they are not much different from the Iranian people. But your government is the villain. Colonel, do you think it will take long for the American people to organize demonstrations and force your Carter to send the Shah to Iran for trial and execution?"

Hossein, obviously a political zealot, is giving me a chance to discuss politics. I decide to give it a try; it's better than going for another "walk." I tell him the Vietnam War was a very divisive war, and many Americans were opposed to our involvement. In a free and democratic society, the will of the people ultimately prevails. I warn him, however, that this is not like the Vietnam situation, and the seizure of our embassy is a clear violation of international law and the Treaty of Amity between our two countries. I

50

advise him that Americans generally are aware of the Shah's alleged crimes against the Iranian people, but that we're tough and do not enjoy being backed into a corner.

Then I ask Hossein a direct question. "You say you want the Shah for trial and execution. How can you be so sure he will be executed if you intend to give him a fair trial?"

Hossein has the anti-Shah and anti-U.S. rhetoric down pat. He insists the Shah is guilty of killing more than seventy thousand Iranians. He claims the Shah will be given a "fair" trial and then will be executed because it is the will of the Iranian people. He also claims the taking of hostages and the attack on our embassy represent the will of the Iranian people. He says Khomeini will support the takeover.

My guess is that he's correct about Khomeini supporting the attack and the seizure of hostages. I don't think the militants would have gotten the attack off the ground without the cooperation of the Iranian security forces and at least the tacit approval of the Islamic clergy, including Khomeini.

Each breath I take causes me almost to double over in pain. My chest and rib cage feel as though I've been beaten with a crowbar. The constant kicks to the groin have left me feeling sick, and I have to go to the bathroom. I'm too tired to continue this very much longer, but Hossein apparently is willing to participate in a free exchange of philosophies indefinitely. So I decide to try and find out what role the Bazargan government is playing in the embassy takeover. "You say the takeover was the will of the Iranian people. What about Bazargan's government?" I ask. "Is he supporting your violation of international law, too?"

This irritates Hossein a little, but he can't resist another opportunity to spout the party line. His reply to my direct question is defensive and high-pitched. "I should not answer your questions, I am asking the questions!"

Nonetheless, Hossein lapses into a rhetorical

tirade on the Bazargan government's leadership of the revolution. He says his group represents the "will of the Iranian people," while Bazargan has been headed toward the resumption of normal diplomatic relations with the United States. He claims the "people" will not tolerate this. They want the United States out of Iran once and for all. That's why there were all the recent demonstrations in front of our embassy. But, according to Hossein, we did not respond to their cue.

Hossein is talking so fast that he's having to pause in mid-sentence to catch his breath. The room is silent during his pause, and I decide not to reply to his jumbled discourse of paranoia.

Then the silence is broken. Hossein speaks slowly and deliberately as though what he's saying is profound and historically important. "We want America out of Iran. We want to continue our revolution without worrying about your subversion. The Imam* will lead us back to an Islamic society, free of Western corruption and influence. Then we will lead the other oppressed peoples of the world out of their shackles. We are especially dedicated to freeing the peoples of other Islamic countries that are oppressed by kings as they are in Saudi Arabia or like Saddam Hussein's in Iraq."

Hossein looks me straight in the eyes, as opposed to his usual style of appearing to be studying papers on the desk. His tone stiffens and his delivery accelerates, as though he's trying to make his words slip past me. He says they also will get support from minority groups in America, especially blacks, who have been oppressed for two hundred years. "They will revolt, too," he says.

I don't agree with him, but having him talk political philosophy is certainly better than being kicked in the

---

*Honorific title bestowed on Ayatollah Ruhallah Khomeini by his followers.

gut. I ask him if he's saying that he and his mob are also against the revolutionary government. He replies in the affirmative; they will not listen to anyone but Khomeini, and if the revolutionary government tries to rescue us, he and the others are ready to kill us and face death themselves. But, he continues, that will not happen, because the people of Iran made the decision to take over the embassy, and the government will have to support their decision or the government will fall.

Hossein is really sure of himself, leading me to believe even more strongly that they made careful preparations before their attack. "We know we are right in what we are doing and God is on our side."

Now Hossein is invoking the deity as an active accomplice in this terrorism. I think about all the historical examples of oppressive movements that have killed and plundered in the name of "God." I decide to argue this point, even though I'm sure it will do no good. I tell him that some of the most bloody and costly wars have been fought by those who claimed they knew what God wanted for all of us. I tell him again that we're not meddling in Iran's internal affairs. In fact, we were doing nothing against the regime.

Hossein's reply is unrelated to my last comment. I wonder if maybe he's getting tired, too, as he seems to pull a comment out of the air: "We will not take orders from Bazargan or anyone else who does not agree with us."

"You sound like a mob of anarchists," I respond. "If you will not obey your own government, who will you listen to besides Khomeini?"

Hossein replies that they are *Daneshjuani-Is-lami-Khati-Iman* [Islamic student followers of the Imam's line]. "We follow Khomeini and no one else," he says. "We are not anarchists, but we will not tolerate opposition to the establishment of an Islamic state."

The other interrogators are getting edgy. Pig Face is playing with a ghastly-looking knife and staring at me. His eyes shine with a sadistic glint from behind the peepholes of the black ski mask. The one who speaks like a Palestinian understands everything being said, but I get the idea that he has been told to let Hossein do most of the questioning. He doesn't like it, judging from the hateful look in his eyes, but he has the discipline to live with it. Hossein begins to lecture me again on the futility of noncooperation. He says his people are merely staging a sit-in, and they will stay, with us as hostages, until the Shah is returned. I can't help myself as I interrupt him: "This is *some* sit-in."

Hossein is angered by my butting in. "We *are* staging a sit-in, and you are a prisoner arrested by the people. You will be a hostage for the rest of your life if the Shah is not returned."

I answer sarcastically: "Nice countries don't take hostages."

The Palestinian is enraged. He jumps to his feet and lectures me for twenty minutes on his belief that hostage-taking is justified in this case. How else could the Iranian people get the Shah and judge him? He claims that the United States controls all the international courts, so the people had to act on their own. He repeats himself several times, seeming to think that if he persists, I will begin to see the situation as he sees it. I ask if he has ever heard of international law.

Hossein interrupts, speaking in a higher pitch than his normal voice. He's irritated and excited. "You speak about international law; where was your international law when the Shah was killing thousands of innocent Iranians? We are revolutionaries; we do not have to abide by your international laws. We did not make them. We live only by the laws of Islam."

I tell him that I've read the Koran, too, and if I remember correctly from my study, it is not right for a Moslem to hold diplomats and emissaries from other countries for ransom. It also is against Islam to punish any person for a crime he did not commit. They're holding us prisoner without charges. I look Hossein in the eye and say, "I don't think you are very good Moslems — you have shown by your actions that you are terrorists, not followers of Islamic doctrine."

Hossein is losing his composure. "You cannot say what is Moslem and what is not Moslem. The Imam is the judge of that and we will do *whatever* he says. If the Shah is not returned, you will be charged for the crimes you have committed against the Iranian people, Mr. Lambrikis. We are not terrorists. If we were, you would already be dead. With us, you have no rights; your diplomatic passport means nothing at all!"

I'm exhausted, but I've got to keep him talking. So I challenge him by saying, "What makes you think you represent the views of the Iranian people?" I tell him again that they're terrorists, and that's the way they'll be perceived by the world.

"We are *not* terrorists! You Americans are terrorists! You do it with bombs from your B-52s on poor people of Vietnam, and you do it by making coups like Iran in 1953."

Hossein is leaving out the definite articles — a sure indication that he's getting excited. I launch into my version of how the Shah was restored to the Peacock Throne. I tell him that his good friend Mohammad Mossadeq, after nationalizing his oil, got Iran into a real economic mess. The rest of the world stopped buying Iranian oil from 1951 to 1953, and consequently the economy was in about as bad a shape as it is now after his Islamic revolution. The poor of south Tehran, who demonstrated to support his revolution, are the same people who marched in 1953 to oust Mossadeq and put the Shah back in power. They got hungry and they were not satisfied with what Mossadeq had done for them or for their country. The U.S. government wanted a stable government in Iran. The Tudeh Party [communist party of Iran] was strong then and it appeared that the dissatisfaction with Mossadeq would lead to a communist takeover, so we fanned flames that were already burning by helping the pro-Shah demonstrations here. We paid the demonstrators then, just as his people do today. If we had not taken action, I tell him, he would be singing the communist "Internationale" now instead of screaming *"Alloh-Akbar!"* [God is great!]

"You want to blame the U.S. for everything that has gone wrong in Iran over the past twenty-five years," I say, "but if you really knew your own history, you would see this is not true. You overestimate the capability of the United States to interfere in Iranian affairs, and you always blame others for your problems. You are xenophobic and paranoid."

Hossein is puzzled; he doesn't understand. "What means this word you say? Sen - oh - phobic?"

He really wants to know. I try to answer calmly. "It means you hate and fear all foreigners, and you do." I tell him that I understand why, though. If he has read his own history, he knows that his people have been conquered by practically every major power since the great Persian Empire withered after Cyrus the Great almost twenty-five hundred years ago. The Mongols, the Arabs, the Ottoman Turks — they all conquered his country. And in this century, Iran was under the influence of the British and the Russians until the United States began to play a major role after World War II. His people are suspicious of *all* foreigners, and they always blame others for everything they think is wrong in Iran. "Look at the mess you have now — and for this you can blame only your revolution. Your economy is in a sorry state, and, if you persist in holding us, you will end up isolated from the rest of the world. Even the Russians don't run around attacking embassies and holding diplomats hostage."

Pig Face, whose sadistic appetite seemed to be

temporarily satiated by the beating he gave me in the embassy yard, has had enough of our philosophical exchange. He doesn't understand most of it, even when it's translated for him. He lunges out of his chair with great anger and emotion. In a heartbeat, he's all over me with punches and threats. He knocks the wind out of me with a right to the diaphragm, and I fall off my stool. He emphasizes his caustic remarks with a series of kicks to my groin. I try to protect myself, but I can't. He rants and raves incoherently for what seems like an eternity as he continues to kick and punch me.

Finally, one member of the gallery, which has watched the entire interrogation while standing and sitting on the floor behind me, comes to my rescue. I'm dazed, but I can see my rescuer clearly as he pulls Pig Face off me. He tells him in Farsi that he's going too far; what he is doing is not necessary and is not Islamic. The terrorist appears to be in his late twenties, tall and skinny with a big nose that bends to the left, destroying the balance of his otherwise sharp features. He is soft-spoken and apparently has the respect of the other terrorists. I have seen this man somewhere before, but I can't remember where or when.

Pig Face cools down, and Hossein tells the militant who came to my rescue to sit down. Hossein calls him Akbar, and he speaks to him with a modicum of respect.

Pig Face, standing directly in front of me ready to give another kick, screams, "You are a pig! You are not being polite! You are a prisoner and you must only answer our questions! Everything you say is full of lies! You must tell the truth or you will die! We will cut off your arm! We will kill you, *slowly,* and get rid of your body. You have been here before; you know that is no problem."

I do not answer. Then Hossein and Pig Face begin a discussion which goes on for more than an hour. The gist of it is that Pig Face wants to get more physical and Hossein is enjoying the exchange of ideas and philosophies. Hossein has all the answers and doesn't fear the outcome of the exchange. He's convinced that he can wear me down over time. Finally Pig Face returns to his seat and the questions continue. As Hossein begins to speak, Akbar and another militant lift me from the floor to my stool. I'm unsteady, so they remain standing next to me, holding my body in a sitting position. "Mr. Lambrikis, my friends are angry with you and they would like to make you speak the truth. I will try one more time to be nice to you, but if you do not cooperate, I will have to give in and let them have you. You must tell the truth and stop being impolite to us. Do you understand?"

I'm exhausted, but I go on. "Yeah, I understand perfectly well, but it doesn't change anything. I'm Charles W. Scott, Chief of the Defense Liaison Office. I'm not George what's-his-name. And I never will be. I was in Iran only to help your military get spare parts for your equipment."

Hossein answers with more of the same rhetoric, only worse. "It would be best for you if you admitted the truth before it is too late. I will give you a chance to be polite. You will write a letter to the American people telling them Shah is criminal and telling them to send him to Iran for trial. You will do this for me? If you do only this, we will let you alone. You can have a nice room with a radio and good food and we will not hurt you. What do you say?"

I'd sure like to get some rest — this has been going on literally for hours — but I remember my goals. They must be my rock and my salvation; they must not float. I tell him that I won't write anything for him. Even if I did, the American people would realize it was done under pressure. They wouldn't believe it. I cannot write anything political because I'm a soldier, I explain. I can't say, write, or do anything that would be against my country or my government. I have taken an oath, and I must live — or die — by that oath.

Hossein hesitates, pretending to be engrossed in

papers on the big desk, then he speaks. "I will give you some time to think all this over. But we will have you back for more questions. Next time it will not be so easy for you. You must admit who you are and what you were doing in the embassy spy nest. Then you must write letters for us to help get Shah back for trial and execution. Think about it!"

Pig Face moves quickly, blurting out instructions in Farsi to a couple of the hangers-on. He tells them that I will be moved to an isolation area and that I will sleep on the floor without blankets. My hands will be tied and I will be awakened every fifteen minutes to make sure I don't get any rest. My blindfold is replaced, and I'm dragged out of the room by a couple of heavies. As we move outside the building, I can tell that it's broad daylight, which means my interrogation must have lasted at least sixteen hours. I'm so tired that I'm getting confused. I wonder how many sessions like this I'm going to be exposed to before they really get tough on me. I keep hoping something will break — and that it will not be me!

Pig Face was right; I have been awakened every fifteen minutes and my hands are tied so tightly behind my back that I've lost feeling in them. It has been impossible to sleep, and the floor is so hard and cold that I'm totally miserable. I have prayed for strength to endure. I can't decide which hurts the most — my back or my guts. My nose hurts, too, but it's bearable. If only I could be moved to a warm place and be allowed to sleep for a few hours, I'm sure I could handle the rest.

My blindfold is so tight that I have a constant headache. I feel sick to my stomach — I'm not sure if it's a result of the beatings, the blindfold, the tension, or the lack of rest. I recite the Twenty-Third Psalm softly to myself: "The Lord is my Shepherd. . . ." O God, please give me the strength and the will to endure. Somehow I *must* get through this ordeal.

November 10, 1979

"Maybe you'd better teach him some manners," says Hossein to Pig Face and two other militants who have been standing by listening to my interrogation for hours, hoping for a chance to use the solid rubber hoses they brandish.

The last five days are an endless blur of inter-rogation, punches, kicks, arm-twisting — like a broken film-strip that keeps showing the same frame over and over. I have not been allowed to sleep for more than fifteen minutes at a stretch. My will is holding, but my body is aching.

Suddenly, I'm snatched back to reality by a blow across my back. The pain is intense, but I manage to retain my position on the stool. Hossein and some of the gallery members leave the room, allowing Pig Face a free hand.

"We will kee-el you. You are pig." Pig Face has learned a few words of English. He spits in my face and pulls on my ears as two of his eager helpers lay on their rubber hoses. I begin to feel faint; my stool topples over with me still tied to it. Everything goes blank for what seems no more than a minute.

It must have been longer, though, because I awake tied over the top of a desk. I am unable to move my arms or my legs, and my face and hair are wet. They must have dumped cold water on my face to revive me. My head hurts and I'm vaguely aware that I hit it on the floor earlier when I fell with the stool.

Pig Face is standing directly in front of me. His helpers are standing on either side of the desk, ready to go to work with their hoses again. He grabs a handful of my hair and pulls my head up again, sneering in Farsi: "You cannot take it! You are weak like all Americans!"

I should know better, but I can't help myself. "Fuck you!"

I instantly feel tremendous pressure on the side

of my face. I can't see what he hit me with, but it must have been a blackjack. I see stars, but I don't lose consciousness. The pressure turns to excruciating pain in my jaw; I taste blood and feel something in my mouth. I move my tongue around and find pieces of broken teeth. I spit them out on the floor, along with a mouthful of blood. I swear at Pig Face in Farsi, questioning his ancestry. He winds up again and I see what he hit me with — a length of one-inch steel pipe about ten inches long, with a rope passed through it and knotted on the business end, the other end folded over into an improvised handle.

"Don't hit him again!" shouts Hossein as he reenters the room. He tells Pig Face he has gone too far; they do not want to inflict any injury that would make them look bad if it were discovered. Pig Face continues to brandish his homemade weapon as he argues with Hossein, saying it would be better to go ahead and kill me and dump the body before they're asked for a list of names of those they have "arrested." Fortunately, Hossein wins, and Pig Face and his goons leave in a huff.

Hossein says he's sorry about what just happened and asks to look inside my mouth. I'm untied and told to sit on the floor. I ache all over as I try to find the least uncomfortable sitting position on the cold floor. Two of my teeth have been broken off at the gum line. The tooth between them seems to have been broken off below the gum line, and I've been swallowing lots of my own blood. I spit again. Hossein tells one of the militants to get some ice. I'm escorted out of the interrogation room by two guards and led into the next room without even being blindfolded.

The guard brings ice wrapped in a dirty towel, which he instructs me to hold against my jaw to stop the bleeding. He then reties my blindfold and leaves me alone.

Within an hour, my jaw is throbbing so much it's impossible to sleep.

November 18, 1979

Keeping track of time is difficult, but I know it has been about two weeks since my interrogation began. I'm alone in a cold, dark room somewhere inside the embassy complex. I think this is one of the servants' rooms in the ambassador's residence. My hands are still tied tightly behind my back, my feet are bound together with coarse rope, and I'm tightly blindfolded. I am physically and emotionally exhausted. I'm not sure how much more of this I can take. I've been given very little to eat since this ordeal began, and I can feel a great loss of weight.

Prayer and the constant realization that I must live up to the goals I set have been my salvation. A number of times, I would have given in if I hadn't set my simple goals earlier. Several times I have decided that anything would be better than the beatings, the relentless questioning, and the threats, but there also have been a few moments of hope and reinforcement, even amid all this pressure and mental anguish. The other day, when my interrogators got tired and decided to quit the questioning, I was blindfolded and moved along with several other hostages to a dark room in the big warehouse we have always called the Mushroom Inn, because it's a bleak underground structure. Marine Sergeant Billy Gallegos was resting on a mattress and offered it to me as soon as my blindfold was removed and he saw what kind of shape I was in. At first the guards would not allow him to give me the thin mattress, but Billy insisted and finally one of the guards let him switch places with me. We had a chance to exchange glances later, and I could tell Billy was genuinely concerned about me. I flipped him a thumbs up, as best I could with my hands tied, and he responded in kind. Billy's grin was a strange combination of fear and determination. But he did manage a smile, and it made my day. But now I'm alone again, and I have no idea when the questions and the beatings and the threats will continue.

I know in my heart that if it goes on long enough, I'll reach my breaking point. I have not reached it yet, but I'm surprised when I consider how long I've been without any substantial sleep or a decent meal. My beard is at the stage where it itches constantly, and my mouth tastes the way I imagine goat drippings must taste. I'd do almost anything just to brush my teeth. But I know this is all part of the breaking-down process the interrogators are using to try to get me to do or say what they demand. I wonder if any of the others are being interrogated and, if so, how they're holding up under the pressure.

The terrorist named Akbar, the one with the big nose who rescued me from Pig Face's wrath the first night, has been to see me a couple of times during breaks in my interrogation. I wonder if he's a plant. He claims he's against the physical abuse, and he has even offered to get water and soup for me. But he's one of them; he's a terrorist and I must be very careful. I can't rule out the possibility that he's looking for a soft spot that he and the others can exploit. But even in my confused and exhausted state, I have sensed that he is different from the other really nasty, sadistic ones like Pig Face. Akbar has the revolutionary rhetoric down pat, too, but he seems more human than any of the rest. He even apologized for the beatings and claims that he was tortured in the Shah's prisons and is against such treatment. Maybe he's the best of a sorry lot — or maybe he's trying to get next to me to discover my Achilles heel. I just don't know.

Someone enters the room and I hear the light click on. Even blindfolded, I can detect light and see shadows.

"Colonel Scott, do you need anything?" It is Akbar speaking in a soft, almost patronizing way.

"Yeah, I need about twenty-four hours sleep, a big steak, and a one-way ticket out of this hellhole you people call a country. I don't even care where the ticket is to, as long as it's to a destination outside Iran."

Akbar doesn't speak very much English, so I have talked to him in Farsi. I wait for him to answer, but he apparently is at a loss for words. "You people have really grabbed a tiger by the tail this time," I tell him. "Do you really think you can blackmail the United States? Do you think the rest of the world will understand you and your revolution after this? And do you think you'll get away with it?"

Akbar is calm and so understanding that it's disarming. "I understand how you feel. My brothers have been very bad to you, but you must understand their hatred. They hate you because you are an American government employee. I do not hate you. I think you are a very strong man, but I hate your country for its support of the Shah. We do not recognize your diplomatic immunity. I should tell you to cooperate with those who question you or they will kill you, but that would not be true. Colonel, they will not kill you unless the Imam orders it. You must be patient. They will eventually stop questioning you, and as soon as the Shah is returned to Iran you can go home to America and your family. You do have a family?"

I'm not going to tell him anything, in spite of his friendly approach. "Yes, I have a family. A wife and nine children. Do you have a family?"

Akbar laughs half-heartedly at my claim to nine offspring. "Oh! You have *nine* children? That's funny, your records say only two. I have a family, too. A mother, father, a brother, and two sisters, but I am much too busy with the revolution to see them very often. Perhaps when this is all over I will have more time."

"Yeah, if you're still alive when it's all over."

Akbar's reply is more formal. I have touched a sensitive spot in his revolutionary armor. "Unless it is God's will that I not survive this, I will return to my family when it is over. You must be patient and not talk too badly to the questioners. You know they enjoy making you hurt. But

64

believe me, it will end and you will live. You will return to America some day if you do not force one of my brothers to kill you. Do you believe in God?"

"Yes, I believe in God. In fact if you study Islam, you will know that I believe in the same God you and your friends claim to follow. That's why I can't understand why you people treat fellow humans the way you do."

Akbar thinks for a minute before he replies. "I believe in God, Colonel, just as you do. But I have seen what happened to my country under the Shah, and I must fight to make a country that is free from oppression."

I think of Voltaire's words: "Beware of he who says to do as God says or God will punish you, for he would leave say do as I say or I will kill you." I've got to make my next statement one that Akbar will understand and think about. He moves closer to me, removes my blindfold, and I see him staring down at me. His eyes are not those of a killer. They're soft and almost kind. He's so damned sincere — a rare attribute for a terrorist. I focus on Akbar's eyes as I say, "If you believe in God and the teachings of Islam, how can you justify the taking of hostages? Your holy Koran teaches this is wrong. Am I to think you're merely using God to seek power? What kind of man are you, anyway? Do you realize the danger you have brought to your country by taking us prisoner?"

Akbar averts his eyes in apparent shame for a moment, then gazes at me with a look that is more of sorrow than hatred. "Colonel, I am sorry for what has happened to you, but you must have faith in God. Everything will turn out all right in the end. Please believe me; I am not a terrorist. I believe in God, but I also believe in my country. I do not hate you," he says, and then asks if I would like a drink of water. I nod yes, and Akbar leaves the room.

For the first time, I have a chance to see that I'm in the cook's assistant's room. The bed has been removed, and the tables and lamps have been stacked in a corner. The room is about ten feet by ten feet. There are bars on the single window, and the glass has been painted black to deny the light. The room is filthy and shows signs that other hostages have occupied it. A black suit and white shirt, which the cook's helper had all ready to wear before the takeover, still hangs neatly on a hook behind the door.

Akbar returns with the water and actually excuses himself before leaving. He says he has work to do but that he will check on me later. He replaces my blindfold; thankfully it's not nearly as tight.

I wonder about this young man, how someone like him could get involved in the takeover of an American embassy. He claims to have spent time in the Shah's prisons, and I try to imagine what he did to end up in jail. He doesn't seem the type. He seems fairly intelligent and he doesn't fit the terrorist mold of most of his "brothers."

His name — Akbar — means *God* in Persian, but is he really a believer, or is he just another terrorist? Would he kill me if he were told to kill? I wonder, as I doze and anticipate my next interrogation, what kind of man he really is, how he could possess such hatred. What experiences in his short lifetime could have made him so resentful and bitter?

The Making
of a Terrorist

3 EAST

TEHRAN, IRAN
OCTOBER 15, 1973

Sharp, commanding blows rattled the door of the small, immaculately clean house at No. 16, Kuche Saadi, violating the serene autumn air which covered the south Tehran neighborhood like a protective shroud. A light breeze from the desert east of the city carried the lingering aroma of a variety of Persian dishes prepared earlier in the evening, blending the fragrances into a potpourri of odoriferous delight. A sensitive nose also could discern the pleasant, albeit faint, perfume of late-blooming roses in a nearby small garden. But it was not to be a night for smelling the sweetness of roses.

The stillness of the night was ruptured by another, even louder and more demanding knock on the door.

"Daro baz kon!" [Open the door!] shouted a tall, apelike policeman. He and his two partners, one from the dreaded SAVAK, the other a plainclothes member of the Iranian National Police, were becoming progressively more impatient. They had other arrests to make this night and resented the lack of response to their deliberately terrorizing intrusion.

The second series of knocks awakened Parviz Houssini — father of four, husband, hard-working laborer, and devout Moslem. Parviz's heart jumped as he slid from his pallet on the floor and scurried as quickly as he could toward the front door. Fear became stark terror as the weathered plastic and plywood door splintered open from the well-placed blow of a rifle butt. Now the entire family was awake and in a state of terror, hurriedly dressing against the chilly night air.

Parviz confronted the big police officer as he entered the main room of the house through the broken door.

The two men stared at each other awkwardly for a moment, mesmerized into momentary speechlessness by the spontaneous, almost nose-to-nose meeting.

"What do you want? Why are you here? Why didn't you wait for me to come to the door?" Parviz's voice, initially tinted with a combination of outrage, resentment, and the authority of a man in his own home, gradually fell off to an apologetic whisper as the gravity of the situation sank into his uneducated peasant mind. "You awakened me — I was coming as fast as possible!"

The look in the eyes of the huge policeman was unmistakable — Parviz or some member of his family was in big trouble with the police. Parviz was only too aware of what usually accompanied a nocturnal visit by the Shah's security forces. His mind reeled with a panorama of memories of the tales of horror he had heard: tales of midnight arrests, without warning or specific charges, grisly accounts of the harsh treatment meted out to those who were arrested and accused of opposing the Shah or his policies.

He felt a hollowness, then a churning in his stomach. His eldest son, Akbar, had been somewhat active in the anti-Shah movement, but he had engaged only in acts that best could be described as simple mischief. Akbar had gone with other boys his age to anti-Shah rallies at the mosque. He had painted a few anti-Shah slogans on walls around the city and distributed anti-Shah propaganda leaflets. But to Parviz's knowledge, Akbar never had been involved in any really serious act. He had not realized, at least not until now, that even this childlike participation in activities against the government could bring such a visit from the police.

Suddenly the burly cop shouted again at the laborer. "Shut up! It does not matter, old man. Which one of you is Akbar Houssini?"

A slender, hard-muscled, big-nosed, yet quite

70

handsome twenty-year-old with doleful, penetrating eyes spoke immediately. Akbar believed that if he readily admitted he was the one they were seeking, he could spare his beloved family any more unpleasantness.

"I am Akbar Houssini. What do you want with me? I have done nothing wrong."

Before the policeman could respond, Parviz spoke again. "What do you want with my son? He has done nothing wrong; he is only a college student. He is studying to be a chemical engineer."

The big policeman bellowed, "Shut up! We have no business with you! We are here to arrest your son for his terrorist activities — he is in big trouble. If you mind your own business and get out of the way, you will not be arrested. If you don't shut up, we will take you with this son of a camel you call your son."

By any standard, Akbar was a good son and a source of considerable pride to his family. Born of an ethnic Persian mother and an Azarbaijani-Turkic father at Ardebil in Azarbaijan Province in northwestern Iran, he moved to Tehran with his family when he was eight years old. The *Englabi Sefid* [White Revolution] was in its infancy then, and hundreds of thousands of Iranians from rural areas and small villages were migrating to the larger cities in search of jobs and a better life.

The White Revolution was so named by the Shah because it was part of his master plan to prevent a bloody revolution by peacefully changing the conditions of abject poverty and illiteracy, hunger, unemployment, and corruption that historically have incited masses to rebel. But in Iran, the White Revolution also brought about drastic and unpopular changes in the traditional Islamic society. This caused progressively more resentment by the fundamentalist Shiite clerics initially, and eventually by a majority of the people, especially those at the lower end of the economic

spectrum who continually benefited least from modernization and Westernization. For them, the plan was a nightmare
of disappointment and continued subsistence living. Mini-
cities of shacks and hovels sprang up outside the big cities to
house these unskilled thousands who had believed the tales
of a better life but found them to be false.

The White Revolution was criticized, first covertly in the mosques by the clergy, then openly in the
mosques and meeting places around the country, especially
in the major urban areas, as the opposition gained strength
and support by the mid-1970s. To the Shah's opponents, it
was another example of a sellout to foreign interests, a sub-
jugation of Iranian national interests to foreigners, and a
deliberate deterioration of the traditional Islamic culture in
favor of Western ways. The Shah was blamed for everything
that went wrong in the wake of the White Revolution. The
United States government was blamed along with the Shah,
because many Iranians viewed the Shah as a puppet of the
United States.

It is an open secret that the United States sent
Kermit Roosevelt and H. Norman Schwartzkoph of the CIA
to Iran to organize pro-Shah demonstrations during the summer of 1953, after the Shah was forced into exile by pro-
Mossadeq demonstrations. Following his election as Prime
Minister in 1951, Mossadeq, the charismatic nationalist
leader who opposed the Shah, gradually usurped the Shah's
traditional prerogatives until a showdown was inevitable. He
nationalized Iran's oil industry, displeasing the British so
much that they, along with most of the rest of the oil-consum-
ing nations, boycotted Iranian oil for more than two years.
The oil boycott wreaked havoc on Iran's foreign exchange
position, and economic chaos gripped the country. Dissatisfaction with economic conditions significantly eroded
Mossadeq's popularity by mid-1953 and set the stage for a
showdown in which the Shah was returned to power.

Historians remain divided on the Shah's

chances for victory in this power struggle if he had not been helped by the CIA. After the ouster of Mossadeq, many Iranians blamed the United States for the failure of his Nationalists to win in August of 1953. This thesis gained popular appeal as revolutionary fervor grew in the 1970s, and SAVAK and the other police organizations got more and more heavy-handed with the opposition. Blaming the United States for all the Shah's alleged crimes is perfectly logical to Iranians; they have heard it preached for years by the mullahs, who used their position to mold public opinion. The important thing is not whether or not the Shah would have been returned to power in 1953 without U.S. help, but rather the perception that many Iranians have been schooled to accept — that the U.S., through the CIA, returned the Shah to power. To a majority of the Iranian people, this view is accepted as an article of faith.

Akbar was one of those who had been taught to hate the United States. An unusually sensitive, hard-working, and conscientious student, Akbar was well-liked and highly respected by his fellow students and his teachers. During his secondary school years, he often was singled out for positions of leadership because of his popularity, sincerity, and diligence, and he graduated from *daberistan* [high school] near the top of his class. He was also a good listener, with a knack for drawing out the views of others and impressing them with his willingness to listen to their ideas. He had an almost charismatic quality that won him many friends and supporters. Akbar was always willing to accept the most difficult tasks. He also was a devout Shiite Moslem.

From early childhood, as is the custom in Islamic Iran, he went frequently to the mosque with his father. As a youth, he listened to the mullahs' Friday sermons and developed an abiding respect and deep admiration for them. He believed everything the clerics of the Shiite sect of Islam said, whether it dealt with matters of religion or with political issues.

In fact, he never really could distinguish between the two. It actually made little difference, because Shiite Islam, as it is practiced in Iran, encompasses all aspects of one's life. As Akbar was taught to see the world, God had revealed the Koran, the holy book of Islam, to Mohammed, the greatest of prophets, so that man would use it not simply as a *guide* for all aspects of his life on earth, but as a *directive*. There was nothing optional about the teachings of Islam as Akbar learned them. Everything had to fall within the proper order of things, in accordance with the dictates of the Koran, or a man's life was unacceptable to God. The individual who did not obey the laws of God would be punished by God after his death. The punishment of sinners by man, acting for God on earth as directed by the mullahs, also was seen as the natural order of things. Thus, the idea of flogging, stoning, and execution for infractions against Islamic piety did not seem brutal or offensive to Akbar. He saw these punishments as a positive cleansing of the spirit.

Over the years, he was taught that technological advances were not only acceptable but desirable to the Moslem world, but that one must be ever vigilant to the inherent dangers which accompany progressive programs, especially if they were engineered by foreigners who were not "believers." The mullahs saw the Westernization of Iran as a threat to their traditional power and influence on society. The clergy had impressed Akbar with the notion that any action to prevent this Westernization was both moral and fully justified.

To Akbar, the United States was stripping Iran of its natural resources and its traditional society and replacing it with neonlighted dance halls and night clubs, where alcohol flowed like water in a lush oasis. That the sanctity of Iranian womanhood could not be protected against this corrupting environment was evident by the number of fashionably dressed and heavily made-up young Iranian ladies who frequented these "dens of sin." These establishments were seen as monuments to the depravity of Western culture, and Akbar felt a moral obligation to oppose them.

Akbar also was an incurable romantic. He often fantasized about the great society which would be established under Islam in his beloved homeland after the satanic Shah and his henchmen were ousted. He was not only willing to participate in activities against the Shah, he looked forward to the day when he would be old enough to join the Society of Islamic Students, a militant anti-Shah organization which was dedicated to overthrowing the monarchy and establishing an Islamic state.

To reinforce his animosity and hatred, Akbar listened with fascination to the horror stories of the arbitrary arrest, imprisonment, torture, and execution of anti-Shah suspects at the hands of the various internal security forces, the most dreaded and feared of which was SAVAK. Several of his school chums were arrested for anti-government activities while he was in high school. Two were sent to prison for three years for the seemingly innocent possession of a copy of a letter from the exiled Ayatollah Khomeini. And one of his closest friends was arrested in the middle of the night and never was seen again.

Akbar joined the Islamic student organization when he was barely eighteen, during his first year as a chemical engineering student at Tehran University's College of Engineering. Because of his academic excellence, he had been awarded a scholarship. He would have loved to be selected for study abroad, but his grades and family influence were not quite strong enough for that. He also had not done very well in foreign-language study in high school, primarily because he resented the mandatory study of English.

The majority of Akbar's college classmates were members of various political groups, ranging from the loyalists (who supported the continuation of the Pahlavi monarchy), of which there were very few in his college of engineering, through the Mujahiddin Khalk and the Fedayin Khalk (both leftist organizations, the first socialist and the second Marxist in orientation), to the Tudeh party (the pro-Soviet Communist Party in Iran). For Iranian students, joining political groups was as much a tradition as joining a fraternity or sorority was in the United States.

As Akbar became more involved, he found that he enjoyed the thrill of participating in such trivial activities as painting anti-Shah slogans on walls and displaying subversive posters. It was exciting in a way that he didn't quite understand. But, more importantly, he sincerely believed that what he was doing was right. The people had to be encouraged to believe that they could oppose the regime and get away with it, or the support necessary for the eventual overthrow of the Shah certainly never would materialize.

About a week before the night of October 15, 1973, when the silence was shattered by the sound of the police at his father's home, Akbar and several members of his militant association had distributed leaflets in an area adjacent to the bazaar in downtown Tehran. The police intervened after spotting the youths and tried to catch them as they fled through the maze of alleyways. One of Akbar's friends was caught, arrested, and taken in for questioning. Akbar was sure that his friend never would reveal the names of the others in the group, even if it meant the loss of his freedom or even his life. But Akbar did not yet know that the human will can be broken if enough pressure is applied. And the Iranian security services unquestionably were experts in applying pressure to extract information from their detainees.

As the electrically activated heavy steel door slammed behind him in the interrogation center of Khomeiteh prison, Akbar felt a sickness in the pit of his stomach. His slender body quivered with a degree of fear that he had never experienced before — fear brought on not by the unexpected, but by the expected. He never had felt so alone or so helpless. He looked around, attempting to survey the situation, but almost immediately he was blindfolded. Darkness seemed to make the situation even more dreadful. He could hear voices in the cell-block corridor where he was standing with a burly guard holding his arm tightly. Men inside the cells were mumbling softly to themselves and to each other. He couldn't hear what they were saying, but it was clear from their tone that the despair and helplessness he felt was typical of the mood of the other inmates.

After standing in the corridor for about twenty minutes, Akbar was told to strip completely. Still blindfolded, he removed his clothes and piled them on the floor. Brutal hands grabbed him and put him through a humiliating body search. He heard the sound of his clothes being ripped and the contents of his pockets dropping into a metal dish. He was moved to another small room; his clothes were thrown at him and he was told to dress quickly. The blindfold was removed and Akbar noticed that his belt, shoes, comb, and the rest of the items he carried in his pockets were missing. He also noticed that his prayer beads were gone.

Then Akbar made his first mistake as a prisoner — he pleaded with the guards to give him his prayer beads. His answer was a sharp punch to the bridge of his nose. He heard the bone crack as he literally saw stars; a warm rush of blood began to flow down his face.

"You will not have time to pray while you are here, terrorist. You are in much trouble and you'd better keep your mouth shut except to answer our questions — and when you are asked a question, you'd better answer with the truth or you will wish you had."

Akbar was thrown into a five-foot-by-seven-foot cell with a solid steel door and no window or other means of circulating air. The cell was barren except for a dirty, worn blanket and a filthy plastic bowl. A small light bulb hung from a bare wire in the center of the cell. Surveying his surroundings, a feeling of loneliness and uncertainty overpowered him. He never had been alone before, and the idea of not seeing another human or knowing if it was day or night instantly demoralized him. But he also realized that the environment was specifically designed to instill such fear and uncertainty. He prayed and tried to fight back his fears about the interrogation which he was sure would come. He wondered what would be done to him and whether he would be able to endure pain and suffering without disclosing the names of his accomplices. Or had they, too, been arrested already? There was no way to find out. He wondered about his family and hoped they were safe.

There was graffiti all over the wall of his cell. He read a slogan written in Farsi by a former occupant, a member of the People's Strugglers. It said, "The pain of the whip cannot erase the will of the people." Other slogans were written close to the floor, apparently by men no longer able to stand. He tried to sleep, but the pain in his nose was too intense. His head was throbbing and the area under his eyes hurt intensely. Finally he lapsed into an uneasy sleep.

About 8:30 the next morning, a guard entered Akbar's cell and told him to put on his blindfold. He was led to a toilet where there were other prisoners and was given two minutes to go to the bathroom and wash himself. Akbar said hello to a man in his late twenties; the man did not answer, but a guard rushed from the other end of the bathroom and pounced on Akbar with a flurry of hard punches to the head. He was stunned. Before his turn at the toilet came, another guard entered and told him to replace his blindfold for the trip back to his cell. On the return trip, the guard told him he would be allowed to use the toilet only three times each day.

Back in his cell, Akbar saw that his bowl had been draped with a large piece of *sang-yak* [Persian stone bread]. The bread wasn't fresh, but it wasn't too stale, either, and Akbar was very hungry. He had just begun to eat when another guard entered the cell with a tea kettle in each hand. One contained strong tea, the other boiling water. Akbar was instructed to present his bowl. The guard filled the bowl half full of pungent tea, then began to add water from the other kettle. As he poured the boiling water, he deliberately spilled it on Akbar's hands. The bowl fell to the floor as the laughing guard admonished him to be more careful or he would never enjoy his tea. Akbar looked down at the empty bowl and vowed that he would suffer the burning water next time rather than lose his tea. The dry bread stuck in his throat.

He spent most of the morning and early afternoon fighting loneliness. It would be so much better if he could talk to someone — anyone; then maybe some of the mystery of this horrible place would disappear. But he was all alone with his thoughts, fears, and uncertainties.

About mid-afternoon he was served a lunch of rice and *khoresh* [a Persian vegetable similar to spinach]. An hour later, the same guard who brought the tea in the morning returned with the two steaming kettles. Akbar cautiously presented his bowl; this time the hot water was carefully poured into the bowl. As the guard left the cell, Akbar tried to show his appreciation for not having his fingers burned by thanking the man. "Thank you," the guard replied in a mocking voice as he slammed the steel door behind him. After drinking the tea, Akbar was very uncomfortable. He still had to go to the toilet, but he had to wait another hour before he was allowed to relieve himself. When his time finally came, he did not speak, but hung his head and quietly waited. An older man noticed Akbar's signs of intense discomfort and motioned him to step in front of him. Akbar nodded his thanks and tried to smile.

Finally, on the eighth day of his confinement, Akbar was taken from his cell to a large room on the first floor of the prison. When his blindfold was removed, Akbar saw several guards standing around the room.

"Welcome, terrorist," growled a mean-looking guard with a three-foot length of rubber hose in his hand. "You think you are a big man, don't you? You engage in acts of terrorism against your country and its people, and you think you will not be punished, but you are wrong. You will be punished. But not today. Today we only want to play a little game with you. Do you know how to play soccer?"

Akbar didn't answer soon enough. His hesitancy was immediately punished with a kick to the groin. Screaming in agony, he slumped to the hard concrete floor.

"We are going to play some soccer, but, unfortunately, we forgot to bring a ball. You have volunteered to be our ball."

For the next forty-five minutes, he was kicked and punched by the guards. They appeared to take almost fiendish delight in the "soccer game" they played, and Akbar thought they never would stop. He ached all over, especially after a blow to his already broken nose. A solid punch early in the game had closed his left eye completely; he could feel his face and head swelling. His chest and rib cage hurt so badly that each breath he took made him feel faint.

At last he was blindfolded and jostled back to his cell. There, fatigue overcame his pain, and he managed to fall asleep. When he awoke, he was so sore he couldn't stand. The first time he tried, he passed out; the second time he managed to stay up. He tried to make an estimate of his injuries; none appeared to be too serious, but the nose was so badly swollen that he couldn't touch it without causing even greater pain.

His nightmare had begun.

3 WEST

GUNZENHAUSEN, WEST GERMANY
OCTOBER 15, 1973

West German Chancellor Willy Brandt, his Defense Minister, Georg Leber, and a host of American high brass — including NATO Commander General Andrew J. Goodpaster and U.S. Army in Europe Commander-in-Chief General Michael S. Davison — boarded helicopters after their visit to my battalion in the field. The huge CH-47 double-rotar, heavy-lift helicopters, which also had brought in more than eighty reporters, revved for takeoff. Those who were not wearing steel helmets held their soft caps against the chinooklike winds created by the noisy air taxis. The weather was typical for Germany in autumn — rainy and cold.

Late the night before, a confidential message had notified us of the chancellor's visit, and our battalion position had become a beehive of activity. This was the fifth consecutive year that we had participated in these large-scale maneuvers, moving entire combat units from stateside military posts by transport aircraft to Germany, and this was the first time that the German chancellor had visited an American unit during the exercises. Brandt's staff had briefed him very well; I'm sure he didn't remember meeting me when we reinforced Berlin after the construction of the Berlin Wall in August of 1961, but the chancellor, who was then Lord Mayor of Berlin, thanked me for what we had done then and asked how I was doing.

We were honored that our 860-man battalion was chosen from a force of eleven thousand men for his visit, and morale in the unit was as high as it possibly could be.

We had moved from our home station at Fort Riley, Kansas, to Germany for the maneuver. In an actual emergency, this was where my battalion would have been deployed. There is something about training on the actual terrain where it might be required to fight that brings out the best in any combat unit, and the battalion's performance during this mission was superb in every respect.

World events had given the maneuvers a new sense of urgency and realism during the two weeks prior to the chancellor's visit. The attack on Israel by her Arab neighbors had begun on October 6, just as we had started the wargame phase of our deployment. Reports of a Soviet military alert caused our government to place us on a high state of alert, too. We conducted reconnaissance missions of the positions we would move to initially if hostilities were to break out in Europe. It was very realistic training, indeed. I told my soldiers as soon as we were alerted how proud I was of them and that, if we had to fight the Russians, I believed the battalion was as ready for combat as any unit I had ever seen.

There were reports that we would not return to Fort Riley on schedule the next week, after the exercise was over, because aircraft requirements for the Israeli resupply mission were so heavy that there wouldn't be enough planes available to ferry us home. The initial war scare in Europe had subsided, but we had two or three weeks on our hands before we could go home. During this time, we planned to turn in our equipment, conduct limited training, and give as many troops as possible a few days furlough in Germany. I hoped the schedule also would allow me time to rest.

Pirmasens, West Germany

The maneuver ended on October 16, and we went to Grafenwohr for live-fire exercises before moving to Pirmasens to turn in our equipment and wait to go home. The countryside in that part of Germany is beautiful, with its forested mountains, fast-running brooks, and small rivers. I felt very much at home, having spent more than seven years in Germany during my military career.

But with the October War in progress, my mind frequently drifted back to places and friends in the Middle East, an area that had captivated my imagination and interest for years. It had been only seven years since I served in Iran as an assistant military attaché and developed very special friendships with men like Amir Fateh and Major General Ali Hojat-Kashani, but with combat duty in Vietnam and stateside assignments since then, it seemed much longer. I had heard from Amir and his lovely British-born wife, Monica, at Christmas, and they were doing fine. Amir's construction business was booming, and he and Monica seemed happy. Yet there was a hint of anxiety evident between the lines in Amir's letters. I got the distinct feeling that he was worried about the impact the rapid growth in Iran was having on the poor, who were not any better off now than they were before the Shah's Westernization and industrialization campaign began in the early 1960s. Amir was not a political animal, but he always seemed to keep an ear tuned to what was going on at the grass-roots level.

I had never heard him speak for or against the Shah, but I had heard him expound at length on what he believed to be best for the people of Iran. His solutions to Iran's growing pains involved a complex mixture of carefully developed and gradually implemented modernization and industrialization, while retaining and protecting Iran's traditional Islamic culture and society. He was truly an Iranian nationalist.

I recalled the many good times Betty and I had with Amir and Monica when we were stationed in Iran. They were among our closest friends. Even with Amir's building projects, which spanned the length and breadth of Iran, and my busy travel schedule as an attaché, we managed to spend many wonderful weekends together. Monica always said Amir needed to learn how to relax and get his mind off the business, and with us, he really seemed to enjoy himself.

Amir had known hard times when he first returned to Iran from Oxford University, where he earned a master's degree in civil engineering. He had married Monica in England and brought her and their firstborn son back to Iran when he graduated, only to be turned away by his wealthy importer father, who disowned him for marrying a non-Moslem foreigner. Amir worked first as a day laborer on the construction of the Tehran Hilton Hotel. Then he managed to pull himself up by the bootstraps, start his own successful construction company, and eventually get back in the good graces of his traditionalist father, who developed a real affinity for Monica and, by then, the Fatehs' four children.

Amir had built a beautiful home in his father's extensive compound just north of where I lived in Tehran. Here Monica and Betty took turns carpooling Amir's son and my daughter, Beth, to a British nursery school, and through them I met Amir. We became the kind of friends who never run out of subjects to discuss. He learned from me about America and the life of a soldier, and from him I added to my knowledge of the land which he loved so very much. I even accompanied Amir on several business trips and never ceased to enjoy his company and typical Persian sense of humor and hospitality. Amir knew I thoroughly enjoyed the Iranian national dish, *chello-kebab* [tender lamb filets broiled on a very hot charcoal fire and served on a bed of Persian long-grain rice with succulent native seasonings], so on special occasions he would bring his best cook from one of his construction sites in the Persian Gulf all the way to Tehran to prepare a special dinner for us. Amir, in turn, loved roast turkey, and I always made a special effort to have turkey when he and his family visited my home. Our friendship became so close that it was difficult for Betty and me to leave Iran when my volunteer letter for combat duty in Vietnam finally was approved. I had been trying for more than a year to go to Vietnam, because, as a professional officer, I considered it my duty to fight. But while my application was pending, my son Gregory Blake Scott was born in Tehran on July 15, 1966.

I had called Amir early that morning on my return from the hospital to tell him the good news. Amir dropped the phone, jumped in his car still wearing pajamas, and raced to my house. I finally got Monica on the other end of the phone and asked what had happened to Amir. She laughingly told me that he was on the way to my house to congratulate me — a typical Iranian reaction to the birth of a male child. To Amir, I was part of his family. We celebrated Greg's birth all that day, visiting all Amir's relatives and sharing the good news with them. It was a day I never will forget.

One week later, I received orders for Vietnam. It wasn't possible to have the orders changed because of Greg's appearance on the scene, so we hastily prepared to leave Iran amid the sorrow of saying goodbye to Amir and Monica.

The day before the movers came to our house to pack our furniture and belongings, Amir stopped by the house, ostensibly to get my help in making a decision on a rug he was considering purchasing. Acting like a typical Iranian rug merchant, he brought four beautiful Persian carpets into my marble-floored living room and unfolded them flat on the floor. "Chuck, I know you have studied our rugs, so I want you to tell me which of these is the best buy. The price tag on each of them is about the same. What do you think?"

Assuming that Amir was on the level, I set about the task of carefully examining the carpets. They all were exquisite examples of the Persian rugmaking art. Each was hand-knotted and unique. But the silk Isfahan, with its superb pattern and top-quality workmanship, was not only the most beautiful, it also was the most valuable. I told Amir that the Isfahan, if it were in fact equally priced with the others, certainly was the best buy. Amir's reply told me a lot about the value he placed on our friendship, but it also revealed a great deal about the legendary generosity of Iranians. "Chuck, I thought you would select the Isfahan. It is not only my favorite, but I had my father check them over, too, and he also selected the Isfahan." Then, looking me straight in the eyes with a warm smile beaming on his handsome face, Amir concluded in Persian, *"En khoda hafezi bayre shoma"* [This is a farewell gift for you]. The rug had to be accepted in accordance with Persian custom. I told Amir that it always would be displayed prominently in our home as a constant reminder of two wonderful people we had come to know and love in a land so far away from our roots in America.

The evening before we left Iran, Amir drove all night from a job site in Bushire, along the Persian Gulf, to say farewell to us at the airport. I was glad he made the trip, because he had to help detach our son from our Armenian maid who had fallen in love with the infant in just four weeks of caring for him. Amir and I shook hands, then hugged with teary eyes as we said goodbye. I boarded the flight for Rome, en route to a stop off in America before going to Vietnam, and Amir jumped back into his waiting Mercedes and drove back to Bushire, five hundred miles away. We wrote to each other occasionally in the ensuing years, and our friendship remained as strong as it had been that day at the Tehran airport.

I wondered if my next assignment would give me an opportunity to visit Iran again. I wanted so much to see Amir and Monica. So much had happened in my life since last we met.

My other dear friend, Major General Ali Hojat-Kashani, was the kind of man who would have risen to the top in any army. The son of a peasant, he had enlisted in the Imperial Iranian Army when the Shah's father, Reza Shah, was King of Kings. As an exception to tradition, because of his outstanding leadership abilities and native intelligence, Ali had been granted an appointment to the Iranian Military Academy. He was a physical fitness buff and a devoted family man. His wife was a beautiful woman, about twenty years his junior.

They had four children. Many would not consider the general a good Moslem because he enjoyed an occasional Scotch and water, but to me his code of ethics and his high moral standards marked him as a man among men. He did not speak English and had a reputation for being reserved in the presence of foreigners, yet I developed a close friendship with him from our first meeting.

His wry sense of humor and satirical preoccupation with protocol and the privileges of rank provided me with many a deep belly laugh. Ali would call my office mid-week and ask if I were standing at attention. As soon as I told him I had risen from my chair and was awaiting his orders, he would command me to load Betty and Beth into the car and travel to his summer home high in the mountains about sixty miles north of Tehran. I've never experienced anything more serene and blissful than those quiet weekends with just our two families high on the mountainside near Ab Ali, Iran. The air was so pure and the environment so still and peaceful that we often said those weekends were our only possible glimpse of Shangri-La. We would sit for hours enjoying the serenity of the mountain hideout, away from the cares and the noise of Tehran.

Ali enjoyed demonstrating his considerable physical strength when he was in a playful mood — which came often when he was enjoying the relaxing days and nights at Ab Ali. He would entice me near the edge of the ice-cold swimming pool and then throw me in. One day I decided I had had enough. When he grabbed me, I wrestled with him and, due mainly to my considerably larger size and heavier weight, I dumped the general in the pool. As I saw him splashing around, I wondered if I had just blown a beautiful friendship. Until then, I had always called him "General Hojat" and he had called me "Major." As Ali rescued himself from the freezing water, springing out with unusual agility, he extended his hand to me saying, "Chuck, from now on, you may call me General Ali." I did, and he called me Chuck from that moment.

Since then, he had been promoted to lieutenant

general and had moved from his assignment at the Military Academy. He wrote to me in Farsi several times while I was in Vietnam, and one weekend a doctor who was serving there with an Iranian medical team visited me at my Special Forces camp and delivered a box of pistachios from the general.

The Middle East had become the focal point of world interest in 1973, as many of my professors in the foreign-area specialist program had predicted it would many years earlier. I knew there had been many changes there, and the things I remembered most fondly might not be the same, but my inquisitive and romantic nature seemed to be beckoning me to return to the land of the rose, and the nightingale, and Omar Khayyám.

November 5, 1973
Fort Riley, Kansas

The five-week stint in Germany had been professionally rewarding, but it was nice to be home. With little to do but explore the local culinary delights at Pirmasens and the surrounding area, I had gained weight, so I went back to running every day. The battalion still occupied my attention, but I was becoming anxious about my next assignment. I wanted to stay in a command job, but those tours were tightly regulated so that more lieutenant colonels would get an opportunity to prove themselves as battalion commanders. The answer to my question was quick in coming.

"Sir, you've got a call from some colonel in the Puzzle Palace [the Pentagon]. He says he wants to talk to you about your next assignment." Sergeant Major Waller, the battalion's senior noncommissioned officer and my strong right arm, entered my office as he spoke. "Sir, tell him you want a soft ROTC job in Florida. Don't you let him send you to Washington or to one of those crazy Middle East places where people don't even speak English."

We both laughed as I pressed the button and picked up the telephone. "This is Lieutenant Colonel Scott."

The officer on the other end of the line had all the answers I'd been waiting for. A number of people in the intelligence business in the Pentagon had been relieved and shuffled off to other assignments as scapegoats; they, along with the Israelis, had been surprised by the well-coordinated Arab attack on October 6, 1973. It wasn't their fault, certainly, but that was the way things were done in Washington. I was to be assigned as the Middle East Desk Officer in the Defense Intelligence Agency in Washington, responsible for all the attaché offices at our embassies throughout the Arab World, Israel, and Iran. My new job began on December 1 — not much time to turn over command of the battalion, pack the family, and move halfway across the country. I was told that I would be making a trip to the Middle East as soon as I was briefed on my new duties.

As I hung up the phone, I figured I would have an opportunity to see Amir Fateh, General Ali, and other Iranian friends sooner than I had anticipated.

4 EAST

TEHRAN, IRAN
APRIL, 1974

"Akbar Houssini, you are guilty of the crime of engaging in terrorism against the state. You are hereby sentenced to three years in prison. I pray Allah will forgive you; the state will not. We will not tolerate your disregard of Iranian law."

The well-turned-out army colonel who uttered those words was head of the Third Military Tribunal, established to try cases such as Akbar's under military law, which was in clear violation of the Iranian constitution. From his comfortable chair, centered behind the table at the head of the small courtroom, the colonel meted out Iranian-style justice to alleged offenders. He and his two assistants, an Imperial Iranian Army lieutenant colonel and a major, were both judge and jury. The Iranian flag — with its horizontal green, white, and red tri-stripe, and the crown of the monarchy superimposed in gold — was prominently displayed behind the judges. The colonel, Ahmad Sayas, was an overweight, nervous little man whose flushed face betrayed his elevated blood pressure. His loyalty to the Shah and his regime was unquestioned. To his subordinates, he was a tyrant. To his superiors, he was an overly solicitous yes-man. Sayas was, in every possible connotation of the term, a consummate, self-serving opportunist. Unfortunately, he was not unusual in the Shah's military bureaucracy.

In 1964, Sayas was one of the three judges on a military tribunal which condemned to death four young soldiers from the Imperial Guard Brigade who were involved in the Marble Palace assassination attempt against the Shah. Despite the secrecy of the trial proceedings, which were not open to the public for fear of demonstrations by opposition elements, Sayas provided a daily, blow-by-blow account of the entire episode to a young American military attaché. The colonel was looking forward to his retirement years, and more than anything else in the world, he wanted a permanent U.S. visa. Two of his children were attending college in California, and he dreamed of spending his retirement in America with them, far away from the fears which haunted him each time he thought about the thousands of young people he had sent to prison. The fifty-five-year-old colonel never had considered passing secret information to a foreigner as treason. To Sayas, his actions represented premium payments on an insurance policy.

The courtroom was quiet following the sentencing except for low moans from the Houssini family, seated on benches in the rear of the courtroom. Other than a limited number of family members of those on trial and the guards who escorted the prisoners from various prisons throughout the city, the courtroom was empty. The newspapers received a list of the sentences only after the trials were over and those found guilty were already in prison.

Akbar stood at the docket, stunned by the cavalier manner in which more than three years of his life had just been forfeited for what was at most a nuisance offense.

Sayas' mind was elsewhere, however. He glanced at his watch in anticipation of a 1:30 meeting with his American attaché friend of several years ago, who was visiting Tehran for a few days from his new post in Washington.

Colonel Sayas decided to move on to more important matters. "Take him away!" he commanded, breaking the moment of silence. There were several other prisoners waiting for their "day in court," but they would have to wait. "Court will adjourn until tomorrow at the usual time," said Sayas as he rose and headed for the side door and his meeting with the American. He planned to retire within a year, unless he was promoted to brigadier general, and the meeting with the American was important to him. It was time to collect on his earlier favors and get his visa. The American who was to meet him was by then a lieutenant colonel. Since leaving Iran, he had served in Vietnam, commanded a mechanized infantry battalion, and was now stationed in the Pentagon in an intelligence job. Sayas was convinced that his American friend might be in a position to help his dream become a reality. Anyway, it was worth a try. After all, that was what friends were for, wasn't it?

"Put out your hands," commanded the senior guard who had escorted Akbar from his cell at Khomeiteh prison. Akbar complied automatically. Six months in prison had taught him only too well the cost in pain and suffering of the slightest hesitation in obeying the guards. Cold steel handcuffs were fastened to his wrists as he tried to catch a glimpse of his parents. He looked over his shoulder just long enough to see his mother being led gently out of the courtroom by his father. His brother and sisters were not permitted to witness his trial, and it was probably just as well — they were too young and would not understand their older brother's predicament.

Akbar was led out the rear door, down the hall, past groups of people standing outside other courtrooms, out the main entrance of the building, and down the pretentious marble steps to the waiting prison van. As he prayed for the strength to survive the next three years, he saw a foreigner racing up the courthouse steps. The man was in a business suit with a white shirt and blue tie. He had a military haircut. Akbar glanced at him for a moment and guessed that he was an American. His heart filled instantly with resentment and animosity. Perhaps everything he had been told about American influence was true. Why was this American in an Iranian court? Was the United States so deeply involved with the Shah's regime that it even monitored the number of Iranians sentenced to prison for activities against the Shah? As the American passed by, he looked directly at Akbar for a fleeting moment. Akbar was surprised. The stranger's eyes were not those of a jackal — they seemed saddened by the sight of the handcuffed prisoner. Akbar averted his glance. He did not want to change his mental image of Americans as oppressive supporters of the Shah. It was better to hate in order to survive the next three years. As Akbar entered the prison van, he glanced one last time at the courthouse. The American was talking to the military judge who had just sentenced him. The sliding steel door of the prison van slammed shut.

Akbar was caged in a twenty-five-foot-by-twenty-foot prison cell with twenty-six other prisoners. He had one battered and worn army blanket, a plastic bowl, and a plastic dish. The air was foul and many of his fellow prisoners were sick. Three times a day he was taken to the latrine to wash his bowl and glass and to take care of his personal needs. Each day seemed an eternity, but at least he had not been beaten by the guards or subjected to the tortures of the special basement room since his trial. The spontaneous beatings which he had received frequently before his trial never would be forgotten, but they were nothing compared to the horrible sessions he suffered through in the torture chamber when his tormentors tried in vain to get him to divulge the names of others in the anti-Shah movement. There were permanent scars on the soles of his feet, where he was flogged with steel electrical cable until he lost consciousness. His broken nose had healed crooked, but it no longer hurt. After talking to his cellmates and seeing the condition some of them were in, Akbar realized that he had been luckier than many. Some of the others told stories of their ordeals in the chamber of horrors that made Akbar's beatings seem trivial. Some were strapped to steel bed springs, sprayed with water, and then subjected to electrical shocks. Others were fitted with adjustable metal helmets used to encase the human head and squeeze it until the victim confessed or until his skull was crushed.

His fellow prisoners represented various political persuasions. Many seemed to have nothing in common philosophically except their shared belief in the need for a major change in the government. From the Marxists, through the Islamic socialists and the Islamic fundamentalists, to the secular democrats, there was but one common thread: hatred of the Shah and his government. Akbar was an Islamic fundamentalist by training and by choice. He did not agree with the Marxists or the Islamic socialists, but he knew that if the anti-Shah movement was to be successful, there had to be a strong coalition of opposition elements. Akbar's hatred of the regime and the United States was intensified by his exposure to the political discussions in his cell with older, more experienced, and better educated opponents of the regime. He never realized how many people opposed the Shah until he went to prison.

Akbar had been permitted a visit from his mother and father twice since his trial. It was good to see them, but he wondered if it were really worth it when he remembered the worried look in his mother's eyes. She, of course, had asked him not to get involved in politics. But it was too late for that. He would work to oust the Shah when he finally was released. Meanwhile, he would pray to Allah for strength to survive so that he could make a contribution to Islam later.

Akbar prayed five times each day. In the tradition of all devout Moslems, who wish to demonstrate their willingness to submit to Allah, he would prostrate himself on the ground, facing in the direction of Mecca as he prayed. Most of his fellow prisoners were also practicing Moslems, so in their overly crowded cell, it was difficult for them to make room for everyone during these acts of surrender to their God. But Akbar and his cellmates were cooperative with each other and managed to continue their prayers, even after an order had been issued that they weren't allowed.

When the prisoners failed to obey the order, the guards began entering the cell, swinging their wooden clubs to stop the praying. Akbar was beaten several times, but his resolve only increased with each beating. He believed he was doing what God would have him do. During confrontations with the guards, in which his cellmates urged him on, he even tried to appeal to the guards' sensitivities as fellow Moslems. He became informal spokesman for his cell, and it was usually he who paid the price for the prisoners' rebellion against orders. But in a way that he couldn't explain, he enjoyed the respect which he gained from the other prisoners for his religious zeal.

Then one day the guards adopted a new strategy. When they entered the cell, they didn't hit any of the other prisoners who were praying. Instead, three guards grabbed Akbar, dragged him out of his cell, beat him senseless, and then dumped him in another wing of the prison. As he regained his senses, he saw that he was in a sitting position in a hot, stuffy, cagelike cell so small that he couldn't even lie down. It would be impossible for him to pray, he realized, and he began to cry.

At about 2:00 that afternoon, a guard opened the Judas-hole cover on the door of his cell and demanded his bowl. But Akbar didn't have one. "My bowl is still in my other cell, I guess," said the famished Akbar, hoping his jailer would get another for him.

"Oh, yes, you are the terrorist who would rather pray than eat. Let's see if you can pray now. You'd better pray that I remember to bring you another bowl when I come with food before you starve." The steel slot was slammed shut. Akbar was alone, without food or water. And he couldn't even pray.

Two days later, he finally was given a bowl and

rice. He wasted no time devouring the white substance with his fingers.

       After two weeks in the cell, Akbar was taken to a shower room and told to bathe. He was told that he was going on a "little journey." He was issued standard prison clothing and loaded onto a bus with about forty other inmates. As the bus was winding through south Tehran, Akbar passed familiar sights. He was in his old neighborhood, but not close enough to catch a glimpse of his father's house. He was homesick, and he wondered where the bus was taking him. One of the other prisoners said he had heard that they were being moved to the national prison at Bushire on the Persian Gulf.

       After about an hour and a half, the bus passed through the holy city of Qom, where the exiled Ayatollah Khomeini once taught theology and overtly opposed the Shah. Several hours later, they passed the fabled city of Isfahan, which the poets of old called "half the world" because of its splendor. Akbar had never seen Isfahan before, and the sights and sounds of the city made him yearn to be free. The prison bus continued to move with its human cargo through Shiraz, the City of Roses, where Akbar's view of the flowered boulevards caused him to think of poetry and of other days when he was free and at home with his beloved family. Contrasting this beauty with the life he was leading was almost too much. But after what he had been through at the hands of the Shah's bullies, he had a sense of commitment that was extraordinary for a man of his years.

       As the bus descended the steep and winding Kazerun Pass, the heat and humidity became almost unbearable. Akbar knew very little about this part of his homeland, but the road sign was unmistakable; the man who had speculated on the bus' final destination had been correct — "Bushire 25 km."

Two and a half years had passed since Akbar arrived at Bushire National Prison. He had survived in spite of the oppressive heat, the crowded cells, and the unpalatable food. There was bread and tea in the morning, rice and occasionally a vegetablelike stew at midday, and bread again in the evening. He was permitted to shower once each week, but he had not been allowed to have any visitors. The main reason he had been sent off to a prison so far away from his family, a guard told him, was so that prison officials would not be bothered with bleeding-heart visitors who spread rumors about the treatment prisoners received. He had spent his time reading, when he was allowed to have books, and had tried to teach himself English from a textbook given to him by one of the older inmates who befriended him. Although he still opposed the mandatory study of English in school, he had come to realize that this knowledge could help him in his battle against the Shah and Western influences. He really hadn't been abused or harassed in Bushire. In fact, a few of the guards actually had been kind to him. When sugar was doled out for the weekly ration, he usually was given more than an ample allocation by a guard who gibed him about being too skinny. "Here, take some more, young man; you look as though you need all the sugar you can eat. Try to gain a little weight or you will give this prison a bad name — if you are ever freed."

The guards in this prison are essentially men just like me, Akbar thought. They were not as hateful and sadistic as those in Tehran had been. Perhaps they were far enough away from the political intrigues and corruption of the capital to be able to relate easier to their charges. In any case, in spite of the boredom and deplorable living conditions, imprisonment here was better than in Tehran. And here, at least, Akbar was permitted to pray. A mullah spoke to the occupants of Akbar's cell one day just before the Shah's birthday as a special form of amnesty. The mullah gave Akbar a copy of the Koran, which he studied from then on. The mullah was accompanied by a guard, so he was not free to speak his mind, but he did tell Akbar to keep faith and to pray that God's will be done.

The mullah also brought Persian dates and pistachio nuts, which he distributed to the prisoners. Akbar kept his as long as possible, eating only two or three each day as a welcome relief from the standard tasteless prison food. He tried not to think about his mother's cooking and his home.

Akbar reckoned his three years were about up, but he had heard nothing about his release. He was beginning to wonder if he had been forgotten by the prison officials in Tehran. He heard of others who had rotted in prison for a year or so after their sentences were completed, but there was nothing he could do. If he asked too many questions, he knew he would only attract attention to himself and reap the wrath of the guards.

"Akbar Houssini, come with me. You are being sent back to Tehran for a hearing on your sentence." Akbar was elated. He guessed he was going to Tehran for release.

The trip seemed to take forever. Akbar wondered what it would be like to be free again. He had survived and he was stronger and more mature than when his sentence began. He also was more resolved than ever to work to overthrow the Shah. But Akbar was too excited to think very much about politics. He just wanted to return to his family and enjoy being with them for a while before he tried to go back to college — and before he became active in the opposition movement.

In Tehran, Akbar was returned to Khomeiteh prison, which was even more crowded than when he had been there before. Many of his new cellmates were still being interrogated, and fear filled his heart each time the guards entered the crowded cell to pluck another victim for torture. Akbar had learned how to be low-key and not to try to be a hero. He knew he couldn't help these poor souls, so he didn't try.

After about ten days, Akbar was summoned before a military tribunal. Two of the judges had been on the court that originally sentenced him. Only the senior judge was new: a younger colonel with an immaculate uniform and a chest full of decorations and awards. He was soft-spoken and looked Akbar in the eyes when he said, "You must return to your cell and write a confession of all the things you did for which you were originally sentenced. You must also tell everything you have learned in prison. After you do this and I have time to read your statement, I will decided whether or not you are now a man and not a young boy seeking trouble and confrontation."

Akbar was flabbergasted. "But my three-year sentence was up more than a month ago. I should be set free. Three years of my life have already been wasted. I am sorry, but. . . ."

The young judge seemed to relish his power over this helpless individual. "If you are sorry, then write that also. I will then decide if you are a man or a boy."

Back in his cell, Akbar wrote as though his life depended on it. In a way, it did. He wrote a detailed account of the mischief he had engaged in before his arrest, and he lied about his intended future. He knew he had to convince the judge that he had learned a lesson and would toe the mark for the rest of his life if he were to gain his freedom. To have the decision on whether or not he was to be freed rest solely on his "confession" seemed unfair, but he would satisfy the requirement. He was told by a cellmate that if he really wanted to convince the judge, he should close his paper with "long live the Shah" or "God protect the Shah." Even at that point, Akbar had trouble writing such words. But he wanted to go home. He ended the fifteen-page testimonial with the clincher: "Long live the Shah, [signed] Akbar Houssini."

A week later the court summoned Akbar from his cell. The judge again looked Akbar straight in the eyes as he addressed him. "I have read your confession — it is pretty good." Akbar tried to stifle a grin, but the judge was not finished. "It is pretty good, but it is not good enough. You are not yet a man. You need more time to think. That is all; take him away."

Akbar's heart sank, but he knew there was no rebuttal. Anything he said would only add time to his indeterminate sentence. He wondered if he would ever go free.

This time, he was taken to Evin prison, north of the city. It was also a maximum-security prison with a reputation for terrible mistreatment and cruelty. Robbers, murderers, sex offenders, and political prisoners were not separated here, and the guards treated their captives worse than animals. Akbar was put in a cell with about thirty of the most ragged and motley-looking human specimens he had ever seen. One of them was a crazy homosexual who almost immediately made advances at Akbar. One night, after the small light bulb in the center of the cell was turned out by a guard, the homosexual sneaked around the sleeping horde of suffering humanity and pounced on Akbar. Like a young virgin, Akbar fought for his virtue. He finally overpowered the man, but it was too late. The guards heard the disturbance, rushed into the cell, and began to club Akbar. "What is going on here? Can't you people even get along with each other?" they shouted. The guards asked the other prisoners what had happened, but they were too prison-smart to take sides and professed to know nothing. Akbar was hauled out of the cell, beaten, and thrown into solitary. He was told that he was a troublemaker, and that if he ever was caught fighting again, he would be executed. He told the guards what had happened, but they only laughed and told him that all the prisoners were a little crazy, and he would have to get accustomed to it.

On a bright, cloudless summer day fifteen months later, Akbar was summoned from his cell by one of the special guards from the administrative office of the prison. A number of prisoners had been released during the previous month or so — the result of a new amnesty program which the Shah's government had initiated to dispel criticism of the regime for its deplorable human rights record. Akbar had heard rumors that the American president, Jimmy Carter, had needled the Shah about Iran's political prisoners. Akbar had heard rumors there was seething unrest in the country, and that the Shah might be trying to deflate the charges of inhuman treatment of political prisoners by releasing captives not considered a real danger to the regime. Akbar prayed all of this was true and that he would be among those selected for release. The wait outside the administrative office was interminable, but there were some good signs — others were leaving the office with broad grins, mumbling as they passed him, *"azade"* [freedom].

"Next." It was Akbar's turn. He entered and immediately was summoned to a large desk in the far corner of the office. "Congratulations, Akbar Houssini, you are being released on probation today." He was told to sign his release papers, and that he must have a copy of them with him at all times. "You are to stay away from all organizations that are involved in any way against your government," he was told. "Do you understand?"

"Balle, gorbon" [Yes, sir], was Akbar's instant reply. He was given one hundred rials for bus fare and escorted to the main gate of Evin prison. Peering at the high brick wall with its watchtowers, he realized why thoughts of escape from this prison were only an exercise in futility. But he no longer needed to dream of escape. He was escorted through the heavy gate, past the guards, and onto the busy street, which was filled with multitudes of Iranians pursuing ordinary daily activities. He was so happy and thrilled that

he had to fight back tears. But it wasn't a time for tears; it was time to rejoice and thank God for His wonderful gift of freedom.

As Akbar waited for the bus in his prison clothes, he was checked several times by passing policemen. In each instance, he produced his release papers and was told to be careful and stay out of trouble. He was surprised at how little notice was made of his prison clothes by the other passengers on the bus. The people had grown accustomed to seeing recently released prisoners heading home in the wake of the new amnesty. In a moment of deep thought just before he darted off the bus for the final walk to his parents' home, Akbar contemplated freedom. He realized that he was not really free; he was simply no longer in prison. His vision of true freedom never could be realized as long as the Shah and his police wielded power in his homeland. He had been punished, but he had not been reformed or rehabilitated. His hatred was stronger than ever.

4 WEST

TEHRAN, IRAN
APRIL, 1974

The pilot of the Saudi Arabian airlines flight from Jiddah to Tehran announced that we would be landing at Mehrabad International Airport in about five minutes. As we circled the field at an altitude of about five thousand feet, I peered out the window trying to catch a glimpse of the city below. The Tehran skyline was liberally dotted with newly constructed high-rise buildings, and for each new building there were two more under construction. A few of the cranes were still at their labor, lifting huge steel beams into place. It was as though there were a great competition under way to determine who could build the highest and most pretentious structure.

In the three months I had been on my new job as the Middle East Desk Officer at the Defense Intelligence Agency, I had been to the Middle East three times, but this was my first visit to Tehran. Most of my effort had been directed toward Israel and the reopening of our embassies in Cairo and Damascus. We had been asked to leave Egypt and Syria during the June Arab/Israeli War in 1967, but after the Arab/Israeli hostilities in October, 1973, we had resumed diplomatic relations with these two Arab countries. Our embassies, which had been vacant for six years, were freshly painted and staffed by a new group of diplomats, eager to demonstrate their prowess by somehow getting along with the same Egyptians and Syrians who had thrown us out years earlier. So goes the cycle of diplomatic machinations in the Middle East, I thought as we began our final approach.

It was difficult to believe that I was finally back in Iran. When I was in combat in Vietnam, I had often thought of old friends here, and I had been looking forward to this visit now for a long time. In anticipation of my trip, I had written to Amir Fateh and General Ali Hojat. Their replies had been cordial and enthusiastic.

Amir asked me to wire him when my plans were definite, so he could meet my flight and welcome me properly. He had insisted that I stay at his home north of the city. He also said I should try to take a week or two of vacation while in Iran, so we would have more time to visit and see firsthand the great changes that had taken place during my seven-year absence. I got the feeling he was as excited about my visit as I was.

General Hojat's letter, written in Farsi, had been more formal than I expected, but it, too, was friendly. The general, in accordance with his usual manner, had ordered me to call him as soon as I arrived and had a spare moment, so we could make specific plans for our time together. As a professional soldier, he also expressed an interest in hearing about my experiences in Vietnam. He philosophized that wars in the future would be more like the one we had fought there than the second World War. He stressed the importance of learning how to fight guerrilla and insurgency wars.

As I reminisced about these two very different but very dear friends, I was reminded of a truism I learned years earlier about Iranians: They're slow to make friends, but once you are accepted, you are their friend for life. And with them, absence really does make the heart grow fonder. Like so many of us, they forget the bad times and remember only the good, so friendships seem even more valuable after a period of separation. As much as I had enjoyed getting back to Morocco, Tunisia, Lebanon, Saudi Arabia, Jordan, Egypt, and Syria, not to mention Israel, it was going to be really great to be in Tehran for five days. I had intentionally

arranged my itinerary so I would be in the city over the
weekend. My other option would have been to visit Tehran
first, then go to Jiddah for the weekend. No difficult decision
to make in that case, I thought as the plane stopped in front
of the terminal.

The Iranian and Arab passengers bullied their
way past me and scrambled toward the door as though it
were a matter of honor to be first off the aircraft. I had
grown accustomed to this machismo characteristic of Middle Easterners, so I waited. I planned to take a cab to the
Semiramis Hotel, directly across the street from the embassy on the busy corner of Avenue Takht-e Jamshied and
Avenue Roosevelt. We had stayed at the Semiramis in 1964
when we first arrived in Tehran and again on our way out of
Iran in 1966. The hotel owner, Abbas, and his wife Parven
were old friends, the rooms were not bad, and the prices
were much better than the newer hotels. The location also
was ideally close to the embassy and within walking distance
of the main bazaar. And I had always enjoyed having dinner
at the rooftop restaurant, with its excellent view of the
downtown section of the city.

I had asked the attaché office not to bother having someone pick me up at the airport — I looked forward to
a little time alone as my nostalgic sojourn began.

Abbas was on hand to greet me when I arrived
at his hotel. He had a hundred questions. How had I been?
How was my family? How long would I be staying? Did I
want to have a nightcap with him before I retired for the
evening? It was almost midnight before I was able to overcome Abbas' hospitality and turn in for the night. I figured it
was too late to call Amir and certainly too late to call the
general.

The-eight-and-a-half-hour time difference between Washington and Tehran had an effect on my sleeping
patterns. I was wide awake at 3:30 and anxious to get busy
with the day's events. After breakfast with Abbas and his

wife, I checked in at the embassy. Amir already had been pestering the attaché secretary for information on my whereabouts. I called him at his home, catching him before he left for his downtown office. Amir insisted that I not remain in the hotel — I would have to stay at his home so we would have more time to talk. I finally agreed and we arranged for him to pick me up at the hotel on his way home from work.

At nine o'clock, I met with Ambassador Richard Helms, former director of the Central Intelligence Agency. He was cordial and happy to receive the copy of the *Playboy* magazine interview with him which had hit the newsstands as I was leaving Washington. The Watergate affair had spilled over onto the ambassador, and he was anxious to read about himself to make sure that the interview had not gotten twisted in publication. I spent the rest of the day at the embassy dealing with problems our attachés had encountered, and I picked up a couple of invitations from old acquaintances who had found out about my visit.

One was an invitation to have lunch with an Iranian Army colonel who had voluntarily provided tidbits of information, not available from other sources, when I was stationed here earlier. His name was Sayas and he was a nuisance. He always went out of his way to ingratiate himself with those he thought might be in a position to do him a favor. The favor he wanted was a green card — a permanent residency visa for the United States. I had told him several times in the past that I had no authority to grant something like that, but he had persisted in keeping our relationship alive. Colonel Sayas was an acquaintance, not a friend. I didn't like him, and I didn't trust him. He had no conscience. If his motivations for passing his country's secrets to foreigners had been political, perhaps I could have understood. But he was not against the Shah or his government. He wasn't really against anything, as far as I knew. He was *for* Sayas, and he would do anything to gain favor with those he thought he might be able to use. I wondered why he wanted to see me.

The other was a formal invitation to dinner at General Ali Hojat's residence. That one would be a pleasure, but I was puzzled by the formality. The invitation had been sent through the Iranian Foreign Liaison Office of Iranian G-2 [Intelligence]. It had an official approval stamp and more sets of initials than a Russian travel permit. Dress was to be "informal," according to the invitation, so I assumed it was going to be a large dinner party. We had never had to go through this kind of red tape to have dinner together before.

Amir was right on time. That was unusual for most Iranians, but Amir had learned punctuality as an Oxford student. He had been overweight and paunchy when I last saw him, but the protruding stomach was gone. His massive shoulders and thick neck looked more imposing than ever with his slim waistline. He was a bundle of energy, friendliness, and classic Persian manners.

"Chuck, you look great," he said. "How are Betty and the kids? Why did you not call when you got in last night? I waited up for you."

He embraced me in a brotherly bear hug as he spoke, and people in the hotel lobby turned to witness his exuberance. We laughed and discussed all the things he had planned for me during my visit, both of us talking at once. Some of the spectators began to laugh with us. Amir was very Westernized, but he retained the old Iranian ways when it came to greeting a friend. He was emotional, and he was genuinely warm and caring. "You must be tired after your long trip; let me take your bag. We must hurry. Monica is having a special dinner for you."

He picked up my heavy suitcase as though it were empty, waving off the hotel bellhop. His new Mercedes was illegally parked directly in front of the hotel. Amir opened the trunk and dumped the suitcase inside as passersby detoured around the offending auto. We headed north through the rush-hour traffic toward Amir's house at Shimeran, an upper-class suburban residential area overlooking the city.

After filling each other in on all that had happened to us and our families since our last meeting, Amir was uncharacteristically silent for a moment. I asked him in Persian the equivalent of "a penny for your thoughts," and after a bit more superficial chatter, Amir became very serious and intense. "Chuck, you can see signs of change everywhere. We are building a new country here, but I sometimes wonder if we are moving too fast for our people." Amir voiced his concern that the traditional Persian society was having great difficulty in the new Iran orchestrated by the Shah and his ambitious plans. His fear was that too much of the traditional lifestyle and values was being eroded by the rapid changes. He didn't say anything against the Shah, but he made it very clear that he was afraid those who opposed him might be gaining strength precisely because of the changes which had not brought about a better life for the masses. Amir spoke of shantytowns that had sprung up all over, where poor villagers had moved to the city in search of jobs but found none. According to Amir, these people were developing into ideal listeners for those who opposed the drive to industrialize and modernize the country. Amir believed that as long as the opposition groups were not permitted a voice in government, there was an ever-present danger that they might unite and use force to slow the rate of change, or try to overthrow the monarchy.

I asked Amir if he thought there really was a possibility of some group overthrowing the Shah in the foreseeable future. Amir was thinking about my question when we entered the alleyway leading to the main gate of his father's huge, walled compound. He honked his horn four times, and the gardener ran out to open the gate from the inside. He drove past his father's house, through the well-tended gardens, until we arrived at the spacious home. As we were getting out of the car, Amir asked me to wait a minute. He had had time to think about my question, and he wanted to answer it before we went inside. I suspected that he didn't want to alarm Monica with his candid estimate of the possible troubles that he thought might be ahead. Amir grasped my left upper arm with his right hand as he spoke. "Chuck, there is much resentment building among the lower classes here, and I am afraid that if some means is not found to permit a free expression of opposing views without fear of reprisal, there could well be major trouble and bloodshed within the next few years." He spoke as a son mourning his father's serious illness. Amir was afraid that the Shah's increasing heavy-handedness against opposition voices would be his undoing. He did not see any way of avoiding a bloodbath in Iran, unless the Shah was willing to win over his opponents by listening and then acting on their grievances.

As Amir finished speaking, I became aware of a barking dog in the background and then a female voice speaking Farsi with a delightful English accent. *"Khosh omadien, Chuck"* [Welcome, Chuck]. It was Monica, deeply tanned and more beautiful than ever. I got out of the car and embraced her. She kissed my cheek and hugged me tightly.

Inside, Monica instructed the houseboy to bring in my suitcase from the car and put it in the guest room. The house didn't look much different from what I remembered. It was a big, well-furnished home, but it looked cozy and very much lived in. It was great to be back with these special people.

I arrived at General Hojat's residence a discreet ten minutes late, in compliance with Iranian custom. I was the only guest. The general had aged, but he still looked as though he could whip his weight in mountain lions. His wife was elegantly dressed in a white knit suit that did not camouflage her eye-turning figure. She had not aged; if anything, she, like Monica Fateh, was more beautiful than I remembered. Her creamy white skin seemed to emphasize the black sheen of her hair and the darkness of her exquisite eyes. Her smile was as genuine as her personality. I told her as she kissed me that she and the general were still the best-looking couple in Tehran. The general's reply was typically Iranian: *"Taarof nakone, Agoya Sarhang"* [Don't be so polite, Colonel]. But I was serious, and I sensed that he appreciated the compliment. I spent the evening chatting with the Hojats about my family and things that had happened to us during the seven years since I saw them last. As it got late, and I finally told the general I had to leave, he enjoined me to linger a little longer. After Mrs. Hojat excused herself and left us alone, he immediately explained the formal invitation, which he knew would cause me to wonder. All visits with foreigners, even those from friendly nations, by senior Iranian military officers had to be approved in advance by Iranian intelligence, he told me. General Ali didn't like it, but that was the way it was, so he had to comply. He said it wasn't really a problem, just an inconvenience. The reason — growing resentment by the Shah's opponents to close ties with the West, especially the United States. They saw these friendly relations as sinister foreign interference in Iran's internal affairs, especially in cases where Western diplomats were given preferential treatment. So the Shah had decreed that all contacts had to be approved by G-2 or the Ministry of Foreign Affairs. It was an attempt to take the wind out of the sails of those who were using these routine foreign contacts as propaganda to undermine the Shah.

General Ali also had a friendly word of caution: "Chuck, be very careful. You know about the two American colonels who were assassinated last year. It is no longer safe for you to wander about the city alone as you did when you worked at the embassy." General Ali admitted that he was genuinely concerned for the safety of Americans in Tehran. He said he expected to see an increase in terrorism, and Americans were prime targets. Opposition to the Shah had become synonymous with opposition to the United States. America was being blamed for every action the Shah ordered, especially actions that dealt with suppression and neutralization of the anti-Shah movements.

On our way home the previous night, Amir had pointed out the exact spot where the two colonels had been gunned down. They had been driving to work at the ARMISH MAAG [American Military Advisory Mission] Headquarters when they were sprayed with machine-gun fire.

"Sir, do you think these groups have the capability to strike at will, or do you believe SAVAK can stop them?" I asked.

General Ali spoke cautiously. He didn't want to be an alarmist, but he seemed to feel an obligation to be honest. "Chuck, no matter how tough SAVAK may be on these terrorists or how good a job they do of maintaining surveillance of the main groups, there is always a chance of additional killings. There are so many Americans here, and they are so easy to identify." Ali also said Americans were creatures of habit, which made it very easy for assassins to select the time and place to strike.

I was getting tired and it was late. I thanked General Ali for his hospitality and told him that I was looking forward to having lunch with him on Friday. We shook hands, then he reached out spontaneously and embraced me in a bear hug.

I was running late the next day. My meetings at the embassy had lasted much longer than anticipated, so it was almost ten minutes after one by the time I raced out the Chancellery to the parking lot, where my driver was waiting to take me to my rendezvous with Colonel Sayas.

The downtown midday traffic was laboriously slow. There was no way to get around it, so we sat for minutes at a time, amid the blaring horns and the impatient drivers. It

was 1:30, and we were still two blocks from Sayas' court —
and we weren't moving at all. I decided to walk and have the
driver meet me at the court building after lunch. I jogged down
the busy street, dodging pedestrians like a running back. When
I approached the building, I decided to run up the long, marble
courthouse steps and then walk calmly once I was inside the
building, to appear more dignified.

Halfway up the steps, I saw a group of uniformed
men escorting a handcuffed prisoner down the steps. I wondered if he was one of Sayas' victims. I recalled how Sayas had
bragged about how easy his job was because he didn't even
have to decide on sentences. That was all determined by his
superiors before the trials began. The sentence depended on
the Shah's mood, and it varied according to his changing
perceptions of the opposition.

I slowed my pace just enough to catch a glimpse of
the prisoner. He was a young man, probably not more than
twenty years old, but he clearly showed the strain of what he
had been through. His eyes met mine for a split second; they
were filled with a hatred and frustration that was beyond
description. His bigger than average nose was slightly askew,
as if it had been broken, and he walked strangely, as though he
had a pound of carpet tacks in his shoes. I felt sorry for him. I
continued to stare at him, but he turned away.

As I reached the top of the steps and began to
slow my pace on the landing, I saw Colonel Sayas walk out the
main door. He was even fatter than I remembered, and he
looked nervous. How I loathed this supercilious man.

Sayas greeted me warmly, in customary Iranian
fashion. I apologized for being late, and he replied, "You are
not late at all. I just this minute finished my last trial of the day
and decided to greet you here."

I couldn't help myself. "Did you sentence him to
life, or did you give him a really stiff sentence?"

Sayas still had his cavalier, warped sense of humor
when it came to his work. "You are still very funny, Colonel.

No, this time I only sent the guilty man to prison for three years." He enjoyed his power over others' lives. He expanded his chest with a sense of pride and continued, "Sooner or later, we will have all the troublemakers in prison, and then I can retire with a clear conscience. We have been very busy. The rabble do not ever seem to learn that they can do nothing against the government."

My luncheon meeting with Sayas produced nothing new. He wanted me to put in a good word at the appropriate places to get him a resident visa for the United States. I told him again that I was afraid I would be no help. He also said there had been a significant increase in the number of arrests for minor offenses against the regime, such as possession of anti-regime literature and the destruction or defacing of government property. He thought tough sentences would solve the problem. He claimed that all of the opposition groups were supported by the Communists. Sayas believed that if a Communist label were attached to every member of the Shah's opposition, the United States government would be less critical of Iran's growing prison population.

Once again, Sayas proved himself to be a man who needed no encouragement to cut corners. As I was leaving him after our meeting, he cautioned me not to mention to anyone that we had met, because he had not bothered to get permission for our meeting from the Intelligence Office. I guessed he had permission but wanted to impress me with his influence and independence.

Aboard Pan Am Flight Number Two, headed for Beirut, I reflected on my first trip to Iran in more than six years. Old friendships remained strong, and, all in all, my visit was a success. But I had an uneasy feeling about Iran that I had never before experienced. I had always thought that the Shah would stay in power as long as he continued to curry favor in the Armed Forces. After this visit, I wasn't so sure. Things were changing rapidly, and what bothered me most was the haunting realization that our continued presence in Iran depended solely on the Shah's retaining power. We had become so identified with the Shah that it would be almost impossible to disassociate ourselves from him if ever he lost his throne. I had clear images of Amir, Monica, General Ali and his lovely wife, Colonel Sayas, and others in the mosaic of memories of that visit as I dozed off to sleep. But I also saw the image of that young prisoner being led down the court steps. What did he represent? And, more importantly, what impact would men like him have on Iran's future?

5 EAST

TEHRAN, IRAN
EARLY AUGUST, 1978

The bus ride from Evin prison to his downtown neighborhood was a thrilling eye-opener for the young revolutionary. Although rumors of demonstrations and riots against the Shah's government had reached Akbar in prison, he was surprised by the scope and destructive power of these clashes. Movie theaters, banks, liquor stores, and establishments selling luxury goods had been burned, looted, and closed by the rioters. To the mobs, these were arrogant symbols of secular influence, or outward manifestations of Western penetration of the traditional Islamic society. After more than four years in the Shah's dungeons, Akbar was excited by the prospect of rejoining his beloved family. But he also was genuinely elated by the sight of these burned-out monuments to the effectiveness of the opposition in directly challenging the regime.

Only five blocks separated Akbar from his family as he got off the bus. The mood of the people in the streets was different from the sullen, subdued attitude he remembered from his preprison days. There was no fear of the authorities apparent as people discussed the latest riots, strikes, and demonstrations. Akbar was torn: He would have enjoyed lingering for a while to eavesdrop on these captivating discussions of recent events and speculation on the future, but his first priority was dictated by his blood and his feelings for his family. He wanted to get to his father's house without delay. He began to perspire and his breathing became hurried as he got closer to home. He realized that he had subconsciously increased his gait from a walk to a jog as he turned onto Kuche Saadi, his father's street.

No. 16, Kuche Saadi, looked about the same as he remembered, except that the door — battered down by the police in what seemed an earlier lifetime — had been replaced by a heavier, stronger blue-painted door. Akbar knocked gently. *"Janabali?"* [Who is it?] It was his mother's voice, and the hardened, dedicated fighter for change melted inside. In spite of the satisfaction he got from seeing his comrades' handiwork against the dreaded Shah, and his compulsion to join them at the earliest moment, he was once again a little boy, anticipating his mother's warmth and tenderness.

"Pesar-a-shoma, Madar – Akbar." [It is your son, Mother — Akbar.] His voice wasn't as strong as he thought it should be; he was choking with emotion. In the split second before she replied, he added, "I am home, Mother."

Akbar's mother was simultaneously laughing, crying, and shouting to alert the rest of the family as she quickly withdrew the heavy bolt and opened the door. Relief, happiness, and love nearly overcame her as she embraced her son. Akbar had waited so long for this moment. There had been times in the chamber of torture and in the long, lonely years in prison when he wondered if he would live to experience this minute. He wiped tears from his eyes as he finally broke away from his mother to greet his excited sisters and his younger brother.

As the initial excitement of Akbar's unannounced return subsided, his mother took a good look at her son. She wept at what she saw. He had lost so much weight and looked so sickly that she pleaded with him to forget politics and stay at home. She peered into his previously warm and affectionate eyes and was distressed by what she saw. Those eyes she had known for so long had changed. They were filled with hate, resentment, and an eerie melancholy. She realized that her son was not the young man she had seen go off to prison. He was one who was destined to take part in the revolutionary drama

116

which was beginning to unfold in their homeland. She was afraid for his safety, but she knew in her heart that she couldn't change either her son's involvement or the destiny of the land she loved.

　　　　After the rest of the family retired for the evening, Akbar had an opportunity to talk to his father, who had been at work when Akbar arrived. The devout Moslem father spoke of a sermon he had heard in the mosque which contained another message from Ayatollah Khomeini. In an *i'ilamiyah* [list of instructions], sent from his exile at Najaf in Iraq, Khomeini had called for devout Moslems to boycott all government institutions, since the government had no claim to being an Islamic one; to avoid helping the government in any way; not to cooperate in any activity endorsed by the government; and to initiate new Islamic institutions in every field. Khomeini was calling for the establishment of a government within a government. Although Akbar's father never had been interested in politics, he felt it was his duty to get involved when specific involvement was called for by the Moslem clerics. Akbar was pleased to see his father caught up in the wave of anti-government feelings, even though he realized that this was the result of his religious discipline and nothing more. Akbar would have liked to discuss his political philosophy with his father, but he was sure the illiterate laborer wouldn't understand. During his more than four years in prison, Akbar had heard a wide range of political views from virtually all the divergent anti-government groups. Many of these ideologies had little appeal to him. He flatly rejected the Tudeh [Communist Party of Iran], because he believed in God and found the Communist doctrine totally alien to his views of man's trust in and reliance on God. He also found that he had little in common with the Fedayin Khalk [a Marxist-oriented anti-Shah movement allied with George Habbash's Popular Front for the Liberation of Palestine], for essentially the same reason. Akbar couldn't see getting involved with any organization that didn't revere

God. He had been very much impressed by the writings of Dr. Ali Shariati, a noted Islamic scholar who had died in London a year earlier. Shariati had written more than a hundred books, spent time in the Shah's prisons, and finally fled the country. Although Shariati was reported to have died from a heart attack or from ingesting an accidental dose of poison, Akbar, like most Iranians, chose to believe that his idol's death came at the hands of SAVAK. In Akbar's view, Khomeini was to be the great leader of the new day in Iran, and Dr. Shariati's writings were destined to be the philosophy which would provide the link between Islam and the militant actions required to overthrow the government. Shariati was closely allied with the Mujahiddin Khalk, drawn almost exclusively from Shiite families of the upper and middle classes. His writings concerned the revolutionary content of Islam, particularly Shiitism. According to Shariati, a good Moslem should strive for happiness through conflict with the world. If an individual wanted to achieve *azadegi* [a state of freedom and spiritual union with God], he had to be willing to struggle to destroy ungodly governments and institutions. Even Shariati admitted that his philosophy was a twentieth-century amalgam of Islam, Marxism, and a tenth-century Persian mystic's teachings.

Akbar told his father that he intended to devote his life to action against the existing system in order to fulfill his destiny and find both freedom and grace with God. Akbar's father cautioned him of the danger involved in the path he had chosen, but he also wished him well.

"I admire what you plan to do, my son. But you must be very careful. Many are being killed, and it would be hard on your mother if you should become a martyr." The laborer spoke with mixed emotions. He was proud of his son, and he had a general understanding of his aspirations, but he didn't want to see him in harm's way.

It was getting late, and the older man had to arise early for work. Akbar bid his father good night and rolled out his pallet on the floor, tired after his busy and exciting first day out of prison. As he fell asleep, he reflected on how good it was to be home. His last conscious thoughts were of the ripple of overt actions against the hated Shah of which he had seen evidence that day. He prayed that the ripple would turn into a wave, and that he would be part of the sea that one day would drown the monarchy.

August 18, 1978

Akbar was discussing the latest news with a group of young men from the college of Chemical Engineering at Tehran University. He had enrolled in the college, hoping to resume his studies and to seek out others who were intent on toppling the Shah. However, this day he was more interested in political action than in chemical engineering because of the recent tragedy in Abadan. The day before, the Rex Cinema in that Persian Gulf oil-refining city had been set ablaze by arsonists. More than four hundred people, many of them teen-agers, were killed. The newspapers, controlled by the Shah, were calling the outrage the work of terrorist enemies who had struck against symbols of Western influence in the past. Akbar and his friends did not believe this. They believed the story circulating the streets that morning: The dreaded SAVAK set the fire to discredit the Shah's opponents and to try to drive them apart.

Although the various groups within the opposition movement had little in common, they all agreed that this terrorist action was a disgrace. "The Shah ordered the fire and the murder of all these innocent people in order to cause friction within the coalition of his enemies," said Akbar's friend Hossein, a third-year engineering student who had a tremendous capacity for hatred and a convincing way of elaborating his provocative, uncompromising views. "We must not let him succeed. He is our sworn enemy, and his SAVAK set the fire. There is no question."

119

Akbar sipped tea from his glass. He was listening intently to the older men, and his hatred was being fed by their words and accusations against the government. But he was a man of action. He had spent too much time meditating and discussing politics in prison. He yearned to get into the fight against the enemies of God — to Akbar, that meant the Shah. His words were a combination of deference to his more eloquent and street-wise friends and a challenge to action: "It is not enough for us to sit and condemn the Shah for this terrible deed. What are we going to do? We have passed the time for talk. I want to fight."

Hossein surveyed the surprised group and then, realizing that he had become *de facto* leader, spoke with authority and purpose. "I'll tell you what we can do. We can help organize demonstrations and protests. It is not time to fight now; it is time to show support and strength by rallying the masses."

Akbar was beginning to understand the strategy. It was as his father had explained Khomeini's instructions on his first night at home. The government was to be weakened by major acts of civil disobedience. No cooperation also meant a total disregard for orders from the authorities prohibiting marches, demonstrations, and strikes. The government must be frustrated into either using the iron fist, which would serve only to increase the strength of the opposition, or doing nothing, thereby demonstrating weakness which would be exploited by the people. "Very well; how do we help organize the people for what is to come?" Akbar asked.

Hossein was convinced that Akbar would be an asset in rallying people for the next big demonstration in a few days. "Akbar, you may work with our small group. We will meet at the mosque to discuss plans with Mullah Sadeghi tomorrow night. Meanwhile, stay out of trouble. You cannot help if you are dead or back in jail."

Akbar was elated; finally he would get a chance

to make a contribution to God by working against the Shah. On his way home, soldiers were everywhere with weapons, tanks, and trucks. People were not directly confronting them or giving them trouble. Instead, they were calling the soldiers "brothers" and asking them to remember that they, too, were Moslems who were oppressed by their leaders. Akbar didn't hate these men who wore the uniform of the Shah's army, but he wondered if they were ordered to fire at the demonstrators whether they would obey their officers or take sides with the people.

The next evening, Akbar joined the others at the small neighborhood mosque, where Mullah Sadeghi explained the philosophy behind the demonstrations. The mullah believed that the people would be successful in winning over the Army, and in a short time, soldiers would begin to desert in droves. He was aware that some blood might be spilled before these desertions began, but they would begin. And those who were killed would go immediately to paradise and become martyrs. Akbar understood all this, but he didn't want to die.

September 8, 1978

The demonstrations had intensified during the previous three weeks. Akbar had been among a cadre of young people who helped to organize a large demonstration on September 4 to commemorate the celebration of the end of the holy month of Ramadan. He was surprised at the restraint shown by the military. Thousands had marched and demonstrated all over the city, and there were very few clashes with the soldiers, who had been ordered by the Shah's generals to stay in the background and avoid direct confrontation with the mobs. Akbar heard talk of numerous efforts at reform and compromise during this period, instigated by the government in an effort to defuse the mobs. Instead, these actions were seen by Akbar and his associates as signs of weakness and an absence of resolve on the part of the Shah. Akbar was convinced that the government would not do anything drastic to oppose the people during these increasingly frequent marches.

An excited mob had gathered at Jaleh Square in downtown Tehran. Akbar was told by several in the throng that the Shah had declared a state of martial law, but the demonstration would continue anyway. Opposition leaders were convinced that the Army would not act, and that this would be another example of the will of the people prevailing over the dictates of the ruler. There were thousands gathered in the square and on the streets leading to it. His mission was to shout encouragement to the demonstrators if the Army tried to disperse the crowds. Akbar's excitement grew as he saw so many of his countrymen shouting defiance at these instruments of the Shah's power. How often he had dreamed of a day like this when he had been a prisoner, he remembered now, as the mob chanted slogans of hatred and defiance.

The soldiers were lining up in a row at one end of Jaleh Square when Akbar heard a voice on a bullhorn demand that the demonstrators disperse. The voice of the battalion commander reminded them that they were violating the law, because martial law had been in effect for more than twenty-four hours. Akbar shouted words of defiance along with the rest of the mob.

"We do not recognize your martial law. Death to the Shah!"

The distraught lieutenant colonel was pleading with the demonstrators to give up the rally and go home, but his pleas brought only new courage and defiance to the more militant participants. Akbar heard a cry of surprise ripple through the sea of humanity. Some of the demonstrators were fighting with the soldiers, and those in the vanguard of the demonstration were cheered on to greater, more aggressive actions. The voice on the bullhorn issued an ultimatum:

"If you do not disperse, I will be forced to give the order to make you retreat. You are endangering the lives of my soldiers. You must go home!"

Akbar tasted fear. He couldn't see what was going on, but he realized that the mob was out of control. Emotions were running so high that some of the most zealous demonstrators were baiting the soldiers, daring them to shoot. They were convinced that their brothers in Islam would not obey any command to fire on them.

Scuffles between the soldiers and demonstrators continued for half an hour; Akbar finally managed to position himself where he could observe the disorder throughout the crowd. A soldier was pushed to the ground, and his weapon quickly was grabbed by a demonstrator before one of his fellow soldiers could retrieve it. A lieutenant demanded the weapon's return and, after an exchange of threats by both sides, the weapon was handed back to the soldier, who was brushing off his uniform and trying to regain his composure. The demonstrators were more vocal and unruly as they continued to chant and rave.

Suddenly a sea of humanity began to push toward the line of soldiers. The lead demonstrators were being prodded from behind. Some moved forward willingly, as though possessed by some mystical force; others went forward only because they weren't able to extricate themselves.

Shots rang out. Men fell, and panic and disbelief spread. The soldiers were firing into the crowd with heavy bursts of automatic fire from their American-made M-16 rifles. In a matter of a few minutes, what had seemed an invincible mob was reduced to a panic-stricken mass of human beings, running for their lives, with a steady volume of deadly fire picking them off as they retreated. Akbar was surrounded by screaming and cursing countrymen. He managed to move with the mob, away from the killing zone to the relative safety of a nearby street. He was afraid, but he also was incredulous and angry. One of the men he had talked into joining the demonstration accosted him. "You said the soldiers would not fire. We will have to get guns; we can't fight the Shah's army with only our blood."

Akbar didn't know what to say. He had been wrong. The mullahs had been wrong. They all had been wrong. More than one hundred unarmed men and women were killed in Jaleh Square, and hundreds more were wounded. That day would come to be known as "Black Friday," and Akbar and millions of other Iranians never would forget it.

When the shooting stopped, Akbar volunteered to help get the wounded to hospitals. The sight of the ghastly bullet wounds and the battered bodies of those who were trampled to death by the retreating mob appalled him. He was sick by the time he had finished his grisly task.

On the way to his father's house, Akbar thought about the events of that terrible day and felt a wave of helplessness and defeat. How could the people win against the might of the Shah's army? Would the Shah continue to use the iron fist, killing thousands of his own countrymen? Akbar was confused and bewildered. He wanted the Shah out, but at what price? The blood he saw spilled that day had taught him a bitter lesson: The overthrow of the monarchy and the establishment of an Islamic state in Iran would not be easy. It would come only after anguish and bloodshed. He never questioned the righteousness of his cause when he was in prison, even when he was tortured. But now, for the first time, he wondered if it would be worth the price he had seen paid that day in blood. Although he was fatalistic about his own life, he found himself asking God why so many had to die. As he walked the last block, he gathered his strength and realized that there could be no turning back after that day — no compromise with the "forces of evil." He would fight, but he didn't want to be among those who sacrificed themselves to discredit the regime by daring the soldiers to kill them. Even as a devout Moslem and a disciplined follower of Khomeini's instructions, he could not bring himself to agree that that kind of sacrifice was worthwhile. Akbar realized that he was, after all, only human, and the human law of self-preservation would continue to be a strong motivation in his life. If he were to lead in the future, he rationalized, he must protect himself and live.

In the weeks after Jaleh Square, Akbar was more careful. The strikes and demonstrations continued, but the government's reaction to them did not approach the violence of "Black Friday." Khomeini ordered his followers to avoid confrontations, which was music to Akbar's ears. He didn't understand exactly what was going on, but he wasn't alone. Everywhere, people discussed the situation, but they were at a loss to figure out what would happen next. The economic situation was getting worse each day. Akbar's father had been laid off from his job as a construction laborer, and the family was finding it difficult to get by. The government was doing nothing to feed the poor, but the mullahs were working hard to make sure their followers were fed. It appeared to Akbar that more and more people were being won over to his side as the situation worsened. At the mosque each Friday with his father, Akbar heard political speeches denouncing the Shah as an "ungodly oppressor" and enjoining the faithful to follow only the instructions of Khomeini, who had moved to Paris. With the worldwide communications facilities available there, he was in a better position than ever to lead the opposition. Akbar was elated to hear that his hero was getting wide coverage in the international media.

Early each morning, Akbar joined a group of militants ranging in age from eighteen to thirty-five. Many of them were students in the various engineering colleges of Tehran University, and most had memorized long passages of the revolutionary writings of Dr. Ali Shariati. Like the dead philosopher, they believed in an interpretation of Islamic doctrine that glorified militant action against political and cultural oppression. Akbar found in this group a mirror image of his carefully thought-out views of both his Islamic faith and his compulsion to work for the establishment of an Islamic state — which, of course, could become a reality only after the "satanic Shah and his henchmen" were overthrown. He was willing to fight for his beliefs, and if that meant he would have to kill his avowed enemies in the name of God, so be it. But in his heart, he didn't relish the idea of killing. His romantic nature seemed to blur reality. He wanted to see a world where all men were friends, a world where all men were free to worship God and obey His law. Of course, the only religion he knew anything about was Islam, so he considered other faiths heretical. He considered breaches of Islamic law blasphemous. But he often wondered why everyone didn't see things with the same clarity that he did. Akbar really believed that after the Shah was gone, his country would be free to develop an Islamic society. He dreamed about this society and saw it as an almost utopian way of life. Whatever it took to make this dream a reality, he was ready. That was why he had decided to be an active member of the organization called "Islamic Students — Followers of the Imam's Line."

It was early November. Akbar and other members of his group had been up most of the night working with other anti-government organizations to complete plans for a demonstration at the British Embassy. They planned to take advantage of the Shah's recent permissiveness by staging a bold attack on the embassy to prove that the regime was unable to protect this symbol of foreign intrigue in Iran. The primary target was to have been the American embassy, but the clerics and others who were orchestrating the opposition decided that wasn't feasible; the U.S. Embassy was well protected by the Shah's army, and there was no sense in deliberately confronting them.

Hossein, the vocal leader of Akbar's cell in the organization, was giving the young revolutionary last-minute instructions as the two sipped hot, sweet tea. "You will be positioned in front of the embassy, and you must make sure the crowds continue to shout slogans when they are instructed to yell by the leader with the megaphone," he said. "We will try to get inside the embassy and hold it long enough to make our point."

"I understand what I am to do, but what if the police or army begins to fire? What do we do then?" Akbar responded.

Hossein was impatient. He didn't have time to play "what if" with this man who seemed to have so little stomach for bloodshed. "If they fire, you will run and try to get away. But we do not believe they will shoot."

Hossein went on explaining the plan. "If we can get close enough to the main building, we have prepared Molotov cocktails, which we will use to burn the British out."

Hossein said they didn't intend to kill any of the staff, but they wanted to scare them and have the world press report the incident to emphasize the Shah's ineffectiveness.

Akbar and his cell members were dispersed from the university to the British Embassy compound. There was not time for morning prayers, because they wanted to get moving before daylight to take up their prearranged position in preparation for the day's event.

Akbar, who was not personally involved, was surprised by the daring actions of some of the members of the various groups participating in the embassy attack. His task of rallying people to create a disturbance in front of the embassy, so others could try to get inside, sack the offices, and start fires, was easier than he had anticipated. People seemed to converge on the embassy from all over south Tehran, and they were more than willing to join the crowd.

Other more daring and violent members of the group set fire to the main Chancellery. Akbar could see the smoke and the fire from his vantage point about seventy-five yards from the flame-engulfed symbol of British influence in his homeland. There was some small-arms fire, but none of Akbar's band of militants had been injured.

Although he was very much involved in keeping the mob busy shouting and chanting their rhetoric, Akbar found he was thinking about the people inside the embassy. He knew they must have been afraid, and he secretly hoped that none of them would be seriously injured or killed. Akbar could not seem to muster the bloodthirsty, vengeful attitude of his compatriots. As the crowds chanted and the air filled with acrid smoke, Akbar decided to work his way to the rear of the crowd so he could get a better view and make an estimate of the immediate danger he and the others were in.

"It is over; tell them to disperse," shouted Ahmad, messenger for Hossein, as he ran through the crowd. "Hossein says more soldiers are on the way and we have completed what we set out to do. Praise Allah!" Akbar was relieved and felt a new sense of pride and achievement in having been a part of this dramatic attack. After the massacre at Jaleh Square, he had been afraid that he might not live to see the Shah's downfall. But after the successful embassy attack, he felt better about his chances for survival and sensed that the revolutionary movement was growing stronger as the power of the Peacock Throne seemed to fade.

The British Embassy attack was not the only overt operation against the regime to take place that day. All the way home, Akbar was treated to a spectacle of the results of mass participation by the people in unlawful political action. Everywhere cars were burning and crowds were gathered, in blatant violation of the Shah's martial-law edict. On cue, crowds were shouting for the death of the Shah and the expulsion of Western influence. To Akbar, it was exhilarating to witness the wave of revolutionary action against his avowed enemy. He hardly could wait to join his friends the next morning to listen to the BBC's shortwave broadcasts about the attack on the British Embassy.

The two months that followed were filled with spectacular news for Akbar and his fellow revolutionaries.

On January 16, 1979, the Shah left with his entourage, including the Empress Fara Diba. There had been a news blackout for more than two weeks concerning his travel intentions, but when the announcement finally came, the streets quickly filled with hundreds of thousands of people in a carnival mood. They laughed and congratulated each other with typical Persian abandon. Within an hour, special editions of every newspaper in the city hit the streets with the long-awaited headline: "THE SHAH IS GONE." Seeing this in print had a spellbinding effect on the masses, and the tempo of the celebration intensified tenfold. Merrymaking continued well into the night. Akbar, of course, was among the celebrants. After all he had been through in the previous five years, he felt it was time to rejoice. He felt a sense of pride and accomplishment that he had never known. He also felt a special closeness and camaraderie in being part of that spectacular celebration. Through it all, the iron fist of the Shah's mighty military machine was nowhere to be seen.

Even as the celebration continued, speculation was building about the return of the Ayatollah Khomeini, or, as he was called by then, the "Imam," the chosen one of God on earth. Many were saying that he would return to Tehran from Paris within a few days. The only holdup was uncertainty about what the military might do to prevent his return. Would they interfere with his arrival, or would they welcome him? Khomeini, from his position of safety in Paris, was calling for a *jihad*, a holy war, against the army or anyone else who opposed the revolution. He had presented his movement as a religiously inspired war of good against evil. He had refused to negotiate or compromise with those loyal to the Shah or with the more moderate secularists. He demanded full power, and he skillfully worded his messages to entice the military to lay down their arms and join their Moslem brothers in this triumph over the "satanic Shah and his foreign puppeteers." America was singled out more frequently as a scapegoat for all that the Shah was accused of doing against the people of Iran, but there were no overt attacks against American citizens in Iran or the American Embassy.

Akbar looked forward to the return of Khomeini, but he also had become more realistic. He believed there still would be a series of bloody clashes with elite units of the Shah's army before the revolution would completely control the country and his patron saint could return in safety to the adulation of his worshippers. Akbar, Hossein, and other Followers of the Imam's Line were ready for these clashes. They considered it the highest calling they would ever receive.

In early February, there were pitched battles in the streets, and Akbar and his friends were in the middle of the fighting. A few of his friends had been killed by the soldiers, and several had been wounded by gunfire or by accidents caused by their careless use of gasoline in Molotov cocktails.

One morning Akbar, Hossein, and Fazollah, another member of their group, were working as a three-man team. They were several blocks from Hossein's home in south Tehran. Hossein knew the area very well, including the rooftops they were using as a vantage point from which to lob flaming bottles of gasoline at tanks and armored personnel carriers, sent in to restore order. The smell of burning vehicles ascended to these rooftops from below, where small-arms and machine-gun fire raked the streets.

Revolutionaries knocked out the lead tank with a Molotov cocktail. As the tankers opened the hatches and tried to flee the burning inferno, they either were picked off by small-arms fire or captured by the angry resistance fighters. Behind the knocked-out tank, there were three armored personnel carriers filled with soldiers, who were afraid to dismount their vehicle and face the wrath of the mob. Another tank brought up the rear of the column; it was Akbar's target. The personnel carriers couldn't move forward because of the disabled tank. If Akbar could set the rear tank afire, there would be no escape for the soldiers.

He ignited the fuse of his improvised fire bomb and hurled it down at the tank. The bottle exploded in a burst of flame about ten feet in front of the tank. Hossein lit another Molotov cocktail and hurled it below; this one landed directly on top of the tank, between the turret and the chassis. Flames erupted instantly, and in a flash the auxiliary, exterior fuel tank was on fire.

The military column had been stopped, and those inside the other vehicles were helplessly surrounded by screaming fanatics calling for their surrender. Akbar, Hossein, and Fazollah abandoned their perch on the roof and raced down the interior stairway to the fiery combat zone in the street. Hossein had a G-3 automatic rifle, but Akbar was unarmed. Fazollah had a .45-caliber American-made pistol, which he recently had been given by Mullah Sadeghi. He had never fired the weapon.

The three men posted themselves near the burning rear tank and waited for the crew to dismount and surrender. Akbar felt pity for the men who must have been suffocating inside.

The commander opened his hatch and scurried out of the tank. He quickly jumped to the ground, followed by the rest of the crew. The commander was a brigadier general — tall, erect, and very military-looking in his combat fatigues and tailored, olive-drab tanker jacket. He wore the gold logo of the Monarch's crown on each shoulder, mounted on a fancy-looking epaulet along with his star of rank.

"Get your hands up, murderer," demanded Hossein as he leveled his G-3 rifle at his prize.

"Go ahead and shoot; it does not matter." The reply by the officer surprised Akbar and the others. The general was poised and dignified. He refused to raise his hands in surrender to the marauders.

Hossein was baffled. He didn't want to shoot the general. If he were guilty, that would be decided by a revolutionary court. Besides, Hossein thought, he had fired his weapon only once, and he wasn't sure whether it was set to fire automatic or semiautomatic. Again, he demanded that the general raise his hands, and again the general refused. The rest of the crew was out of the tank and being led away by revolutionaries, but the general stood firm. Akbar, Hossein, and Fazollah approached him with both weapons at the ready. Hossein said, "If you do not raise your hands, I will shoot you."

The defeated but unbowed general stared directly into Hossein's eyes and said, "If you want to shoot, shoot. You have won. If it had been the other way, I would not have hesitated to shoot you."

Hossein was perplexed. He decided to discuss the problem with Akbar, whose judgment he respected. "What shall we do?"

Akbar thought for a moment before he replied, "Let's just tie him, blindfold him, and send him off with the others. He probably will be executed anyway, but we should not shoot him. It is against Islam to kill a defenseless man, and he has surrendered."

Hossein nodded concurrence. He and the two others approached the general, who did not resist. They tied his hands behind his back with rope and fashioned a blindfold from a piece of dirty cotton cloth given to them by another militant. The general was led to a nearby house where prisoners were being kept temporarily. He was turned over to a group of young fighters, who were responsible for securing officers until they could be dealt with by the recently activated Revolutionary Courts.

On the way back to their position, Hossein had second thoughts about the disposition of the general. "Perhaps we should have shot him. He is one of the Shah's generals and he refused to do as he was told, the prideful son of a pig."

Akbar was firm in his conviction that they had done the right thing. "We had no reason to shoot him. That would have been against Islam. We must always remember who we are." Akbar then related a parable about Ali, one of the prophets of the Shiite sect of Islam. Ali, in a battle against heretics, was hit from behind and slightly wounded. One of his followers subsequently disarmed the culprit who had wounded Ali and brought him before Ali for execution. Ali admitted that he was angry at the man, but he declined the opportunity to get revenge. He instructed his followers to remember that it was acceptable to "kill for God" in battle against enemies of God, but it was not right to kill in anger. To Akbar, the distinction was very clear, and the story of Ali and his treatment of his enemy paralleled the situation between the general and Hossein.

Hossein also had heard the parable before, and he refused to let Akbar have the last word. "You are right, Akbar, but you did not finish the story." Hossein said that Ali then went for a walk to cool his rage. Later, he returned and killed the man without remorse, rationalizing that it was an acceptable act since he no longer was killing in anger.

Akbar acknowledged Hossein's argument, but added, "If the general is to be punished, let it be done by those whom God has chosen to mete out punishment, not by us."

The two men laughed as they remembered an

old Persian saying: "The devil can quote the Koran for his purpose."

Khomeini's triumphant return to Iran after a fifteen-year exile was cause for a tremendous outpouring of affection and adoration. Akbar was among the millions who turned out to greet him and drown him in an unabashed sea of love. To the Iranian people, the return of their idol signalled the beginning of a new era in Persian history. The twenty-five-hundred-year reign of one dynasty of shahs after another was history. Many believed that Khomeini, after staging and inspiring the overthrow of the Shah, would return to Qom, the religious center sixty miles south of Tehran, to act as the patriarch of a secular, democratic government. But Akbar and his band of Islamic zealots were not among these; they believed that only Khomeini could lead the continuing revolution. They weren't sure exactly what type of government would emerge, but they wanted it to be Islamic. Akbar dreamed of a utopian society and culture that never had existed in Iran. It was a figment of the fertile imaginations of men like Dr. Ali Shariati, but Akbar was convinced that it could be. Although he was glad that the revolution had progressed so rapidly, he considered the ouster of the Shah as only a first step. Before the revolution was completed, Akbar visualized the establishment of an Islamic republic, rich in oil revenues, but totally independent of the "corruption and decadence" which he associated with "help" from the capitalist countries. As the revolution had mushroomed toward success, his ambitious dreams of what must follow also had grown.

On February 9, Khomeini's guerrillas routed the elite Imperial Guards Division at Doshan Tappeh Airbase, in Tehran. Two days later, General Gharabaghi, chief of the Supreme Commander's Staff and the senior military officer in the country, sent the following message to the news media:

"To avoid bloodshed and chaos, the Armed Forces declare themselves neutral in this political conflict and order their troops to return to their barracks."

The army had been neutralized before this official withdrawal from the conflict. Junior officers, noncommissioned officers, and soldiers were deserting and joining the opposition in droves. That order simply made the army's ineffectiveness official. There was no authority left in Iran except for an eighty-one-year-old Islamic scholar, and he became the focal point for all decision-making. Iran had shed an autocratic shah and replaced him with an autocratic ayatollah.

The provisional revolutionary government struggled to grasp the reins of power in the weeks following the capitulation of the army. Mehdi Bazargan was installed as acting prime minister, and a small group of Western-educated Khomeini disciples, including Ibrahim Yazdi, Abdolhassan Bani-Sadr, and Sadegh Ghotbzadeh, was given cabinet positions by its benefactor. Akbar and his friends were skeptical of these secular leaders, whom they suspected were tainted by Western values and ideas.

On February 15, Akbar read in a newspaper that a force of Mujahiddin and Fedayin militants had stormed the American Embassy the previous day and held the diplomatic staff prisoner for several hours. Finally Ibrahim Yazdi, newly appointed Deputy Foreign Minister for Revolutionary Affairs, had arrived at the embassy and persuaded the attackers to release their hostages. Akbar wanted the United States out of Iran once and for all. He didn't understand Yazdi's actions and was afraid that it might be an indication that his distrust of Bazargan's cabinet was justified. Later Akbar had an opportunity to discuss his perceptions of the

Yazdi rescue mission at the American Embassy with a group of his more militant friends. They, too, were displeased and would have preferred to see the Americans escorted to the airport and the embassy closed. As usual, Hossein was the most vocal and adamantly hateful. "Yazdi should have kicked them all out of Iran," he said. "We will have to watch this new government to make sure there is no conspiracy with the United States." Men like Bazargan and Yazdi, he said, might be "working for the CIA."

Although Akbar knew very little about the CIA, everything he had heard from friends and other prisoners in jail indicated that it was an extremely powerful organization with an almost limitless capability to meddle in the internal affairs of other countries. He agreed with his compatriots — the sooner the U.S. was out, the better for the security of the revolution.

Two weeks after the collapse of the Shah's regime, it appeared to Akbar that there were two parallel governments competing for power in Iran: the committees set up by and responsible only to Khomeini and the clerics, and the secular government of Mehdi Bazargan. The committees held the real power, and nothing was accomplished without their approval and support. Quickly constituted revolutionary courts were meting out "revolutionary justice" to a wide variety of culprits from the old regime, ranging from former SAVAK officers, through senior military officers, to former members of the *Majlis* [Parliament].

Akbar read the name of the brigadier general whom he and Hossein had captured at the peak of the fighting in a newspaper list of twenty-one senior officers who recently had been executed. Akbar, the romantic, was saddened by the news. He secretly had hoped that this man, who had demonstrated such courage and the fatalistic attitude Akbar respected, would be spared. However, he reflected, it was not up to him to decide appropriate sentences for offenders. That had to be the prerogative of the Islamic revolutionary courts. There had to be strict discipline if the revolution were to be continued and an Islamic state established. Nevertheless, he was disappointed by the callous newspaper article announcing the execution.

During the next few months, Akbar was disappointed on many occasions by news reports of continuing problems within the revolutionary government. Unemployment was in excess of thirty-five percent, and prospects for improvement did not seem good. Bazargan was prime minister in name only; the real power continued to rest with the committees, which controlled virtually everything within their jurisdictional areas and responded only to orders from Khomeini. Revolutionary courts continued to keep the firing squads busy executing those summarily found guilty of such unspecific offenses as "corruption on earth," "crimes against God," and "crimes against the revolution."

Shortages of Western-manufactured consumer goods, and even food, resulted in a thriving black market. Edicts issued by Khomeini were withdrawn if the mobs took to the streets to oppose them. A requirement that all women wear the *chador*, covering the face and the entire body from head to toe, was withdrawn after thousands of women marched to oppose the return to this ancient garb. Confusion about who was responsible for what within the society created a state of near-anarchy. Excuses were made for every problem. Scapegoats were sought to parry blame away from the revolutionary government. "Everything is the fault of the satanic United States and its imperialist henchmen" was a frequent cry.

In the midst of this revolutionary turmoil, Akbar was becoming less optimistic about the possibility of his Islamic dream state ever becoming a reality. His frustrations were compounded by inactivity. Now that the Shah was gone, there was little for him to do. All the colleges were closed. He didn't want to join the army because it wasn't doing anything, either. Soldiers — those who had not deserted — were confined to barracks because Khomeini and his followers were afraid of a pro-Shah coup by the military. So eager was Akbar to do something that he even considered joining the Pasdaran, the Revolutionary Guards, but they seemed to him to be an undisciplined, poorly trained, paramilitary organization loaded with self-serving, vengeful, and ignorant young men. Reports of corruption and strong-arm excesses against the people by the Pasdaran upset Akbar's sense of fairness. He would not join the Pasdaran and would go to the Army only if drafted.

Akbar's father was still out of work, and the family was forced to accept handouts of food and heating and cooking oil from the government. His father was a proud man who, even under the Shah, had always managed to find work, and the charity he was forced to accept had demoralized him. The older man and Akbar argued frequently about the situation. Akbar saw an irritability in his father that was new and unusual. The laborer frequently asked Akbar, "You worked to overthrow the Shah; is this better than the Shah, or are we not worse off now? At least under the Shah I was able to work so I could feed the family."

Akbar always answered these questions by imploring his father to be patient — things would get better, but it would take time. He still wanted to believe that, but he was doubtful.

Akbar had walked by the British, French, West German, and American embassies frequently during that time, and they still were open and operating. If foreign influence and intrigue were responsible for the economic and political instability, why had they not been closed?

To avoid arguments with his father, he spent his days wandering the streets and meeting with members of his student group. Many of them also were concerned that the revolution might be bogging down because the secular leaders were maintaining ties with America. They listened to

Khomeini and read the papers, and they came to believe that diplomatic ties between Iran and the Americans had to be severed to prevent a repeat of the events of 1953.

The Islamic Students — Followers of the Imam's Line had expanded its membership dramatically since the revolution. It was popular among young devout Moslems who were convinced that a secular government composed of Western-educated intellectuals was not going to move the revolution toward the theocracy they dreamed of. As their name revealed, they stood ready to receive Khomeini's orders and to follow his "line" — whatever the consequences.

5 WEST

FORT MCPHERSON, GEORGIA
JULY - SEPTEMBER, 1979

"Colonel Scott, you have a call from a Lieutenant Colonel Meadows in Colonels' Branch at the Department of the Army."

What could Colonels' Assignment Branch want with me, I thought as I picked up the phone and pushed the lighted button. I had been assigned to Forces Command Headquarters in Atlanta, Georgia, for only three weeks, following a two-year stint as chief of the Readiness Group at Redstone Arsenal, Alabama. I was sure the call couldn't have anything to do with another assignment.

After an exchange of amenities, Meadows got down to business. "Colonel Scott, we're looking for an officer qualified in the Persian language to take over as Chief, ARMISH MAAG [the Army Mission to Iran], in Tehran."

This had always been a major general's position, he said, but with the reduced American presence in Iran, they were going to send a full colonel. According to their records, he explained, my Farsi was excellent, and I had been away from Iran long enough that I wouldn't be too closely associated with the Shah's regime.

Then he added, "You're a War College graduate, and you're still competitive [military jargon for "you are still in the running for promotion to the next higher grade" — in my case, brigadier general]. Although you've recently been assigned to Atlanta, you're the best-qualified officer for the job."

I stalled for a minute before asking my first

question. "Are you asking me to volunteer for this assignment? Or, if you aren't looking for a volunteer, what's the story?"

"Actually, it would be best if you were willing to volunteer, but that's not absolutely necessary."

Meadows said that he knew I had just returned from Redstone and had been promised an assignment in Atlanta, but the needs of the service could override my personal desires, and I could be sent to Iran anyway. He pointed out that I had an excellent Middle East record of service, and that I had not had an overseas tour in a number of years. Then he asked if I was interested in the job.

I decided to lay all my cards on the table, face up. "It's not that I'm not interested. On the contrary, it sounds both interesting and challenging. But I'm on the alternate list for a brigade command. If I take this assignment, what happens to my chances for command?"

I knew that without a command at the brigade level, my chances for promotion to brigadier general were close to nonexistent. I told Meadows that I had been seriously considering retirement within the next year or so if I didn't get a command. I also told him that I wasn't going to volunteer for the assignment.

Meadows was letting me do the talking, so I decided to add a postscript: "If I could do anything I wanted in the next two years, I'd be out commanding a brigade somewhere. Not for the 'ticket punch,' but because I love working with soldiers, and I think I'd be a good commander. After that, if I don't make the grade, I'll willingly wrap it up and retire. I don't ever want to be one of those old colonels who've been passed by the parade but hang on until mandatory retirement, anyway. I guess what I'm asking is, if I end up going to Iran, what's in it for me from a career angle?"

There was another brief pause, but I opted not to throw more grist into the mill. I figured I'd given him enough to work with already. Lieutenant Colonel Meadows was composed and well-versed in all the rhetoric that a man in officer assignments had to know. He was smooth and low-key. Meadows said he heard what I was saying, but that he was in no position to make any promises. He would pass my remarks to his boss and get back to me as soon as he had additional information. "We need to get the position filled as soon as possible. We're looking at a reporting date of August 1."

I got a bit icy. "August first is not much time. When can you let me know whether or not I'm off the hook?"

"I'll get back to you as soon as possible."

How was I going to break this to my family? My last set of orders had upset our plans and our lifestyle. We had purchased a house in Atlanta, only to have me trans-ferred at the last minute to an important job at Redstone in Huntsville, Alabama. I'd been commuting on weekends for the past two years until I was finally reassigned to Atlanta. And now, after less than two months under one roof, this bombshell had hit.

Then I considered the current situation in Iran, and I decided my best course of action was to sit tight and do nothing. If the fundamentalists got their way, we might be out of Iran before they got around to cutting orders to send me there. No sense in getting my wife and children upset over an assignment that might never materialize.

On the way home that night, I thought about what it would be like to return to Iran. I thought about the potential for a rapprochement between our countries, and I fantasized about the role I might be called upon to play in making American policy goals for that relationship a reality. The Iranians had purchased almost twenty billion dollars of American-made military hardware before the Shah's ouster, and it seemed to me that providing spare parts for that equipment could give us the only real leverage possible with the new government. I knew many of the emerging military leaders, who had been my contemporaries when I lived in Iran, and I thought this would be an asset.

I found myself thinking about the challenges the assignment to Iran portended, but I decided that I still would not volunteer for the job. If they really thought I was the best-qualified officer for the job, they could make the decision for me. They always had done so in the past.

But if they did decide to send me, I felt it was time to stand up and be counted. I wanted to know what impact the assignment would have on my chances for promotion. I was a foreign-area specialist, and officers in my specialized field actually had less chance for promotion to top grades than generalists with all the traditional "ticket punches" — the high-visibility jobs where they could be observed regularly by the senior officers who sat on promotion boards. I wanted to see that trend reversed, because I believed we needed more high-quality, foreign-area experts, and that they should get a chance at promotion. We had only a handful of generals with foreign-area expertise. I decided to make an issue of the effect the position in Iran would have on my future, if the assignment became firm.

July 18, 1979

"Colonel Scott, that lieutenant colonel from your Branch in Washington is on the phone again. . . . I hope it's good news for you."

It was good news: Meadows told me I was no longer being considered for the assignment. An Air Force colonel had volunteered for the position, and the Army had withdrawn my name. The services had been competing for the position, which had been rotated between the Army and the Air Force for a number of years. The incumbent at the time was Major General Philip Gast, an Air Force officer. I asked Meadows if the Air Force colonel spoke Farsi. If he did, there was a good possibility that I knew him from my earlier assignments involving Iran. Meadows said he didn't speak the language, but otherwise was qualified for the position.

I was pleased with the news, but I already was having second thoughts by the time I hung up. The Air Force nominee didn't even speak the language. He would be at a tremendous disadvantage in Iran, where foreigners have been condoned but never really accepted. I wondered if he would be able to do the job without an understanding of the language and the culture. As I thought about it, I began to feel like a draft dodger because I hadn't volunteered for the assignment. I knew I was well qualified for the job, but I still didn't want to make another move so soon and risk family turmoil and personal inconvenience.

August 30, 1979

"Sir, it's the colonel from Branch again. I thought that was a dead issue."

It was, as far as I was concerned. I picked up the phone and my life began to change instantly. It was Meadows.

"Sir, the Air Force colonel was not accepted by the Joint Chiefs of Staff. The Chief of Staff, General Meyer, has personally gone over your records and you are his choice for the job. We're late on this one, as you know, so we need to have you come up here for briefings within the next week or so. We want you to be in Iran by September 5. You don't have to volunteer. It's already gone too far for that."

I had a dozen things to say at once, but I was stunned speechless by the sudden turn of events. After an awkward moment of silence, I said, "That's very interesting and also quite a shock, after your telling me I was off the hook. It will be tough to pack, get briefed, and do all the other necessary things before I go. As a matter of fact, I'm not sure I'm going at all. I may just submit my retirement papers rather than accept this assignment."

I was interrupted by Meadows as soon as I mentioned retirement. "Sir, I'm not sure you'd be permitted to exercise the retirement option, given the importance of this assignment. The Chief has personally been involved in your nomination, and you're the best-qualified and available officer for the job."

I was upset by the short notice and the threat that I might not be allowed to retire instead of going to Iran. It was starting to look like a no-win situation.

"So when do I come to Washington to get some answers? I'd like to talk to the Chief personally, since he supposedly handpicked me for the job. I've never even met him."

Meadows was trying hard to be smooth, but I sensed that I was beginning to get to him. He had a slot to fill, and if I retired, he still had a problem. The Army had a problem, too: They needed a colonel with a list of specific qualifications to go to Iran in a hurry. They had decided that I was their man. Meadows didn't want to go back to square one. He was just trying to do his job.

"Sir, I'll pass your request to see the Chief of Staff to my boss. I'm sure that can be arranged. I'll notify your current commander of this assignment as soon as we get off the phone. I'm personally sorry for the short notice, but I'm sure you understand."

I understood the short notice, but I also understood that Iran at this time could be more dangerous than Vietnam at its worst. The Iranian radicals would love to assassinate the American officer in charge of helping get supplies for the Iranian army — and that was going to be my job. I decided again to be blunt.

"Before I accept this assignment — and I have not accepted it — I believe I have a right to some answers. You can tell the Chief that Colonel Chuck Scott wants to know what's in this assignment for him. And if that sounds like it's self-serving, so be it. I also want a briefing by the NSC staff to make sure our current policy of keeping the Shah out of the United States is locked in and not subject to change while I'm in Iran. The vibes I get from Iranian friends and reading the newspapers tell me the fanatics will go wild if the Shah comes to the U.S. They already took over our embassy once in February. Colonel Meadows, this is not just another assignment overseas, in my opinion. This could be the most dangerous I've ever been on, and coming as it does in the twilight of my mediocre career, I believe I have a right to a few answers before I take the plunge."

"Sir, I know now why they want you for this assignment. You have an unusual understanding of the situation over there. I'll call you as soon as I have an itinerary approved for your briefings, and I'll pass the word up the chain of command that you want to see the Chief while you're here."

As I drove home that night, I had time for some serious thinking. The assignment to Iran was shaping up to be an exciting and challenging adventure. But, if I had a choice, I would rather command a brigade than go to Iran. Commanding a brigade could get me promoted, but no matter how well I did in Iran, I knew that all I would get out of it would be personal satisfaction. I had changed from my days as a young soldier and junior officer, when blind obedience was my style and I really believed in the "system." For the first time in my military service, I wanted to ask a few questions before I marched off to the beat of the drum; I felt I had a right, considering my length of service and the danger the assignment to Iran portended. If the Chief of Staff really had handpicked me for the assignment, he should be willing to discuss my future with me before I moved to Iran.

I decided to tell Betty precisely what I planned to do. I would go to Washington, go through the briefings, and talk to General Meyer. If I didn't get some pretty positive comments from him on the Iran assignment and its effect on my future, I would apply for retirement. At least I'd try to retire and put the monkey on the Army's back.

There was one bright spot in the days that followed. Betty was not taking the tour as hard as I thought she might. She had been very pragmatic about the Iran duty. She said that if it was a stepping-stone to a brighter future in the Army that I had loved for so many years, then I should go and do a first-class job. On the other hand, if it was just another overseas slot, where I'd be forgotten while I was there and totally forgotten when I returned, then I should go ahead and retire. We even had a new will drawn up by an attorney — not out of a fatalistic attitude either of us had about the assignment, but because it made sense to plan for the worst in the constant hope that it would not come to pass.

September 2, 1979

On the return flight to Atlanta from Washington, I thought about the briefing and the people I'd talked with during my four days in the nation's capital. The Army had arranged meetings and briefings with the Air Force, Navy, National Security Council staff, State Department, and CIA. I also had extensive discussions with LTG Frank Graves, the Deputy Assistant Secretary of Defense for Security Assistance, and his staff, and I met with Major General Bob Sweitzer, the Chief of the Army's Security Assistance Office. My meetings ran the gamut from exceptionally professional and enlightening to a total waste of time. I was appalled by the general absence of understanding of the unquestionably anti-American nature of the Iranian revolution in the highest offices of the U.S. government. Very few seemed willing to accept the reality of the situation: The United States had lost Iran, and as long as Khomeini was in control we would be considered an enemy. It was alarming how much senior diplomats and members of the intelligence community were hoping for a miracle — that pro-Shah elements would somehow topple Khomeini and his fundamentalists, and that another pro-Western government would emerge. They wanted so much to believe it was possible, or even probable, that they were reluctant to face reality. Our long-term support of the Shah and his regime would not be forgotten soon by his enemies.

Yet, amid all the optimism, there seemed to be an acute awareness of the personal danger inherent in the assignment. During a number of meetings, I got the feeling that senior officials were well aware of the tenuousness of our position in Iran and felt sorry for me because I was on the way there.

My meetings with General Sweitzer started out rather coldly and warmed considerably as they progressed. Bob Sweitzer was a bona fide hero of the Vietnam conflict. He had been wounded so many times that his Purple Heart ribbon was covered with oak leaf clusters. He was one of the Army's brightest stars — a Distinguished Service Cross attested to his heroism, and a doctorate pointed out his intelligence and personal drive. After we had a chance to exchange views, he told me that he had called officer assignments and said he didn't think I was the right man for the job because of my "negative attitude." When he was told that I was the Chief's choice and that my record of service had been personally reviewed by him, he backed off and became very supportive.

The general went out of his way to make me feel welcome, insisting that I use a desk in his private office between scheduled appointments. He sponsored a luncheon for me in the General Officers' Mess and introduced me to all the senior Department of the Army staff. He promised to call Betty if the situation in Iran deteriorated and told me to have her call him anytime there were bad reports from Iran.

I had an intuitive feeling that I could trust Sweitzer, and I left his office feeling very good.

The meetings with the Department of State's Iran desk officers opened my eyes to the root cause of our failure to accept the realities of post-revolutionary Iran. From their Washington vantage point, they told me that they were working to dispel the "siege mentality," which they said was prevalent on the embassy staff in Tehran. They were trying to sell the impression that things were rapidly pointing to a return to "business as usual" in our dealings with the Iranians.

I had read Khomeini's writings in Farsi and had talked to a number of Iranian scholars in the United States, and I was convinced that Khomeini was anti-Shah, anti-West, and ardently anti-American. Nothing I had read or heard about his philosophy had dissuaded me from believing that he never would be receptive to friendly relations with the United States. I also questioned the capability of Bazargan's provisional government to control the masses, who responded only to orders from their hero, Khomeini.

I never got to see the Chief of Staff, but I spent thirty minutes with General Jack Vessey, the Vice-Chief of Staff. He ran the day-to-day operations of the Army, while the Chief worked on matters involving the other services with the Joint Chiefs of Staff. General Vessey's reputation as a man of courage, great integrity, and candor made me trust him from the start. He never said that I would be promoted if I went to Iran. I knew he couldn't say that, even if he had wanted to. But what he did say was even better: "You're concerned that if you don't command a brigade, your chances for promotion are slim. Chuck, this job you're going to is more important to the Army and the United States right now than any five brigades you might command. No matter how the assignment in Iran works out," he said, "as long as you do your job, you come out a hero. The Army *does* take care of its own."

That was good enough for me, coming from a man of General Vessey's stature and reputation. I was going to Iran, and I was going to do the best job I'd ever done. The business of being a professional soldier never had been easy, and I always had done very well under pressure and adversity. I was ready, I thought, as I recalled the words of Teddy Roosevelt:

> Better it is to dare mighty things,
> To win glorious triumphs,
> Though checkered by failure,
> Than to take rank with those poor spirits,
> Who neither suffer much nor enjoy much,
> For they live in that gray twilight,
> That knows neither victory nor defeat.

I was looking forward to the intrigue and hard work which I understood were waiting for me in a land that I had known for two decades and had learned to love and understand.

6 EAST

TEHRAN, IRAN
SEPTEMBER - NOVEMBER, 1979

In early September, when the university re-opened, Akbar again enrolled as a chemical engineering student at the Tehran University's College of Engineering. Returning to the world of academics after his mentally debilitating time in prison proved to be a real challenge for him. But he was no stranger to hard work, and sometimes he thought that his time in prison actually had made him a better student. He had matured, and he realized the importance of completing his education.

However, he frequently was torn between the demands of two strict mistresses: his studies and his political activities. In mid-September, the conflict crested; his studies were relegated to second priority.

On September 16, Hojat al-Islam Musavi Khoeiny, a short, bespectacled man with an unkempt black beard who was responsible to the Revolutionary Council for student activities, stood at the head of a group of about fifty men. Akbar was among this carefully selected group which had been invited to attend the meeting. They were called the *Murabitun*; in the early days of Islam, this name referred to men who manned the outposts on the frontier against Byzantium. Khoeiny was an Islamic scholar whose title, *Hojat al-Islam*, indicated a higher degree of scholarship than that of a mullah but not as high as that of an ayatollah. Although Khoeiny was not a member of the Revolutionary Council, he had a direct line to the Ayatollah Khomeini through the Imam's son, Ahmad. He was highly respected and admired by those who had come to hear him speak. As Akbar surveyed the crowd, he noticed many of his student activist friends in the audience, but he also saw a number of older men who certainly were not students. He recognized one man who had received training in the Soviet Union and had close ties with a leftist element of the PLO. Two of the others he spotted were Iranians who had received training in Lebanon and Syria with PLO cadres. He also saw Ahmad, a man who had been in prison with him at Evin. Ahmad was a graduate of an American university who had been arrested by SAVAK upon his return to Iran. Although he spoke excellent English, including American slang, he was violently anti-American.

Khoeiny began by telling the group that they must never discuss what they were about to hear with anyone outside the Murabitun. He said that he had received information from the highest levels of the Revolutionary Council that the United States was developing plans to admit the Shah. He claimed that SAVAK had a spy inside the American Embassy, and that the spy had been exposed by the former SAVAK chief, General Nassiri, when Nassiri made a full confession in order to try to save his life. The information from his agent, which he passed on, was provocatively revealing, but the chief of the Shah's secret police had been executed anyway. Khoeiny had a fascination with intrigue and intelligence operations, and he seemed to enjoy relating this story in minute detail. He went on to say that the Revolutionary Council had documentary proof that the Americans were planning to admit the "despised ganster Shah." He had been asked by certain unnamed members of the Council to develop a plan for an assault on the American Embassy to capture additional "proof of this satanic American conspiracy." The Murabitun was to work with him on this plan and be ready to execute it on order.

Khoeiny already had prepared a list of key "students" selected to work on various elements of the plan.

When the meeting broke up into smaller groups to discuss implementation of the plan, there was an undercurrent of chatter about a sinister countercoup planned by the Americans to get the "puppet Shah back his throne." Memories of the anti-Mossadeq coup in 1953 were on the lips of everyone as they began work.

Sketches of the embassy were distributed for examination. These detailed drawings of the compound depicted every building, guard post, doorway, and gate. Potential weak points also were listed, as well as priority targets for the assaulting force to secure in order to prevent the destruction of sensitive documents and material.

Akbar was impressed by the amount of information available in the drawings. Several of those he had identified earlier as having received training abroad seemed to be natural leaders during this development phase. They had ideas which seemed practical and clever to Akbar and the other members of the potential assault force.

The plan was developed in detail over the following weeks and approved by Khoeiny. But it was just a plan. Akbar and his friends didn't know when, if ever, they would receive final instructions to storm the embassy. In the meantime, a good deal of time was spent going over the operation in order to anticipate problems. The thoroughness of the planners impressed Akbar. They seemed to have thought of everything. For example, a number of cloth signs with Khomeini's picture on them were being prepared to be worn as bibs, or shields, by the attackers. The idea was that if there were a fight and blood was shed by some of the "students," the news media would get pictures of red blood invading the sacred black and white likeness of the revolutionary leader. This would symbolize to the Iranian people, and to the world, the cold-blooded brutality of the Americans. The overall objective of the plan was to humiliate the United States and to obtain additional proof of American involvement in actions against the revolution.

As part of his preparation for the attack, Akbar walked near the American Embassy to observe the daily activities. He noticed that there was a lot of traffic in and out of the compound during business hours. The busiest area was around the American Consulate, where hundreds of his countrymen lined up each day to wait for visas to America. Akbar watched as Iranians tried to bribe police and others in line in order to advance their position. He was puzzled by this manifestation of his countrymen's desire to get out of Iran. If America were, in fact, akin to the devil, why were so many seeking to go there? To Akbar, there could be only two explanations — the would-be emigrants were criminals and oppressors left over from the Shah's regime, or they were heretics who couldn't face Islamic law.

On October 23, Akbar received the news of the Shah's trip to America. According to the newspapers, the Americans claimed that the Shah was a very sick man, but Akbar didn't believe that story. He thought it was a lie to cover up the real intent of the Shah's visit, which clearly was to conspire with the Americans in order to return to power in Iran. Wasn't that what Khoeiny had told them was planned, according to information obtained by the spy in the embassy?

The following morning, Akbar and other select members of the Murabitun gathered in the foothills of the Elbruz Mountains, north of the city and south of Shemshak, to review their plan of attack. They considered this latest event as proof of the conspiracy they feared.

But even a week later, they had not received the green light from their mentor to launch the attack.

On November 1, Akbar heard of a meeting in Algiers attended by the Iranian Prime Minister, Mehdi Bazargan, his Deputy Prime Minister, Ibrahim Yazdi, and the American National Security Advisor Zbigniew Brzezinski.

Rumors abounded that this meeting, which had been requested by the United States, was only the most recent in a series of attempts by the Americans to undermine the revolution and subvert the Iranian government. Bazargan and Yazdi, who had been suspect by Akbar's radical Islamic group from the beginning, had showed their true colors by attending that meeting. They were supposed to have been attending the anniversary celebrations of Algerian Independence Day, not meeting with the Americans. Akbar was caught up in the wave of outrage and sense of betrayal exhibited by his contemporaries. He was beginning to wonder what it would take for the order to be given to begin the attack against the "den of spies."

The next day, while the Algiers meeting was still in progress, Ayatollah Khomeini issued a proclamation to the students and young people of Iran to "open their eyes to the conspiracies of that malignant enemy, the United States." In a radio message marking the observance of the anniversary of the student protests that had occurred on November 4, 1978, Khomeini asked the students to "expand with all your might the attacks against the United States and Israel, so that we may force the U.S. to return the despised and cruel Shah."

That exhortation from Khomeini was what they had been waiting for. The Murabitun was hastily assembled at the university, and the Revolutionary Committee inside the Tehran institution, along with Khoeiny and his delegated lieutenants, completed plans for the attack. It was too late to complete the last-minute details that night, so the attack was delayed until Sunday, November 4. Initially, the attack force was to be five hundred strong. As soon as they penetrated the embassy compound, others were to canvass the nearby area for volunteers to rally in front of the embassy in support of the takeover. The original objective of the mission — to capture documents incriminating to the U.S. — had been changed. The new objective was to hold the Americans inside the embassy walls as hostages until the United States was forced to return the deposed Shah.

Ropes for securing captives were cut to the right length, and handcuffs were distributed. Akbar was as excited as the rest of the Murabitun. The plan was complete in every detail.

6 WEST

ATLANTA, GEORGIA
TEHRAN, IRAN
SEPTEMBER - NOVEMBER, 1979

As Betty and I left our home in Stone Mountain, Georgia, and headed for the airport, there was a long, awkward silence. Then, suddenly, we both spoke at the same time. It was as though we realized simultaneously that if there were something we wanted to say, we had better say it before we reached the crowded concourse.

"Chuck, you know how I wish this assignment had been changed, but remember that you're a survivor. I guess I never realized that until Vietnam, but I know in my heart you'll somehow make it." Betty's words were convincing, but I wondered if she was trying to convince me, herself, or both of us.

I didn't want her to worry. I reassured her by saying that I would not be away for a full year anyway. I had been told that I would be required in Washington periodically for briefings and updates. "I'll be home for Christmas," I said. "I'll set up my travel itinerary so I'll be in Europe for a couple of days in mid-December, then go to Washington for a few days before I take a week's leave to spend the holidays at home."

Our discussion was reassuring to both of us, but I still sensed that Betty knew this assignment could be dangerous. I didn't know what else to say. We had been over and over the Iran tour for weeks, and it always came out the same: I promised to be careful and not take unnecessary chances, and she promised to try not to worry.

We had agreed earlier that Betty would not go to

the gate with me. There is something so final about a good-bye at an airport, when those who remain behind actually watch a flight pull away from the gate and prepare for take-off. I preferred to say goodbye in a less emotional setting. We would part at the concourse, after I checked my four pieces of luggage to New York, where I had a four-hour wait for my Pan Am flight to Germany.

There was a sober moment of looking at each other, then we embraced warmly and kissed. As she pulled away, she said, "Be careful, Chuck. I'll see you at Christmas. Give my love to Amir and Monica, if they're still in Iran."

"Don't worry," I answered. "I'll be careful. You take care of yourself, remember I love you . . . and tell the kids again for me that I love them, too."

Betty turned away and walked toward the door, and I headed for the security area to be checked for my flight.

At EUCOM [European Command] Headquarters, I was given the VIP treatment. I had a suite at the bachelor officer's quarters usually reserved for visiting generals. I met all the senior staff chiefs and was briefed on everything I was supposed to know about my new assignment. Although the perceived danger and uncertainty of my assignment was not discussed directly, it was obvious from the preferential treatment I received from headquarters personnel, including the senior generals, that they were well aware of the risk involved in going to Iran. Some of them were so considerate that I felt I was attending my own wake. I was promised a blank check for my operation in Iran.

The nonstop Pan Am flight from Frankfurt to Tehran was crowded. The man who sat next to me was an Iranian Jew who fled the country during the revolution and was going back to settle his personal affairs before returning to live in England. He related stories of Jewish friends in Iran who were finding it progressively more difficult to live side by side with the Islamic zealots. Khomeini had promised earlier to treat all Iranians equally under the law, but the situation for Jews and other minority groups was worse as the revolution solidified its power. My seatmate was afraid to return, but he didn't want to leave his property and personal treasures, gathered over generations, to be pillaged by the new regime.

A very pretty Iranian woman in her late twenties or early thirties sat across the aisle from me. I spoke to her in Farsi, and she smiled and responded in kind. She had been visiting relatives in France for two months and was looking forward to getting home. After twenty minutes of small talk, she asked my nationality and where I learned to speak Farsi so well. When I told her I was an American, she cooled instantly. End of conversation. I noticed in the next few minutes that she was rubber-necking around to see who else was seated near her. She obviously didn't want to be seen talking to an American.

When the captain finally announced our approach to Tehran, Iranian women crowded into the restrooms and the aisles, putting on their tentlike *chadors* hiding their expensive Western dresses, high heels, designer jeans, and everything else, except for their huge, brown eyes. There was an almost mystical change in these animated and gregarious ladies as soon as they donned their *chadors*, those ancient symbols of modesty and subservience. They were role-playing as they deliberately and consciously camouflaged the great strides women had made in Iran in fifty years under the two Pahlavi Shahs, who had outlawed the long veils in an effort to bring women into the twentieth century. It was as though our landing in Tehran signalled a return to ancient times, customs, and mores for these women.

One thing had not changed: Every Iranian passenger was pushing and shoving to be among the first to deplane. Charles Dickens wrote in *Our Mutual Friend*, more than a century ago, "We must scrunch or be scrunched." Profound, I thought, for a man who never took a trip to Iran on a jumbo jet. As for me, I left the "scrunching" to others, and I had no desire to be "scrunched." I opted to wait and avoid the crush of sweaty bodies.

As I waited for my baggage, I surveyed the terminal building and watched the hundreds of Iranians who stood around, waiting for friends to arrive. The large portraits of the Shah, which once decorated the airport along with replicas of the crown, were gone forever. A large, ugly, black and white likeness of Khomeini had been draped over the position of honor where the Shah's picture had been. Revolutionary slogans had been painted all over the white terminal walls. If a contest were conducted to find the graffiti champions of the world, I decided, the Iranians would win hands down. A clean wall becomes an instant challenge to these people, who take a perverse delight in defacing public property. Everything in the airport looked makeshift and temporary, and the relative neatness and discipline of the Shah's era were gone without a trace.

I helped a lady remove her heavy bag from the baggage ramp, and she thanked me. My bags had not yet arrived, so I offered to help her carry hers to the customs inspection station. At first she accepted, then, realizing I was a *kharaji* [foreigner], she took the bag from me and struggled on her way. Finally my bags were dumped on the baggage ramp. With my diplomatic passport, I cleared customs without a hitch. There was no sign of my military driver, so I decided to take a taxi to the embassy. I rented an old Mercedes taxi, driven by a middle-aged man from Tabriz. He was Turkic, but his Farsi was good. As we drove toward the center of the city to the American Embassy along Avenue Eisenhower, my driver informed me that the names of all the streets had been changed to honor the revolution and to purge the country of regal and Western influence. It appeared that they had also purged the garbage collectors and street cleaners. The once-clean avenues and broad boulevards were strewn with garbage and trash. Signs of the revolution were everywhere. As we passed through the circle at the junction of Eisenhower and Amirabad avenues, I noticed the burned-out marquee of a large theater, boarded-up bank buildings, and other evidence of the destruction and havoc brought by the mobs of several months ago. As I viewed these vestiges of the raging revolution that had swept this ancient land and turned its people into looters, eager to destroy what their own hands had built, I remembered a quatrain from Omar Khayyám:

> Then said a Second—"Ne'er a peevish Boy
> "Would break the Bowl from which he drank in joy;
>   "And He that with his hand the Vessel made
> "Will surely not in after Wrath destroy."

But they did "in after Wrath destroy" these theaters and other places of recreation and entertainment, which many of them had helped build and most of them loved to frequent.

As we turned off old Pahlavi Avenue and on to Takht-e-Jamshid Avenue, which had been renamed Avenue Taleghani, I was on familiar ground. I used to walk along this street daily when I worked at the embassy, several blocks farther down the street. The traffic was heavier and more undisciplined than ever. People raced through red lights with police watching, as though daring them to do anything about it. The always individualistic Iranians, who in the old days obeyed only out of fear of the consequences of not adhering to the law, seemed to have taken the departure of the Shah as a license to do exactly as they pleased. The old fear was now replaced by a new aura of abandonment, approaching anarchy.

The embassy compound looked like a fortress in the middle of a hostile country. The gates were all locked, and it took several minutes to convince the local guards to allow the taxi through the gate so my baggage could be delivered to the Ambassador's residence, where I would be staying.

Major General Philip Gast, Chief of the American Military Mission to Iran during the Shah's last two years, was waiting to greet me. He had volunteered to stay to wrap up loose ends after the forced evacuation of his staff at the peak of the revolution. General Gast and I sat in the library to get acquainted. He was articulate, efficient, and friendly — not at all what I had expected. During my briefings in Washington, a number of his former subordinates had bent my ears with bits and pieces of information critical of Gast. As the revolution had crested and it had become obvious that Americans, especially those in the military, weren't welcome in Iran, Gast had refused to "rock the boat" to get his people out of the country. Some said he unnecessarily risked the lives of his men by keeping them in place long after it was obvious that they were in imminent danger. The other side of that coin, however, is that any early withdrawal of U.S. forces would have been interpreted as the end of our support for the Shah. Consequently, they probably were kept in place as a matter of national policy, whether Gast personally agreed with the decision or not.

We talked about everything from the spare parts business to the revolution as it had been lived by General Gast. I was fascinated by his stories of the final months of the Shah's reign and saddened by his ticking off of old friends in the Iranian military who had remained loyal to the end and were executed by the revolutionary winners. He urged me to sleep late in the morning and try to get over my jet lag. I told him I would try, but I was anxious to get to work.

I was up for breakfast at 7:30 with Bruce Laingen, the acting ambassador, and the general. We ate in the informal dining room, overlooking the gardens and the pool.

Luigi smiled when he entered through the swinging door from the kitchen. I got up from the table and shook his hand. He greeted me in Farsi, and we ended up in a bear hug. Even though the two senior members of the embassy staff were eating breakfast with me, I felt most at home when I saw the cook I had known for years. As Luigi returned to the kitchen, Bruce said, "Chuck, I get the impression you know your way around here pretty well already. How long have you known Luigi?" I told him about my earlier duty here, when Luigi was my only real link with the ambassador's big house . . . and was my source of coffee and snacks.

Bruce was gracious, exceptionally friendly, and down-to-earth for a senior State Department officer. So many of them were stuffy and egotistical; it was refreshing to meet an exception to the norm. Bruce gave me a rundown on the house and told me that it was my home, and I should enjoy it as much as possible.

I walked the tree-lined lane to my office in the Chancellery building. It was a pretty walk, especially early in the morning. The lush gardens, with their shrubbery, green grass, and tall trees, were particularly comforting when juxtaposed with the hustle and bustle of the rush hour I could hear in the city outside the high embassy wall.

Colonel Ron Davis met me as I entered our suite of offices on the second floor. It was still early, and I had seen very few people during my short walk to the office. Davis was a very young Air Force full colonel who had been assigned here for about three months on temporary duty. He was sharp and businesslike — perhaps a bit too businesslike for my blood, and somewhat aloof in his dealings with subordinates. Davis introduced me to the rest of the office. There was Navy Commander Don Sharer, an expert on the Navy's F-14 fighter. Don was a sandy-haired, quiet man with a quick sense of humor and a pilot's instinct for precision in performing his job. He was an individual with an insatiable appetite for fun and a tremendous capacity for getting a job done without fanfare or supervision. I liked him on sight. When the General and Davis left, Don would be my next in command.

Navy Lieutenant Commander Bob Engelmann was a mild-mannered logistics expert who was in Iran on temporary duty. Bob, a bachelor, had an excellent reputation in his field. Air Force Captain Paul Needham also had just arrived for three months temporary duty from the States. He was a professional supply officer with plenty of experience in his job.

Master Sergeant Regis Ragan, U.S. Army, was a holdover from the big Military Mission of the Shah's days. He left for a short time when others were evacuated, only to return as a volunteer. Having spent five years in Iran, he knew where all the skeletons were hidden and was worth his weight in gold. He was a typical first-rate Army noncommissioned officer, totally dedicated and hard-working — the kind you have to order out of the office at night and never can beat to work in the morning. We had instant rapport.

Air Force Staff Sergeant Jim Hughes had just arrived from his permanent duty station in Germany. He would replace Army Sergeant Bill German, who was due to leave in a few days to return to his permanent unit in Europe. German was a regular "Sergeant Bilko"; he had a finger in everything and knew exactly what he was doing. I sensed right away that we would miss his efficiency and his wisecracks. Hughes was new, quiet, and unsure of himself — at least, that was my first impression.

Davis said we were supposed to have an Air Force Master Sergeant Vincent arrive within the next few weeks to be our chief administrator. We also would be getting an Army lieutenant colonel by mid-November.

I was pleased with the staffing. In a small operation, everyone has to pull his weight and get along with the rest, and this team seemed to have been carefully selected. I told them that I looked forward to working with them and asked for their help in getting oriented in the new job.

As the day progressed, I met other members of the embassy staff, including Air Force Colonel Tom Schaefer, the Defense Attaché, and Colonel Lee Holland, the Army Attaché. Both of these officers were veterans of the revolution and the attack on the embassy last February 14. I also met Ann Swift, the senior political officer who was sitting in for Vic Tomseth while he was in the States on home leave, and Bill Daugherty, the political military officer from the State Department, whom I had met in Washington. Bill also had just arrived.

Lolli, the pretty, tall, brunette Iranian girl who had been in the attaché office for years, was still at her desk, as were many of the other longtime Iranian employees. I was reminded of Robin Moore's book *Dubai* when I saw Lolli, and I asked if she had read it. She said she had heard about it but had not seen a copy. Ironically, in that novel based on research Moore did in Iran and other Middle East countries, an out-of-favor young military attaché, who speaks fluent Arabic and Farsi, quits the service and gets involved in a series of exciting adventures as a private consultant to a Gulf sheik. He eventually returns to Tehran and wins a pretty embassy secretary's heart, marries her, and takes her to the Gulf with him. My old boss, Colonel Bill Cavness, told me that he had granted Moore an interview during his visit to

Iran — after my departure for duty in Vietnam. According to Cavness, I was part of the composite character of the young attaché, and Lolli was the secretary. Compared to the girl I had known before, Lolli now seemed nervous and worried. This was probably only a natural effect of the past year's turmoil, I thought as I walked to the finance office in the basement of the Chancellery.

Another young woman I vaguely remembered was working there in embassy finance. She remembered me and said, "Welcome, Colonel Scott. What brings you back to Iran? Are you going to be here very long?"

"Yes, I'll be here a year, unless we get kicked out before my time is up."

She smiled at me and said, "You speak good Farsi, and you know this country very well. Are you working for the CIA?"

I told her I wasn't working for the CIA. She laughed, but she didn't believe me. She had listened to too much propaganda; she thought most of the embassy staff had CIA connections. Paranoia has penetrated even to the local employees, I thought as I walked up the main stairs to my office on the second floor.

I had been unable to get a current phone number for Amir Fateh. The operators were less than cooperative when I called from an embassy telephone, so I decided to get help in locating him. I waited until after dark and left the embassy by the motor pool gate. The big Kurdish guard remembered me from the past, and we chatted about old times. Then he hit me with the same question as the girl in the finance office. I told him I was not CIA, and he chuckled to himself as if to say, "I bet."

Abbas, the owner of the Semiramis Hotel, was in jail, according to his wife. He was accused of corruption and was awaiting trial by a revolutionary court. I suspected that his only crime was being a successful businessman who had worked hard and accumulated some wealth and property. Abbas' wife, when I told her of my difficulties in locating Amir, agreed to make inquiries for me. She tried the operator and the special locator number but without success. She said she had heard the name "Amir Fateh" or had read something about him in the paper within the last year or so, but she couldn't remember what it was. She agreed to do some more checking for me, and I told her I would stop in again within a day or so. As I left, she cautioned me: "Remember, this is not the same Iran you knew. You are an American, and you are not safe here, I am sorry to say. God go with you."

The streets were quiet as I walked back across the avenue to the embassy. I wondered about Amir and Monica, and I found myself hoping they had managed to get out of Iran safely. Amir was the epitome of a successful businessman, and I questioned his chances for survival if he was still in the country.

"Hey, sir; don't plan anything for Friday. We're going on a picnic to the mountains with Erika, Heidi, and some others from the Austrian Embassy." Don Sharer was not only good on the job, he also was rapidly becoming my unofficial social secretary. He could organize and plan a successful party for a Syrian and an Israeli if he decided it would be fun.

"Sounds like a super idea," I said. I hadn't had a day off since I'd arrived, almost five weeks earlier. "What do I need to bring?"

Don explained the plan to me: A group of about ten of us would visit one of the old *Imam Zadehs* [tombs of religious leaders purported to be related to Mohammed] in the mountains about fifty miles west of the city. We would have a picnic in the mountains and then return for supper at the home of one of the Austrian women.

The day of the picnic was absolutely beautiful.

167

The air in the mountains was clear and quite cool. We hiked through two villages on the way to the summit of this breezy mountain and the *Imam Zadeh*. We saw no signs of the revolution and few signs of the modern world. The villagers, with their mud huts built into the mountainside, looked as if they came unchanged from the twelfth century. For these poor, illiterate mountain people, little had changed in hundreds of years. The revolution did not appear to have touched them, and they were friendly and went out of their way to welcome us. It was a world apart from the hatred and resentment of Tehran. As we ate our picnic lunch, the family of the old Iranian man who was caretaker of the site arrived with his noon meal. They joined him at an old table to share the special Friday meal of rice, spinach cakes, and yogurt made from goat's milk. They insisted on sharing their meal with us — typical old-fashioned Persian hospitality. I finally accepted a spinach cake and a helping of yogurt. We chatted with the caretaker's family; Jon, an excellent linguist from the Norwegian Embassy, and I translated for the others.

These poor people had so little, yet they were more than happy to share with us, total strangers from another world. This was the Iran I remembered. This was the Iran I loved. This was the culture that had won my heart and my respect during my trips to the countryside years ago. I had to find out what they knew of the changes in their land, so I asked, "Do you know of the Ayatollah Khomeini?"

The family members looked at one another before the caretaker answered my question. He hesitated like a schoolboy about to recite a difficult verse before a stern teacher.

"Yes," he said finally. "We have heard of the Ayatollah. He chased the Shah away, and now he is the leader in Tehran." He spoke of Tehran as if it were a million miles away. To these simple, proud people, it was.

Driving back to the city, I felt more relaxed than I had since my arrival. I was pleased to see that some good things about Iran remained, still untouched by the dramatic changes in the cities. The fresh air, the exertion of climbing the mountain with happy, friendly people, and the chance to see another side of the Iranian scene was a good tonic for me.

To repay the debt for our wonderful trip to the mountains, Don and I invited a few friends from the Austrian Embassy to watch *All the President's Men* with us one night at the residence. Bruce was attending a reception and dinner at the French Embassy, so we had the house to ourselves.

Since General Gast had left, it generally was quiet at the house when Bruce was busy with diplomatic functions. I declined most invitations to these big functions as part of my effort to keep a low profile. It was unwise to flaunt American military presence.

That night, Erika brought her Iranian boyfriend to the movie. Hassan was a handsome, upper-class, well-educated, successful engineer. I asked him if he had ever met or knew anything about another engineer, my friend Amir Fateh.

He said that he and Amir had cooperated on several business ventures a few years earlier, and that he had known and admired him. He asked if I knew how much Amir had done for his country with his philanthropy — he had sponsored more than a hundred bright young men and women without money, sending them to colleges in Iran and abroad to study engineering. I told him I knew of Amir's goodwill. Hassan was uneasy, and I sensed there was something he wasn't telling me. "Do you know where he is?" I asked. "Did he leave the country?"

Hassan spoke softly, almost reverently. "Amir, his wife Monica, and three of their children were killed last December in an airplane accident at Mehrabad Airport. I am so sorry."

169

Amir's private twin-engine Beechcraft had exploded on takeoff, Hassan said. There had been no survivors, and no cause of the accident had ever been established. Hassan suspected that the airplane had been sabotaged by revolutionaries who resented Amir's success. The "accident" happened during the big riots and demonstrations, just before the Shah's departure. He also told me that Amir's father had been killed in an ambush several months earlier, while driving across a bridge from one of his factories in the city of Yazd, south of Tehran.

I was speechless with grief and disbelief. That wonderful man, my close friend, was dead . . . and I had wanted so much to see him again, or at least to know that he was alive and safe. I excused myself before the film was over and went to my room. I remembered Amir's love of poetry, and recalled one of his favorite quatrains from Kayyám:

Ah, with the Grape my fading Life provide,
And wash the Body whence the Life has died,
And lay me, shrouded in the living Leaf,
By some not unfrequented Garden-side.

I could only pray that he was resting by some "not unfrequented Garden-side," as he would have wished.

October 23, 1979

Henry Precht, the State Department's Country Director for Iran, was visiting for a few days. I saw very little of him except at mealtimes, but I was impressed by his helpful attitude. He spent a good deal of time closeted with Bruce Laingen, and I got the impression he had secrets which he preferred that I not know. Bruce told me one night that they had been discussing his next assignment. He had been offered the senior State Department post in Jeruṣalem but was inclined to turn it down; he had been an ambassador already (in Malta) and preferred to return to his family in Washington if he didn't land another ambassadorial position. At breakfast the next day, Henry entered while Bruce and I were talking. It was obvious that he wanted to talk with Bruce alone, but Bruce told him that if the discussion concerned his assignment, he could speak freely, that I already knew about it.

Before Henry could answer, however, Luigi informed Bruce that he had a phone call from the communications center at the embassy. It was a "flash" message from Washington — the highest possible priority that can be given a message. Bruce took the call, returned to rush through the rest of his breakfast, and dashed to the office.

At the nine o'clock staff meeting, we learned the contents of the flash message. Bruce was at his diplomatic best as he announced, "The Shah is at this very moment on his way from Mexico to New York for medical treatment." Bruce had been instructed to meet with the Prime Minister as soon as possible to pass this blockbuster to him. He was told to emphasize that the Shah was being admitted to the U.S. for humanitarian reasons only, and that he would not be permitted to engage in any political activity. Bruce also was supposed to seek assurances from Bazargan that the American Embassy would be provided with whatever additional security this startling news might warrant.

The usually noisy conference room was unsettlingly silent. I surveyed the room. There were looks of disbelief. Barry Rosen, from the International Communications Agency and one of our few Persian linguists, placed his head in his hands on the table, in deep thought. The usual wisecracks and trite remarks didn't surface. I personally felt that we had been betrayed by our own people. How could they admit the Shah and leave us in Iran to face the angry wolves? It made no sense to me. My mind flashed back to my briefings at the State Department when I was told there were no plans to permit the Shah to enter the U.S. I had been lied to, and I didn't like it.

Finally the bad news sank in and the initial shock abated. Colonel Lee Holland, who had been through it all before, had a "here we go again" look on his face. Al Golacinski, the security officer, announced that he would be issuing two-way portable radios as soon as possible and advised all of us to lay low and take no unnecessary chances. I planned to do just that, as I left the meeting and hurried to inform my staff of the worrisome news.

Initial Iranian press reaction to the news was subdued and fairly straightforward. People at the embassy were counting the hours and days that passed without action by the angry Iranians. Some felt that if we didn't see some action by anti-American groups within a few days, we might have weathered the storm. The old Iranian hands, however, felt otherwise. We wondered what they were planning and why it was taking them so long to respond. The local press was becoming loaded with inciting propaganda accusations against the U.S. The newspapers claimed that the Shah was not sick, that he was in the U.S. working on a coup to restore his throne. Iranian doctors demanded permission to examine the ex-King of Kings, but the U.S. refused to allow it.

Thursday, November 1, 1979

"Sir, there's a woman on the phone for you. She called three times this morning while you were out, but she wouldn't leave a message. She speaks only a few words of English, and she seems very anxious to talk to you."

I picked up the phone and answered, "*Salam arz mekonam, Sarhang Escott*" [Hello, this is Colonel Scott]. The voice on the other end of the line spoke beautiful Farsi. I had heard the voice before, but I couldn't place it.

"Colonel Scott, I am a friend of a very dear

172

friend of yours who is gone to his reward. It is dangerous for me to be seen with you, but I know he would want you to know he died as he had lived — a soldier."

I still couldn't place the voice, but she obviously knew a lot about me. She asked about Betty, Beth, and Greg, and she congratulated me on my promotion to colonel. She asked if I remembered the big party in Tehran when I was promoted to major many years ago. We talked some more, and I agreed to meet her the next evening. She promised to call early the next morning to give me the address.

That afternoon, I had a meeting with Colonel Kamkar, the Deputy Minister of Defense for Armaments. I enjoyed the ride to his office with my driver. The air was clearer as we drove north, and the streets were busy with Iranians shopping for their weekend, which for most of them had begun at one o'clock that day. The next day was their sabbath, so all offices and stores would be closed. It was nice to observe people going about their normal daily activities. There were sandbagged weapon emplacements manned by revolutionary guards all along our route, but people seemed to take them in stride. I wondered if they really were returning to a semblance of normalcy after the long months of revolution and demonstration, or if demonstrations had become so routine that they were an accepted element of life.

At the Ministry, on my way to Kamkar's office, I met an Iranian Special Forces master sergeant I had known for years. He had run the Iranian jump school parachutist refresher course when I went through it in the mid-sixties. He greeted me warmly, recognizing me instantly in spite of my civilian clothes.

"Major Rockne told me you are a colonel now. Excuse me for not saluting, but it would not be wise these days."

"You're right, Sarge, that's part of the reason I'm not in uniform."

The sergeant had gained weight and had not

aged very well, but he still looked as tough and fearless as ever. I wanted more time to talk to him. "Maybe one of these days we can get together and talk over the fate of many of the people we both knew," I said in an effort to end our chance meeting and get to Kamkar's office on time.

"*Shayad*" [Maybe], he said, "but in the meantime, God go with you. You are in danger in my country now, and there is nothing I can do to help."

Kamkar had his civilian assistant join us as soon as I entered his office. He apparently was not allowed to speak to an American Army officer without a witness. My host offered us tea, as usual. We sipped our drinks and made small talk for the first five or ten minutes before we got down to business. Kamkar was concerned about spare parts shipments needed for the campaign against the Kurds in the north, and he also wanted the U.S. Congress to remove the ban on the shipment of lethal items to Iran. I told him I would like to help, but the Congress was concerned about the oppressive use of U.S.-made weapons and ammunitions and wasn't likely to change its mind about the ban as long as anti-U.S. propaganda remained at a high level. I told him that I understood his position, but that some of Iran's actions and the media coverage of them wasn't helping his case for better U.S. cooperation in obtaining these vitally needed items. The colonel tried to finesse the touchy subject by saying, "We are soldiers; we should not worry about political issues. They do not mean anything. What has meaning is what we do, not what they say in the newspapers."

I told him I hoped he was right, but that the level of inflammatory propaganda in the press was bound to have an effect on the Iranian people and on those in the U.S. who made decisions regarding our sale of military hardware to Iran. Kamkar spoke of the U.S.'s showing some sign of goodwill and cooperation with the revolution. He mentioned his ace in the hole — the five million dollars that had just been deposited in an American bank for spare parts. "That," he said, "is a sign of Iranian goodwill. Now it is up to your government to settle quickly the old issues, if you want to get along with us."

It was the same line I had been hearing all along. Nothing new today, I thought as I bid Kamkar and his assistant farewell and wished them a happy weekend.

My expected phone call came through early the next morning, as promised.

At the high-rise apartment building on Avenue Pahlavi, I rang the bell for apartment 911. A female voice answered on the small speaker in the security system. I identified myself and entered as the buzzer unlocked the heavy steel door. Upstairs, I knocked lightly on the door. A beautiful pair of Persian eyes I remembered so well looked into mine as the door opened — eyes that once had reflected happiness and lightheartedness, but now appeared as sad, hurt, and dark as a moonless night in a war zone. Beyond the eyes, even in her sorrow, Mrs. Hojat was more beautiful than I remembered. Her long, shiny, pitch-colored hair, her satiny white skin, high cheek bones, gleaming and perfectly shaped teeth, and her slim, well-maintained figure made her one of the loveliest ladies I had ever seen. Her warm and friendly personality was still intact, but there was an overpowering air of mourning that wrapped around her like a black cape.

She poured tea as we sat in the living room with its Louis XIV furniture. "Chuck, General Ali would have wanted you to know how he died. I know you respected him as a soldier, and he did you." So she told the story.

General Ali Hojat-Kashani was arrested by the revolutionaries shortly after they seized power. He was accused of murdering hundreds of innocent civilians. He had been a brigade commander in 1963, when the riots against the White Revolution took place. At one point, he had ordered his troops to fire into the mob, when their lives were threatened by the rioters. There were casualties; there was

175

no question about that. General Ali spent two months in Evin prison before he finally was brought before a revolutionary court.

Ali was a close friend of Ayatollah Taleghani. When the ayatollah was being hunted by the Shah's police, the general had provided him with a hiding place in the mountains at his summer home. But Taleghani had no authority with the revolutionary court — only the Ayatollah Khomeini could intervene to spare Ali's life. Mrs. Hojat had obtained a letter from Taleghani explaining the help he had received from Ali during his time of great peril. She raced against time to Qom to ask Khomeini to read Taleghani's plea and spare her husband's life. It took a good while to get an audience with the revolutionary patriarch, but he finally agreed to write the necessary letter.

Mrs. Hojat then rushed back to court in Tehran, where she was refused entry until the trial was over. She pleaded with the guards, but to no avail. As soon as the trial was over, she presented the letter to the court. It was too late. General Hojat was taken to the roof of the court building and shot within minutes of the trial's conclusion. The court apologized to her by saying, "We are sorry, but the anger of the people must be vented."

Ali, according to information received later, had refused a blindfold. He stood at rigid attention before the firing squad until his lifeless body fell to the ground.

On my way back to the embassy, I thought about my friend. I had always said that he was an exceptional soldier who could have been a general in any army. Whatever he may have done in 1963, he certainly had the right to a fair and impartial trial. His death was Iran's loss. My most disturbing thought was imagining what must have gone through his mind during his time in prison and at the trial. He had loved his country more than life itself. The unfairness must have been difficult for him to comprehend.

The next day was November 2 — a regular day off for the embassy staff — but I planned to work on a message report for Washington. The Shah had been in the U.S. for ten days. Except for the usual demonstrations, the Iranians had done nothing. Considering their treatment of men like Amir and General Ali, doing nothing was out of character for them.

Akbar Houssini -- a terrorist without a taste for violence

United States Embassy Compound

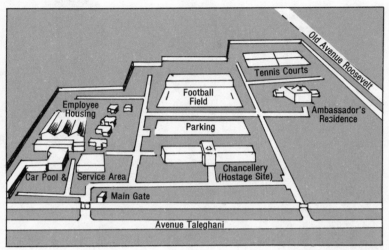

Old Avenue Roosevelt

Tennis Courts

Football Field

Employee Housing

Ambassador's Residence

Parking

Car Pool & Service Area

Chancellery (Hostage Site)

Main Gate

Avenue Taleghani

Walter Cumming

AP/Wide World Photos

Col. Scott reads from Bible during second Christmas telecast

Wearing his eagle freedom shirt, Scott deplanes in Germany

Former President Jimmy Carter greets the freed officer

Billy Downs, courtesy Atlanta Journal/Constitution

Well-wishers celebrate with Scott and wife Betty

President Ronald Reagan commends Col. Scott at White House

Back in uniform, a proud soldier is honored by his comrades

WELCOME HOME
COL SCOTT

Col. Scott leaves a press conference and soon left the service

The Long,
Lonely Year

7

U.S. EMBASSY, TEHRAN
NOVEMBER 24, 1979

"Take him away, but do not let him sleep!"

I can barely hear the interrogator's sneering instructions to the guards. His voice is only a background
sound that seems far away and detached from reality. It has
been a long questioning session, but I haven't been beaten
this time, and there have been fewer threats of physical
abuse, torture, and death. They're no longer insisting that
I'm a CIA operative. I've been subjected to at least twenty
interrogation sessions by four different teams of ruthless,
paranoid questioners. They all ask the same questions and
spout the same accusations and revolutionary rhetoric.
They're trying to wear me down with this grueling procedure and sheer fatigue.

They've taken away my shoes and my belt. I'm
having great difficulty keeping my trousers from falling
down over my significantly reduced hips. My nourishment
has been limited to bread, hot tea, and an infrequent cup of
soup; I'm sure I've lost at least twenty-five pounds.

Physical and emotional exhaustion have taken
their toll; I'm weak and confused. I've lost track of time, and
I haven't seen daylight since I became a hostage. After each
interrogation session, I'm dumped on the floor of a different
room. Frequently I'm left blindfolded between sessions. The
few times I haven't been left blindfolded, I've seen some of
the other hostages but haven't had an opportunity to communicate with them. We're under constant surveillance to
keep us from talking. Except for a few incidents when the

guards were negligent in doing their duty, I have been awakened every fifteen minutes to keep me from getting any real sleep.

I'm led into a room where I stumble over someone lying on the floor. My guards find an unoccupied spot and push me down. As a welcome relief, my hands are tied in front this time. My ankles are securely bound with coarse rope and my blindfold is removed. I'm in a room with several other sleeping hostages. I look around, trying to identify them in the dark. A guard sitting in the doorway tells me to go to sleep, and my fatigued body responds to the order.

"Get up quickly!" The guard emphasizes his command, which startles me from the soundest sleep I've had in three weeks, by poking at me with a stick. I'm physically exhausted, and I still hurt all over from the beatings during my interminable interrogations. I pray there will not be another round of questioning.

"Move quickly. You must to hurry!" The guard probes me again with his broom handle. I'm the only one who is jostled from sleep. Two of the other hostages are awakened by the noise, but they roll over and go back to sleep. I envy them. Sleep is the only relief from the terror and uncertainty. I wish they were awakening one of the others, who hasn't been interrogated, but it is evident: It's my turn again — for something.

I'm blindfolded, and the ropes which have been tied tightly around my wrists and ankles are removed, but my wrists are quickly pulled behind my back and locked together by cold, steel handcuffs. I'm pushed toward the door. A heavy blanket is tossed over my head and upper torso and tied in place around my neck by a guard who says, "This will keep you warm; you are going outside." I am moved down a hallway and then told to be careful of the stairs. As I'm led down the stairs, I hear a door opening. Guards speak in whispers, warning each other not to say anything important because "this one speaks Farsi." I can feel the cold ground on my bare feet. After a few minutes of standing and waiting, I'm forced inside a vehicle — probably a van. A surly voice orders, "Sit still and do not talk, or you will be shot." My ankles are tied together with a length of rope.

I sit shaking in the cold for about half an hour. There are no sounds inside the vehicle; I assume I'm alone. Suddenly there is movement and noise as another hostage is pushed inside and takes his place beside me. There are other sounds, so I presume one of the guards has remained inside to make sure we don't communicate. I decide to question the guard so that my companion will know he's not alone. He may be able to recognize my voice. "Where are we going?" I'm sure I won't get an answer, but it's worth a try.

The guard is upset by my audacity in daring to speak. "You must not know, and you must not to speak!"

His use of the infinitive form of the verb tells me that he doesn't speak much English. He emphasizes his directive by tapping my head with his stick.

There's more movement as additional hostages are loaded and told to sit still and be quiet. After a long, uncomfortable wait, someone enters the cab, slams the door, rolls down the window, and receives last-minute instructions in whispers from someone outside. I can't make out what they're saying. Breathing is difficult through the dirty blanket. I feel perspiration on my face and back, but my feet are like ice. Am I really this warm, or is it, once again, a symptom of the uncertainty and terror? I sense that this could be our last ride, but there's nothing I can do about it. All I can do is try to make myself as comfortable as possible and pray.

As the van maneuvers along the winding roads of the compound, negotiating the speed bumps, it seems that we're leaving the embassy grounds. I anticipate the worst: Are we going to a real prison? This has been on my mind for some time, and I mentally have prepared myself for this eventuality. But I know in my heart that if we're moved to a real prison, it will be an indication that we're going to be stuck in Iran for a very long time. Maybe even for the rest of our lives.

We stop at one of the embassy gates, and I hear the heavy steel structure squeak open. The driver speaks to someone outside, and I hear traffic on the street in front of us. I assume, by the volume of traffic, that we're exiting the main motor pool gate along Avenue Taleghani. It sounds as though we're one of a group of vehicles moving as a convoy — probably for additional security, I think as we begin to move more rapidly. After about ten minutes, I'm convinced that we're heading north because we've been moving uphill most of the way. I have a sick feeling in the pit of my stomach. Are we going to Evin prison in north Tehran? As usual, the total absence of information adds to the terror of the moment, and possible scenarios begin to flash across my mind.

What's going on in America? Have we been written off and forgotten? I can't visualize the United States giving in to the demands of these Islamic fundamentalists, but I can't see the Iranians releasing us without getting the Shah, either. I try to divorce my thoughts from this situation which I can't control. As the vehicle speeds through the quiet streets of Tehran, I concentrate on happier days when I was on maneuvers in Germany. I thought then that the lack of sleep and cold were difficult, but I thrived on the challenges of soldiering. The personal satisfaction of knowing that I was making a contribution to my country's defense was more than adequate compensation for the rigors of duty in the field. But at least then I could see what was going on, and I was in control of my own life. Now I know that my sole mission, my greatest challenge, is to survive.

The vehicle is slowing. The echoes of the engine's noise and the vehicle's movements, bouncing off walls, indicate that we're in a built-up area with narrow streets. We

184

stop, apparently at a gate. Then we begin to move slowly along a bumpy narrow road inside the gate. It must be a driveway. Finally the van stops and the driver opens the door and gets out, slamming the door behind him. The guard (or, perhaps, two guards) in the van with us continues to sit in silence. Time passes slowly. I guess we've been sitting here for about thirty minutes when the door slides open and the terrorists unload their human cargo. We move inside a building, where I feel thick carpeting under my feet. It's cold, and the room we're in seems very large. I am told to sit. A cold wall is behind my back.

In about half an hour, my blanket is removed, and I'm told by a guard to sleep. I try to arrange the blanket so that it's both under and over me, but it's difficult to do with my hands behind my back. I catch a ray of light through my blindfold, so I decide to try to work it loose. Rubbing the back of my head against the wall, I maneuver the cloth blindfold enough to catch a glimpse of the big room. It's a large drawing room with an ornate chandelier and beautiful Persian carpets. There is a huge ebony desk at the other end of the room, and expensive-looking French provincial dining room chairs are stacked in a corner. My imagination plays tricks on me. I see a judge seated at the big desk. He's wearing the robes and headdress of a mullah. I picture this room as an improvised courtroom. Are we going to be tried here? The uncertainty is, in itself, frightening. I realize that I'm so tired, I'm not thinking rationally. I try to sleep, but I'm too cold and unnerved to rest.

Hours pass. I try to get another look at the room. There are eight other hostages here. All are blindfolded and they, too, are trying to keep warm enough to sleep. I see Bob Blucker and Colonel Tom Schaefer, and I think I recognize Captain Paul Needham. I hear furniture being moved upstairs, and I wonder if they're preparing that area for us. But why have we been moved from the embassy? Is it a good omen or a bad one? I don't see anything positive about it. To me, it's a signal that they're preparing for a long stay. I can't rule out the possibility of trials, and I know what that will mean. I think of home and family, but that only increases my anxiety and depression. I find solace only in prayer, asking God to continue to give me the strength and resolve to endure. I begin to feel a little more relaxed. I have managed to convince myself again that there's no use worrying about things I can't control. Finally I doze off.

Judging by my feeling of intense fatigue, I'm sure I haven't been asleep more than an hour when I'm awakened by a group of guards and told to get up. They escort me up a long semicircular staircase, along a hallway, and into a room. I'm pushed along, turned around, and told to sit. There are no other voices or movements of any kind for about half an hour. Then a guard enters and removes my blindfold. He replaces my handcuffs with a length of strong rope, tying my hands in front of me. I'm in a medium-sized bedroom of a private home that probably belongs to some well-to-do Iranian who has been dispossessed by the revolutionaries. I'm on a king-sized bed with a mattress and no sheets or blankets. The room is very cold and apparently hasn't been occupied for some time. There are heavy dark drapes covering the window.

Within a matter of minutes, I'm joined by three other American hostages — Tom Schaefer, Paul Needham, and Bob Blucker. They're seated in the corners of the room, and their blindfolds also are removed. The ever-present admonition "Don'ta - espeak!" is repeated several times by the guards. We also are cautioned not to look at each other for any reason. A guard with an automatic rifle is posted outside the door, and a guard with no weapon is seated directly inside the door, to make sure we don't talk. For the first time in our captivity, I have the most comfortable spot. I actually have a bed! I haven't even seen a bed in almost a month. I decide to take advantage of the situation and sleep.

186

After about an hour, I give up. It's just too cold to sleep, and my mind is working constantly, still wondering why we've been moved away from the embassy. I glance at my fellow captives when the guard's eyes are averted. They all look starkly pale, hollow-eyed, and unkempt with their long beards and matted hair. Weight loss is readily apparent, even in those like Paul who had little surplus to lose. I know I look at least as bad as the rest. I finally realize that the bed is not the best place to spend twenty-four hours a day, but the guards won't let me up except to go to the latrine. When we have to use the bathroom, we're led one at a time, blindfolded, downstairs to what was once a fancy powder room. It's now a filthy mess. The Iranians are using the same facility, and they refuse to sit on the seat. They apparently squat above it and their aim is off the mark more often than not. The stench is almost unbearable. There's no toilet paper, and the only water is a low-pressure cold faucet. We're required to wash off our plastic bowls for eating in this same latrine; I wonder how long it will be before we're sick. I'm sure there are other hostages in this building, because we have heard them from time to time, but we haven't seen anyone else.

I smell the sweet odor of pipe tobacco, and it is a constant reminder that I haven't been allowed to smoke my pipe. I recognize the tobacco as John Graves' blend. Bob Blucker complains constantly to the guards about the "stink" from the smoke. I think it smells fine and wish he would shut up.

One of the guards enters the room and passes out some old paperbacks. Most of them are trashy novels, but at least we'll have something to read to help pass the time. I select the thickest book from among those available, figuring it will last longer than the short westerns by Louis L'Amour. It is Judith Krantz's *Scruples*. I have no trouble getting involved in this fast-moving, racy story about the world of fashion. I pause in my reading frequently to reflect on how far we are from our normal lives, even though my normal life is nothing like those portrayed in this novel.

To pass time, I go through the mental gymnastics of figuring what day it is, and suddenly I realize that tomorrow is Thanksgiving. I wonder if the militants will stage a big propaganda show for the holiday, complete with turkey and all the fixings. We could use a decent meal. I can tell that the lack of protein in our diet is causing me to lose muscle as well as fat. My guess is that we're secreted away here for some special reason, that there will be no special meal, and that we're just going to remain here, away from the others, in a state of limbo. I wish I could find an opportunity to speak to those in the same room with me, but it's impossible with the alert guard looking on all the time.

Tom is in good spirits, but Paul is complaining to the guards about dizziness. Paul is an exceptional runner and was in excellent physical condition before the takeover, but this sedentary life is getting to him. Thin before, he now looks gaunt and drained. Bob Blucker is enjoying himself by trying to make the guards think he's mentally deranged. He yells at the guards for smoking and spends most of his time trying to block the smoke from coming in under the door connecting our two rooms. Smoke is poison to Bob, even if it's in the next room. I think how funny it is for someone in our situation to worry about tobacco smoke and lung cancer, when our immediate and most imminent threat may be a firing squad.

It's Thanksgiving Day, but there are no indications that the guards are even aware that it's a special holiday for Americans. I think of Thanksgivings I have celebrated with family and friends. It's a tradition in our home that I stuff the turkey and start it baking in the oven before Betty and the children are even awake. How I wish I were repeating that ritual today. I start worrying about my family, but then I catch myself in time. It's not good to think of home and family in this situation; it is counterproductive and depressing to reflect on how they must feel. I know they're as helpless in this situation as I am. All they can do is wait and pray. My spirits are low as I try my best to avoid thoughts of them, and home, and freedom.

My thoughts return to this spacious and elegant house. I'm sure that, until a few months ago, it was the happy home of a wealthy Iranian. I wonder if he managed to escape Khomeini's firing squads and find sanctuary in America or Europe. I recall a quatrain from Omar's "Rubáiyát." It applies so well to my thoughts on the fate and destiny of the usurped owner of this once-lovely home.

> Think, in this battered Caravanserai
> Whose Portals are alternate Night and Day,
> How Sultán after Sultán with his Pomp
> Abode his destined Hour, and went his way.

Whoever lived here certainly must have lived in the image of the sultans of old, with the pomp and material trappings of pre-revolutionary Iran. But, after having abode his hour or two, he too went his way. If this bed could speak, I wonder what it would tell of happier days. The feeling that I already know the fate of the former owner is depressing. He's probably rotting in some prison dungeon left over from the Shah's regime, awaiting the firing squad, which is the most common outcome of revolutionary "justice." Or is he already dead? If so, I wonder about the family of this man, who provided so well for his loved ones. It's ironic, I think, how often I'm comforted by the poems of Omar Khayyám as a prisoner here in his native land.

I review the hundreds of lines I've memorized from his "Rubáiyát" over the years, as I continue to reflect on the profound impact that my loss of freedom has had on me. Then I see a clear image of a special verse I haven't recalled in years.

> I sometimes think that never blows so red
> The Rose as where some buried Caesar bled;

That every Hyacinth the Garden wears
Dropt in her Lap from some once lovely Head.

In this simple verse, I realize that one must know adversity and pain, one must experience a loss of liberty, in order to fully appreciate the freedom we often take for granted. My appreciation of liberty has been nurtured by its absence. I've learned the true value of freedom by losing it. I know that if Divine Providence smiles on me and I return to America, my appreciation and love of such freedom will be stronger than ever, and this perception of the beauty of liberty will be with me for the rest of my life.

The interior guard is called outside by one of the other militants, and Tom and I decide to take advantage of the situation. We simultaneously look toward the door to reassure ourselves that we have a moment for surreptitious dialogue. I decide to defer to Tom, allowing him to speak first and wondering, with great anticipation, what he'll consider most important to say during this precious moment without Big Brother listening.

Tom whispers out of the side of his mouth, his eyes twinkling mischievously: "Goddamnit, Chuck, you sure are ugly."

"Tom," I answer, "if you could see yourself, you wouldn't criticize me." Tom is prematurely gray, and with his shaggy white beard, he looks ten years older than his fifty-one years. We both chuckle as the guard returns, admonishing us, "Don'ta - ta - espeak." It has been a revealing exchange of information — Tom still has his sense of humor. This is his way of saying, "Hang in there; we can still joke, even under these conditions." Tom is smiling broadly, and we both feel good about our short dialogue. But I think of other, more important things I should have said. It's too late now. I'll try to talk to Tom again later, but next time I'll plan ahead so our exchange can be more substantive. I wonder if he has been interrogated and, if so, how it went for him. He doesn't seem to be physically hurt at all, but I can't be sure.

My thoughts are interrupted by the arrival of lunch. I wonder what kind of meal we'll be given today, Thanksgiving. Our plastic bowls are rounded up by the guard and taken outside. I'm hungry and cold. How I would enjoy a big turkey dinner!

As the guard reappears with our plastic bowls, my morale takes a nose dive. We're given a very small serving of cold canned spaghetti, just as it came from the embassy cooperative store. The spaghetti is almost frozen. It sticks together in wads. I know it'll give me indigestion, but there's nothing else, so I eat it. "Happy Thanksgiving," I think as depression engulfs me.

It's more than an hour before the hot tea arrives. The cold spaghetti has upset my stomach and made me thirsty. I hope the tea will help. The guard seems to be more alert than usual, so there's no opportunity even to look at the others. It's hard to adjust to prison life, but at least my interrogation seems to be over — for now. During the last two or three interrogations, the militants were almost apologetic for what they had done to me during the first two weeks. In the last session, we discussed politics, and I had a chance to elaborate on the futility of their blackmail scheme. They still think they can force the United States to give in and return the shah, but I believe they're beginning to realize that it may not work. I was warned that they're not through with me yet, and that if I expect to get out of here alive, I'll have to cooperate by writing letters to American newspapers condemning the Shah and asking for his return to Iran. The talk of spy trials for some of us, me included, has persisted throughout the sessions. I find this frightening and unnerving.

I think about the raw courage of our Vietnam prisoners of war. I have great respect for what those brave men did, and I know I must consider their example, no matter how rough it gets for me. I recall a quote from Alfieri's *Orestes*: "Often the test of courage is not to die, but to live."

I realize that dangerous missions I've had in the past required courage because they portended a possibility of a quick, violent death in combat. But this situation is different; it would be easy to give up, to tell the Iranians anything to save my skin, and hope for better treatment. It also would be relatively easy to provoke them into killing me by attempting a futile escape. But the real test of courage here is not to die, but to live. My mission, as I see it, is to survive physically, mentally, and emotionally. To do this, I have to develop a routine to pass the long days and nights. I have to keep myself as physically strong and ready as humanly possible, so that if a chance for escape ever appears, I'll be prepared. I must concentrate on positive and healthy thoughts, keeping all this in perspective, so that when it's over, the entire experience will be seen as a strengthening period in my life. To die here would take no courage at all — it would be easy. I can't afford even to think of death. I must concentrate on keeping faith and hope alive. I *will* live through this, and when it's over, I'll still have my dignity. This is my mission: to survive and maintain my human dignity and my integrity.

The food is getting worse: bread and tea in the morning, cold rice at lunch, and cold soup at night. I know I'm still losing weight, and the others are looking thinner each day, too. Tom Schaefer looks pretty bad, and so does Paul Needham. We all exercise by running in place for an hour or so each morning and again in the afternoon, but the guards allow us to do it only one at a time. They're afraid to have two of us standing at once. The exercise helps tremendously by working off our nervous energy. It also warms us for a little while against the intense cold of this room. Tom and I have exchanged a few comments in the last few days. I've learned that he hasn't been interrogated yet. In the beginning, he refused to talk to them, saying he was a prisoner of war and was required to give only his name, rank, serial number, and date of birth. That ploy didn't work for me, and I wonder how long he'll be protected by it. He probably was smart to delay his questioning for as long as possible. The Iranians stopped the beatings during my final sessions, as though they were told by their leaders to cut out the physical abuse. Hopefully, if they do interrogate Tom later, it won't be a repeat of what I went through. But Tom is tough, and I'm sure he can take it. My mind flashes to Joe Subic's "introduction" of me to the militants, and I feel my fist clench without any conscious order from my brain. I'm sure Joe's actions put me at the top of their list for interrogation.

I wonder what the Iranians would have done if I had flatly refused to talk to them. Given their mood of anger and hostility, I suspect that I might have been badly disfigured or even killed in the first few days. I've spent a lot of time going over my interrogation. I never gave them any information, and I had an opportunity to learn a great deal about their organization and motivations. I just hope that phase is over and I won't have to live through that kind of ordeal again.

Paul is still complaining of dizziness, but the Iranians have refused to do anything to help him. For some reason, my broken teeth haven't caused me any great pain since the swelling went down. Of course, there's been no sugar in our diet to irritate the nerve endings, and the rice and soup we eat don't require much chewing. Bob Blucker continues to give the guards a hard time at every opportunity. He was pulled out last night for questioning because he refused to give them the address of his apartment, located away from the embassy. He told them they could kill him, but he wouldn't give them the address. I suspect he spent an uncomfortable night, but he says he didn't give them the address. To me, it seems silly to hold out that kind of information, because they can get it anyway. Bob is tough, though, and he's determined not to compromise or give in to their threats. He's a confirmed bachelor who says he prefers to be alone. He hasn't taken part in any of our covert infractions of the "Don'ta - espeak" rule, but I do admire his guts, his tenacity, and his fighting spirit. His obsession about smoke and bad air drives the guards crazy. They think Bob is off his rocker, so they pretty much leave him alone. He may be the smartest one in the group, if he can keep the Iranians off his back by making them think he's gone around the bend. The only bad thing about his antics is that his bitching frequently awakens the rest of us in the middle of the night. Tom really let Bob know how he feels about his nocturnal outbursts earlier today, when the guard was distracted for a moment. I've never seen Tom angry before, but he was really riled up over Bob's constant complaining at our expense. Bob couldn't care less — he's going to cope in his own way, and that's all there is to it.

Our guards have the curiosity of small children. There is a dresser and a night stand in our room, and each new guard inquisitively rummages through the drawers of both pieces of furniture. It's comical to observe their fascination with each object they find. They often get so preoccupied with their searches that Tom and I have a chance to cheer each other a bit by making faces or obscene gestures behind the guard's back. We've nicknamed each of the guards based on his personality — or lack of one. The skinny kid in his late teens with apparently very little between his ears, if the blank look in his eyes is a valid indicator, we have dubbed Space Cadet. The officious little man who claims he is a medical student and pretends to have all the answers, regardless of the subject, I've named Hitler. He's one of the worst. No matter what we say, his standard reply is "It does not matter; it is not important." I have a genuine hatred where he's concerned. I catch myself fantasizing about encounters with him under more equal circumstances. I picture myself walking down Peachtree Street in Atlanta; I spot Hitler walking in the opposite direction with two or three

194

other Iranians, usually Pig Face and Hamid the Liar. I gloat over the possibilities. Sometimes being a good Christian is not easy. Anyway, I'd love to have an opportunity to deal with some of these people one on one.

My thoughts are interrupted by the arrival of supper — if you can call it that. Tonight it's not even the usual cold cup of chicken noodle soup. All we're having is a cup of bouillon, and it's cold as ice. I decide to raise hell about the lousy food we've been getting. The worst they can do is put me in solitary. I'm convinced that they won't kill me unless they're ordered by Khomeini to kill all of us, so it's worth a try. I complain to the guard in Farsi, "You people treat us worse than dogs. This is not a meal. We wouldn't feed this to a pig in America. Why can't you get some decent food for us? Starving us will not bring back your Shah."

He's taken aback. He tells me to shut up, but I continue my loud tirade. "If you have a leader, I want to talk to him. If this is the best you can do, I'll stop eating. If I'm going to starve, I prefer to have it happen as quickly as possible."

The guard decides to debate and appeal to my sense of decency. "Many people in Iran are eating less than you. This is not a hotel. You cannot order anything you want. You are a hostage; you have no rights. If you do not shut up and stop complaining, you will be in much trouble."

"Thanks to you, we're all in much trouble already. Starving us will not help your cause at all."

The guard is angry. He screams his words, and the veins in his skinny neck protrude as his blood pressure soars. "You Americans eat too much anyway. All you want to do is eat, sleep, and make love."

I tell him he's right, that we do eat very well in America. We have worked hard to produce the greatest abundance of food in the world. I tell him that as far as sleep is concerned, there is little else to do here, and that's his fault, not ours. And I tell him that if he thinks we make love too much, he must have seen too many movies.

"You terrorists are not human or you would

provide us with some decent food," I continue. "There's plenty of food at the embassy; you don't even have to buy it. Or are you selling that on the black market?"

The guard is joined by a couple of militants from the hallway who have overheard the loud exchange of insults. One of them points his G-3 automatic rifle at my head. The other speaks in English. "Colonel, you'd better shut up and eat, or we will make it very hard on you. You are a troublemaker, and we know how to deal with those who give us trouble."

All but our regular guard leave. He takes his seat at the doorway and decides to stare me down. I dump the cup of bouillon on the floor next to my bed, never taking my eyes off his. He says nothing. We continue to stare each other down for about ten minutes. I feel intense hatred and revulsion toward this terrorist. I will not give in. After a while, he averts his eyes.

I've made my point, but there's no more food tonight. As usual, I go to sleep hungry.

Something smells good. It smells like an American hamburger with onions. I wonder if I'm losing my mind or hallucinating. Suddenly, a guard with a box full of hamburgers comes in and gives two to each of us. Another guard enters with bottles of Pepsi-Cola; they're even cold. By American standards, the hamburgers are greasy and not very good, but to us they're a veritable feast. I try to pace myself, eating slowly to savor every morsel. I wash the sandwiches down with the cold Pepsi. My morale soars.

I wonder if my act yesterday prompted our feast, or if there has been a turn of events which the Iranians see as positive, so they're celebrating by giving us something to eat that American movies suggest we'll enjoy? In any case, the hamburgers are a welcome change from the steady diet of cold spaghetti and lumpy rice.

196

The difference between total depression and a ray of hope is sometimes quite subtle. Tonight I feel better than I have in a long time. I feel a sense of hope, prompted by our captors showing a little consideration for the first time. I drift off to sleep with a full stomach, dreaming of our release and return to freedom.

It has been a week since our hamburger and Pepsi feast, and the food has gone back to "normal." It's as bad as ever. I'm tired from spending so much time in the prone position on this bed; my shoulders and back ache constantly. We continue in our round of reading, exercising, and sleeping, and there are no indications of a breakthrough in our situation. The thought of remaining here for months or even years is hard to dismiss. Once again, sleep begins to ease my troubled mind. I feel a sense of peace and tranquility as I dream of other places and other times.

But my sleep is interrupted by a guard shouting, "Get up quickly!" There are four guards in the room, three of them armed. They seem more nervous and excited than usual. We're dragged to our feet, handcuffed, and tied. We stand like sheep waiting for the slaughter. Moments pass, but nothing happens. A guard detail escorts the others out of the room. Then it's my turn. I'm hustled down the stairs, only to wait another half hour or more. A door is opened and closed. I smell fresh night air from outside; it's pleasant and refreshing. Suddenly I have a blanket tossed over my head and secured around my neck with a rope. We're on the move again. I wonder where it will be this time. Are we off to a real prison? Are we going back to the embassy? Are we going to the airport for release? Or are we being taken somewhere for trials?

I'm loaded into a van. I sit in the cold and wait, as usual, not knowing.

8

THE MUSHROOM INN
DECEMBER, 1979 - EARLY FEBRUARY, 1980

We've been traveling, blindfolded and securely tied, for about half an hour. My bare feet are numb from the cold. Circulation in my hands and feet is cut off by the tight bonds, causing my hands to feel as if they've been plunged into a bucket of sharp needles. Breathing under the blanket is laborious; my chest and face perspire while the rest of me freezes. So far, our ride has been mostly downhill, an indication that we're headed south, toward downtown and the embassy. I hope we're going back to the American compound and not to one of the mid-town prisons. I'm still afraid that if we end up taking one of these "no-frills excursions" to a prison, it'll be a very bad omen — especially if we end up at Khomeiteh or Evin prison.

Other bound and blindfolded hostages are on the floor next to me. None of us has spoken, so I don't know who they are. There's a sense of security in knowing I'm not alone, but I wonder if the others are as tired, uncertain, and afraid as I am. They must experience the same terror I do each time we're moved.

Our van screeches to a halt, apparently at a gate or check point. *"Khosh-omadien, be sefarat"* [Welcome to the embassy], says the voice outside to the driver. I'm somewhat relieved. People are noisily milling around where we stop. It's as though our arrival has not been expected; excited discussion in whispers goes on for more than an hour. I hear part of what they're saying. Initially, they're not sure where we are to be taken; then they agree that the area is not yet ready for us. Meanwhile, we sit shivering in silence, wondering what's next.

At last, the slow process of unloading us is begun. One by one, my fellow hostages and I are manhandled out of the van and away from the vehicle. We stand outside in the cold for about fifteen minutes. I can't see anything, and I can hear very little. My high-frequency hearing loss seems to have gotten worse, probably as a result of the blows to my head during my interrogations. It's frustrating to understand Farsi and still not be able to make out what they're saying. Finally I'm led down a long flight of cold, steel stairs by a guard steering me in the direction he wants me to go. We descend still another flight until we reach a sub-basement. The only building in the embassy with a sub-basement is the old communications building, which more recently has been used as a warehouse. We call it the Mushroom Inn because it's cold and dark, ideal for growing mushrooms, but not suitable for human habitation. I remember this building from the 1960s, when we had a major communications monitoring operation here. Even in those days, the men who worked in this underground hellhole eight hours a day cursed it.

A guard tells me to sit down and lean against a wall. He removes the blanket over my head, and I hear shuffling as the same is done to other hostages. Another guard checks my handcuffs and blindfold to make sure they're tight.

Hours pass slowly. I hear some kind of activity in the center of the room; it sounds like the cutting of cardboard or heavy construction paper. The militants apparently are making some kind of charts or signs. They seem to be relaxed and preoccupied with their work, whatever it is. My curiosity is aroused; I want to confirm my assessment of what they're doing. Why would they be making posters or signs in the same room where they're holding a group of hostages? A picture of a typical Iranian firing squad flashes through my mind. I see enemies of the revolution standing before a firing squad with signs tied to their chests listing their crimes against Khomeini's regime, as though this written manifestation of guilt somehow justifies their fate at the hands of their executioners. God, I hope they're not preparing us for execution. I must find out what they're really doing, so I slip completely to the floor and pretend I'm sleeping so I can work my blindfold loose enough to see over it.

This has to be done slowly, and it must appear to be the result of natural movement of sleep. I don't know whether or not I'm being watched by the guards, but judging from the past performance of these security-conscious paranoids, I'm sure at least one of them is observing my every move.

It takes more than an hour, but finally I work my blindfold loose enough to get a peek at what is going on in the middle of the room. I sit up as though I've just awakened from sleep. I simulate as much stretching as I can with my hands bound together, and then I peer over the blindfold. There's a guard looking right at me, so I decide to cool it for a few minutes and just act naturally, like I'm a good hostage obeying the strict cloister rule. When I think I've waited long enough for the guard to look away from me, I peek again. They *are* making signs, and they're working from a list. Each sign is about a foot square or so, and each has a number at the top in Farsi. Other writing is carefully being lettered below the numbers. As the signs are completed, they're placed in a row, side by side, so the ink can dry. Each letter is about two inches high. And each sign is just the right size to be placed on our chests or backs. My pulse quickens, and again I smell the pungent odor of the perspiration of fear.

The guard still isn't looking in my direction, so I survey the rest of the room. We're definitely in the Mushroom Inn. There are about twenty hostages seated along the outer walls. The others also are blindfolded and tied. They all have beards, and they all look miserable. I wonder if they're as scared as I am. It would be so much easier if we could speak to each other to allay our fears, or at least share them. I spot Don Sharer, Al Golacinski, Joe Hall, Tom Schaefer, Greg Persinger, Lee Holland, and a really tall man whom I assume is Bill Keough. He has lost so much weight that it's hard to tell for sure, but he's the only six-foot-seven-inch hostage.

Hamid the Liar enters the room and walks directly to the center where the militants are still hard at work. He speaks to one of the workers, but I can't hear what he says. Then he looks around the room, focusing his stare on each of the hostages. As his gaze approaches me, I lower my head as though I'm falling asleep. I wait for a few minutes, until I'm reasonably sure he hasn't noticed my loose blindfold, and then I take another peek. Hamid has been watching me, waiting for me to look again. When I do, he quickly summons one of his henchmen and I hear them walking toward me. Hamid is too cowardly and cautious to approach even a tied hostage without reinforcements. They stand directly in front of me, as Hamid speaks in his usual intimidating tone. "What are you trying to see, Colonel? What is going on here is not your business. You were told to be still and be quiet. You have worked your blindfold loose. I will make sure you do not see again."

Hamid reties my blindfold so tightly that I get a headache almost immediately. I say nothing. I've seen what's going on, and I don't like it. I decide to try to sleep, but I can still see the image of all of us standing before a firing squad with our neatly printed signs attesting to our "crimes."

Just as my fear abates enough to allow light sleep, I'm awakened by guards who order me to get up. They lead me into another room, where I'm told to sit on what seems to be a mattress. I sit for about half an hour before my blindfold is removed.

The large, subterranean room is well lighted by

fluorescent bulbs. The Iranians have separated the room into about fourteen cubicles, each about six feet square. The cells are separated by large improvised bookshelves, so each hostage has his own small cubicle. In each square is a twin-size embassy mattress and a chair. Most of the chairs are the large, overstuffed living-room type from the embassy furniture warehouse. Cubicles line both sides of the long room, so that there's an aisle in the center. A guard is seated at a folding table, about every ten feet in the center of the room, to keep us under constant observation. As opportunities present themselves, we glance at those in opposite cubicles and exchange "thumbs up" gestures. Dick Morefield is to my left front, then Don Cooke, Al Golacinski, Greg Persinger, and Bert Moore. On my side of the room from left to right are Don Sharer, John Limbert, Tom Schaefer, me, Dave Roeder, Paul Needham, and Sam Gillette. I'm sure there are others in the adjoining rooms, but I can't see them. We're like animals in a zoo. The guards enjoy walking up and down in front of our cells, even when they're not on duty.

The Iranians have gone to a great deal of trouble to set up this new prison. We're obviously going to be here for a long time. It's depressing to think of the future, especially when I realize that our hostage status is being institutionalized in this underground prison. But the mattress is soft and quite comfortable, so once again I try to lose my depression in sleep.

My slumber is interrupted by a guard who tells me my breakfast is ready. It's the usual Persian bread, a pat of butter, and a little something extra today — grape jelly from the embassy cooperative store. It tastes good, and I'm hungry. I can see some of the others eating, too, but still others sleep away their captivity. I decide to continue my routine of reading and vigorous exercise to while away the days, weeks, and months which I now believe lie ahead. Like our captors, I'm digging in for the long term. I've felt, since the last few days of my interrogation, that the militants have been told by their government that they may continue to hold us and harass us, but that they had better not kill or permanently injure any of us. There are still some advantages to being a citizen of the most powerful nation in the world — even as a hostage in revolutionary Iran. Our captors seem to realize that they're not going to get the Shah for trial by holding us hostage. But they're stuck in a situation from which they can't extricate themselves without losing face. We're just going to have to dig in, I decide. At least here in the Mushroom Inn I have company, and we'll find a way to communicate with each other. I want to learn how the others are holding up and what information they've gathered in the last six weeks. The more we all know, the better off we'll be.

We all realize that Christmas is fast approaching. In our clandestine communications network, we have speculated on the possibility of our release during the holiday period, but there are no indications that this will happen. I'm not looking forward to spending Christmas as a hostage. It's depressing to think of the large, vaulted-ceilinged family room in my home in Stone Mountain, with a beautiful Christmas tree and a roaring fire in the fireplace, and of my family trying to carry on in the traditional holiday spirit while they're filled with uncertainty about my safety. I realize that Christmas is going to be a very tough time, a real obstacle which must be overcome if I'm going to maintain any kind of positive attitude.

There are rumors of a religious service during the Christmas season, but the guards, as usual, have not given any definite information. Al Golacinski has been the most vocal in demanding a mass or church service. I suspect he's trying to convince them that he's Catholic to keep our anti-Zionist captors from finding out that he's really Jewish. Not a bad idea, especially considering the kind of hatred we have seen in their dealings with Barry Rosen.

It's Christmas Eve, 1979, and our spirits are lower than a snake's arches. It's hard to think about Christmases I've known in the past and contrast them with my anticipation of a totally nothing day here in our underground cell. With the eight-and-a-half-hour time difference, it's Christmas Eve afternoon on the east coast of America. I think of millions of children excitedly anticipating Christmas Day, and parents looking forward to the smiling faces of their offspring tomorrow morning, while wondering if they found just the right gifts. I ask God to give my family the strength to make it through these trying times without bitterness or resentment. I think about my neighbors, and I'm comforted by the certainty that they're doing all they can to make it easier for Betty and the children.

A group of guards enters the doorway at the end of our room of cubicles and begins to distribute candy bars and nuts. I almost subconsciously begin to hum "Silent Night." One of the guards approaches and tells me not to speak or make noise. I tell him in Farsi to go screw himself. He doesn't react as I anticipate; he merely walks away, looking a bit ashamed. I have an intuitive feeling that he has some understanding of Christmas and has decided to leave me alone. I hum louder, and then I begin to sing. I'm a lousy singer, but I try. "*All is calm, all is bright*." Others join in softly, and the guards get fidgety; they're afraid we may be starting something they can't handle. They finally quiet us down, but not before we all have felt the camaraderie and unity that's generated by singing this wonderful song. I do not feel alone; somehow, millions of Americans were with us at that very moment when we joined in singing "Silent Night." Akbar appears with two candy bars and some assorted nuts (all from the embassy store). He looks at me with a kindness that is most unusual for a terrorist. "Colonel, I wish you a merry Christmas," he says.

"Merry Christmas, my ass. You people are terrorists. You're holding us for blackmail, and you have the audacity to wish me a merry Christmas. One of these days you'll all pay for this."

Akbar is visibly hurt by my outburst, but he seems to understand why I'm angry. He takes it all in stride. "I am sorry, but your government is at fault. If they had answered the will of the Iranian people and returned the Shah, you could be home now with your family. Do you have a family, Colonel Scott?"

"Akbar, we've talked about my family before when I was being worked on by your interrogators. Remember? As you know, I have a wife and two children. My son was born here in Tehran thirteen and a half years ago, when you were probably in grammar school. He can even claim Iranian citizenship, but who would want to be an Iranian in this screwed-up land your revolution has created?"

Akbar's reply is soft and deliberate. I'm disarmed slightly by his sincerity. "Colonel, I know you are very angry and you are sad, but you must have patience. This will end when the Shah is sent back by Carter; and then you can go home to your precious family. I have a family, too, and I spent more than four years in the Shah's prisons because your country kept him in power. I love my family, too, and I missed them while I was in prison. I know how you feel, please believe me."

"Akbar, how can I believe anything you and your people say when you're holding all of us prisoners? If you actually spent time in the Shah's jails, I feel sorry for you. I know of the mistreatment meted out by the Shah's security forces. But the Shah was not an American puppet. If he had been, do you think we would have allowed him to quadruple the price of oil in 1974? In your Koran, there is a quotation you should memorize. It says, 'Man is governed as he deserves to be governed.'"

Akbar is nonplussed by my reference to the Koran. "What do you know of the holy Koran, Colonel? You may read it in Farsi or English, but you have no idea what it means. I have trouble with the meaning of some of it myself, but the Imam tells us who follow him what it means. And it means we must throw off the oppressors and fight for our freedom. Your country is an oppressor of the Iranian people. Please believe me when I wish you a merry Christmas. I am a Moslem, and in my heart I do not wish you any harm. I want this to end as much as you do. And I want you to return to your family; I will pray for this to happen. Goodbye, my friend. Be patient, and you will be free when the time is right."

Akbar gives me a stilted smile as he hands me two more candy bars and dumps some more nuts in my plastic bowl. He moves down the line to the next cubicle. He really isn't like the rest, I think as I begin to unwrap my candy bar. I'm hungry, and the candy bar looks good, even though it's so stale that the plain Hershey chocolate has turned gray. It has been a long time since I've had anything sweet, and I can't help being moved a little by this militant who seems to sense the spirit of Christmas and who made a sincere effort to cheer me up. My thoughts are interrupted as Akbar returns.

"Colonel, I forgot to tell you. The Imam has arranged for a Christmas celebration for you. It will be sometime tonight, and there will be priests from America to help you celebrate and pray." With this, Akbar is on his way.

So they're going to parade us before a group of American clergymen. I can see it now — a big Christmas celebration complete with ministers, priests, and, of course, television cameras. It'll be a propaganda spectacular in the grand Iranian tradition — an attempt to show the world how kind and considerate they are toward their captives. But there's no alternative. I'll have to face the ministers and the cameras.

It's Christmas morning, and a group of hostages from one of the rooms behind our large bay is being led blindfolded past our cells. I surmise they're being taken somewhere to celebrate Christmas. In about forty-five minutes, they return laden with candy, fruit, and nuts from the party. Another group from our cell block is taken out next. They, too, return in less than an hour. It's my turn. I'm blindfolded and escorted down the hall where, as we approach another room, my blindfold and wrist ties are removed and I'm told to enter the room. There's a decorated Christmas tree and a table full of fruit, cookies, and candy bars. There's also a robed clergyman. I'm not sure at first whether or not he's an American. He appears to be a very light-complexioned black. Lee Holland, Tom Schaefer, Paul Needham, Regis Ragan, and I are told to sit in a row of folding chairs positioned for the occasion. We all have beards and look unkempt and pale; we're also showing signs of our imprisonment — especially weight loss.

The minister is resplendent in his long, flowing, clerical robes. I wonder what religious denomination he represents. He's articulate and friendly. He introduces himself as the Reverend William Howard and says he is the president of the National Council of Churches. The TV lights are bright and the cameras are rolling. It's precisely the spectacle that I anticipated. It irritates me to think of the American clergy being taken in by these Moslem terrorists. Howard says, "I'm here to help you celebrate Christmas. I bring the best wishes of the American people. You are not forgotten; we as a nation are praying for all of you. Would you like to sing some Christmas songs, just conduct a brief service — I don't know your individual religious backgrounds — of a nondenominational nature to celebrate Christmas, or would you like to ask me questions?"

There's a pause, but no reply. Finally, Howard speaks again. "It's up to you; what would you like?"

We all reply in unison. We would like to ask questions. Howard advises us not to ask political questions. I speak up quickly: "What's the price of gas in America today?" I know, as an intelligence analyst, that I can derive a good bit from this tiny shred of information. But instead of quickly blurting out the answer, Howard looks toward the gallery of militants and says, "I don't suppose I should answer that question, do you? I mean, he may be able to determine a number of things, political in nature, from that kind of information. What do you think?"

I'm mad as hell. Whose side is he on, anyway? He could have answered me directly, instead of referring my question to the militants. Howard obviously is instructed not to tell me the price of gas. He asks if we have other questions of a nonpolitical nature. He answers general questions with worthless information for the others, but I'm still smarting over the way he missed an opportunity to give me some meaningful intelligence. What is he afraid of? I crawl into my shell, and this doesn't go unnoticed by the reverend. After a few minutes of meaningless chatter, he mentions that I'm from Georgia. I acknowledge, and he goes on to tell me how difficult it was for a black man to travel through Georgia just a few years ago. Is he trying to blame me for past racial injustices in America? I've never been accused of being prejudiced in my entire life, and I certainly don't like it now, under these conditions. I get the impression that Howard is enjoying the fact that he's free and I'm not. This pompous minister in his regal clerical robes angers me, and I find myself hoping this charade will end soon. The cameras continue rolling, and the lights seems brighter than ever, but I'm oblivious to what's being said around me.

Finally the party is over and we're returned to our cells. Hamid the Liar stops by my cell to chew me out for asking about the price of gas. When he has vented his rage, I ask him simply, "Hamid, what *is* the price of gas in America?" Hamid leaves in a huff, without so much as a farewell.

All day there has been a lot of activity in the cell block. Visitors have entered and glared at us as though we were specimens. The Iranians are enjoying our holiday more than we are. They stuff themselves with cookies and candy and seem to be in as festive a mood as they can be without letting down on their relentless security. It's late afternoon, and a special Christmas dinner is being served, when the Ayatollah Montazari, Khomeini's heir apparent, appears with a large group of militants following him as though he were a direct representative of the deity. He rants and raves for about fifteen minutes. The gist of his tirade is that he "prays the American government will come to its senses soon and return the criminal Shah, so you hostages can go home and we can get on with the important work of our revolution." I understand what he's saying, but John Limbert, who speaks better Farsi than any of the militants, interprets for the other hostages. John summarizes the cleric's rhetoric each time he stops to catch his breath. Montazari is jokingly called the Crazy Professor because of his propensity for speaking on any subject or issue *ad nauseam* — prior knowlege never being a consideration. He acknowledges Jesus Christ as a prophet and claims that he understands the importance of this day to the Christian religion. Essentially, he's doing his best to be friendly to us, but there's no mistake: The Iranian Shiite clergy is holding fast in its determination to keep us prisoners until the Shah is returned for trial. His inflexibility and uncompromising attitude are depressing.

John Limbert reminds the ayatollah that they have met before, when John acted as interpreter for a meeting between him and Henry Precht held at the cleric's house ten days before the embassy attack. No doubt, the two-faced revolutionary knew of the planned attack when he met with Precht. Montazari finally runs out of jargon and leaves with his forty-man entourage.

The propaganda show continues with a "special" Christmas dinner. I suspect it was prepared by Luigi or catered by one of the international hotels. Turkey, cranberries, mashed potatoes, and tomato aspic. The turkey is rare and tough. I pick at my drumstick, but it's too uncooked to be enjoyable. I finally get it down. At least it's better than the cold, canned spaghetti we had for Thanksgiving dinner in north Tehran.

Supper is served later in the evening. It consists of leftover tomato aspic and a glass of hot Iranian tea. Some of my compatriots don't like it, so there's plenty of second helpings for those of us who'll eat almost anything.

Akbar has told me that "tons" of mail addressed to the American hostages are arriving at the embassy. He says that this is a problem because they don't have the time to read and censor it. But as far as I know, none of us has received any mail. Shortly after our "aspic feast," however, Akbar and Ahmad, a terrorist educated in the United States, bring a few pieces of mail to each of us. We've been hoping for news from home during the holiday season. I'm very concerned about the well-being of Betty and the children. During my interrogations, the Iranians had showed me pictures of my Stone Mountain home and threatened to burn it to the ground and kidnap my children if I didn't cooperate with them. I'm sure my family is well protected, but it would be wonderful to have written proof that they're safe.

I quickly scan the return addresses of the five pieces of mail I've been handed by Akbar, but my hopes fade; there's no mail from anyone I know. It's all addressed to "American Hostage, American Embassy, Tehran." On closer examination, I see that each letter has been opened and inspected by our captors. All five are Christmas cards from concerned and thoughtful Americans, who write that they're praying for us. I appreciate their thoughtfulness and kindness, but these cards are no substitute for the reassurance that I need from my family to ease my worry. What if they have burned my home or kidnapped my children? The idea is totally terrorizing, but I'm helpless. I try to escape my thoughts by taking a mental excursion to my first Christmas away from home. I was an eighteen-year-old soldier stationed in Germany, and I spent Christmas Day with a German family. I discovered that in many ways they were very much like Americans. From then on, I always tried to learn the customs of the people in countries where I was stationed. I enjoyed learning foreign languages, which to me are keys to unlock the gates that separate and polarize people of different nationalities and beliefs. As a result, I learned to love and appreciate the hard-working, fun-loving German people. I developed the same affinity for the people of Vietnam and Iran.

It's eerie, though, when I think about the friends I've made in Germany over the years and then recall the horrors of the Holocaust. I remember visiting Dachau in 1950 while I was stationed in Germany, and how repulsed I was at seeing this extermination camp with its gas chambers. The Germans I talked to in the villages nearby denied any knowledge of what had been going on inside. I found that impossible to believe then, and I still do today. How could people stand by and witness the systematic destruction of an entire race and not do anything to stop it? Conditioned hatred is the answer — a mesmerizing, all-consuming vilification of one nationality by another. The Holocaust was orchestrated by men possessed by a tremendous hatred and an insatiable thirst for power. I see similarities between the mood in Germany then and the mood of these fanatics in Iran today. How far will our captors go in seeking revenge against their perceived enemies? The thought is upsetting. Sleep is my only comfort. And so goes Christmas as a hostage.

We have been hostages for two months. We're still not permitted to communicate with each other in any way, and we're denied access to news of any kind. I spend my waking hours reading, praying, and trying not to dwell on our predicament. We've been given books from the piles of

211

volumes which are stored in another basement room of the
Mushroom Inn. They were in the Tehran American High
School library until the revolution, when the school was
closed. Literally thousands of books were dumped in this
building for storage until they could be packed and shipped
to another American overseas school. Bill Keough, the huge
former Tehran American School superintendent, was visiting here from Pakistan to arrange for shipment of these
books when he got caught up in the embassy seizure and
became a hostage.

I'm reading Irving Stone's biography of Clar-
ence Darrow. It's a fascinating story of one man's fight
against the power of big corporations and the system of law
that protected them and suppressed the rights of workers for
many years in America. It's a story of courage and disappointment, determination and failure, and it's a touching
account of the tremendous impact one man can have in a
free society. I enjoy rereading this classic; it has given me
some refreshing insights into our heritage that I normally
wouldn't have time to think about in my busy life as an Army
officer.

I decide to make reading a cornerstone of my
plan for survival. It is essential, if I'm to retain my sanity,
that I gain something from this experience rather than let it
be an entirely negative one. And so I read, exercise for an
hour twice each day in my six-foot-by-six-foot cell, and concentrate on positive and happy thoughts as much as possible.
My exercise consists of running in place, push-ups, and sit-
ups. It's not the same as having the freedom to jog outside,
but it'll have to do for now. The physical exercise is like a
tonic for me. It relieves the stress and anxiety of not knowing
how or when this horrible experience will end.

In spite of our captors' ruthless, full-time surveillance, we manage to communicate secretly with a simple
code. There really is not much news, but we want to have a
way to communicate so we'll be ready when we do get word

about what's happening. It's also good for morale. It proves that our captors don't have complete control, and it gives us something to do. The Iranians have an aversion to anything relating to the toilet, so we plant messages in the toilet paper rolls in the common-use latrine, where we're taken individually to wash our plastic bowls and wash ourselves. The main thing we've tried to do is pass on the word about how to use the visual and tap code, so if we're moved again, we'll be able to pass messages from room to room.

Our code is the same as that taught at military service survival schools. You draw a square and divide it with four horizontal lines and four vertical lines, thus producing a box with twenty-five squares — five rows of five squares each. Then you write the letters *a* through *e* in the first line of boxes, *f* through *j* in the second line, and so on, until you've filled all the boxes. The letter *z* is left over. Then you number the rows of boxes, both vertically and horizontally, with the numbers one through five. That's all there is to it. To use the visual code to send the letter *c*, hold up one finger, pause for a second, then hold up three fingers (first row, third letter). Taps can be used the same way to produce an audible code that can be heard through walls.

I have heard guards talking in Persian from time to time when they thought I was asleep. They've mentioned the possibility of moving us to locations outside the embassy complex. I also have heard references to moving us to a prison to facilitate our security against opposition groups, who would like to kill us to embarrass Khomeini. There's a power struggle going on in Iran, according to conversations I've overheard, and our captors are concerned that they may lose their human prizes to one of the opposing factions. Ironically, the same militant Moslems who may execute us at any time also are protecting us to prevent others from snuffing out our lives and taking that prerogative away from them. The freedom to move about as they choose is also denied these so-called "students," who are responsible to Khomeini for our security. Our captors, it seems, have become pawns in this game, just as we are. Initially, they didn't believe this affair would last so long. And now some of the less zealous guards are becoming bored with their mundane duties. Several of them have visited my tiny prison cubicle and talked to me in Farsi. They're interested in learning about life in America and about life as an army officer. One young man, about twenty, asked if I thought it would be possible for him to attend college in America "after the Shah is returned and you are set free." I told him it would be difficult to get a visa, inasmuch as we have no embassy in Iran. He informed me that the Iranian Embassy in Washington is still in place and working. It seems absurd to me that our government would permit Iran to continue operating an embassy in America after what they've done here. I'm never one hundred percent sure that I'm not being set up by those who do talk to me, but I continue to encourage conversation anyway; I always get bits and pieces of information from them during our discussions. They're impressed that I speak Persian and seem to enjoy talking to me. However, only a few terrorists are in this category. Most of the others are hard-core revolutionaries who would just as soon shoot me as look at me. They speak only to threaten and give orders.

It's the third week in January, 1980. Another seven days and we will have been prisoners for three months. I'm really getting concerned about my family. It seems that we've been here a lifetime, and the tension is intensified by our not receiving any information from the outside world.

I notice that some of the other hostages are being blindfolded and taken out of their cells. Don Cooke, who is almost directly across from me, catches the sentry off guard and moves his lips to signal what's going on. He doesn't make a sound, but the word he's mouthing is unmistakable: "MAIL."

Several groups are led out and then returned, but I'm not among them. Finally the procedure is halted. I should have tried to keep better account of who made the trip and who didn't. But I'm sure just about all except three of us have made the "mail call." For the next few hours, message after message is sent via our clandestine communication system. Most of my fellow hostages have been permitted to read mail from home, but they weren't allowed to keep the letters. All had been opened and censored, but at least they got some word from home. I'm totally depressed. I'm sure my family must have written to me by now. Could it be that the militants are playing cruel mind games by giving mail to the others and withholding mine? That's certainly a possibility.

The mail-call routine is repeated the next week, but still I receive none. I complain to Ahmad and Hamid the Liar, the two top leaders who seem to run the operation as far as we're concerned. Ahmad tells me in his Americanized English that I have no mail. When I tell him I don't believe him, he replies, "Maybe your wife has found someone else — that happens in your country, you know." I would like to have a chance to fight him, one on one. God, how I hate this surly little man with the giant ego.

Akbar, who is learning a little English, later enters my cubicle and asks, "How are you, Colonel?"

"Akbar, I'm concerned about my family. It's bad enough to be held here against my will, not knowing if I'll ever be set free, but it's even worse when you people don't give me my mail. What are you trying to prove?"

Akbar seems ashamed, but he's still one of the terrorists. In spite of the rapport we have established, he is careful in what he says. "Colonel, you must not have any mail, or my brothers would give it to you. There is no reason for them to keep it from you." Akbar says that when he was in prison, the Shah's people often kept his mail from him for more than a year at a time. He says he understands how I must feel, but there is nothing he can do. Then he seems to have an idea. "Colonel, if you want to write a letter to your family, give it to me and I will send it international mail. It should get to them in about a week or so."

I'm desperate to hear from my family, and I'm sure the letters I have been permitted to write so far (two in all) never have been mailed. So why not give this a try?

"If you'll really send a letter for me, I'll write. Please give me a pencil or a pen."

Akbar fumbles through his field-jacket pocket and finds a ball-point pen. He hands me the pen and rushes off, saying, "I will find some paper and an envelope."

He returns shortly with paper and an envelope. It's a franked State Department envelope from the embassy. I write a very distressed letter to Betty, pleading with her to write to me as soon as possible and asking her to send the letter by international mail. I tell her that I have heard nothing from her since the embassy attack, and I'm worried about her and the children. I tell her I'm doing all right, but I miss them more than they ever will know. My letter is short and pitiful, I think as I read it over and wait for Akbar to return to pick it up. I do not seal the envelope, knowing it will be read by my captors, anyway.

In about an hour, Akbar returns as promised. "Do not worry," he says. "I will send this tonight. You should hear an answer to this letter within two or three weeks." I thank Akbar for his help, hoping my small exhibition of trust in him will have the desired effect and that he really will mail my letter.

Our third "mail call," Iranian terrorist-style, is in progress. Four separate groups of hostages have been led from their cells. I still await my turn, but I've almost lost hope.

Hamid the Liar approaches my cubicle. "Come with me, Mister Colonel Escott; don't you want your mail?" He is wearing his patronizing look, as though he's imploring me to thank him for being such a thoughtful individual when he just as well could order me shot. I follow the ritual by handing him the blindfold, which he secures around my head. I'm led out of the room and stopped in the doorway of another room about forty-five steps down the hall. My blindfold is removed by Hamid, and I'm told to enter the room but not to speak to any of the hostages. Ahmad and another man I haven't seen since the first week of my interrogation are seated at a folding table piled high with mail. I walk to the table and wait for Ahmad to shuffle through the stacks of mail. He is deliberately taking his time. "I don't see anything for you, Mister Scott. Are you sure your wife has not found another man?"

I say nothing. The other man doesn't seem to be amused by Ahmad's antics. He hands him several letters and directs Ahmad to give them to me. Ahmad would like to play games, but he does as the other man directs. "Here is your mail. Read it quickly and then bring it all back up here when you are ready to return to your room." There's no sense in antagonizing Ahmad; it will only cause trouble for me. I take the letters and find a spot on the floor, where several other hostages are reading letters. There's no talking, but even without it, it's obvious from the facial expressions that all are deeply engrossed in letters from home.

I have five pieces of mail. I scan the opened envelopes, looking for a letter from home. The first two are from people I've never heard of, but they are addressed to me — at least they're close enough. One is addressed to "Lieutenant Colonel Charles W. Scott." Perhaps I've been reduced in rank from full colonel for allowing myself to get captured. The next one is even worse — it's addressed to me with the rank of lieutenant. I decide to read these later. The next one is a letter from my sister Edie, postmarked December 23, Lawrence, Kansas. I'll read this in a minute. The fourth is a letter from Betty, but it's postmarked October 26, 1979, a week before the embassy attack. The last piece is another letter from Edie. I read the letter from Betty, and my spirits slide even lower. She writes of my plan to return to Stone Mountain for Christmas, and says that she and the children are counting the days until the holidays. Our hot-water heater had to be replaced a few weeks after I left home for Iran. Nothing else. Nothing to give me any insight into how my family is handling this situation. I read the letters from Edie in order. They contain words of encouragement I'd expect to receive in this situation from someone who has been a source of tremendous support for thirty years. Edie apparently has been told not to mention anything political in her letters, and she has rigidly complied with this instruction. I reread the letters looking for some mention of Betty and the children. There's none. It's as though they've ceased to exist. There's not even a casual mention of them. My concern for my family's safety is only heightened by these letters. What could be the problem? Have they been moved to some isolated area for their own safety? Have the Iranians made good on their threat to burn my home and kidnap my children?

My last letter is from a little third-grader named Pamela from Omaha, Nebraska. It's the one addressed to "Lieutenant Scott." She says her class in school, composed of fifty-three students, has been assigned to study about and write to the hostages. She drew my name, so she had to learn about me and write to me. She writes in a direct, uninhibited style, and I find her letter a real morale booster. She's praying for all of us. She thinks it's stupid that we're being held, and she thinks it would have been better for President Carter to have sent the Shah back to Iran rather than let him escape to Panama. So the Shah is no longer in the U.S. . . . . That *is* interesting. Little Pamela ends her very revealing epistle with an amusing aside. She says she knows

I'm forty-eight and that I'm a lieutenant in the Army. Then she asks, "At your age, shouldn't you be higher than that?" So much for my first mail. I still wonder if letters from my family are being deliberately kept from me, or if this is an indication of some serious problem at home.

I stall as long as possible before returning the letters to Ahmad. I look through all of the letters one more time to see if I may have missed some important clue which may reveal something about the fate of my family.

"Mr. Escott, give me the letters. It is time to return to your room."

"You mean *cell*, don't you?"

"Room, cell. It does not make any difference. It is where you are going and where you will stay until the Shah is returned or you are tried by the Iranian people and shot. Get moving."

"Thanks, Ahmad, I really appreciate your courtesy and consideration. Perhaps someday I can return the favor."

Ahmad is not amused by my sarcasm. He rises from his improvised desk and assists the guard who is busily retying my blindfold. Ahmad pulls the blindfold tighter than is necessary as he sneers at me: "You'd better learn to shut up or you will never get another letter."

Back in my cell, before I even have a chance to think about the mail I've just received, I am startled by still another move in this macabre game. Colonel Tom Schaefer is not in his cell next to mine. I wait for the ever-present guard to avert his eyes for a minute so I can try to make visual contact with Al Golacinski or Don Cooke, my "neighbors" across the room. After about half an hour, I query Al by hand signal, and he acknowledges my message by nodding his head just as the guard looks directly at him.

"Don'ta - espeak!" yells a tall, thin, ugly character with a Uzi machine gun slung over his shoulder under his field jacket. He has a hair-trigger temper and is even more

219

paranoid and strict than most of the guards. I lay low until he's off duty. His replacement is a man of Turkic ancestry from Tabriz who smiles a lot and doesn't seem to take himself as seriously as the tougher militants. He has spoken with me on a number of occasions and is very interested in learning about the United States. Don Cooke diverts his attention by asking him a question. The mannerly little Turk moves from his position in the middle of the room to Don's cell before he answers the question. Al immediately begins to send me a message about where he thinks Tom has been taken. "I-N-T-E-R-R-O-G-A-T-I-O-N." My heart sinks. God, they're starting the interrogations again. Then I remember Tom's telling me when we were in north Tehran, away from the others, that he had refused to talk to his interrogators at all. They're just beginning to try to get to him now.

"Wake up and eat your breakfast." The guard drops a large piece of Persian Barbari bread on my blanket. I get off my pallet and pretend to be stretching in an attempt to see if Tom has been returned to his cell. I catch a glimpse of Al across the room and he shakes his head from side to side. Tom is not in his cell.

I have difficulty concentrating on my book. I'm reading Nancy Friday's *My Mother – Myself*, learning things about the symbiotic relationships between a mother and daughter that I will never need to know. But it's the only book I have for now, so I'm trying to read and study it as though my life depended on it. I'm very much demoralized by the thought of more interrogation.

At about noon, Tom is returned to his cell. He looks tired and drained. I immediately decide to run in place, my only legitimate excuse for standing in my cell. Tom also is standing up, trying to adjust his clothing and look around at the others he can see, while being as inconspicuous as possible. I wink at Tom and he returns my

220

wink. He manages a half smile. His eyes show his fatigue and anxiety, but he doesn't appear to be hurt physically.

About two hours later, the guards come for Tom again. He is blindfolded and led away. They're not letting him get any rest — the same tactic they used on me.

In mid-afternoon, Akbar pauses in front of my cell. He says he's very busy but asks if I'm doing all right. I tell him I'm fine, but that I'm wondering what's going on. He asks what I mean, and I tell him about Tom being taken away twice during the last twenty-four hours.

Akbar looks around to make sure he is not being overheard by any of the other militants, then he says, "It is nothing. He is just answering some questions. He will not be hurt."

"Yeah, Akbar, just like I wasn't hurt, right?"

"No, Colonel, you were hurt in the beginning, but do not worry; none of you will be hurt anymore unless a decision is made to punish all of you because your government will not do as we wish."

"So we're O.K., unless Khomeini orders that we be tried and shot to get the attention of my government. Is that right?"

"Yes, that is right, just as you say. But it will not happen. I pray it will all end soon and you can go home to your family. Have you news from your wife?"

"None, except for a letter that was sent before your attack. Did you send my letter by international mail?"

"It was sent the day you gave it to me."

"Do you know that for sure? Did *you* send it?"

"I told you I would, and I did."

I intuitively believe him. I've always considered myself a fairly good judge of character; I had to be to work with soldiers most of my life. I've been wrong, but not very often, and I don't think I'm wrong about Akbar. If nothing else, he's the best of this sorry lot, and the only one who shows any signs of human kindness. I will keep working on him; he's my only source of information — and we need all the news we can get.

There's something unusual going on this evening, January 24, 1980. Hamid the Liar is overseeing the distribution of cookies and candies, stale pretzels from the embassy cooperative store, and a second glass of hot tea. Hamid even has a half grin on his sneaky-looking face. He's bouncing around as though he's celebrating a great victory. As he dumps some goodies in my plastic bowl, I try to elicit some news. *"Khabara taza chea?"* [What's new?]

He answers in English, "Something good is happening, but I will not tell you what it is."

"Are we going home?"

"What has happened is good for us — it is not good for you." It's no use; Hamid isn't going to tell me anything. The other guards also are bouncing around like their home team has just won the world soccer cup. The "party" lasts an hour or so, and then Hamid and his henchmen leave. The usual guards remain at their posts to make sure we don't talk. Later, Akbar enters my cubicle. His eyes are glowing and he's smiling, bubbling over with news of some kind.

"Akbar, you look so happy. Did the Shah die, or did Panama decide to send him back here?" Akbar is surprised.

"Who told you the Shah is in Panama? He is still in America."

"I don't remember who it was, but it was one of your friends. He told me more than a week ago that the Shah had gone to Panama." I disguise speculation as fact. "And your country is trying to have him extradited to Iran."

"He should not have told you that, but it is true. We expect to arrange with the Panamanian government to have the Shah sent here for trial. That is why we are so happy."

"If he's returned, does that mean we can go home?"

Akbar thinks for a long moment before he replies. "Maybe, but there are other matters to be settled with your government besides the Shah. When they are settled, you can go home. Be patient; it will happen."

It is our eighty-ninth day in captivity. The jolly mood of a few nights ago has been replaced by sullen suspicion, as our guards engage each other in long whispering sessions. Individual weapons are more in evidence than at any time in the last month. I'm watched more closely than ever when I stand up in my cell to exercise. The slightest evidence of a hostage looking at another is cause for a major outburst by the guards. Tom hasn't returned from his interrogation sessions for the last four days. The last time I saw him, the bounce was missing from his step and he was a very tired-looking colonel.

Akbar passes my cell for the first time in three days. His smile is gone, replaced by a very serious look. He moves back the other way without looking in on me. Almost as an afterthought, he pivots around and enters my cubicle.

"Colonel, your friends the Canadians have done something very bad. It does not look good for you."

"What did they do, declare war on Iran?"

"No, they violated international law by making false visas for some of the Americans who escaped when the rest of you were arrested at the embassy. This will only make it more difficult for you ever to be released. The Iranian people are very angry. None of you can be trusted."

I'm thrilled to hear that some of our people avoided capture. That explains a multitude of questions during my interrogation about the number of people working in the visa office. I tell Akbar that he and his band are in no position to talk about violations of international law after what they've done to us. I tell him that he and the Iranian

223

people are only angry because the Canadians put one over on them.

"When hostages are taken," I say, "anything that is done to free them is morally and legally acceptable. I would not be surprised if one of these days the U.S. government decides to forget trying to save our lives and settles for punishing Iran, to teach the lesson that terrorism does not pay."

It's the wrong time to try to reason with Akbar. He's angry that the Canadians were successful in getting some of us out of Iran. "I must go, Colonel," he says angrily. "I have much work to do."

I feel good about the news that some of our people escaped, but I feel depressed that I wasn't one of them. Tomorrow will make three full months since this ordeal began, and I'm beginning to wonder if it ever will end. I sometimes think that I would rather die than spend the rest of my life as a prisoner. But I must not allow myself to dwell on thoughts of death or prison. I must have hope . . . that's the key to survival.

9

THE MUSHROOM INN, TEHRAN
2:00 A.M., FEBRUARY 5, 1980

By all indications, the hostage ordeal is about to end suddenly, but not in the way we all hoped and prayed that it would.

We are rudely jostled from sleep by an awesome new terror. A stormtrooperlike platoon of armed and masked terrorists appears, seemingly from out of nowhere, and descends on us like a pack of wolves. They wear the traditional snowwhite Moslem execution masks and new military fatigues, complete with military field jackets and well-shined combat boots. And they're all armed with imposing G-3 automatic rifles. I don't recognize any of them as being part of our normal cadre of guards. My pulse quickens as I'm told to move quickly out of my cubicle. I try to stall, telling them I need a shirt or sweater against the cold night air. I'm manhandled out of my cell at gunpoint without a sweater or anything to cover my feet. I'm told that I won't need a shirt or sweater again. "Ever!"

Other prisoners from the Mushroom Inn also are being led out of their cells and dragged or escorted at gunpoint. None of the hostages speaks, but the terror of imminent death is evident in their eyes and in their facial expressions. With the others, I'm forced by three masked gunmen out of the room and down the hallway to what seems unquestionably to be my final moments of life.

The expressions of our regular guards show an eerie combination of sadness, shame, and apology. They are not active participants in this drama and appear to be as surprised and stunned as the rest of us. One of the regular guards who has been less sadistic than most of the others — and on occasion almost friendly — averts his glance as I'm forced to pass directly in front of where he stands. He looks upward toward me only for a split second, as if to say he is personally sorry that it's all to end this way. I instantly translate the pained and apologetic expression as additional evidence that my greatest fear is to be realized: We *are* going to be executed!

I find myself gripped by a degree of terror surpassing any I've ever experienced in combat. Only this time I'm not even cast in the warrior role; I'm not even a combatant, only a helpless pawn. The frustrations of the early days of captivity return, intensified tenfold. My heart is pumping so hard and fast, I can feel my rapid pulse in every sinew. I realize I'm on the verge of being overcome by fear.

"Don'ta - espeak" echoes through the large warehouse room I'm forced into by my tormentors. I catch a glimpse of several other hostages already spread-eagled against a long wall of the cold, dank room. I also see the artificial Christmas tree, used for the propaganda show with the visiting clergymen in this very same room. We're going to be shot where we celebrated Christmas before TV cameras, so the Iranians could convince the world that we were being well treated. What a farce!

Diplomatic efforts to secure our release obviously have failed. Or has the United States lost patience and launched a military operation against Iran, or seized the oil fields or the Straits of Hormoz? Are we going to be shot in reprisal for an action by our government against Iran? That at least would make it more bearable. Or have opposition forces inside Iran scared the militants into this final, desperate act? The real frustration comes not from facing certain death before an Iranian firing squad, but in having absolutely no idea what has precipitated this final nightmare.

226

My mind is thrown into high gear, trying to find some logic to what's going on. But there's no logic to it at all.

Now I too am spread-eagled against the wall and ordered to stretch my arms even more. I tell the guards I can't because my hands are tied too close together. A guard reaches for my hands, forcing them higher up the wall, as another guard kicks my legs farther apart. It's as though they're making every effort to position us so that all vital organs will receive maximum exposure for the convenience of the marksmen, who already are manipulating the bolts and firing mechanisms of their weapons. As several of the firing-squad members clear their weapons, I hear ammunition fall to the floor, confirming my greatest fear.

I feel slightly dizzy and sick, but I realize it doesn't matter at this point. I try my best to resign myself to my fate, but I'm unable to comprehend fully that this is really happening! All the suffering of the past three months, all the hopes of eventual release which have sustained me to this point, are about to be snuffed out, along with my life, against the cold brick wall of a warehouse room in a land most Americans couldn't even find on a world map until late last year. I'm not reviewing my life as one facing certain death is supposed to do, according to most accounts I've read. I'm still trying to understand why this is happening. I begin to pray, not asking God to spare my life — I'm conditioned by my training never to beg, not even to God — but seeking some explanation and meaning for all this. Some purpose that all of this will serve to make the world a better place for mankind. But I find no meaning and no purpose. Suddenly, out of my racing mind springs the memory of comforting words from Omar Khayyám:

> We are no other than a moving row
> Of Magic Shadow-shapes that come and go
>   Round with the Sun-illumined Lantern held

227

In midnight by the Master of the Show;

But helpless Pieces of the Game He plays
Upon his Checkerboard of Nights and Days;
   Hither and thither moves, and checks, and slays,
And one by one back in the Closet lays.

The Ball no question makes of Ayes and Noes,
But Here or There as strikes the Player goes;
   And He that tossed you down into the Field,
He knows all about it — HE knows — HE knows!

The Moving Finger writes; and, having writ,
Moves on: nor all your Piety nor Wit
   Shall lure it back to cancel half a Line,
Nor all your Tears wash out a Word of it.

      How incredibly ironic: My first spark of resignation and inner peace comes from the brilliant words of a Persian poet who lived, loved, and wrote his poetry about four hundred and fifty miles east of here at Naishápúr, seven hundred years ago. I'm reminded, even at this moment, that all Persians are not terrorists. I reflect on the scores of Iranians I've befriended over the past twenty years, and I try my best to feel hatred toward them for what's happening to us now, but I can't seem to generate that emotion at all. I simply have known too many truly fine Iranians to feel hatred. It still doesn't make sense to kill us after holding us for three months . . . it simply doesn't make sense! But it's happening. We're going to be executed right here and now. I exhale, resigned to my fate, and continue to pray.
      I thank God for the forty-eight years of life He has given me. I thank Him for giving Betty and me two wonderful, bright children. I remember when Beth, our daughter, was born in Germany, and how I felt closer to God on that day, when I witnessed the miracle of birth, than I had ever felt in my life. I think about our son Greg's birth right

here in Tehran fourteen years ago, and what a big deal it was to my Iranian men friends because I had fathered a male child. How will my children take the news of their father's execution? How will Betty feel? Will the great strength that always has been characteristic of our family prevail, even after I'm gone? Or will it simply be too much for them to understand and endure? I'm confident that the family will make the adjustments necessary and will do just fine. I thank God for granting me this insight into the future, and I ask that He forgive all my sins and shortcomings.

It's quiet now, except for the constant whispering of our tormentors. Apparently we all have been moved into position for what is to come next. The sick feeling returns. Why don't they go ahead and get it over with? I figure they're going to stay in character and drag out the mystery and the drama as long as possible in order to flaunt their power over us. Surely the United States will be compelled to take strong military action against Iran to punish them for the cold-blooded murder of American diplomats. In my mind's eye, I picture the United States attacking Iran in reprisal for our summary execution, but this vision doesn't provide any comfort to me at all. Strangely, I'm beginning to get impatient. The waiting is almost unbearable. I almost want to have them go ahead and do what I'm thoroughly convinced they're going to do — shoot us down where we stand. My impatience is shortlived.

"*Hazer kon!*" [Get ready!]

I brace and inhale, hoping the end will come quickly. I don't want to give them a spectacle. If it must be, let it be clean, fast, and final. I wonder how long it will take to die. My knees are actually shaking out of control. I try to stop the shaking, but it's as if my knees don't belong to my body anymore. The fear and frustration peak as my mind fills with a complex combination of anger, hate, and tenacity. My belief in God and in eternal life provides a degree of courage, but I'm angry at President Carter and his entire administration for admitting the Shah in the first place. How could a president of the United States be so utterly naive? It should have been apparent that if the Shah were admitted to the United States, the Iranian people would react violently. The embassy had even reported that if the Shah were given asylum in the United States, irate and irrational Iranians might take hostages. I'm also angry at my executioners. How can they be so stupid? Don't they realize that if they commit this act of war against the United States, America will be compelled to lower the military boom on them? Haven't they carried this desire to be martyred a bit too far? Or do they really believe that if they're killed while carrying out Khomeini's orders, they automatically will go to paradise? I even feel pity for the innocent Iranians who most assuredly will pay with their lives for our deaths.

At this moment I realize that we're all standing tough and tall against this final threat. So far, not a single American has cried out, pleaded for his life, or in any other way outwardly displayed the fear which I know we're all experiencing. I feel a deep sense of pride in and comradeship with these men, whom I have come to respect and admire during the past three agonizing months. They truly are a cross-section of the American people. They've been raised and educated in a fiercely competitive society, and they've learned well the lesson that one suffers with dignity and in silence; one accepts death at the hands of the enemy without crawling or begging. Each of these men has made an individual decision to go out in style. We will die as men and as Americans, and our final courageous silence will haunt our executioners for the rest of their lives. I feel an almost uncontrollable urge to curse our tormentors, to cry out to them and let them know that we're aware of what's happening and to condemn them to eternal damnation for their cowardly deeds.

Suddenly I think of the six million Jews who perished in the Holocaust, virtually without resistance. How row after row of them could march quietly to their deaths had always been a puzzle to me, but now I understood why those brave Jews chose to die with a degree of dignity, by not making fools of themselves attempting to fight a hopeless situation. At this precarious time, my respect for them and what they were forced to endure increases dramatically.

I think of the idea of a noble death. I had always considered such a death to be the result of combat with an enemy; but isn't that what this is, too? By showing courage now, we're doing our best for our country. Without so much as a glance at each other or the reinforcement of a word of encouragement from our comrades, we all have decided to stand tall and show the Iranians American toughness. I realize that I'm in very special company.

"*Hadaf sho!*" [Take aim!]

One more command, and it's all over. My life will end. I'll never again see my children. I mentally tell them good-bye, tell them that I love them, tell them to take care of their mother. I'm saddened as I recall all those who have loved me in my lifetime. Not because they loved me, but because I never got around to telling them often enough how much I loved them and how much I appreciated their caring for me.

Damn it, go ahead and shoot! I'm getting angry. What in the hell are they waiting for? I can almost feel the searing pain as the bullets rip through my back and out my chest. I project my mind away from my body momentarily, and I see my body literally blasted closer to the wall as the bullets impact, then slumping lifeless to the floor. I find myself wishing they would give the final command to fire. No human should be forced to suffer through an extended execution like this. If it is to be done at all, it should be done without stalling.

But still the command to fire doesn't come.

I hear the Iranians begin to snicker and whisper to each other. The dirty bastards — they're enjoying themselves at our expense. I vow again that I will not allow myself to fall apart. My knees are no longer knocking. Once again I'm in full control of my nerves. One can get only so scared, and then he becomes angry, I think, angry at those who are creating the fear. I remain resolved to wait this out without showing any emotion at all.

"*Hazer kon*!" [Get ready!]

They're going to start all over again! Damn them; what are they trying to prove? Why don't they just get on with it?

I'm becoming more relaxed; I've made my peace with my God. And again I feel a sense of pride as I realize that my fellow hostages, to a man, have remained silent. Most of them do not speak Farsi, so they may not understand the fire commands, but they must know what's going on.

"*Hadaf sho*!" [Take aim!]

My body is numb. My mind is protecting my sanity by detachment and mental excursion; it's a kaleidoscope of experiences and memories from my past. I await the sound of shots, but again there's only silence. Suddenly I'm aware of time. This torment has been going on for a long time — maybe half an hour. My arms are numb. I no longer care whether they shoot or not; I only hope this ordeal will end soon.

There's motion to my left. The shouting of commands has ceased. The hostage next to me is being moved away from the wall and apparently out of the room.

I'm grabbed by the shoulder, manhandled into an adjacent room, and told to strip completely. Are they going to strip us and then shoot us? No, that would be too much even for these characters. I'm searched thoroughly. They check every body cavity and thoroughly search my clothing. Money I had secreted in my pocket lining is ripped out and flaunted before me as though I had just murdered Khomeini.

"What are you doing with this money? Have you been planning an escape?" Everything is taken from my pockets, even the toothpick I have salvaged for three months and used to clean my fingernails. Then the search is over, and I'm told to dress and move quickly. I am not blindfolded as I move through the room where the firing squad played its terrorizing games. I move past the others, some of whom are still lined up against the wall in the spread-eagled position. I'm pushed quickly past them and back to the cell block. The area is a shambles. Styrofoam mattresses are thrown everywhere, and everything has been thoroughly searched. I am not returned to my old cubicle, but to the one on the end directly under the air vent — the coldest spot in the Mushroom Inn. Tom Schaefer had been in this cubicle until he was moved out for interrogation. We haven't seen him since.

Slowly the rest of the hostages are returned to their cells. They are silent. The few I can see appear to have been resurrected from the dead. Their faces are drained of all emotion, and they move more like robots than like men. But there's a glint of pride deep in their eyes that seems to be shouting, "We can take anything you bastards can dish out. We are Americans!" My eyes mist as I catch a glimpse of Sergeant Greg Persinger. He winks at me as he passes my cell on his way to the latrine. He's tired and drained, but he's walking tall and proud. I instinctively expand my chest and pull my shoulders back. I've never been more proud of a group of men. They have stood up to a firing squad apparently designed to make us break and beg for our lives.

We never will forget this night as long as we live. The men who staged this cruel drama never will forget it either. They will remember the quiet dignity we demonstrated under conditions of almost unbelievable stress. On this night, it was the American hostages who won and the Iranian terrorists who lost.

10

THE MUSHROOM INN, TEHRAN
FEBRUARY 5 - MARCH 4, 1980

After the mock firing squad we faced last night, today is a day for reflection and prayer. More than anything else, this episode as a hostage has taught me to appreciate each day of life — to live it fully and to share love unabashedly with those who are special to me. But as a prisoner, I can't fully exercise my new resolve, and that creates tremendous frustrations.

But just when I think my spirits have reached rock bottom, I'm given a book by Joseph Wambaugh, *The Choirboys*. It's a tale of the ridiculous antics of a group of Los Angeles policemen, and it's hilariously funny. I've been reprimanded by the guards three times today for laughing out loud. Dave Roeder, who's in the cell to my right, manages to whisper to me, "I don't know what you're reading, but if it's that funny, I sure need to read it." Like many of the books I've read here, I hate to finish this one because it's such a relief from thinking about our situation. After I finish each book, there's an emotional letdown until I manage to get engrossed in another one. I particularly enjoy history and biographies, but I'm also soothed by a good novel like *The Choirboys*. I wonder if Wambaugh will ever realize how much laughter and happiness he brought me when I needed it most.

The guards must have been talking to a psychiatrist about our treatment, because suddenly there's a new arrangement. We're still not allowed to talk or communicate

234

in any way, but once a day we're permitted to move to a folding table in the hallway to play checkers with one of the other hostages. I've played with Regis Ragan, Don Sharer, and Joe Hall, an Army warrant officer who worked in the Defense Attaché Office. Regis is the undisputed champion. Don and I are about evenly matched. Joe Hall I can usually beat. Several days into the new arrangement, however, there's a change: Don and I no longer are permitted to play against each other.

Meanwhile, Tom Schaefer has not been back to our cell block in almost two weeks. I wonder if his interrogation is over and he has been moved somewhere else, or if he's still going through hell somewhere here in the building. Up until three days ago, the guard with the food cart routinely took a meal out of our cell block down the hall to some other area. I'm sure it was for Tom, but now it has stopped. I decide to make an issue out of the change in the checker rules to see if I can flush out any information on Tom. The guard who told me about the new restriction is a diminutive man we call Little Ali. He must be under five feet tall. He loves to give orders, but he's scared to death to be too close to any of us unless he has a backup with a weapon. I challenge him on the decision not to allow Don and me to play.

"Why can't we play anymore? We've played together before. What are you people afraid of, anyway?"

Ali doesn't appreciate his order being questioned. "You cannot play with him; he worked for you and neither of you can be trusted. That is all. Shut up!"

I go into my animal act, swearing at Ali in Farsi. I intentionally violate all the rules, shouting and shaking my fist at a very upset Little Ali. He retreats toward the doorway where the armed guards sit and play with their automatic rifles. A tall guard with a nasty disposition and a propensity for menacingly pointing his weapon at us rushes in from the hallway, along with three or four other armed terrorists. Ali is brave now. He threatens me with some undefined punishment, then he says I will be moved to solitary confinement if I don't shut up.

I don't, and Ali makes good his threat. I'm taken out of the cubicle and moved to another room down the hall. I'm locked in this freezing room with nothing but my slacks and shirt. The room is empty except for a high stool. The walls are covered with pictures of tiger cages in Vietnam with human occupants, glossy prints of starving Biafran children, and prints of the mutilated bodies of some of the Shah's generals, executed by the revolutionaries. I assume this is where Tom was interrogated. Before I can check the room over for signs of Tom, a group of militants with weapons and a length of solid rubber hose enters the room.

I'm ordered to sit on the stool. One of the militants apparently is a member of the elite leader's committee. He doesn't speak English. As two of the others hold my arms and shoulders, he grabs a fistful of my cheek and lectures me on all the terrible things he can cause to happen to me if I don't roll over and play dead. I'm angry, too, and I don't give him much satisfaction. He orders Ali to take the rubber hose and beat me with it. Ali takes the length of solid rubber and waves it around. The two characters who are locked on my arms and shoulders back off a little in deference to the hose. Ali begins to lecture me on my serious misconduct, while brandishing the hose as though he'll hit me in the face with it at any moment.

"Hit the son of a pig!" The leader wants to see some action. My stubbornness has infuriated him.

"I will not hit him this time," says Ali, "but if he ever talks back to me again, I will kill him."

"If you're going to kill me, do it and get it over with. It would be better to die than be your hostage forever."

They all back off and go into a huddle to decide my punishment. I can hear them whispering and snickering, but I can't make out what they're saying. Finally Ali approaches me and tells me I will be left in this cold room with nothing "for a long time, until you learn to obey the rules."

They all leave, locking the steel door behind them, and I immediately begin to look for signs that Tom has been here. There are rows of steel wall lockers around the room. I feel along the tops of them, since they're too high for me to see. About halfway through the lockers, I find some papers and a short pencil. On one sheet is a list of songs Tom apparently was trying to remember. Another is a list of garbled notes concerning changes in the Iranian military he probably gleaned from his interrogators. The last piece of paper is a calendar of sorts, prepared by Tom to keep track of the days and jot down other routine items, such as what he was given to eat, when he was allowed to go to the toilet, and so forth. We all try to do this to see if we can develop intelligence about changes in our situation by analyzing these changes in the routine. Tom was good at it. I can even tell when he exercised. From Tom's scraps of paper, I deduce that his interrogation lasted thirteen days, and then he was left here until about three or four days ago. My guess is that he was moved outside this building, thus the change in the meal cart schedule.

I'm cold and uncomfortable, and I'm beginning to think this wasn't such a good idea. Alone with my thoughts, my mind races over the events of the last few days, focusing always on the firing-squad incident. I'm still unable to force that experience out of my thoughts. I'm concerned that it may have been a practice for the real thing. Any seemingly insignificant action on the part of our government could lead to our execution. But, then again, I don't want to freeze in this bare room for an indefinite period, either.

Ali arrives on the scene as I try to find some way of getting comfortable on the cold floor. He asks if I need to go to the toilet. I tell him I don't. He says to bang on the door if I have to go. He returns in about half an hour and asks again if I have to go to the bathroom. He's afraid to enter the room alone, so he stands just outside the door, next to the armed guard. I tell him how cold it is and ask him to bring me a blanket. He refuses, but adds, "If you will say you are sorry for being bad, I will see if you can go back to your room." I believe Ali is actually trying to be nice. I tell him that compared to what they've been doing to us for more than three months, I have done nothing for which I should feel sorry. Ali leaves in a huff. He thought for sure that I would be willing to eat a little crow to avoid staying in the cold room.

I'm fed the same cup of soup I would be eating if I were in my regular cubicle, but tonight it's far from enough. I have burned calories trying to stay warm in this icebox, and I'm still cold. It's going to be a long night.

Later, Akbar comes by my new cell with a piece of news: Iran has a new President. Abdolhassan Bani-Sadr recently has been sworn in as the first elected president of the Islamic Republic of Iran. I ask him when all this happened, and he looks at me very sheepishly.

"It was the day after you were all taken from your cells to be searched."

"Akbar, that was no search. Your hoodlums stood us before a mock firing squad. If that was an example of Islam and your new republic in action, I'm glad I am not part of it."

"Colonel, I had nothing to do with that night. It was wrong for our people to do that . . . it was not Islamic. I am sorry it happened."

"Akbar, you are part of it, so you must share responsibility with those who actually wore the masks and staged the whole thing," I answer.

"I am sorry you feel that way. I was against it and had no part in it. I think you should be held until the Shah is returned, but there is no reason for us not to treat you well. I do not hate you; I only hate your government."

238

"I do not hate you either, Akbar. As a Christian, I'm not supposed to hate, but sometimes it is hard not to want to strike out in retaliation for the way we have been treated."

"I understand how you feel. Come, I will take you back to your room. It is too cold in here." Akbar has more authority than I realized. He places my blindfold around my eyes and ties it loosely. He says nothing as we move, but when we reach my cell and he removes my blindfold, he says simply, "Be good."

As I try to sleep, I think how much some of these militants are like children. They're playing a game, the stakes of which are higher than they have realized in their wildest dreams. But they have guns, and they can kill with the same deadliness as mature men.

I really feel like a hobo. I haven't had a haircut or a shave in more than three and a half months. My beard is so long that it's hard to keep it clean, especially when I eat my soup at night, yet they won't allow us to use a razor. They say they're afraid we'll slash our wrists. I have heard that one of our people did try to kill himself. I don't think I'll ever reach that point. If I die here, my death will be on their hands, not on mine. Mahmoud, a young Turkic-speaking militant from Ardebil who occasionally talks with me, claims that he has been trained as a barber. A small man with an unusually round face for an Iranian, he is one of the few with a sense of humor. He asks if I am trying to compete with the Imam by growing such a long beard. I tell him I'd love to have a haircut and a shave, but his brothers will not allow it. He promises to try to get permission for us to shave. He says if he does, he will give me a haircut.

Later Mahmoud arrives with scissors and a dirty comb in hand. He says that he has set up a barber shop in one of the small rooms down the hall, and he asks if I still want to have a haircut.

239

"Yes, Mahmoud, I would like to have a haircut and a shave, but I have no money; it was all stolen by your friends."

"You can pay me when you are free again. I will trust you," says Mahmoud with a chuckle.

Wearing my ever-present blindfold, I'm led to "Mahmoud's barber shop." It's a filthy mess. There is a pet rabbit jumping around the room, and evidence that the bunny has been here for some time is all over the floor. Mahmoud is slow and not very professional in his work, but he gets the job done. He hands me a dirty, cracked piece of mirror so that I can check his artistry.

"Thank you, Mahmoud. Now if your people decide to shoot us, at least my corpse will look better." I know instantly that I've hit a sore spot with my barber. "You will not be shot, Colonel, if your government will do what it should. If you are shot, it will not be our fault; it will be your government that should be blamed." Persian logic at its zenith, I think as I'm escorted back to my cell. Now if only I could get rid of the beard.

Another dramatic mail call is in progress. One by one, hostages are being led out of the bay to receive their precious envelopes from home. This time I'm one of the first to be taken, and the news is good. I have seven letters from Betty, five of them written in the early days of the takeover. She and the children are doing fine. The new hot-water heater apparently works. She says I am missed and that she is praying for my safe return. The final letter is in answer to my plea for her to write, the one Akbar promised to send by international mail. He came through after all. My spirits rise. Knowing that my family is safe and well makes a big difference in the way I feel. I can take anything if they're all right. There has been no crisis at home. My examination of the envelopes reveals that the letters were returned to her by the Department of State, which claimed I was "not known at the State Department address." Thanks a lot, I think as I return to my cell.

Late yesterday afternoon, Hamid the Liar brought a new hostage to our row of cubicles: Sergeant Joe Subic, from the Defense Attaché Office. On top of his performance on our first day of captivity, rumors circulating through our clandestine communications network say that Subic made a TV broadcast for our captors, in which he pointed out sensitive electronic equipment captured by the Iranians. I don't know if these stories are true, and I have decided not to hold my earlier experience against him. Besides, he has been somewhere else, and it will be good to compare notes as soon as we have an opportunity to communicate with him. I wonder what he may have learned about our chances of getting out of here. Joe asks the guard if he can play checkers with me. The guard approves and we face off in a game. Joe is no competition at all, even for me. We have a chance to whisper each time our less-than-attentive guard turns his attention away from us, and we take advantage of the opportunities. Joe already has most of the information we've managed to elicit from our guards. He knows that the Shah left the U.S. for Panama. He knows that Bani-Sadr is the newly elected president of Iran. And he has some news that we previously have not been privy to, including a report that America is up in arms over the hostage situation and that it is consistently a major news story at home. He says Walter Cronkite ends his evening news each night by saying how many days we have been hostages. He also has a basic understanding of our secret communications network.

Akbar is passing out envelopes, one to each hostage. They are fairly large, about ten by fifteen inches. The return address is a Doctor Englemann in Indiana. The one I'm handed has not been opened by our captors. Inside is a red T-shirt with a profile of an American eagle's head in

white superimposed on the shirt and the word "America" in
large blue letters under the head. I look around and see that
Greg Persinger already is wearing his new shirt. I'll try to
keep mine in good shape to wear home, if we ever get out of
this place. I wonder how the Iranians let these slip by their
censors. But I don't wonder for very long.

Hamid and his band of goons come to collect the
shirts while I'm in the bathroom. As soon as I return, I hide
mine by stuffing it inside my jockey shorts like a sanitary
napkin. Within ten minutes, one of the guards returns to
collect the missing shirts. I tell him I already gave mine to
Hamid, hoping he won't know the difference. He passes me
and repeats his demand for the shirt at Don Sharer's cell.
Don tells him he already gave his back to "one of the other
guards." Later Don manages to catch my eye as we both run
in place. "I've still got my eagle shirt," he says, moving his
lips without any sound. "Me too," I reply. I know intuitively
that Don has the same idea I do — to hide the shirt until
we're on our way home, then wear it to show the world that
we're proud to be Americans.

Subic has been with us only three days and two
nights when Hamid the Liar approaches his cell and beckons
him to follow. Joe already has his belongings packed in a
plastic bag and rolled up in a blanket. He must have known
he was being moved. Instantly, I get a strange feeling in my
stomach. Was he planted here? If so, did I make a giant error
by letting him in on our communications system? It's too late
to do anything about it; I'll just have to wait and see.

Within an hour, Hamid is back ordering his
guards to be more alert. He is followed by a group of guards
carrying stacks of books. Soon our bay in the Mushroom Inn
is more isolated than ever. Between each cell, books are
stacked to form a solid wall all the way to the ceiling. Wall
lockers have been brought into the room and placed in a row
between the two rows of cubicles. Hamid is tightening his

242

security noose to prevent any possibility of our passing messages to each other. I think I've been had.

"Get up quickly, move!"
The stormtroopers with the masks and the guns who staged the "execution" exactly one month ago are back again. We're prodded out of our cells and lined up against the same wall. My pulse races uncontrollably, but I'm less fearful than a month ago when we faced our first firing squad. After that horrible episode, I refuse to be intimidated. As I wait for the commands to begin, I have a sick feeling of desperation.

But there are no commands. There is only silence and waiting. After about ten minutes, some hostages are moved to the strip search room. I didn't have time to hide my eagle shirt; it's still in my cell in my plastic bag. My turn to be searched arrives. Three masked gunmen who enjoy their work check me thoroughly. Then I'm told to put my clothes on and be quiet. I'm blindfolded, handcuffed, and moved to a cold hallway, where I'm ordered to sit on the cement floor. A blanket is thrown over my head, and I sit and wait for more than an hour. I think there is another hostage seated next to me, but I can't be sure. I hear guards passing by every few minutes, and I sense that one is next to me.

Finally I'm led up the hall by two guards who say nothing except to give me directions. We go up two flights of stairs and outside. I feel the chilly night air as it rises up under the blanket that is draped over my head. I'm jostled inside a car and told to be quiet. I sit and listen. Another hostage is loaded and then another.

After the usual thirty-minute wait, we drive a short distance, over two speed bumps, and stop. The others are unloaded first. Then it's my turn. I'm taken inside a building which I assume is the Chancellery, down a flight of stairs, through another hall, and into what seems to be a very small room. The echoes of the guards' whispers bounce off the walls with a metallic ring. The blanket is removed from my head, but the blindfold and handcuffs are left on. I'm tired and demoralized as I sit and wait for the next act to begin. I sense that I'm alone in this tiny room. Alone with my thoughts and what little remains of my hopes.

11

AMERICAN EMBASSY, TEHRAN
MARCH 4 - APRIL 11, 1980

The jailer is another kind of prisoner —
Is the jailer envious of his prisoner's dreams?

Fragments de Faust
Gerard de Nerval

After about twenty minutes, my blindfold is removed. I'm in a room about seven or eight feet square. Hamid the Liar is here with four of his flunkies, all pointing automatic rifles at me. My new prison is a vault with a steel door and no outside light or fresh air. It's bleak and dismal, but there's a desk, an office chair, a thin styrofoam mattress, and a four-drawer high-security safe that has been torched open in a most unprofessional manner.

Hamid is even more irritated and threatening than usual. He says I will remain in solitary because I'm guilty of the "serious crime of communicating with the other hostages." I instantly and dramatically deny the charge. My rule is never admit anything, even if caught red-handed. If he has been given information by one of us, I want to know who it was, and the best way to find out is to continue to profess my complete innocence. Hamid says he has proof that I was sending written and verbal messages. He sneers, "You will not be allowed to read or write letters. We will give you food, but you must learn you can't disobey the rules. We have been nice to you, but you have not cooperated with us at all. You are a very bad man. There is no reason for us to be nice to you. You will stay totally alone until you are either released or tried as a spy."

Hamid's evaluation of my lack of cooperation with them is just as it should be. But I want to know how he found out about our communications system. I know I was foolish to share information with Joe Subic in view of his shaky past performance as a hostage, but I never dreamed he would stoop so low as to tell the guards about our covert information network, which was pretty effective in the Mushroom Inn. I will continue to deny any involvement and perhaps Hamid, in one of his "I know it all" moods, will slip and tell me who blew the whistle. Meanwhile, I'm fairly sure that we've been sold out by one of our own.

I'm not looking forward to being alone again, and it will be rough not having anything to read. What am I going to do all day? It has been four months since the embassy takeover, and my instincts tell me that it could go on for months or even years — forever.

After Hamid and his band of protectors leave, slamming and locking the huge steel door behind them, I survey my depressing surroundings. Just as I realize there isn't a light switch anywhere inside my new cell, the light is turned off from outside. I wonder if this is to be the routine, or if they're going to leave me in the dark all the time. That would be too much. I'm very tired, so I feel my way over to the mattress and try to get some rest. I haven't talked to any of the other Americans directly for four months now, except for my brief discussions with Tom Schaefer when were in north Tehran. But at least most of the time I was in a position to observe one or two of the others, and there's a certain amount of comfort and security just in that. The mind can play cruel and strange tricks when one is isolated and denied all human contact. I knew this before, but now I realize it more than ever. This will be yet another test of my will, patience, and strength. I vow not to let this isolation get to me. I will continue to think healthy thoughts, no matter how long I remain alone. After all, I'm pretty good company, and I've lived an interesting and exciting life. I will continue my routine, starting tomorrow morning. I'll exercise and concentrate on positive things. I'll relive some of the best moments of my life and critique some of those that didn't work out quite so well. I'll think about those who have been an inspiration to me because of their courage and dedication. I'll also try to con the guards into providing me with books. I will not write any letters for the Iranians, and I will remember who I am and what I am. I'm not going to let them turn me into a vegetable.

I tick off another day on my do-it-yourself calendar. I've been in solitary for three weeks. It's lonely, but it hasn't been unbearable. Hamid came in with two of his soldiers about a week ago and tried to tell me that the other hostages had been released, and that if I would write a few letters condemning the Shah and asking the American people to return their former leader for trial, I also would be set free. He was lying — I could tell by various signs when I was taken to the toilet that others were still here. I've also heard Mike Metrinko talking in Farsi to the guards — I'm sure he's in the next cell — and I've heard Courtney Barnes shouting at the guards. I figure he's on the other side and down the hall about twenty feet from my cell.

Reflecting on the past three weeks of solitary, I note with a certain feeling of pride and contentment that the time has passed rather quickly. My routine of sleeping only at night, exercising for at least one hour each morning and afternoon, and concentrating on positive thoughts is quite successful. I'm getting enough to eat to sustain my rigorous exercise program, but I go to bed hungry every night — due more to the feeding schedule than to the quantity of food I'm served. Breakfast is always the same: Iranian bread and tea, sometimes with grape jelly from the embassy cooperative store. God, how I would love to have some good American ham and eggs! Lunch is usually fairly decent, but it wears off by evening, and the bowl of chicken noodle soup which is the routine evening meal doesn't stick to the ribs, as my dad would say. I know I'm not getting enough protein, and I really miss the fresh vegetables and fruits that always have been a part of my diet. But at least I'm not losing any more weight. I estimate that I'm down to about a hundred and fifty pounds — about thirty-five pounds below my normal weight.

Hamid interrupts my thoughts. This time he has a couple of the interrogators with him. I haven't seen either of these characters since the end of my questioning more than four months ago. A red-haired, squat Iranian, whose name is also Hamid, is with the group. He has a notebook and a gold Cross pen, probably mine. Ahmad, one of the key interrogators, is the first to speak. He asks how I'm doing and comments on how lucky I am to have "a room all to myself." His vindictiveness shows through, and it's obvious that he's not here to check on my welfare.

"Do you know Mr. Thomas Ahern?" Ahmad the interrogator is still trying to ply his trade. He looks me straight in the eyes as the others seem to bore in, intent on observing my reactions.

"Yes, I know Tom. He worked at the embassy, too, before you people took over."

Hamid the Liar is not pleased with my answer. He can't keep his mouth shut, even though interrogation is not his area of responsibility.

"Of course you know Mr. Ahern, you worked very closely with him," he says. "We know all about your relationship with him and also with William Daugherty. They are CIA, and you know very well they are, even though you would not tell us of them when you were first arrested. We know all about the embassy, who is CIA and who is not; you worked with these men — we know they are CIA — so you must be CIA, too."

I do my best to act surprised and indignant.

"Bill Daugherty and I were friends; we socialized together. You know, a dinner once in a while, lunch at the embassy restaurant — that sort of thing. I hardly know Tom Ahern at all, but I find it hard to believe he is CIA. He's just not the type. He's very quiet and seems to be pretty much a loner. What makes you think he is CIA?"

Ahmad the interrogator's eyes have not left mine even for a moment. He decides to take over from Hamid. "We know Ahern and Daugherty are CIA, and we suspect you are, too. Sooner or later, we will find out what you were sent to Iran to do. You have been very smart, but eventually we will find out everything. Some of your friends are being very cooperative, because we have told them that if they give the information we need for trials for people like you, Ahern, and Daugherty, they can go home. We do not want to have to question you again. Why don't you tell us everything?"

I don't want to be questioned again, either, I think as I carefully consider my answer. Righteous indignation seems to be the only logical approach. "If either of those men is CIA, it certainly is news to me. I was here to help your Ministry of Defense get spare parts for your military services. If that's a crime, I guess I go on trial. But if you open the trials to the world press and use any kind of rules of evidence at all, you will never convict me of doing anything wrong. Damn it, I was here to help your country! And for that I have been beaten, threatened, and treated little better than you were treated under the Shah. I'm sick of being accused of being CIA — you people would accuse the Pope of being a CIA agent. I was not even in Iran until a few weeks before you attacked the embassy."

Ahmad apparently is convinced I'm telling the truth. His mood changes, and so does the subject of the questioning. "Tell me, Colonel, how long do you think it will be before your government answers to the will of the American people and sends the Shah to Iran?"

"How can I comment on the will of the American people, when I haven't seen a newspaper or magazine or received any mail to tell me what that will is? Even without information, though, I know enough about my country and its people to tell you this: You will not get the Shah back by trying to blackmail the United States. Americans do not like to be pushed around, and when they are, they get very angry. If they haven't already lost interest in us, sooner or later they will lose patience. When they do, Iran will suffer. Do you want to see thousands of Iranians killed and others left homeless because of what you've done?"

Ahmad seems to be interested in the dialogue we're having. He thinks he has all the answers and is not hesitant to let me speak. Little red-haired Hamid seems to be enjoying the discussion, too. Hamid the Liar, on the other hand, is uneasy and nervous. He obviously doesn't like my spouting off, but Ahmad is clearly in charge of this visit, so Hamid remains silent. Ahmad decides to demonstrate his prowess with revolutionary "logic" and rhetoric. He's pretty good at it, and he remains cool and poised, his eyes never leaving mine. The others now are strictly spectators to this debate. Ahmad speaks softly and distinctly.

"The United States government must eventually send the Shah back, or you will be here for a long time. If the American people lose interest and your government continues to do nothing to answer the just demands of the Iranian people, we will have trials for you and some of the others. Perhaps that will create a renewed interest in our cause. If some of you are sentenced to long terms in prison or shot, your government will be forced to listen to us and send the Shah. We will do what we must do. As far as thousands of Iranians being killed, we are not afraid. The Imam has said if your government sends bombers and totally destroys Iran, killing all thirty-seven million people, then you can have Iran. Of course, if this does happen, you will be among the first to die."

"I'm not afraid to die either," I counter, "but it

seems senseless to die — either you or me — over the return of your deposed Shah. He is very sick anyway. What difference does it make whether he dies in the United States on an operating table or in front of one of your firing squads? If he really has been such a despot, God will punish him. You all profess to believe in God. Why not leave it to Him?"

The reference to God is too much for Ahmad. He begins to lose his temper. "God will certainly punish the Shah, but it is the will of the Iranian people that he be tried here and executed for his crimes against the people. We believe God is on our side. Your government is helpless; they can do nothing to save you — even with all their atomic bombs and airplanes. If your government is so powerful, why have you been here for almost five months? The answer is simple — there is a limit to your great power, and it is no good against the will of the Iranian people and the will of the Imam and the will of God. If your government really cared about you, the Shah would have been returned along with his money, stolen from the people of Iran, and you would be home by now."

My turn again. "It is not the lives of a few Americans that are important, and in the final analysis it is not the Shah and his money, either. Our honor is important. Neither the government nor the American people will give in to your ransom demands. We lose more than one hundred people in traffic accidents in America each weekend, so don't get the idea that our government is so preoccupied with the idea of saving fifty or so lives. You are in a no-win situation, and you know it as well as I do."

I've hit a sore spot; Ahmad is uneasy. He's getting red-faced and his tone is louder and more threatening as he decides to end the exchange. "No matter what you say, Colonel, you are the one who will suffer if your government does not meet our demands. We have plenty of time, and your government can do nothing to get you back except return the Shah and his stolen money. We will drive Carter out of power, because the American people will see how helpless he is against us. Even if the Shah never returns, we will destroy your president. That is how much power we have in revolutionary Iran. We can overthrow the American president by keeping you here. That, Mr. Colonel Scott, is real power."

Ahmad and his band turn to leave, but Hamid the Liar has to get his licks in before he departs. "You are still a troublemaker, but perhaps a few months of being alone — or even a few years — without books and a chance to see the other two hostages who are still here will change your attitude. We know you were trying to set up an escape with your sneaky message system. We have this information from one of your friends."

Hamid is livid. This is my chance to make him slip and tell who exposed the communications network.

"Hamid, no matter what you say, I've done nothing wrong. I have had no opportunities to communicate, and if one of our people says I did, he's a liar. I do not believe that one of the hostages would lie about a thing like that. You're bluffing, and you know it."

Hamid doesn't like being called a liar — even indirectly. He finally blurts it out: "Mr. Subic would not lie! He told us how you, Colonel Holland, and Golacinski were passing your messages. Why do you think we put him in with you? We knew something was going on. You are stupid, Colonel; you let him in on your little plan the first day he was with you. You think you are smart, but you are stupid!"

Hamid realizes that he has said too much, but it's too late to retract his words. He leaves in a rage, slamming the steel door behind him. I can hear him shouting at the guard outside. He orders him to turn off the light in my cell and keep it off until he says otherwise. "When we have trials for these spies, he will be one of the first to be tried and shot!" he screams.

I have suspected Subic all along, but I will not

252

pass judgment because I don't have all the facts. I wonder what, if anything, they did to encourage him to become an informer. I'm disappointed that one of us is helping them at the expense of his fellow Americans. What a feeling of guilt he must have.

To get my mind off the objectionable subject, I shift my thoughts to my family and what a trauma this must be for them. I wonder about my neighbors and friends and whether they have been able to comfort my family, or is the whole thing an awkward mess that's just too sensitive to discuss? Thinking about what must be going on at home at this very moment, I realize that my thoughts have none of the usual materialistic overtones. I do not see, in my mind's eye, big houses, manicured lawns, or expensive automobiles. I see only people. People with needs, hopes, and fears. People with plans, desires, and limitations. People with dreams and faith in God. I realize, here in solitary confinement in a land thousands of miles from my roots in America, that I have sorted out my values and reached a degree of peace which I've never known before. I'm conscious of, and somewhat amazed at, the ability I have to adjust to the total absence of material things and still be happy. I have an almost euphoric feeling as I consider the changes that have taken place in the way I look at my world, my God, and my life as a result of this experience. The time in solitary has been, so far, the most peaceful of my ordeal as a hostage. I'm at peace with my God; I know who I am and what I am. I don't really miss the material things I've been denied, because I realize that they're not important. My faith in God and my country are stronger than ever. My faith in myself is stronger, too.

But I still don't like being in the dark, and I'd find it all much easier to bear if I had some books, a pencil, and some paper.

The last three days have been boring and slow.

I've been in total darkness, thanks to Hamid's edict. Eating in the dark is worst of all. Before I always picked through my rice and removed the long black hairs that invariably were in it, but here I just have to eat it "in the rough." The hair is still in the food, but I don't find it until I try to chew and swallow. But I continue to eat anyway, and I continue to exercise and try to stay awake all day so I can sleep at night.

I hear a familiar voice outside my door talking to the guard. It's Akbar. He instructs the guard to turn on the light in my cell. The guard tells Akbar that Hamid says I'm a spy and am not to be treated well at all. Akbar says I'm only a tough old soldier and not a spy. He tells the guard that he already has talked to Hamid, and the light is to be turned on during the day. My cell door is unlocked then, and Akbar enters. He gives me an embarrassed smile.

"Colonel, you should not be surly with Hamid. He hates you and he enjoys making it hard for you. Why don't you just listen when he talks and give him no reason to punish you?"

I speak softly in Farsi to Akbar, letting him know that I appreciate his concern but also trying to make him understand why I feel as I do about Hamid and most of the others. "Akbar, I heard what you said to the guard, and I thank you for your words and your interest in my welfare. But I don't like Hamid, and I refuse to take his threats, propaganda, and outbursts of temper. I know he enjoys his position of power, but I have to fight back. The only way I can is by not letting him get away with thinking that I believe everything he says." Then I ask about him and his family.

Akbar likes to talk about his family, and I know this always breaks the ice with him. He has been quite forthcoming with me, and much of that openness, I believe, has come because I'm a good listener. He is the only militant who routinely looks me in the eyes when he speaks.

"My family is doing fine, and I appreciate your asking about them. I see them very little, though. There is so much to do and, in a way, we are also hostages. We have to be here just as you do. I hope and pray this thing will not last much longer. For your information, I think progress is being made, even though my government and the American government are not speaking directly to each other."

"Akbar, what do you think the chances are of some sort of settlement, say by Easter?"

Akbar speaks without hesitation. "I don't know exactly what is going on, Colonel, but I think there is a possibility it could end by then. Our president has said the situation must be resolved, but there are many in the Revolutionary Council who disagree with him and want to put the senior embassy personnel on trial as spies. I do not believe this will happen, but it could. Meanwhile, you must be patient. You must pray, as I am doing, that it will end soon so you can go home to your family. Do not give Hamid and Ahmad a bad time, and I'll do what I can to help you. I know it is not good to be left alone with nothing to do — I had a lot of that in the Shah's prisons. Do you like to do crossword puzzles?"

"Akbar, you're very kind. Yes, I like to work crossword puzzles. But I don't have any. In fact, I don't even have anything to read."

He reaches into the pocket of his military field jacket and pulls out a pen and notebook. He flips the notebook open and begins to write. After jotting down a few notes, he says, "I will try to get you some crosswords and some books. What kind of books do you want to read?"

"I prefer history and good novels, but I'll read whatever you can get. I don't really like science fiction or junk novels, but other than that, anything you can find will be appreciated. I'd also like to write to my family, if you can arrange for paper and pencil."

Akbar again makes notes. "I'll be back within a day or two. Meanwhile, be patient. Do you want some cigarettes?"

I almost answer yes, but I decide against it. There's no fresh air in this cell, and the smoke would be stifling. I've never smoked cigarettes, but I sure miss puffing on my pipe. "Thanks, Akbar, but I don't smoke anything but a pipe, and I don't have one or any tobacco."

"I'll try to get you a pipe and tobacco," he says. "Goodbye. I'll see you later."

Akbar extends his hand and I shake it warmly. His grip is firm and he's very sincere. His eyes do not seem to reflect any hatred at all; on the contrary, they seem to be filled with a genuine concern and interest.

I knock on the cell door, signalling the guard that I have to go to the bathroom. He doesn't respond. I really have to go, so I knock again, but still no response. Minutes pass and I'm getting more and more uncomfortable. Why can't these people let a man use the toilet when he has to without making a major production out of it? I know there is a guard outside, because I can smell the smoke from his cigarette. I look for some object to bang against the steel door; the only thing I can find is the pullout extension from the desk. I slam it against the steel door, and almost simultaneously I hear a scuffling noise outside the door. Apparently the guard fell asleep in his chair, and the shocking sound of the drawer against the steel door has startled him awake. He must have had his chair leaned back against the wall, and the sound I heard was him falling. I'm tickled, but I know there'll be hell to pay for this.

The guard finally opens the door. The armed sentry from the other end of the hall has heard the commotion, too, and runs to the door of my cell, weapon at the ready. The guard who has been jostled from sleep says, "You must not be so noisy; you will be punished for making so much noise. What do you want?"

"I need to go to the toilet. I've been knocking for about twenty minutes."

The guard is angry and decides to make me wait. "You must wait until it is your turn, so be quiet."

I hear the other guard, the one with the automatic rifle, caution the first guard to remain awake; then I hear his footsteps retreating back down the hall to his position. In about a half an hour, the guard finally opens my cell and blindfolds me for the trek to the latrine. While I'm in the latrine, someone else enters. It's Don Sharer, whom I haven't seen in almost a month. He asks how I'm doing and tells me he thinks that most, if not all, of the others have been removed from the Mushroom Inn. He's cleanshaven and looks good, except for his pale coloring and his weight loss. He tells me that he's in a cell with Petty Officer Sam Gillette.

Just then my guard enters the latrine and, seeing Don and me in the bathroom at the same time, admonishes us not to talk. He places my blindfold over my eyes and escorts me back to my solitary cell. He's obviously embarrassed at the screw-up, but he says nothing.

There has been a noise in my cell almost every night for the last two weeks. It sounds like something scratching against the cement wall. Tonight it's louder than ever, and I'm beginning to wonder if someone or something is trying to dig a tunnel into my cell. I've tried contacting Mike Metrinko in the next cell by using the tap code, but he hasn't responded. I wonder what it could be. I rise and move toward the desk very deliberately and as quietly as possible. Suddenly I sense movement, and something brushes the side of my feet. Damn it, there are rats in my cell! I sit in my chair for about an hour, only to be disturbed again by the scratching sound. This time it's obviously coming from two locations along the edge of the cell. I'm unable to sleep the rest of the night. The last thing I need is to be bitten by a filthy rat.

In the morning, I make an extensive search of my cell. Over behind the safe, there's a large crack in the joint between the floor and the wall. There's another one farther along the wall. The rats obviously are entering from these cracks, which they've spent two weeks making bigger to accommodate their bulky bodies. I decide to ask the guard to leave the light on this evening.

About midnight I'm sitting in my chair, with the light on, trying to be as quiet as possible. I hear the scratching, and in a few minutes, a big rat moves brazenly to the middle of the room. He's not at all intimidated by the light or by my presence. Damn it, I hate rats! In Vietnam, we used to shoot them in our team house with Montagnard crossbows, but here I don't have anything to fight them with.

Another even bigger rat appears from behind the safe. He moves to the middle of the room, stopping for a fleeting moment before he scampers directly across my styrofoam mattress. This is too much! I don't even have anything to throw at them. I decide to see if the guard will give me something to plug the entry holes with or help me get rid of them in some way. I knock on the door, and my two "roommates" make a beeline for their sanctuaries outside my cell in the bowels of the building wall.

The guard pokes around in the holes with a stick and proclaims there are no rats in either of the holes. I ask him to give me something to plug them with, but he says that's not necessary. He leaves, locking the cell door and turning out the light. I decide to stuff my socks in the holes and try to get some sleep. I figure I'll hear them if they begin to gnaw through my socks or try to scratch them out of the opening. Sleep doesn't come quickly. The rats have made me think about Vietnam. God knows, we had plenty of them in the central highlands where I was stationed. I have vivid memories of the war and some of the more significant actions I fought in during that conflict, but mostly my thoughts are of frustration and disillusionment. I'll never forget when I returned to a very divided and bitter America in January of 1968. I was as brown as a berry after more than a year of jungle combat when I landed at the San Francisco airport, and I was in uniform — an obvious Vietnam returnee. A little old lady who was protesting the war hit me in the chest with her purse as I got off my plane. She called me a baby killer and a murderer.

As I try to fall asleep and forget about the rats, I recall an "impossible dream" I had when I returned from Vietnam. I hoped to live to see an America as united as the America I had grown up in during World War II, when the men in my lower-middle-class neighborhood in Philadelphia marched off to war without complaint. They did their duty without question. America was truly a nation united in those days, but when Vietnam veterans came home, they found a country that had little or no appreciation for what they had been through or for what they had contributed. I guess, though, that I'll never see a united America again, and I wonder what effect, if any, this crisis has had at home. Based on my remembrances of the Vietnam era, I'm not optimistic. I figure there was high interest in our plight for a month or so, but then the American people probably began to forget about us. As a nation, we generally are apathetic about foreign affairs. I pray that I'm wrong, as I finally find the sleep that has been eluding me.

I'm awakened by something moving across my chest. I swing my arms wild and wide. Damn it, one of those rats was actually on my chest! My pulse races with a combination of revulsion and fear. There'll be no more sleep tonight.

Akbar is true to his word . . . well, almost true to his word. He came by this afternoon with two crossword puzzle books and a half-dozen history books. He also brought some sticks and short metal rods and helped me plug the access routes of my unwanted cellmates, whom I had complained loudly about. He had no real news to relate, but he insists discussions are taking place that he hopes will produce a breakthrough in our situation. He told me again to be patient and not to tell Hamid that he had given me the books and crossword puzzles, but to hide them when any of the guards enter the cell, so they won't take them away from me. He also brought me a can of Half-and-Half tobacco, but no pipe. I opened the can and decided to chew some tobacco for the first time in my life. Even if I had a pipe, it would be too close in here to smoke, but the tobacco tastes pretty good. It seems to soothe me. I think about the advertisement on TV: "Just a little pinch between your cheek and gum; you don't even have to light up." I chuckle for the first time in several days. I'm enjoying the crossword puzzles, and I have read more than half of Irving Stone's *The Passions of the Mind*.

I've begun to look forward to Akbar's periodic visits and our discussions. I wonder if he ever will have an opportunity to finish college and make something of himself. The prospects seem pretty dismal in post-revolutionary Iran. The priorities are directed toward revenge and oppression, not toward education and modernization. I wonder how the mass exodus of educated Iranians has been affected by the seizure of our embassy. When the attack came, there were more than seventy thousand Iranians seeking visas to the United States. I feel sure this has been stopped, but I don't really know. I decide to ask Akbar about this the next time he visits.

"Any more signs of the rats, Colonel?" Akbar asks as he enters my cell.

"No, I think they've run off to join the *Pasdaran* [Revolutionary Guards]."

"Oh, you'd better not say that to Hamid or Ahmad."

"What's new, Akbar?"

"Not very much. The Red Cross may be visiting

you soon. I do not know for sure. Our people are worried about security."

"Are you afraid the International Red Cross may be working for the CIA, too?"

"Yes, something like that." Akbar laughs as he speaks. He seems to enjoy my remarks about their paranoia and never seems to get irritated by them.

"Akbar, do you know that the total denial of information is in itself a form of cruel and unusual punishment?"

"Maybe, but there are things you are better off not knowing." Then he remembers something and reaches inside his field jacket pocket and pulls out a set of beads. "Do you know what this is?"

He is delicately holding an inexpensive, blue plastic set of rosary beads with a white plastic crucifix. A small Saint Christopher medal is attached to the lower end of the beads, just above the crucifix. "Yes, that's a set of rosary beads used by Catholics when they pray." I explain to him that there's a different thought or meditation associated with each bead; the thoughts are recited when praying. They usually describe some event or incident in the lives of Jesus and his mother, Mary.

"Are you Catholic?" he asks.

"No, but when I was a boy, the lady who took care of us while my mother taught school was Catholic, and she taught me about the rosary. The rosary is very sacred to Catholics, and most have one which they use in prayer. They usually are blessed by a priest."

Akbar stares at the rosary, appearing to concentrate on the plastic cross and the image of Jesus hanging on it. He is touched by the religious significance of the rosary and seems a little afraid to hold it. "Colonel, would you like to have this?" he asks, extending his right hand with the rosary. "If you would like it, please take it."

I take the rosary and look at it. Memories of my

youth in a predominantly Catholic neighborhood in Philadelphia race through my mind. I remember some of the young priests who used to play baseball with us, and I remember going to mass with Mother Ward, our baby sitter, when I was a very little boy. My love of God has always been nondenominational, but reflections of this sweet and loving lady and her strong religious example, her faith and goodness, bring tears to my eyes. How long it has been since I had a chance to attend church, to worship in the presence of others who believe in God and in His power and mercy.

"My friend, I am glad I found the rosary and gave it to you," Akbar says. "Please keep it; maybe you can use it when you pray for your family and your return to them."

"Thank you, Akbar; I promise I will keep it always . . . unless Hamid or one of his guards takes it from me."

"If you tell them what it is, they will not take it. They will not."

Akbar is not in a hurry today. He actually asks if he may sit on my mattress and visit awhile. He's in a reflective and talkative mood, and he tells me in detail the story of how he was dragged from his father's house and thrown in prison six years ago. He describes the trial he went through, the beatings, the various prisons he was in, and his release. His story is interesting and too consistent to be a lie. He doesn't complain about his time in prison. On the contrary, he says it made his faith in God stronger, and it hardened his resolve to fight for change in his country.

After a couple of hours, a voice outside my cell summons my jailer.

"Oh, I must go, it is getting late," says Akbar. "I did not realize how long we had been talking. *Khoda hafez* [goodbye]."

I think about Akbar's description of his prison ordeal and realize why he's different from the other terrorists. I'm fascinated with his story, which he told without being overly dramatic or adding phony heroics. While many of his fellow terrorists are hateful, sadistic men, he is sensitive and devoted to his cause. He really believes that they were justified in taking over the embassy, but essentially he is not a violent man. I wonder what will become of men like him when this ordeal is finally over. I sense there are things about this revolution that already have been a disappointment to him. He's naive. He doesn't realize that his deep religious beliefs are being used by power-hungry men to solidify their control of his country.

I look at the rosary for a long time. A gift from an Iranian terrorist.

It must be about two in the morning. I can hear the guard outside my door whispering to one of his buddies who is helping him pass the time. The guard on duty is a huge, dumb-looking young man with a big mouth and a foul disposition. He also is lazy. It's a major effort for him to take me to the toilet, and he doesn't try to hide his distaste for the chore. I decide to play a little game with them.

"Hello, is this Washington? This is Colonel Scott. Hello! Hello! Yes, I can hear you very well now; go on please."

I hear the two guards get up from their chairs and move closer to my door.

"Yes, you say Khomeini is a crazy old man and you will be bombing Iran soon. Yes, start off with Tehran, then the other cities."

I hear a guard run down the hall.

He's back in less than a minute with armed reinforcements. Five or six militants enter my cell. I pretend to be sleeping.

"Get up! Who were you talking to?"

I sit up in my bed on the floor and stretch my

arms at full length. "What are you talking about? I was asleep."

"You were talking to someone. How did you get a radio in here? Where is it?"

"You guys must be smoking something besides cigarettes. I was asleep." I'm hustled outside the cell and forced to spreadeagle against the wall. I can hear them searching my cell. Then they search me. They're really perplexed, but they find nothing. I'm taken back to my cell and the door is locked. I hear nothing outside. I wait about an hour. Still silence outside. Not even the sound of the guard moving his chair.

Another hour goes by. Time for more fun.

"Yes, this is Colonel Scott. I'll have to be very careful; they are listening outside my door."

The door is unlocked and opened in a flash. The light is turned on from outside. The big, dumb guard is frantic. "You have a radio in here; I heard you call Washington. Where is it?" He grabs me by the front of my T-shirt. It's all I can do to keep a straight face. He really believes I'm talking to someone. We go through the same routine again, then I'm put back in my cell. I fall asleep in silence. The guard is posted outside my door, listening for my next "call."

At about eight in the morning, my breakfast of bread and tea is delivered by my very sleepy-looking guard. He says that he is sure I have a radio, and he'll find it sooner or later. I tell him there is no radio, that he must be getting tired from taking too many people to the bathroom. He is not amused, but he still thinks I've found some way to communicate with Washington. Maybe if I continue this charade, they'll move me back with the rest of the hostages.

Ahmad, the militant leader with the American education, is acting totally out of character. He is actually speaking in conversational tones and not threatening me.

264

"We may move you to a better place, where you can see the sunshine and have some company. Would you like that?"

"Fine with me. Where am I going?"

"You will see. You must promise though, if you have a visitor, not to tell him where you have been until now."

"I will say nothing if you move me to a nice place where I can see daylight. I haven't seen daylight in more than five months. That's even worse than your Shah treated his enemies, isn't it?"

"I will not talk politics with you, Colonel. I am being nice, but you must promise not to say bad things about your treatment if I move you and there is a visitor."

"O.K., but who's coming to see us, the Imam?"

"No, he is much too busy with important things to bother with you, but you may have a visitor." Ahmad leaves the cell, saying he will be back to move me within an hour or so.

I wonder what this change of attitude is all about. And if I'm really getting a cellmate, who will it be?

12

AMERICAN EMBASSY, TEHRAN
APRIL 15 - 25, 1980

The light is painfully bright and blinding at first. It's ordinary daylight on a clear Tehran morning in spring, but I haven't seen the sun, a glimpse of daylight, the sky, or even a tree in five and a half months. The sun's rays, beaming through the barred Chancellery office window, radiate hope, optimism, and an awesome awareness of the presence of God that is at once soothing and overwhelming.

Ahmad removes my handcuffs, then leaves me alone. After months of darkened, unventilated cells, this is literally a breath of fresh air. I'll be able to tell when it's day and when it's night. I can breathe clean air and watch the changing seasons. Although my head aches and the intense light seems to sear the retina of my eyes, I move closer to the window. The sky is an infinite, cloudless, pale blue umbrella above the embassy gardens. The line where the trees meet the sky is like a work of art.

Slowly, I become aware of the songs of birds. Their serenade is the most perfect music I've ever heard. I stand mesmerized by it all, oblivious to the bars framing my window. Again, I think of lines from the "Rubáiyát":

Wake! For the Sun, who scatter'd into flight
The Stars before him from the Field of Night,
    Drives Night along with them from Heav'n, and strikes
The Sultán's Turret with a Shaft of Light.

Suddenly I'm aware of sounds outside my cell

door. I snap back to the reality of my circumstances and decide to have a look at this room to see what intelligence I can gather from its contents.

The noise from outside continues, but I'm left alone to examine the place. This was once the anteroom to the embassy administrative officer's office. It apparently has been occupied by other hostages — there are two mattresses on the floor, along with a desk and two straight-backed chairs, left over from before the embassy became a prison. The room is dirty and dusty, and the waste basket in the corner to the left of the door is overflowing with trash and papers.

The waste basket! It seizes my attention. I should be able to tell quite a bit from what's in it. I begin going through it carefully so that my jailers won't know what I'm doing. On top are sardine cans and evidence of other treats taken from the embassy cooperative store. Whoever was in this room before was pretty well cared for. I wonder if the room may have been used by off-duty guards. No — there are some torn papers written in English with a green felt-tip pen. And there are fragments of a memorandum to Hamid the Liar typed in English. I thumb through the paper fragments, each an inch square or so. There is one signed in the same green, felt-tip handwriting as the other paper. It says "Joe Subic."

Someone is fumbling with the lock on the outside of my door. I quickly dump the contents of the waste basket into my blanket, fold it over, sit on it, and try to look natural. It's Ahmad and my new roommate, with his head covered by a dirty white sheet. Ahmad removes the sheet and instructs the tall, lanky hostage to remove his blindfold. It's Bob Blucker.

I haven't seen Bob since we were hostages in north Tehran in early December of last year. He has lost more weight, looks as old as Khomeini, with his long, flowing white beard, and is just as morose as he was in those days when he drove the Iranians crazy with his anti-cigarette-smoke antics. Before Ahmad can leave the room, Bob tells him he doesn't like this setup at all. He would rather be back across the hall, on the front side of the Chancellery, where he had a room to himself.

Thanks a lot, Bob. Here I finally have someone to talk to and my cellmate tells the Iranians he would rather be alone. I decide to let it pass without comment. Bob is not my idea of the ideal roommate either, but he's all there is, and I'll get along with him. I ask him how he's been.

"I'm doing O.K., but I would rather be in the room I just left. It was cool and there was no smoke. And I was actually getting a suntan by opening the windows wide and catching the afternoon sun."

I tell Bob this is my first opportunity to see the daylight since we were captured, and he seems surprised. We compare notes on who we've seen, rumors we've heard, and our best guesses at what's happening both here and in the United States. Bob has received a lot more mail than I have. He's convinced that nothing will break in our situation until after the November elections in the U.S. I hope he's wrong, but I agree that it could take that long for any settlement. Blucker is a die-hard Republican who has nothing good to say about President Carter or his administration.

I sense that he's tired of talking, but I persist. It has been a long time since I've talked to another American, and I don't know how long it will last. I intend to take advantage of this opportunity. Bob obliges.

In mid-afternoon, Ahmad reappears. He is friendly and so soft-spoken that it is apparent he's on his best behavior. "You will be having some visitors very soon. They are from the International Red Cross. You must be nice to them." He is easier to see through than the plot in a cheap novel. "You have been well treated and well fed, so do not complain to the Red Cross."

"Is it O.K. to tell them if we have medical or dental problems?" I ask him sarcastically.

"You should have told us before, Colonel, if something is wrong with you."

"I have, several times, but I have been told it doesn't matter. Some of your people broke three of my teeth early in my interrogation. I'm concerned that one of these days an exposed nerve will begin to ache. I need to have some dental work done before than happens."

"As long as it does not hurt, it does not matter. We can't get a dentist to come here for you."

"That's O.K.; I don't mind leaving to get my teeth fixed. If you don't have a decent dentist left in Iran, I'd be happy to fly to Germany. I promise I'll come back."

"Don't be so smart. And don't forget, you will not tell the Red Cross where you have been until now."

Ahmad actually manages what must be for him a smile as he leaves the cell.

In less than ten minutes, our cell is crowded by a group of four International and local Red Cross representatives in neat business suits with clean, white, starched collars. The fifteen militants who accompany them smile and look at us as though we're their brothers. One of the bullies who worked me over during my interrogation is part of the group. He smiles and waves at me. I do not respond. He waves again, grinning broadly.

The senior Red Cross representative, a stocky middle-aged man from Switzerland, dressed in a smart-looking European-cut wool suit, surveys the room and reports his impression aloud. "This is not so bad."

Without looking at Ahmad and without hesitation, I shoot back, "No, *this* is not bad at all, but you should see where I was being kept until a few hours ago. This is my first chance to see daylight since this thing started."

Ahmad is nonplussed. He glares at me menacingly, but he says nothing and his glare quickly fades away in favor of his painted-on smile for the benefit of our visitors. I assume there will be hell to pay for my comment later, but I said it, and I'm glad. The Red Cross foursome did not miss my remarks; however, they apparently are trying to be nice to our captors and not cause a scene.

A Swiss team member who lives in Tehran passes out Red Cross message forms and tells us we can write a letter and he'll make sure it is mailed home. He winks at me as he volunteers additional information: He has given thousands of these forms to our captors during the past five and a half months, but has had none returned to him for mailing. He says to write a quick note and he'll have it picked up before he leaves the embassy.

The burly leader of the Red Cross visitors asks about health or medical problems. I seize the opportunity to request dental care for my broken teeth. An Iranian doctor accompanying the group interjects, "There will be no problem in having his teeth fixed." The Red Cross chief asks me to open my mouth. He does a quick check of my teeth and agrees that I need dental care. The Iranians, including Ahmad, nod and smile concurrence. These characters really know how to stage a show when it's to their advantage. I'm sure that I am no closer to seeing a dentist than I was the day Pig Face bashed the side of my jaw with his metal club.

The visit is over in less than ten minutes. The Red Cross people bid us farewell and tell us to take care of ourselves. The four Westerners head for the door, followed by the smiling entourage of militants.

As soon as the room is clear, I suggest to Bob that we take advantage of the guards' preoccupation with the visitors and piece together the Subic papers I dug out of the trash can. Bob concurs, and we set to work trying to sort out the tiny pieces by shape and color, as if we were working a jigsaw puzzle. Bob is patient and thorough. I suggest that he must be an experienced puzzle-solver, and he says he used to work them all the time when he was a kid.

Our work creates a good bit of tension; we have to be careful not to be caught piecing together the papers. Bob is much better at it than I am, so he suggests that I listen at the door in case one of the guards approaches. Finally, after an hour or so, Bob has completed his work. The typed page is a letter to Hamid the Liar from Joe Subic. In it, Joe suggests that arrangements be made to release him so he can return to America and "tell the American people the Iranian side of the story."

"It would be best to make it appear I had managed a successful escape," the letter says. "That way I would have a better chance to be on TV to tell your story and convince people to demand the return of the Shah." Joe even has a suggestion as to when the escape would be most appropriate. He apparently wrote this letter before Easter, while I was still in solitary, because he favors pulling his caper during the holiday period when interest in the hostages is high. He even lists those he thinks also should be considered for release, if a limited release is approved instead of the escape ploy. My name and Bob's are not on the list, which doesn't surprise either of us.

The paper written with the green felt-tip pen is even more startling and revealing. It's a list of questions Subic wrote for our captors to ask Colonel Tom Schaefer during his interrogation. One of our own people writing detailed follow-up questions on classified Defense Attaché activities over the past year for the benefit of Tom's interrogators! This is too much. My blood is boiling.

"Bob, let's study these, especially this one, very well. One of these days, we may be in a position to testify against this guy. And I hope we someday get a chance to tell Tom."

271

"Hard to believe, isn't it?" Bob says. "But there it is in green and white."

The food has improved considerably since I was moved to this aboveground cell. I'm sure they have a cook who has worked for Americans. Breakfast and supper have not changed, but the noon meal has been pretty good — spaghetti and meat sauce, hamburgers from the cooperative store, and lasagna. I wonder if this, coupled with my improved accommodations and the Red Cross visit, constitutes some sort of preparation for our release. Are they trying to fatten us up so they won't look so bad if we're set free? I decide to try to find out by working on the guards, especially Akbar.

He has stopped in to talk to me almost every day for the past week. His general mood seems to be pretty much upbeat. He claims there is a plan to turn us over to the Iranian government; that certainly would be a positive thing and very well could be the first step toward our release. Even though the Iranian government has been deeply involved in every facet of the hostage affair, condoning and supporting it from the start, they consistently have tried to make it appear an act of desperation by the Iranian people. To me, this is a typical Persian example of avoiding direct responsibility and future blame by pretending not to be involved. If we are turned over to the Iranian government, I don't see how they can justify holding us very much longer. The decision, of course, rests with Ayatollah Khomeini. If he tells our captors to turn us over to some other group, that's what they'll do. If he orders them to shoot us, they'll do that, too.

The latrine we're using is filthy. Somewhere along the line, the single lavatory drain got plugged. Instead of cleaning it, our captors removed the pipe and placed a plastic bucket under the sink to catch the draining water and waste. There's no hot water, and the single toilet, also clogged most of the time, is so dirty that it has become home for hundreds of filthy flies. As though that weren't enough, we are required to wash our plastic food bowls in this same, foul-smelling room. The large pans the cook uses to prepare our food also are cleaned here. Bob and I have been asked to do a little kitchen police work today. I've heard other hostages cleaning pans in the latrine on several occasions. Bob refuses to help, maintaining that it is beneath his dignity to scrub pans. I tell him it'll give us something to do and it may give us an opportunity to clean the filthy latrine at the same time. He still refuses, saying we should let someone else do it. It irks me that he won't help, but I accept the chore and go to work. I don't like it, but I refuse to live in filth if I can do something about it. The smell is sickening in the latrine. I ask the guard to get some steel wool, scouring powder, and rags from the cooperative. He produces the basic cleaning materials and I go to work.

I'm about half finished when Akbar appears.

"Colonel, it is not right for a colonel to clean latrines. Let me help you."

"I have only one rag," I tell him, "but if you can find another, feel free to pitch in. You could rip the dirty T-shirt off the guard in front of my cell. He needs to change it anyway."

"I will get a rag and come back to help."

Akbar is true to his word. He returns in about ten minutes with several rags and some ammonia. He's a good worker and, unlike most Moslems, doesn't seem offended by this dirty chore.

"Akbar, I always thought you people were afraid to touch anything in a latrine. Isn't that why your toilets are squatters and not sitters?"

"You are right in a way. A Moslem will not sit on a Western toilet because of fear of getting a disease. But there are times when a man must forget his pride and do dirty work out of necessity, as you are doing."

In about an hour, we have the place cleaner than it has been since the embassy occupation. Akbar says I do good work for a senior officer. We both laugh and I ask him what's new.

"There is some news, but I'm afraid it is not good for you."

"Tell me anyway. I can handle it."

He tells me that the Imam has ruled that we should remain with the "students" and not be turned over to the government. "I think the biggest problem is a reluctance on the part of the government to accept full responsibility for you. Releasing you will not be popular with the people, and nobody is willing to take that responsibility," he says.

"I can understand that, but if that attitude persists, we could be here forever."

"I hope not, but you are right. Your government has closed our embassy in Washington and sent the Iranian diplomats home, so there can be no negotiations in your country. And there is no way now for the Iranian side of the story to be told in your country. Carter was angry because you were not turned over to our government." Akbar seems to want to get all this off his chest. He's checking my reactions to his news, but he's not revealing any signs of resentment, only of concern.

"Your embassy in Washington should have been closed on the fourth of November, last year."

"And our diplomats taken hostage?"

"No, that would not be legal in America," I tell him. "We respect diplomatic immunity. If we took your people hostage, we would be as lawless as you were in attacking our embassy. We just could not do that in America, even if we wanted to, and I'm sure it was a strong temptation."

Akbar becomes more serious as he continues. "Carter has also threatened additional economic sanctions

274

against us, and he says if that does not lead to your release, he may use military force."

"I'm surprised that hasn't been done already. Any other American president would have given you a deadline for our release, then blasted hell out of your country."

"But then all of you would be killed."

"That's right, but the crisis would be over and people like you would think twice before pulling a stunt like this the next time."

"I think we would do it again under similar circumstances," he says. "We are not afraid to die. But this is foolish talk, Colonel. It will not come to that. Eventually you will be free again."

"Yes, but I may be too old by then to enjoy my freedom."

Akbar's big eyes fill with a sadness and shame I have seen in them before. "You will not be too old. You must be patient. If you are too old, I will be too old also."

"You're right — you started this game and you're stuck with it. Your future depends on the action of others, and so does mine."

Akbar appears in deep thought for a moment, then manages a smile as he begins to recite in Persian, *"But helpless Pieces of the Game He plays / Upon his Checkerboard of Nights and Days . . ."*

I join him in completing the quatrain: *"Hither and thither moves, and checks, and slays, / And one by one back in the Closet lays."* We both laugh. Akbar is surprised that I know Khayyám in Farsi. "My friends would say, you must be CIA if you know the poets in our language," Akbar says, and then becomes more serious. "But I do not believe you are CIA. You are a soldier and I think you must have loved my country almost as much as I do . . . at least before you were taken hostage, you did."

"I had many friends here. My son was born

here. Yes, I guess I loved Iran. Your takeover has not changed the feeling I have for your people. I cannot hate your country for what you did."

"Colonel, I have watched you and I do not believe you hate me, any more than I hate you." Akbar glances at his watch. We have worked and talked longer than he realized. "I must go; it is getting late. I will take you to your room."

Bob is napping and I have time to stare out the window and think about my exchange with Akbar. In the world in which we live, things are not all black or white. There are shades of gray that must be seen and understood if we are to keep from blowing up our planet. We need not agree with the views of others, but we should try to understand their motivations and their feelings. It is, indeed, ironic that I can exchange philosophies with this terrorist, using lines from one of his country's poets, without either of us misunderstanding the other. Perhaps, beyond the polarization of men that develops from political, linguistic, and national differences, we all are essentially the same human creations of our Maker. I do not regret having learned Persian; this ordeal would be even worse if I didn't have the advantage of knowing the language of my captors. But, on the other hand, if I had not studied Persian, I probably would not have been in Iran when the embassy was invaded. I almost laugh at the thought.

I'm haunted by Akbar's revelations. I do not believe economic sanctions will result in the martyr-worshipping Iranians bowing to our release. They welcome sacrifice and challenge. Even if wiser heads recognize the damage a boycott will inflict on the already shaky economic situation here, the masses will not allow our release in the face of a threat. They're stubborn and full of pride, and they really do believe in the value of martyrdom. And if our president uses military force, we will be among the first to die. The eye-for-an-eye philosophy in vogue here will see to that. But if President Carter were planning some kind of rescue mission, why would he tip off the Iranians by threatening military action? He's probably not planning anything, I surmise. Maybe he has decided simply to wait the Iranians out, hoping they'll tire of the whole affair. Of course, Akbar and some of the others have said that if it goes on too long, the Iranians will have trials and possibly execute some of us to force Carter's hand.

There are so many possibilities, and most of them portend little likelihood of our getting out of Tehran alive. What I told Akbar is true: We are merely pawns, and there's nothing I can do to change that or to improve my chances of staying alive. Perhaps I'm becoming a fatalist, but there's serenity in reducing the situation to these simple terms.

13

AMERICAN EMBASSY, TEHRAN
APRIL 26, 1980

It has been one of my best mornings as a hostage. I'm still enchanted by the sight of the tranquil sky and the beautiful evergreens. I'm sure my cellmate questions my mental competence, because I spend so much time sitting silently, peering out the barred window of our room. But these hours and precious days of daylight have a tranquilizing effect on me. Never have I realized so keenly the beauty and greatness of God's work. I cherish the eleven days I've been in this cell.

When it's time to begin my daily physical exercise routine, I do my push-ups and sit-ups and settle for an hour or so of running in place. As I begin my run, I face the window and transfer all my conscious thoughts from the present predicament and location to another place and time. My imagination transports me half a world away to Stone Mountain. The trees in the embassy yard are not the Georgia pines I prefer, but they'll do. I'm running counterclockwise around Stone Mountain now, and the lake is as smooth as glass. The weather is warm and there are other joggers along my route. It has taken me less time than usual to make the trip, and the scenery I see in the park as I run is in sharp focus. I see a beautiful, long-haired blonde running in the opposite direction. She's in good shape and is running fast — probably a seven-minute mile. She's lovely as she prances along proudly, smiling at me as we pass. Is she smiling to be nice, or is she smiling because she knows she's running faster than I am? My mind jumps back to the present for a moment, and I laugh as I realize why she appears so lovely: I haven't seen a female in five and a half months. Of course, she's a composite of all that I remember as beautiful in the opposite sex.

I pan back to Stone Mountain. I turn left at the bait hut and start up the hill toward the camping area. Today the hill seems to be easier than usual, but I subconsciously take shorter, more deliberate steps anyway to compensate for the uphill pull. I can almost feel the pull of the hill in my calves as I run in place. I'm serene as I reach the bridge and view the lake to my left. The paddle boat, with its cargo of tourists, is lazily making its way around the smooth blue body of water. As I run in place, I'm pondering my schedule for the rest of the day after I complete my run. My mental excursion is a total success — I am, for the moment, no longer a prisoner in Tehran; I am *home!* I'm beginning to hyperventilate, but I want to keep going, because I know that when I stop, I'll be a prisoner in the American Embassy in Tehran again. I want to defer that reality as long as possible, so I continue to run for another ten minutes. Finally, I'm too tired to continue. I stop, and instantly I return to the realities of the present. I'm still here in a prison cell.

About mid-afternoon, there's a dramatic increase in activity in the parking lot behind the Chancellery. Bob and I try to see what's going on without permitting our captors to see us peering out the window. Most of the windows have been painted black, but for some reason they haven't gotten around to painting ours yet, and we don't want to draw unnecessary attention to this fact.

Several van-type vehicles are being loaded by the guards under the supervision of a mullah. It looks as though some of the "students" are going on a camping trip or some sort of pilgrimage. Various camping gear is being loaded, along with blankets and boxes. There's very little talking as the guards busily load the vans. I see several walkie-talkie FM radios being checked and loaded, and various weapons being placed inside the front seats of the vans. The windows of the vans have been painted black, except for the front windshields, and they're putting some kind of curtains between the front seats and the interiors. We're obviously going on a trip, and it must be a long one — otherwise, why all the gear? I'm puzzled. Are we going to be driven to the Turkish or Iraqi border to be released? Are we going to be taken to the airport? No, that's not logical; if we were only going to the airport, we wouldn't need all the sleeping gear and supplies.

I note an air of caution and quiet among the guards. They're more serious than they usually are when they think they're out of sight of their captives. They seem to be afraid of something. Has their bubble burst? Have they run into trouble with the government authorities here? Are they going to simply load up and desert us? If so, what will happen to us? The possibilities are limitless, and most of those that come to mind don't provide much hope for our safe release.

Shortly after dark, and before our usual supper of soup, we hear shuffling in the parking lot, like we hear when blindfolded hostages are moved from place to place. We turn out our lights so we can see outside without making our surveillance obvious. It's unmistakable — they are moving some of us out of the building and into the waiting vans.

Hamid the Liar enters our cell about an hour later. So far, none of the vehicles has left the embassy grounds.

"Roll everything up in your blankets; you may be moving," he says. I immediately fire a barrage of questions at him in Persian, hoping to catch him off guard and elicit some pertinent information on our impending "trip." Hamid doesn't bite. He's even more elusive than usual. "Just pack and get ready. You may move; then you may not move at all. You may move only to another room right here. We do not know your destination yet — it will be decided and then I will let you know." He spins around and out the door. Then, in a split second, he returns and tells us to pack only two books and one blanket. I ask him why we can't take several books and both blankets; he smirks and says, "Everything you need will be available as soon as you get where you are going."

Fifteen minutes after Hamid's visit, Ahmad comes in and tells us to pack everything we want to take with us, including any extra clothing we have and both blankets. He says we can take all the books we can carry, because it may be a while before we again have access to reading material. I complain that we haven't had supper, and Ahmad seems surprised. He pivots and asks one of the guards about supper in Farsi. The guard pleads ignorance, but Ahmad sticks his head inside the door and says supper is on the way. I wonder aloud how he fathomed that bit of information from a guard who said he didn't know. Ahmad tells me to shut up and not ask so many questions. "Just pack all your things and be ready to go; you will be fed somewhere, if God wills." He's in over his head and is having difficulty coping with the administrative requirements of this apparently unscheduled move.

About an hour after supper, Akbar comes to our cell. He also looks more severe than usual. He has a clipboard and obviously is writing our names on some kind of manifest. I ask him questions, too, but he's totally unresponsive except to say we should take everything we can carry. I tell him of our conflicting orders from Hamid the Liar and Ahmad. Akbar responds with a warm, pensive smile. "Just do as I say. I will be going with you. Hamid does not know what he is talking about. Take whatever you want, and I will see you later." That is the only good news we've heard so far today.

It must be about eleven o'clock at night when Hamid, Ahmad, and Akbar enter our cell with two other militants carrying automatic rifles. Akbar, Hamid, and Ahmad are wearing sidearms, which is most unusual. They usually enter our cells unarmed except when there has been trouble. The blatant, open exhibition of revolvers on these three is surely an indication that they're very worried about their own security.

Bob and I are blindfolded and a blanket is draped over my head. While we're standing in the hall, there's a flurry of whispering among the Iranians as they pass last-minute instructions and bid each other farewell. Apparently some are going with us while the others stay behind or go somewhere else. Are we being split into small groups? I'm searched thoroughly before being loaded into a waiting vehicle. I am conscious of another individual to my left; I don't know who it is, but I presume it's another hostage. In a moment, another person is seated to my right. One of the guards orders me in English to put my hands in front of me. I feel the cool steel of the handcuffs tighten around my wrists, and almost simultaneously my feet are bound with rope. I realize that I'm handcuffed to the people on either side of me. The blanket is removed from my head, but with the blindfold still tightly in place, I can't see anything except an occasional flash of light.

Suddenly I hear the sound of cameras clicking, and I see the light of a flashbulb. They're taking pictures of us in the vehicles. The guards change places several times, and each time additional pictures are snapped. It's like a group of hunters or fishermen having their pictures taken with their prizes. Finally the van pulls out from behind the embassy Chancellery. I hear my captors talking on the walkie-talkie in the cab of the van. There are three different voices talking. Pretty soon it's obvious that we have a vehicle in front of us, with a radio, and a trail vehicle behind us — just like a moving military convoy. I'm not sure, but the road surface and the initial absence of hills seem to indicate that we're going west toward the airport. My heart jumps for a moment as I contemplate the possibilities. Is there a plane waiting there to whisk us to freedom? But then the traffic gets lighter and the grade steeper, and these hopes are dashed. The engine strains slightly and the driver shifts to a lower gear. We must be heading north, toward some location where our ordeal will continue.

Our driver becomes a man possessed when he reaches the open road. He must be doing at least sixty-five as he banks into the sharp curves, causing the three of us manacled together to lean from side to side as a single body. I'm not sure who is on my right, but from earlier mumbling, I'm fairly certain that Sam Gillette is joined by the handcuffs on the left. "Is that you, Sam?" I whisper. "How are you doing?" The guard can't hear my muffled whisper because of the noisy bouncing of the van. "This is Chuck Scott. How are you doing, Sam? This is Sam, isn't it?" I say speaking softly and carefully. I tug slightly on the handcuff on my left wrist.

Finally, he replies. "Yeah, this is Sam; who is this?"

I try to be clearer in my speech without raising my voice. "This is Chuck Scott."

"Oh, Colonel Scott. How are you doing, sir? I haven't seen you since the Mushroom Inn in early March. We heard you, Colonel Holland, and Al were put in solitary for communicating. Is that right?"

"Yeah, that's correct; word is that one of our own people blew the whistle on us. I haven't seen Al or Lee since we were hauled out of the Mushroom on March 4. I'm doing fine, but I'd give a month's pay to know where we're headed and why."

"Don'ta - espeak!" A guard behind me pokes the barrel of a weapon into the back of my neck, ending our brief exchange. "You must not be speaking; only sit without talking!" I decide to answer our guard so others can hear my voice, hoping this may facilitate our communication later. "I was only asking the man at my left to give me a little more room. It's crowded and uncomfortable here in the middle. Where are we going?"

The gun barrel pushes punishingly into my neck again, but I've accomplished my purpose. The guard twists his weapon deeper to emphasize his warning. "You must be quiet, Colonel, or you will be punished. You will find out soon enough where you are going. It does not matter anyway."

For the next hour, we sit quietly, swaying back and forth as the van continues to negotiate the snakelike curves of what is apparently a mountain road.

Another hour or so passes without incident. I'm tired and I have to go to the bathroom; we haven't had a rest break, even though the van has stopped several times. It seems that the guards are afraid that either they are being followed or may be ambushed. They're in frequent communication by walkie-talkie with the lead and trail vehicles, and about every half hour they turn off the road, stop, get out of the vehicles, and have a short discussion in whispers. I'm unable to hear what they say, and this frequent stopping adds to the drama and uncertainty of our ride.

When the leader in our van talks on the radio, he's trying very hard to speak softly so we can't overhear. He's pretty successful, but I still can hear the incoming voices fairly clearly. *"Movazeb boshein, momkenny commando dar oonjus!"* [Be careful, there could be commandos there!] What on earth is this all about? What commandos? I've never before heard Iranians use that word except to describe Western military forces. Are they talking about some opposition group? I don't think so. But why would they be worried about foreign — American — commandos unless they have information about some sort of raid?

There must be at least one other hostage in the vehicle, because I've heard him coughing. Finally, in a fit of temper, he asks the terrorists not to smoke. It is, without a doubt, Bob Blucker. Bob also has to go to the bathroom. He's told to shut up, but he doesn't.

"Damn it, I have to go to the bathroom. You people act like you're transporting a load of pigs to the market. Why can't we stop and take a leak?" Bob is really upset and I can understand why. I chime in, too.

"Ma boyard be toilet" [We have to go to the toilet], I say in Farsi. Our guards are not having any of this.

"Shut up! We do not have time to stop every time you want to go to the toilet. We are not on vacation. You must wait!"

I figure there are at least four Iranians in the van, all armed. One of them also has a knife or bayonet, which he pushes at my back every time I make a move.

We stop again. This time we must be near some houses, perhaps in a small village, because as soon as we pull up, dogs begin to bark. The militant in the right front seat gets out of the vehicle and slams the door. The brief moment of fresh air while the door is open is a welcome relief from the heat and putrid air inside the van. The Iranians are dirty and sweaty, and so are we. I'm getting more tired and uncomfortable. I have a headache from the blindfold and the motion of the vehicle. I ask again for permission to go to the toilet, and Bob jumps on the bandwagon.

"Damn it, I have to go to the toilet," he says. "If you won't let me out, give me a bottle!" Bob is really adamant now, but it does no good. My personal antagonist decides to probe the back of my neck again with his bayonet. He pushes just hard enough to impress me without actually breaking the skin.

We've been stopped for about fifteen minutes; this is the longest coordination parley so far. I wonder why they don't let us out of the vehicle to go to the bathroom. What difference could it possibly make to them? Unless they're deliberately trying to be even crueller than usual. I can't relax at all — chains on my wrists, ropes on my feet, and pressure on my bladder. Bob Blucker is in the same predicament, from what I can hear of his utterances to his guard. He, too, is getting angry.

Finally we move out again, this time climbing a long, steep grade. It's still dark, and I tell myself to be alert for daybreak so I can sense the direction of the brightest light, which will tell me precisely which direction we're moving in. More than an hour passes, and I hurt all over. My head is throbbing and my stomach aches. I decide to give it another try — a serious try. I jerk my hands together and manage to pull my blindfold loose. "Damn it, we have to go to the bathroom!" I shout. Bob Blucker, Sam, and Don Sharer — the previously unidentified hostage to my right — join in. I immediately feel cold steel pierce the back of my neck. I turn to face my assailant and see that he's a short, well-built militant I haven't seen in months. He was one of the guards who worked me over during my interrogation; I recall that he enjoyed his work. He sneers at me as he struggles to replace my blindfold. "If you do that again, you will be killed; you are not allowed to take that off. You are a pig!" He is livid. I feel a trickle of blood flowing down the back of my neck onto my shoulder. A voice from the front of the vehicle tells the guard to sit back down and not hurt me. It is Akbar's voice.

There is a long argument between the sadistic guard and Akbar in guttural Farsi, but it's unmistakable from the discussion that Akbar is the boss. He finally agrees with the guard that I should be punished for taking off my blindfold, but not until we arrive at our destination. We seem to grind along forever on this leg of our trip. The guards have settled down; one of them in the rear of the vehicle is snoring. My mind races to thoughts of escape, but with the handcuffs and the bonds on our legs, it's impossible. Not once since we became hostages has there been even the slimmest opportunity to make an escape. These guys understand security.

Dawn is breaking; we've been on the road eight or nine hours. Don and I covertly confirm our observation that we're moving north-northwest. Judging by the speed and length of our tedious ride, we will run out of Iranian territory within a couple of hours. Is that good or bad? For a while I had hoped that we were headed for the Russian or Turkish border and possibly release, but now I don't think so. The suspense adds to our feeling of anxiety and terror. I can't rule out the possibility that we're being taken to some remote part of the country where we will be either imprisoned or executed. And a rescue attempt — which I gave up on months ago — or retaliation for our executions will be virtually impossible if we're spread all over the country. I know other vehicles were loaded at the embassy, and some of them left before we did. I doubt that they all were headed in the same direction, based on the security concerns we've overheard.

It is broad daylight and we seem to be in heavy traffic. I hear truck horns blaring along the highway in both directions and can feel the vibration as we're passed by vehicles travelling in the opposite direction. The traffic noise continues to increase as we seem to leave the major road and wind through city streets, turning right, then left, then right again. We stop, apparently at a traffic light, and I hear people on the street talking. Some are speaking Farsi and others are speaking a dialect of Turkish. We must be somewhere in Azarbaijan Province, I calculate. I try to figure the time it takes us to get through the town. If it's a large town, we must be passing through Tabriz. If it *is* Tabriz and we pass through the town to the north, we may be headed for the Aras River and the Soviet border. If we head west from the city, we may be headed for the Turkish border. Maybe I gave up hope of our release too soon. Then again, the militant who stuck me in the neck probably would not have been as nasty if we were going to be released. We're either going to jail somewhere in Azarbaijan, or we're going to be tried and executed here. I am physically and emotionally exhausted . . . almost back to the state I reached several times during my interrogation and during the first mock firing squad. I want to live very much, but I'm not sure how much more of this I can handle. I hurt all over. I'm hungry. I still need to go to the bathroom. My headache seems to be getting worse — a combination of the blindfold, the movement, the bad air inside the van, and the lack of sleep.

Another half hour or so passes and we still seem to be in the city. In fact, the traffic seems to be heavier as we move deeper into the urban area. I hear children laughing and speaking Turkish. Finally the vehicle stops, and someone tells Akbar to go inside for a meeting with Mullah Mosavi. The same voice orders the other guards to keep an eye on us. After about fifteen minutes, we're led from the vehicle and inside a building, where we're told to sit on the floor. I decide to make my toilet requirements known one more time, and maybe in the process I can learn more about where we are. "I still have to go to the bathroom," I blurt out.

There's a hand on my shoulder. The owner of the hand squeezes, but not very hard. "Colonel, you can go to the bathroom in just a few minutes. You will be staying here for a while, so you can rest." It's Akbar speaking in a firm but pleasant voice. My anger subsides as I recall his argument with the other guard several hours ago. He actually tried to help me by keeping his buddy off my back. I can't seem to be angry at Akbar.

My blindfold is removed. I'm sitting on the floor of a living room in a middle-class home. All the furniture has been removed except for a built-in, wooden display cabinet, very much like those seen in a European living room. All of its contents have been removed. There's a Tabriz rug on the floor. Don, Sam, and Bob Blucker are in the room with me. There's also a mullah, dressed in dark robes with a .45-caliber pistol stashed in his beltline tunic. His arms are folded across his chest and he's smiling. He looks at me directly and speaks in Farsi.

"Welcome. You will be safe here. We will not hurt you. You will be fed and cared for as long as you are our guests — and you will be our guests here until your government decides to send back the Shah for trial by the people of Iran."

I answer that the Shah will not be returned as a result of Iran's taking Americans hostage, so we'll be here forever.

"Then, Colonel, you *will* be here forever," he replies.

"As long as we're going to be your 'guests,' do you suppose we might be able to go to the toilet?"

The mullah is initially offended by my terse comment, but Akbar comes to my rescue: "It has been a long time; we have been on the road and were unable to let them go to the toilet. Please forgive the colonel; he is upset and tired." The mullah instructs the guards to take us to the toilet one by one.

I feel a lot better when I return, even though I'm still tired and hungry. The mullah is almost friendly. We talk about the United States, where I'm from, and what I was doing at the embassy before we became hostages. He tells me that he was one of the leaders of the revolution in this area. At this point, he obviously decides to test me.

"Colonel, you do not know where you are, do you?" The mullah is playing with me; he's sure I have no idea where I am.

"Yeah, I know where I am. I'm in Tabriz."

Mullah Mosavi, leader of the revolutionary court in Tabriz and one of the architects of the anti-Shah and finally the revolutionary movement in all of Azarbaijan Province, is stunned. He was sure that with the tight security, the blindfolds, the frequent stops, and the painted windows in the van, I would have no idea where I was. He's angry — not at me, but at the guards.

"How did he find out where he is? Did one of you tell him? Wasn't he blindfolded all the way? What is wrong with you people? Can't you do anything right?"

Akbar responds without getting either excited or

intimidated by the mullah's outburst. "The colonel has served in Iran before, and he knows the country better than most of us. I am sorry he knows where he is, but what difference can it make?"

Mullah Mosavi takes the cue and softens his tone as he continues. "When did you serve in Iran before? Have you been to Tabriz during the Shah's time?"

I tell him that I have been to Tabriz many times in the past and always considered it one of the most beautiful cities in his country. He is taken off guard, but seems to be enjoying our discussion. He tells me that he has not known very many foreigners who spoke Farsi, especially Americans. I know he's an important man in Tabriz, but I also know he has a killer's instincts. He has sent scores of opponents to the firing squad in his role as head of the Revolutionary Court, and he is known as a tough fighter and a stern disciplinarian. He has an air of authority about him that is unusual in Iran, and he obviously has the respect of the militants. I decide to be as inoffensive as possible with him; I may learn more by being friendly.

A helper enters the room with bread and white goat cheese. He asks me to tell the others to eat, and he will bring tea. The mullah leaves, as do the guards, giving us a chance for the first time in months to swap gossip and try to figure out why we've been moved to Tabriz.

14

TABRIZ, IRAN
APRIL 27 - JULY 11

We have been here in Mullah Mosavi's home for two days. The food has been pretty good and we each have had a hot shower in the mullah's bath. I've been listening to the guards whenever possible, but so far I haven't been able to learn anything specific about our latest move or our future. It's obvious that something big has happened to put our captors on edge, but other than the talk about commandos I overheard on the way here, there's no information about what it is.

Akbar and three or four others enter the room. They're all armed. "Get ready to move," Akbar says. "You are going somewhere else where you will be safe."

"What are we going to be safe from?" I ask Akbar.

He tells me simply, "Don't worry about it, you will like the place you are going."

The trip this time is a short one, lasting no more than thirty minutes. We're still somewhere in Tabriz. When my blindfold is removed next, I'm sitting in a steel and concrete vault. There are American-type 110-volt sockets on the wall. That's all I need to discern that I'm in the communications vault of the American Consulate. I've been in this vault before, when stationed in Iran in the sixties. The desks and the communications equipment are missing, but the vault looks the same. There are no windows, and the heavy steel door provides the only entrance. There is an air-conditioning unit on the upper part of the wall, about ten feet above the floor. Otherwise, the room is empty except for the chair I'm sitting in. Akbar enters and removes my handcuffs. He asks if I'm all right. I tell him I am and then I ask him if we're in the American Consulate. He gives me an affirmative reply, instructing me not to let the other guards know that I'm aware of where I am. He says this vault was once the local CIA office, and admitting that I know my precise location may be considered as "proof" of my involvement with the CIA, if I'm eventually placed on trial.

Big Ali, an athletic-looking Tehrani with an unusually good sense of humor, bounces into the vault with a chair on top of his head. *"Salam, Sarhang, hala shoma chetora?"* [Hello, Colonel, how are you?] Before I can reply, Ali places the chair next to mine and tells me to say hello to Bob Blucker. Blucker is not in the chair, but Ali goes through the motions of removing a blindfold and handcuffs from his imaginary figure. I saw Ali only a couple of times before the trip to Tabriz, but I have the impression that he's one of the few who doesn't take either this situation or himself too seriously. I think he would rather be playing soccer or lifting weights than acting as a jailer. I can't resist the temptation to joke with Big Ali.

"If you were a decent man, you would offer Mr. Blucker a cigarette." Ali knows of Bob's phobia about tobacco, too. He reaches into his pocket, pulls out an American cigarette, lights it, and pretends to be handing it to Blucker's ghost in the chair. He drops the cigarette and laughingly tells me Bob refused the smoke. Just then, Akbar and a little, bespectacled weasel of a man named Mahmoud lead Bob Blucker in and get him settled in the usual way.

As soon as the guards leave, I tell Bob where we are. We both speculate on why we've been brought all the way up here from Tehran. I tell him that Tabriz is almost five hundred miles from Tehran, and it's within an hour's drive to the Aras River and the Soviet border and about two hours from the Turkish border.

"This is interesting," says Bob, "but what does it mean?" I admit that I don't know.

A local Turkic-speaking man enters with two of the guards. He looks over our new cell and tells the guards in guttural Farsi that he will return in a few hours with styrofoam mattresses for us.

Later, Akbar returns with a notebook and pencil. He says we may be here until the hostage crisis is over, one way or another, and promises to make it as easy for us as possible. He will have a plumber come and set up a place where we can shower regularly, and he says he's trying to get permission to set up an exercise area outside, where we can get sun and fresh air when circumstances permit. I ask about mail and he writes a note before replying, " I will see what I can do to have your mail sent up here from Tehran. This move was not planned, so there was no time to worry about your letters."

"If the move up here was not planned, why was it done?"

"Colonel, you ask too many questions," Akbar laughs. "Maybe later I will be able to tell you more." He's still wearing his holstered pistol, and his field jacket pockets are bulging with bullets.

I ask him why he's carrying the gun. "Are you guys afraid of an American invasion or something?"

Akbar is startled by my question. "Maybe we have already had an invasion by your army, and maybe we repulsed the invasion."

"I don't think you would be able to stop it if it did come, but I also don't think you have to worry about an American ground attack. If a decision is made to punish Iran for taking us hostage, all we have to do is push a few buttons in the United States or aboard our fleet of submarines, and your cities will be reduced to rubble. There's no need to risk American lives just to teach your country a lesson."

Akbar is uneasy. He wants to say something, but he hesitates, in deep thought. He stalls for a minute in awkward silence after my boastful assessment of U.S. military prowess, and then he says, "I hope that does not happen, but I am afraid you might be right. Your president is getting impatient, and he is crazy enough to start a war. If he does, though, we are not afraid."

"Akbar, there are cemeteries all over the world full of men who were not afraid, but they died anyway."

Akbar has heard enough. *"Shayyad"* [Maybe] — he stops for a second before blurting out the rest of his sentence — "your president has already learned that invading Iran can cost American lives."

"What is that supposed to mean?"

"Exactly what I said. Maybe I will tell you more later."

Akbar is playing "I've got a secret." There is something he's dying to tell, something he's proud of, and yet he doesn't feel free to reveal it. I stare directly at him and say nothing. Bob asks what we've been talking about, but rather than translate for him, I decide to see just how much English Akbar understands. "Bob, he is talking, but he has said nothing."

Akbar understands. He says in Farsi, "I am sorry, I cannot tell you anything. Do you like Persian dates?"

I ask Bob if he likes dates, and he says yes. "Yes, Akbar, we both like dates."

"Give me a bowl, and I will get some for you." Akbar takes my bowl and departs. Bob asks why he only wanted one bowl, and I tell him I don't know.

Akbar returns in a few minutes with the plastic bowl full of black Persian dates. They're speckled with the yellow straw used in packing them for shipment but otherwise look appetizing. I offer the bowl to Bob, but he refuses. Akbar asks if I would be willing to help him learn English while we're in Tabriz. He says it should be more relaxed here than in Tehran, and he should have more time to study. I tell him I would be happy to help him with his English, and I suggest that he bring in some American magazines to be used in our language sessions. Akbar smiles and says, "I will try to get some recent copies of *Time* and *Newsweek*; however, I will have to cut out all items concerning Iran."

"Akbar, I've told you this before, but the total withholding of information from us is in itself a prime example of cruel and unusual punishment. In America, even people in prison are permitted to read magazines and watch television. Many prisoners have their own radios. You are cruel to deny us news. If we are ever freed, it will not look good for you or for Islam."

Akbar is touched by my argument. "I understand what you are saying, and in a way I agree with you, but I must follow the rules. Our rules are that you are to be told nothing. I am sorry."

Then he changes the subject. "The other students want you to be punished for your bad behavior in the truck. You should not have gotten angry and removed your blindfold. They want to beat you and put you in a very small cell alone for a month. I have told them this would be against Islam and would not change the way you feel, but you will have to be careful, or they will outvote me."

"I appreciate your help. Are you in charge up here?"

"Yes, except for matters of security, I am in charge." For these matters, I find out, they have a representative from their security committee, which is composed of a select group of hardline, self-styled experts on internal security. They're the ones who make the rules against talking and communication in general. They also make sure we're blindfolded and handcuffed each time we're moved from place to place, even to go to the bathroom. The few members of this committee whom I've been able to identify are totally oppressive, paranoid, and suspicious. The militants also have a propaganda committee, a mail and censorship committee, a committee for care and feeding of the hostages, and a leadership and planning committee. Akbar is a member of several of these functional groups but has no voice on the security committee. Anything he wants to do to make our confinement a little more bearable first must be approved by the security people. While he seems to have a good bit of influence with most of the other militants, I sense that he is watched closely by the security committee. Even among these revolutionaries and terrorists, Big Brother is always watching.

After Akbar leaves, I ask Bob why he refused the dates — if it was because we would be using the same bowl. That's right, he says. The next time he will give *his* bowl when the dates are offered. I find his response downright odd, considering our circumstances, but I decide not to make an issue of the dates.

It is May Day, and there's an ear-piercing demonstration outside the building. I hear hundreds of voices screaming the usual chants of "Death to America! Death to the Shah! Death to the hostages!" The people of Tabriz know we're here, and that doesn't do anything for my sense of safety.

Suddenly our cell is alive with activity. An elderly, white-bearded man in the garb of an ayatollah and several mullahs enter and take positions around the room. They're accompanied by the usual entourage of militants, all smiling and on their best behavior. Akbar says the old man is the "Imam Jomieh of Tabriz," the leader of the Friday prayers for Tabriz. He looks like Ayatollah Khomeini and is treated with similar respect and awe by both the clerics and the militants. Akbar says that he speaks no English and asks

296

that I translate his comments for Bob. Mullah Mosavi is among the robed mullahs standing to the left of the ayatollah. He smiles and waves at me like an old friend. I return his wave. The old man gestures for his flock to sit, and at once the militants all sit on the floor in the cross-legged position. The mullahs continue to stand.

When there is silence, the ayatollah begins to speak in a whisper. At first he welcomes Bob and me to Tabriz and says we will not be harmed by the people, as long as we obey our captors and do not try to escape or do anything foolish. Then the volume of his aged, raspy voice increases as he goes into the standard rhetoric about demanding the return of the Shah. I translate about half of what he's saying for Bob, but there's no sense in getting bogged down in repeating his disjointed statements. The old man goes on and on, building up to a dramatic climax, in which he assures all that their cause is just and that God is clearly on their side. The group applauds. Bob and I do not. Akbar tells the ayatollah that I speak good Farsi and asks him if he will consent to speak directly to me. The old man says he sees nothing wrong with talking to me and asks if I have any questions.

"Yes, as a matter of fact, I do wish to ask you a question. You continue to demand the return of the Shah for our freedom. Do you not realize that this will never happen? If you persist in your demands, my government will never submit to blackmail, and we will be your prisoners forever. Is this what your revolution and Islam are all about — holding innocent people in bondage for revenge?"

The ayatollah raises his eyebrows in surprise, and there is a rumble of disbelief in his audience. I glance around the room. Mullah Mosavi is still smiling — he is not upset by my comments. The old ayatollah's surprise wanes, and he moves closer to me, followed by his mullah protectors.

"Colonel, I understand your concern, and I will

be honest with you. We no longer really want the Shah; he is nothing to us." There is another murmur of disbelief throughout the room. The militants and mullahs shift positions awkwardly in anticipation of the ayatollah's next revelation.

The old man says that Iran is being very realistic in this situation; all it wants is a promise of noninterference in Iran's internal affairs, a withdrawal of American military forces from the Persian Gulf, a return of the Shah's money (which he claims was stolen from the people of Iran), and the cancellation of all debts and claims against Iran. He says that if these can be agreed to, then Iran will be willing to talk about freeing us.

When he finishes answering my question, there is loud applause. Akbar nudges me and says it would be nice if I thanked the ayatollah for this good news by applauding too. I am elated — they at least have backed off on their demand for the Shah's head, and there has been no mention of trials or a demand for an apology for alleged American crimes in Iran during the Shah's reign. I translate quickly for Bob and join the others in applauding. The ayatollah has just given me more information in a few minutes than I have been able to gather throughout this entire ordeal. On seeing me applaud, the militants and the mullahs begin to clap all over again. Mullah Mosavi, applauding with the rest, catches my eye and smiles. The ayatollah takes his leave, saying, "If God wills, and your government comes to its senses, you will not be our guests forever."

Mosavi approaches me, asks how I am doing, and extends his hand. It seems crazy, but I shake his hand. He says it's nice to see me again. I tell him it's easy to see me — I'm here all the time. He laughs, places a hand on my shoulder, and suggests it will all be over very soon, "if God wills."

One of the guards delivers our breakfast of

bread and tea and informs us that we must be ready to go outside for *"Hava-khore"* [literally, *eating air*, but it's an idiom for *fresh air*] in fifteen minutes. He says we must both go or neither of us can go, and we must be ready when he returns to escort us. I quickly put on my slacks and shirt, eat my bread, and drink my tea. Bob hasn't started his breakfast and is moping around as though he's in no hurry.

"Hey, Bob, you'd better hurry. If both of us aren't ready, we won't be taken outside. You do want to get some fresh air, don't you?"

"Frankly, I couldn't care less. I'm not going to hurry through my breakfast just to go outside."

"Fine, but I want to go, and if one goes, the other has to go, too. We both have to be ready."

"That's your problem; I'm not going to hurry." I am frustrated. I can't understand his lack of consideration. It is the only chance we've had to see the daylight and the outside of the building. As I think about his statement for a while, my anger rises.

"Come on, Bob, we're in this thing together. I know you prefer to be alone, but give me a break."

"I told you, I'm not going to hurry, and that's it," he answers.

I lose my temper and grab Bob by his shirt front and swear at him. I tell him I'm going outside, and he's going even if I have to drag him. I stop short of hitting him, but I'm beside myself with rage over his behavior. I release him, but we continue to argue loudly. The guard appears with Akbar right behind him. Bob tells them I tried to hit him.

There will be no outside exercise today. I'm immediately taken from the cell to a small, dark room. I'm angry at myself and at Bob. I shouldn't have threatened him, but he should have been more considerate. It's as though he were daring me to do something. I'm also angry because now the Iranians know about our spat, and that's not good. I sit for an hour or so in the dark, then I hear someone at the door — it's

Akbar. "Colonel, Mr. Blucker is afraid that if he is left with you, you will kill him. He says you are crazy."

"Akbar, he may be right. I should not have grabbed him, but if he acts that way again, I may very well hit him."

"You are all getting mean because you have been cooped up too long. That is why I set up the exercise area outside. Mr. Sharer and Mr. Gillette went outside a little while ago, and they enjoyed the air and the exercise."

"So where do we go from here?"

"You will be put in the same room as Sharer and Gillette, and Blucker will be alone. He says he prefers to be alone, anyway. He has been that way from the beginning."

Being with my new cellmates is good for my morale. Don has lost about thirty-five or forty pounds since we worked together at the embassy, but he's still the same unshakable, matter-of-fact professional Navy officer I knew before. His strong will and quiet gift of faith have sustained him thus far. Sam Gillette is an exceptionally astute Navy petty officer, about twenty-five years old. An accomplished gymnast, he doesn't appear to have lost any weight at all. He and Don have shared a cell since they were moved out of the Mushroom Inn in mid-March. Both men have a splendid sense of the need for cooperation in this environment and for playing down petty differences. Although our cell is crowded, we have no problem getting along with each other. We take turns washing our dishes and go out of our way to be considerate.

A couple of hours ago, two young revolutionaries, apparently from the local unit or the *Komiteh* [committee] in charge of the building, came by our cell, inspected our meager accommodations, and announced that they would return with a rug for the floor. They did, bringing a beautiful handmade Tabriz rug that covers almost the entire floor of our ten-foot-by-twelve-foot cell. The rug was left behind by Mike Metrinko when he barely escaped the hangman's noose at the height of the revolution last February and retreated to the embassy at Tehran, only to end up a hostage with the rest of us.

Not surprisingly, in light of the rug, we soon have visitors. Hojat al-Islam Ali Hussein Khamene'i, Deputy Minister of Defense at the time of the embassy attack, and the Imam Jomieh, Tehran, enter our cell with Reza, the militants' security chief for Tabriz. Hossein, Akbar, and just about all the rest of our guards are with the visitors. Khamene'i greets us with a smile and invites us to sit on the floor with him. One of the militants insists that he take a chair, but the Hojat al-Islam wants to be one of the boys and sits on the floor. He begins to tap his Dunhill pipe out in his hand and immediately is presented an ash tray by a guard. Khamene'i is wearing the traditional clerical robes of his station, just below that of an ayatollah. He uses a gold-filled Dunhill lighter to fire his pipe, and he's wearing a gold Rolex watch. He says that he is here only to see that we're healthy and happy in our new home in Tabriz.

I want to laugh. I tell him I hope this is not my home, that I don't want to spend the rest of my life as a kidnap victim in Tabriz or any other place. The mullah gives me the usual argument that it's not his fault we're hostages; it's the fault of the American president for being unreasonable and not returning the Shah.

I can't hold my tongue. Addressing him in my best, most polite Farsi, I say, "Funny, how you say you still want the Shah, sir, while your counterpart here in Tabriz says that is no longer one of your demands. I'm getting confused; please enlighten me, sir."

He answers without hesitation. "That is right, we do not care about the Shah anymore. I know you do not like being held — you would rather be fighting for your country in places like Vietnam — but let me ask you a question. If we were to release all of you now, without any conditions, how long would it be before you could begin to supply us again with spare parts for our military forces?"

"You're asking the wrong man. I have had no contact with either my government or the American people since I became a hostage. I have been kept in the dark by your people. I do not know what they're afraid of if we're given information, but that's the way it is."

"But you have served in your army for many years; what do you think? How long would it take?"

"Frankly, my guess is it will be a long time before you'll get any cooperation on spare parts from America, after what you've done and continue to do to us."

"We're not harming you in any way . . . just protecting you from your enemies here and in your homeland. Did you know that a CIA team of commandos tried to kill you about two weeks ago? Fortunately, they did not succeed in getting inside the embassy, and a number of the invaders were killed before they could escape. Your president was trying to end the crisis by killing the hostages. What do you think of that?"

So that's it! There was an attempted rescue mission, and he says some of the rescuers were killed in the attempt. That explains our being hastily moved to Tabriz, and it also accounts for our guards brandishing weapons and acting even more paranoid than usual.

"No, I did not know about the incident. But why would President Carter bother to send commandos to kill us, if that were his intention? All he would have to do is bomb Tehran, including the embassy, to end the crisis. I do not believe a rescue mission was dispatched, and if one was sent, it was not for the purpose of killing us."

"I am telling the truth. Ten Americans were killed in the desert near Tabas trying to get away after the commandos were discovered by us."

"In America, each man is entitled to his own beliefs. I just don't believe Carter sent a team all the way over here with the mission of killing us."

"You are lucky to be alive, do you know that?"

"We are all lucky to be alive, sir. When my time comes, my life will end as will yours. As you people say, 'It is in God's hands.'"

"Colonel, we do not wish you any harm. We seek only justice under Islamic law. If your government tries another stupid mission, we will be forced to kill you. If your Carter does not comply with our just demands within a reasonable time, we will place you and some of the others on trial as spies."

"If you do that in a fair court trial with observers from the rest of the world, I have nothing to fear, because I was not a spy."

"But you fought in Vietnam and were decorated for your heroism. That means you are guilty of war crimes against the oppressed peoples of the world. It is the same thing."

"Yes, I'm sure if you decide to put me on trial, you will find some rationale for executing me. If you do that, though, you can bet your gold Rolex watch that President Carter will blast Iran off the face of the earth."

"There is no point in continuing this part of our discussion. We are miles apart in how we see this situation. I did not come here to make you angry, only to check on your welfare. Are you getting enough to eat? Have you been getting some good Tabriz *chello-kebab*?"

"The next time I eat *chello-kebab* will be the first since about a week before the embassy attack. We are pretty much living on rice and bread." The visitor is surprised. He turns to our guards and asks them what they're doing with the money they were given to buy food for us. They deny any knowledge of funds for food and tell him we're being fed the same diet as the nearby prison.

"Your diet will improve," he turns and tells me. Suddenly he glances at his watch and announces that he's running late for another appointment. He bids us farewell, shakes hands all around, and is on his way.

Before we can even discuss this unexpected visit, several of the guards enter our cell, armed with G-3 automatic rifles. One of them, whom I call Neanderthal Man, points his imposing weapon at my chest and stands menacingly about three feet from me. Reza, the hot-tempered security chief, says I have committed a serious crime —I have been disrespectful to an ayatollah. I should not have questioned our visitor, and I should not have told him we were not being well fed. I will be punished for my brazenness and disrespect as soon as he and the other "students" have a meeting to decide on an appropriate punishment.

I figure he's bluffing. He's angry because he and the others have been caught with their pinkies in the fund which supposedly was provided by the clerics to supplement our food.

"Why don't you just let the little man with the big gun" (I point to my least favorite guard, Neanderthal Man, who is still hovering over me with his weapon) "go ahead and shoot me and get it over with? If that is what's going to happen eventually anyway, let's get on with it."

"We will shoot you when we decide to shoot you; it is not up to you to say when that will be!" I have called his bluff and he's thoroughly frustrated. I get another fifteen minutes of threats and lectures on my bad behavior, and then the group departs. Neanderthal Man, his eyes glazed with hatred, is the last one out of the room. As he approaches the door, he aims his rifle directly at me and squeezes the trigger.

Click! The sadistic little bastard didn't even have a round in the chamber. He says the Persian equivalent of "I'll get you" and is gone.

The two Turkish revolutionaries who brought the rug to our cell are filling in for our regular guards. They're both interested in America and our way of life. Both are more animated than the rest of the guards, except Akbar,

304

and they don't seem to be as affected by the anti-U.S. propaganda. Reza is a nature lover who says he likes to spend time alone in the mountains around Tabriz. He says he has a trip planned within the next few days, and that his friend Davood will go with him this time to learn about the high country.

I tell him that I have always loved the mountains, too. "I remember driving in this area before your revolution, and I agree with you — there is nothing more peaceful and serene than the mountains, especially when one has an opportunity to go above the snow line in the spring and early summer. Right now it should be beautiful."

Reza is impressed by my knowledge of his mountains. "You can't go with me this time, but if your situation should change while you are in Tabriz, maybe you could take a trip with me."

"That would be nice."

"If you are freed, would you stay for a few days for a trip in the mountains?"

"Sure, I'd love to relax a few days there before I return home."

"Then, if God wills, we will do it."

The fool actually believes I would stay! Sometimes I think I'll never understand these people.

I ask him what ever happened to the restaurant on the small island in the lake at Tabriz. He says that the restaurant was a "palace of sin." Alcoholic beverages were served and girls displayed their bodies in an un-Islamic way by dancing in pre-revolutionary days, so the revolutionaries burned the building to the ground.

"What are you going to do with the site now?"

"We are building another restaurant," he answers. Revolutionary logic at its finest.

Reza and Davood smoke cigarettes and constantly are offering me one. I tell them I only smoke a pipe but don't have either a pipe or tobacco. Davood says he will find a pipe and tobacco for me. He is so polite and thoughtful that it's sometimes hard to realize he's involved in this hostage fiasco at all. His involvement is coincidental; he just happens to be part of the Tabriz *Komiteh*, and we're in his area. He has told me a couple of times that he and Reza do not think it's right to take hostages.

Today Davood has a surprise for me. He has not been able to find a pipe or tobacco, but he has a very nice butane lighter which he presents to me as a gift. He says Akbar is going to get a pipe and tobacco from the embassy the next time he makes a trip to Tehran. I thank Davood for his generous gift and tell him I have nothing to give him in return. He says if I'll stay and make a trip to the mountains with him and Reza after I'm free, that will be my gift to him. Like Akbar, he is sincere and devoid of the kind of hatred and resentment that is the hallmark of so many of the militants.

The menu has changed, at least for today. Akbar, Reza, and a young, exceedingly stupid country boy called Fazollah enter our cell with restaurant plates of *chello-kebab*, covered with large pieces of Persian bread to keep the contents warm. They proudly place the feast on the table and invite us to eat. The Hojat al-Islam came through, I tell Don and Sam as we enjoy the traditional Persian meal of skewered kebabs, seasoned rice, and raw onions. The kebabs are made with ground beef in lieu of the traditional lamb tenderloin pieces, which are in short supply. But after the bland diet we've been eating, we don't complain.

I'm sure this change in menu is a one-time thing because of my comment to Khamene'i. If there's money provided by the mullahs or the government for food for us, it will continue to find its way into the pockets of our captors.

In addition to teaching Akbar English — and pumping him for information in the process — I have undertaken an additional chore. I'm teaching English to young Hossein, a nineteen-year-old militant who is in love with everything military. I call him *"Sarbaz Hossein"* [Hossein the Soldier] because he would rather be a soldier than anything else in the world. He's fascinated by army field manuals on obstacle courses and leader's reaction courses, as well as manuals on weapons. I steer clear of teaching him anything that would help in combat, but I've been learning a great deal about the overthrow of the Shah by listening to his stories of fighting the army in the streets of Tehran. Hossein is anti-American, but he has great respect for American Army training, doctrine, tactics, and equipment.

Hossein is with me, sitting on the edge of my styrofoam mattress. He says he has brought something today which will be of interest to me. It's a book of pictures taken in Tabriz soon after Khomeini came to power. He enjoys looking at these pictures, which graphically show the horrible fate of the enemies of the revolution. They're sickening photos of the mutilated corpses of former members of SAVAK and the Shah's army, who were summarily executed by the knife-wielding locals in a frenzy of sadistic hatred. Hossein says, with unbridled glee, that while the Shah's enemies were either shot or hung in other cities, the good people of Tabriz decided to *"tee-kay, tee-kay"* their victims. They were slowly cut and chopped to death while hanging by their ankles in public.

"Hossein, I find these pictures offensive and sickening. Is this what your revolution is all about? Is this Islamic justice?"

"It is very bad, but the anger of the people had to be vented. These criminals had tortured and killed thousands of people, and they got what they deserved. The people of Tabriz are Turks and they prefer to use knives and axes instead of bullets."

"Put yourself in the place of these men who were chopped to death. Do you think they were treated humanely?"

"They were criminals. They got what they deserved. If you try to escape while you are in Tabriz, the same thing will happen to you."

"But Islam speaks of mercy and kind treatment of prisoners," I argue. "How do you reconcile this kind of atrocity with your religious beliefs?"

"It is hard to do, you are right. But Islam also believes in punishing offenders. It is up to man to punish offenders on earth, and God will punish them by denying them paradise after they die."

"My feeling is that these men in the pictures have already suffered enough."

"Perhaps you are right." Hossein closes his book, somewhat less enthused with showing off his pictures than he was before our discussion. He changes the subject.

"I would like to go to Afghanistan and fight against the Russians. It would be a good experience for me. I would learn things that will help me defend my country."

The Russians have invaded Afghanistan, he explains, and are fighting against the Moslem, anti-Communist rebels. I tell him the same thing may happen here: If Iran continues to be isolated from the Western powers, there will be no security umbrella to protect it from a Soviet move south. Hossein says they're not afraid of the Russians; they will fight them the same way they fought the Shah's army — with their rifles and fire bombs; they will stop Soviet tanks and turn them back. He says God is on their side and they'll win with their lighter arms and their cries of "God is great!"

"You will find that yelling 'God is great' is not a substitute for proper training and weapons. If the Russians decide to move south, you will not be able to stop them."

"We are not afraid to die, but we will not die. We will win."

"Hossein, if you have to fight the Russians or the Iraqis or my country, you'll get your socks blown off. It won't be the same as fighting the Shah's army, which was demoralized and suffering from lack of direction and leadership."

"No, it will not be the same as with the army, but we will win."

Akbar comes through again. About three times a week we're blindfolded and taken outside for exercise. The militants who are not on guard duty at the time join us for the exercise period. We're allowed to talk to each other and our captors, and it gives us an opportunity to check on Bob, who is also brought out of his cell for the festivities. Today Hossein is trying to get me to teach him some of the un-armed defense tactics we use in the Army to subdue an opponent with a knife or other weapon. I show Hossein in slow motion how it's possible to use an opponent's own momentum to render him helpless by using the principles taught in judo. Hossein is armed with a stick, which he uses as a knife in our demonstration. He lunges at me, I step to his right, grab him by his right shoulder with my right hand, then, grasping his forearm with my left hand, pivot to my left and throw him to the ground, using my right hip as a fulcrum. He's amazed how it works so effectively, even in slow motion. But Hossein doesn't like the idea of being defeated so easily — even though it was only a slow-motion teaching demonstration. He trips me with his legs and tries to pull me to the ground. I back off, regaining my balance, and he laughingly lunges at me again with his stick.

I repeat the same moves as before, only this time at normal speed. In a flash, Hossein is flat on his back and I'm holding his stick against his throat. His eyes bulge in disbelief. His ego is crushed. An armed guard outside the barbed-wire fence, which Akbar had built to enclose our exercise area, rushes inside with his automatic rifle. Hossein's fellow militants laugh at him, as do Bob, Don, and Sam.

"Hossein, like I told you, yelling 'God is great' is not a substitute for knowing what you're doing in a fight."

Hossein is still prostrate on the ground. I help him to his feet. He's laughing — the initial shock of his defeat is gone, replaced by an awareness that he has much to learn. Hossein the Soldier shakes my hand and says he's sorry for trying to trip me. It was all in fun . . . but, he says, "Will you teach me? I want to learn to do that fast, like you."

Sam Gillette is going through some of his gymnastic routines, and several of the militants are trying to play "follow the leader." It's the funniest thing I've seen in months. Sam is doing flips and acrobatics, and Big Ali, Akbar, and Fazollah are trying to copy his moves. Big Ali tries a forward flip and lands flat on his back. Akbar follows with the same result. They keep trying, and each time they manage to perform a trick without getting hurt, Sam shows them a more difficult one.

There are beautiful roses in the garden outside our exercise area. I tell Hossein that I love roses and would like to see them close up. He says that's not possible.

We sit for a moment under a tree, tired after our vigorous exercise. Hossein is looking at the clear blue sky, his thoughts a million miles away. I watch this terrorist for a full minute, trying to understand him. If I had a thousand men with his enthusiasm for the profession of arms, I could mold the finest military unit in the world. His dedication, his love of adventure, and his devil-may-care attitude would make him a fine warrior. But he's also a victim of the politics of ignorance. I wonder if he's looking to the sky for some sense of direction for his life. I think of Khayyám's quatrain about the sky, and I recite it softly in Farsi as Hossein peers into the endless blue.

And that inverted Bowl they call the Sky,
Whereunder crawling cooped we live and die,

> Lift not your hands to *It* for help — for It
> As impotently moves as you or I.

Before I finish the verse Hossein is reciting along with me. His meditation interrupted, he looks directly at me and says, "When do you think all of this will end?" I tell him I don't know.

Our spirits are high following our brief outing in the exercise yard. After our lunch of rice and hot tea, Hossein appears with three beautiful roses, one yellow and two red. He says they are for us to enjoy in our cell. Fazollah is with him, smiling in his stupid way. Hossein asks if I remember the quatrain about the thousand roses. I tell him I know it in English, but not in Farsi. He recites it in old Persian:

> Each Morn a thousand Roses brings, you say;
> Yes, but where leaves the Rose of Yesterday?
>   And this first Summer month that brings the Rose
> Shall take Jamshýd and Kaikobád away.

He says that when the petals fall from our roses, he will bring some more. I ask him if we might substitute our names for those of Jamshýd and Kaikobád so that we may be taken away — back to America — by this first summer month that brings the rose. Ironically, it is June, the first month of summer. Hossein and Fazollah leave, Don and Sam read, and I look at the flowers and think of home, my family, and my life, and, as always, I pray to God that this will end soon.

Akbar arrives for his English lesson carrying a copy of *Newsweek* magazine, the first one I've seen since our capture and imprisonment. He says he has censored all the items pertaining to Iran and the hostage crisis. He will leave the magazine for us to read. As an afterthought, he adds, "I may have missed something in my censoring. If I did, will you black it out with a ball-point pen?"

I assure Akbar that I will. Don, Sam, and I are eager to see what we can learn, but we'll have to wait for Akbar's departure so it's not obvious that we're going to analyze every item in it for news pertaining to our situation. Akbar says there have been major riots in America by blacks, and several cities are under martial law. I question him on this, and he says black Americans are engaged in a revolution against the government, according to what he has read in the Tehran newspapers. I tell him that I think his newspapers are exaggerating the situation and ask him for specifics. He promises to bring a newspaper to prove his story.

He also says that the International Court of Justice has ordered the release of all the hostages and has warned Iran against placing any of us on trial. And the court has ruled that Iran must pay reparations out of Iranian assets in the U.S. to compensate America and the hostages. But Akbar says Khomeini and his regime do not recognize the jurisdiction of the World Court or the United Nations, of which it is a part.

"If Khomeini will not listen even to the International Court of Justice, I'd say our chances of ever getting out of here are pretty slim."

Akbar is forever the optimist. "Sooner or later, something will be worked out and you will go free," he says. "I think it is only a matter of time. If your president had not sent commandos to Iran, perhaps it would already be settled."

"I don't think so. I think Khomeini and the rest of you are in the kind of situation where you would just as soon release us, but you can't do it without making it appear that your demands have not been met. You don't want to lose face."

"You may be right in your assessment of us. It would be best for my country if you were set free, but there are many in the Revolutionary Council, and here among the students, who think you should be tried as a way of justifying our attack on your embassy. Do you understand, at this point, if we were simply to release you without getting something in return, it would be seen by the Iranian people as not only an admission we were wrong in what we did, but as a surrender to America? We cannot allow this to happen."

"Meanwhile," I answer, "I can't go home, and you can't go back to school or to a job."

"You are right, but you must be patient and have faith. It will be settled some day."

"You always say that, but sometimes I feel depressed and think we may rot here forever, or worse. . . ."

"It has gone on too long. I am tired of it and want to go home as much as you do."

"Maybe *almost* as much, Akbar, but not *as* much."

"Very well, almost as much." Akbar smiles. I can sense that if it were left up to him, we both would leave Tabriz tomorrow. But I still think that if Khomeini ordered us executed, Akbar would obey the order. He might do it with a tear in his eye, but he would do it. That's the bottom line for us, unfortunately. We can never rest assured that we'll live to see another day. And no matter how considerate our jailers become, they're still our executioners-designate if the order is given.

I tell Akbar about the American Revolution and its anniversary, which will be here in two more weeks. I tell him that will be a very sad time for us, because we usually spend the Fourth of July holiday celebrating our freedom with our families. I tell him that if we're still here on the Fourth of July, it will be yet another bad omen.

I ask Akbar if he would ever consider visiting the United States. He says that he would be afraid of being arrested and shot for participating in the hostage caper. I tell him that in America people are not arrested and summarily shot, no matter what crime they've committed. He asks what I would do if he knocked on my door in Stone Mountain. Would I beat him up, call the police, or shoot him on the spot? I tell him that if I were to shoot him, I would be tried for murder; if I were to beat him up and get caught, I would be tried for assault. I want to win his confidence, so I tell him that I wouldn't call the police, because he personally has not done anything to me; he is only part of a group, some members of which have harmed me. He says, after thinking it over for a minute, that he would like to visit America and see for himself how I live.

At this point, I decide to test an idea I've had in the back of my mind since we arrived in Tabriz. I want to ask Akbar if he would be interested in starting a new life in America as a free man. If he could only work out some arrangement to get us out of here and to the Turkish border, we could take him with us. It would be a great coup if we could escape from here and actually have help from one of the militants. I think Akbar is the most likely candidate for this role, but I have to be careful in my approach to him.

"Akbar, you would love America. There already are many Iranians living there. You could practice Islam in my country just as easily as here, and you could finish your education without worrying about a revolution closing the schools. You could start a new life, never again concerned about poverty or danger from some opposition group. But there would be a cost — nothing in life is ever free."

"What would be the cost to me?"

"Help, Akbar . . . help."

"If nothing has happened by your Independence Day, we will talk some more." Akbar is a little uneasy, but he has taken at least part of the bait. He needs time to mull over my suggestion. Meanwhile, I'll discuss my proposition with Don and Sam. Akbar already is disillusioned with some

314

parts of the revolution. He says he disagrees with the brutal treatment of some minority religious groups, and he's disappointed by the corruption he sees among his own people. The utopian Islamic nation he visualized before the revolution is still a long way from reality.

Today is Sam's birthday and we've been browbeating Akbar, Big Ali, and Hossein about having a birthday party for him. Don and I have told the guards that it's a very important occasion for Sam, who is celebrating one-quarter of a century on earth. We're starting to think that they haven't picked up on our cues — lunch was the same old rice and tea.

About five in the afternoon, Akbar and Hossein enter our cell and tell us we're going to be joined by a new hostage. Fazollah enters with a fairly tall man with a blanket over his head and handcuffs on his wrists. He is seated in a chair and told to be quiet. Whoever it is is laughing under his dirty army blanket. Akbar removes the blanket, Fazollah the handcuffs, and Hossein the blindfold. It's Big Ali, playing games and enjoying every minute of his charade. Akbar says they only wanted to make us all laugh to start Sam's birthday party. He and Hossein rush out of our cell and return in less than a minute with Persian sugar cookies, an assortment of nuts, and carbonated soft drinks. We all sit around eating and drinking, talking about birthdays in Iran and in America. Don mentions that we usually sing "Happy Birthday." Within a matter of minutes we're all singing "Happy Birthday" to Sam Gillette in an unholy mixture of Persian and English — off-key.

Reza, the chief of security, and some of the other more militant members of our guard cadre are absent. Akbar says that Bob Blucker also turned down the opportunity to attend. I tell Akbar that when it is a man's birthday, there are no guarded borders and no politics. He likes the line and asks me to tell the others. We drink a toast with our soft drinks to "birthdays."

It has been a week since Sam's birthday, and our diet has settled back to the normal rice, bread, and tea. Our trips outside for exercise have stopped for some reason, and we haven't seen Akbar for almost a week. Big Ali says that he has returned to Tehran on important business. The two friendly Turks have been forbidden to visit us by Reza, the nasty security man. He has been on the scene more and more since Akbar's departure, and he's as nasty, sullen, and overbearing as ever. When he takes me blindfolded to the latrine, I can always count on standing alone for a minute or two before I realize that we've reached our destination. The big goon escorts me in, then slips out without telling me to remove my blindfold and use the toilet. He seems to enjoy deliberately walking me into partially opened doors — shades of the early days of the takeover. It's either play the game or don't go, so I play the game. But I have a plan in mind.

I bang on the heavy steel door. There's no answer. I bang again as hard as I can without breaking my fist. Finally Reza opens the door, enjoining me not to knock so loudly, and asks what I want. I tell him I have to go to the toilet. "Wait," he says, closing the heavy door and locking it from the outside.

In thirty minutes, I knock again. This time Reza is angry. He tightens my blindfold and pushes me down the hall. I count the paces to the latrine door. When I know I'm just inside, I reach to my right for the door. My judgment of the distance is perfect. I slam the door behind me and I hear the crunch of metal on bone. Reza lets out a yell of pain and surprise. I remove my blindfold in time to catch him reopening the door. Blood is gushing from his nose, and he takes a wild swing at my head. I dodge to the right, and he misses. He swings again, this time hitting one of Akbar's jerry-rigged water pipes. Reza is livid. He doesn't know what to do. I tell him that I thought he was gone and had forgotten to close the door, which is his usual *modus operandi*. Hossein and Fazollah arrive on the scene in answer to Reza's call for reinforcements. Fazollah has his usual blank look, but Hossein is amused by the spectacle of Reza's bloody nose and my look of complete innocence. Reza tells Hossein to take me back to my cell without letting me go to the bathroom. He leaves to get his nose patched up, and Hossein tells me to hurry up and use the toilet — he'll be waiting outside.

On the way back to my cell, Hossein says that I had better be careful, that Reza is a tough man who hates Americans. He adds, "But it was funny to see the two of you standing there, him with the surprised look and the bloody nose and you with a smile only in your eyes."

Another small victory for our side.

It is July 4, 1980. I'm depressed and feeling sorry for myself. It's beginning to look as though there's no end to our ordeal. Holidays come and go, our lives are slipping away from us. "The leaves of life are falling one by one," as Omar has written, but how many leaves can be left to fall? It's going to be a bad day. Akbar is gone and with him my only fantasy of escape from this place. I wonder what Betty and the children will do today? There's usually a big neighborhood cookout and games for the kids and plenty of good food and drink for all. Don and Sam have tried to cheer me, as I do for them when they're feeling low, but I haven't been very receptive to their efforts. I'm down, and that's all there is to it. For about two months, I have thought of this day as a milestone — a day when we would be either out of here or planning an escape to freedom. We're still here and there's no hope of an escape.

Our detailed study of the magazine which Akbar left for us to read produced sad and sobering news. Although he had cut out the article on the rescue mission completely, he had left in the table of contents page, which gave a capsule description of the mission. Eight American servicemen had lost their lives trying to win our freedom. Major General Jack Vaught and Colonel Charlie Beckwith, a native Georgian — both officers I have known during my Army service — were in charge of the mission. All were volunteers, men who knew the risks involved yet persisted in trying to get us out of here. It's a very humbling thought — that others died for us. But they failed and we're still here, and I guess there's little chance for a diplomatic settlement in the wake of this incursion inside sovereign Iranian territory. No wonder they leaned on us during the ride to Tabriz.

I think about those brave volunteers, and I'm reminded of our country's long history of sacrifice, courage, and determination. My mind races over the history of America, and in my mind's eye I'm treated to a panoramic view of the country I've known and loved all my life. Emblazoned in my imagination, one symbol appears in every scene — the flag of our country, the red, white, and blue. I recall how we fought in Vietnam under the Vietnamese flag, but we always kept an American flag hidden away in my Special Forces camp, ready to fly if we were ever in danger of being overrun. My theory was that if it came to that, I wanted the North Vietnamese to know who they were up against. It worked — morale among my men soared, because they knew that if things really got hot, we would fly the American flag. There's a sense of dedication and pride in our flag that goes beyond the pomp and ceremony of watching it fly high from a flagstaff on a national holiday. I recall the sadness and quiet pride I felt when, in the midst of my interrogation, I was dragged outside to watch Old Glory burned by angry Iranians. I realized then, and I recall again today, that the flag can wave in our hearts even when we can't enjoy the strengthening sight of it waving proudly in the breeze.

My depression has lifted. My thoughts about the flag have reminded me that I'm still an American. Men have died for more than two hundred years to defend our freedom. Men have suffered as prisoners of war, too. Those who have not forgotten who they are and what they represent have never faltered in doing their duty with courage and tenacity. I can do no less here. I have to live up to that tradition. I know who I am, and there's strength in that. I'm an American.

Since Akbar's departure, the food has gone from bad to worse. I suspect we're getting leftovers from the nearby prison. The rice we're fed in the afternoon is usually cold and lumpy. The foul-smelling mutton fat that's poured over it is repulsive. Today it was worse than usual. Sam flatly refused to eat it, but Don and I doctored ours with the last of our Tabasco sauce, procured for us by Akbar from the cooperative store. In Vietnam, no jungle fighter was ever found without his bottle of McIlhenny's pepper sauce. We ate it on powdered eggs, rice, and virtually everything else. I never could figure out whether I consumed so much hot sauce to add flavor or to overpower the bad natural odor. Here there's no question — we use it to counter the smell of rancid mutton fat.

Within two hours of consuming a generous portion of the rice and sauce, black hairs and all, Don and I have developed diarrhea, fever, and terrible stomach cramps. I bang on the steel vault door. We both have to use the toilet. Hossein opens the door and says, "You just went to the toilet a few minutes ago."

"I know, Hossein, but we have to go again. We're both sick." Hossein takes us to the latrine and says he'll try to get a doctor to check us.

Reza, the security chief, enters our cell and asks what's wrong with us. I tell him that Don and I are very sick and describe our symptoms to him graphically. "It does not matter," he says. "It will go away in a day or so."

It has not gone away. In fact, it's getting worse. We're both so weak that we're having trouble making it to the toilet. With the blindfold and the dizziness caused by our dehydration and weakness, we almost have to be carried to the latrine. Hossein and Fazollah have tried to help, but Reza seems to think it's funny. Instead of his usual firm guiding hand steering us into doors, he's inclined to bark out directions as he lets us stagger to the latrine on our own. Sam has felt our heads and confirmed that we're running high fevers.

I try to sleep, but it's impossible. I'm doubled over with pain, my intestines are beginning to convulse, and I'm hallucinating. I've lost control of my bowels. The room is pitch-dark as I try to raise up from my pallet on the floor. I manage to find my trousers, but I'm almost too dizzy and weak to get them on. Finally I get my left leg in and try to steady myself enough to get the right leg in. I lose my balance and fall down. Suddenly there's an excruciating pain in the bottom of my right foot. It feels as though someone has driven a wooden tent peg or a punji stake all the way through my foot. I reach for the invaded area of my heel and discover that the toothpick I have carried for months to clean my fingernails is buried more than halfway into a tender muscle there. I feel faint. The pain is getting worse. I try to pull it out by holding the flesh back with my right hand and pulling on the exposed inch or so of the wooden barb with my left hand, but I don't have enough strength to pull it out.

"Hey, Don, wake up. I need some help." Don stirs from his pallet. Sam, who must be president of the Sound Sleepers Association, never moves. I ask Don if we still have part of a candle. Our single forty-watt bulb has been providing power for only a few hours a day recently because of a shortage of electricity. Don fumbles in the dark for a candle. He strikes a match and lights a one-inch candle stub.

"Don, you're going to have to get a grip on this thing with both hands while I try to hold the flesh back so you can pull it out." Don's facial expression reveals his revulsion at the thought of my pain and in anticipation of his part in relieving it.

Sam finally is awake. He holds the candle so Don and I can see the swelling heel and the protruding toothpick. Don grips the exposed end with as many fingers as possible. The pain is unbearable. It's as though the toothpick is growing inside my foot. Don gives it his best effort, in spite of his own illness, and the blood-saturated toothpick finally comes out. I apply pressure to the throbbing heel. There's very little blood, and the pain is relieved almost instantly. Don lies back on his pallet, exhausted by the physical effort and his food poisoning. I rest for a few minutes, thank Don for his help, then knock on the door. It's too late to go to the bathroom, but I want to clean myself.

By morning, Don and I are regressing rapidly. We're both delirious with fever and suffering unbearably from painful convulsions. Reza says he'll get a doctor. It finally occurs to him that we're really sick and may die if we don't get medical help.

A Turkish-speaking doctor enters our cell and examines us. He immediately diagnoses our malady as severe food poisoning. I'm too sick to care what's going on, but I hear him bawling out Reza and the others for allowing this to happen. He says we would have been dead in a few more hours. Don's fever is 105 degrees, and mine is 104.7.

The doctor writes out a prescription and instructs Reza to have it filled right away. We're to be given freshly cooked rice and natural yogurt and plenty of liquids. The doctor tells me that he'll return in the evening to check on us. He says that if we don't feel better within a few hours, to tell our jailers and he'll return. He's ashamed of our treatment and doesn't try to disguise it.

"Pack your things in your blanket. You are going on a little trip." Big Ali and Hossein enter our cell to prepare us for another leg in our seemingly endless odyssey. It has been only two days since we saw the doctor, and even though we're much improved, the prospect of travel is nauseating. Each move also brings a fear and uncertainty that's difficult to describe. We never know when we might be headed for our last journey.

"Where are we going this time, Ali? If it is a long ride, we should not have to wear blindfolds all the way. We get sick from the long moves when we can't see anything." I recall the trip up here from Tehran and don't look forward to a repeat of that.

"You are right. I will check to see if you can take them off once we are on the way."

Don, Sam, and I pack our blankets and meager belongings — a few books and a toothbrush — and speculate on where we're going.

After the usual routine of searching, blindfolding, and handcuffing, we move out toward our unknown destination. Ali is in the back with us to make sure we don't talk. Reza is in the front with the driver. Ali asks if we can remove our blindfolds, but Reza is afraid we may be able to see where we're going. Ali asks what difference it makes, but Reza is adamant. The blindfolds stay on.

We travel all night. Ali tries making wisecracks on the way to keep our spirits high. "Do you know where you are now, Colonel?"

"Yeah, Ali, I'm still in Iran, I'm sorry to say."

I have managed to work my blindfold loose enough to see over it from time to time. Ali knows what I've done; he catches my eye, winks, and holds his finger to his lips, gesturing for me to play it cool. I see familiar sights along our route and assume that we're headed in the direction of Tehran.

Shortly after daylight, about ten hours into our

journey, we enter a large urban area. I'm sure it is the main road from downtown to the airport; we're moving toward the center of Tehran. The streets are littered with trash and there are very few pedestrians. It's Friday, the Sabbath in Iran, and the usual work-day traffic is missing. We turn off onto a side street. I hear a huge clock chiming seven o'clock as we stop in front of a large, walled compound. I catch a glimpse of a sentry. He's wearing the uniform of a prison guard. The gate is opened electrically from inside. We enter. It finally has happened — we're in a real prison. I exhale and my heart sinks. When will it end?

15

KHOMEITEH PRISON
JULY 12 - OCT. 21, 1980

Once inside the prison, I'm strip-searched against a cold steel wall by two very professional-sounding guards. My blindfold, of course, stays on. They dump the contents of my pockets onto a table and sort through them. The only thing that's returned besides my trousers, shorts, and shirt is the blue plastic rosary given to me by Akbar. My comb, handkerchief, toothpick (some folks never learn), and pencil stub are confiscated.

I'm led down a series of corridors and through three steel bulkheads. As I step over the foot-and-a-half high steel dividers, I hear the electrically operated, heavy metal doors slam shut behind me. I'm moved inside a cell and told to sit on the floor. My blindfold is removed and the guards who led me inside leave, locking the heavy door behind them. There's a low-wattage light bulb hanging from a wire in the center of the fifteen-foot-square room. The concrete walls have been repainted recently. Except for an opening above the steel door, there's no ventilation; there's a Judas hole in the door, but it has been welded shut. I know exactly where I am. This cell is precisely the same as the one Akbar described when he told me of his first prison, where he was interrogated, beaten, and tortured.

This is Khomeiteh prison, one of the most infamous and dreaded of all Iranian jails.

In spite of the new paint, signs of the misery endured by previous occupants are evident. The walls are scratched with the graffiti of men without hope, men who were awaiting execution or worse. There are slogans, prayers, and references to virtually every opposition group from the Shah's days. "Prisons are warehouses for the poor," "The people's struggle will go on," and "Islamic Socialism is the only path" are among the still readable slogans. Close to the floor, in a progressively less legible scrawl, are the words of an apparently dying man. He wrote, "Merciful God, please take. . . ." He never finished the message. The place is barren and depressing. I pity the men who have suffered here, regardless of their political beliefs. This is strictly a political prison, closed after the revolution and considered uninhabitable for humans. But it must have been reopened for us. Or is it also used to imprison the growing numbers of Khomeini's opponents?

Don and Sam are led into the cell. Their handcuffs and blindfolds are removed and their escorts leave, telling us once again to keep quiet. There are three styrofoam mattresses, a table, and three wooden chairs in the cell. We shake hands, glad we're still together. We pull the chairs over to the table, sit down, and discuss our latest journey. I tell them we're in Khomeiteh prison, and we discuss the implications of this negative turn of events for more than an hour. We agree that this place is escape-proof and impossible to penetrate by any rescue force with a hope of reaching us before we're killed. Perhaps that's why we've been brought here. We know there are other Americans here because we can hear them. Keeping us spread out all over the country must have been a security problem for our captors, as well as a logistical nightmare. It also was an inefficient use of manpower. We had at least twelve militants involved in the operation at Tabriz to hold four hostages. But we also agree that our move to this prison is an indication that there's nothing in the works that holds any prospect of gaining our freedom.

We'll continue to live day by day, keeping our faith and doing our best to follow a routine of physical exercise, reading, prayer, and conversation. It's the only way to retain our sanity. We discuss the tendency each of us has toward periods of depression, when we're not sure it's worth the struggle. We agree to continue to reinforce each other during these psychological lows. We also will continue to build our own morale and high spirits by passive resistance at every opportunity. We'll browbeat, ridicule, and otherwise harass our captors who treat us badly, but we'll stop short of doing anything that might prompt them to separate us or make life more miserable. In sum, we'll work as a three-man team against the Iranians and for each individual member of our group. We'll give the guards no quarter, but we won't be foolhardy, either. Our mission is to survive and get out of here in as good a mental and physical condition as possible. Everything we do must be aimed toward that objective.

Ahmad, the American-educated terrorist leader, enters our cell with two of his henchmen. He is a prematurely balding, stocky man in his mid-thirties. When we were in the Mushroom Inn, we figured he was second in command to Hamid the Liar. He is an arrogant, two-faced man with a nasty disposition and a short temper.

"Welcome. How are you doing? Did you enjoy your nice ride through the Iranian countryside?" Admad's English is good.

"Yeah, it was a blast," says Don sarcastically. "What's going on out there that you're so afraid to have us see?"

"Nothing, we are only trying to insure your safety. You know about the mission that was sent to kill you."

"Come on, Ahmad; save the bullshit for your own people who may believe you. We don't," I add wearily. We've heard this story many times, and the deaths of those eight men is still a touchy subject with us."

"Anyway, you will be safe here until your Carter comes to his senses or you stand trial," says Ahmad.

"While I'm awaiting my trial," says Sam, "do you suppose it would be possible to get something to eat? We weren't given supper last night or breakfast this morning." Don and I both look at Sam, surprised to hear the normally shy personality speak up aggressively.

"I will get you some cheese and bread," says Ahmad without argument as he turns to leave. I'm unable to resist the opportunity to comment on our new status as occupants of a real prison. "Hey, Ahmad, I thought Khomeiteh prison was closed because your revolution declared it not fit for humans. What are we doing in a place like this?" Ahmad is flabbergasted. He never figured I would guess exactly where we are.

"This is not a prison; it is not a prison anymore. You are right. Khomeiteh was closed."

"But this *is* Khomeiteh and we *are* prisoners, so you and your revolution have lied again."

"O.K., so this is Khomeiteh. But it is not a prison; it is only a place to keep hostages."

"Yeah, great, sometime when I have a slack month or two, maybe you can explain that logic to me. Meanwhile, we're in the prison you people admitted was the worst in the Shah's inventory."

"It doesn't matter," says Ahmad, slightly irked by my comments but managing to remain very much under control — at least for him.

Ahmad, for once, is true to his word. He brings slices of cheese from the cooperative stockpile and fairly fresh Persian bread. We eat and discuss our plan for making contact with the hostages in the adjacent cells. We're almost certain that both cells on our flanks hold Americans. Sam thinks he heard Joe Subic being led into the cell on our left, but we have no idea who's on the right. The walls are about

327

three feet thick, so it'll be difficult to communicate. We decide to be careful for a week or so, until we are sure we're not being set up by either the Iranians or Subic before we make contact with our neighbors. We would like to find out where the others have been; anything they've learned could help us piece together a mosaic of our current situation.

The way we see it, there is little or no hope of a release on the horizon. The rescue mission more than likely drove an even bigger wedge between the U.S. and Iran. It must have been approved in an atmosphere of frustration over constant failure to free us via diplomacy. The Iranians must have realized the logistical and security problems inherent in secreting us at distant locations, not to mention the possibility of a vehicle accident killing one or more of us, or a poorly disciplined guard shooting one of us in fear or anger. But after they were totally surprised by the attempted rescue mission, they were willing to take those risks.

There has been another result of the aborted attempt to rescue us: The Iranians now realize that Uncle Sam is tired of fooling around and not getting any results. They do not know what our government may do next. This has them scared and puzzled. I suppose that's precisely why the Imams of Tabriz and Tehran both told me of the new conditions for our releases — conditions that no longer require the return of the Shah.

The worst indication of the futility of our situation, however, is the fact that we're now residents of the worst prison in Iran. Just the thought is depressing. Ironically, when our future is most threatened and in doubt, we want to talk about it, perhaps to reassure ourselves that there is a future. In any case, we talk frequently about what we want to do with our lives if and when this is resolved. Sam would like to get out of the Navy and go to college. Don and I both have encouraged him to return to school, but to get the Navy to sponsor him. He's an intelligent, sound thinker with all the attributes necessary for a successful career as a Navy officer. Sam likes the idea of being able to stay in the service and complete his education.

Don is dying to return to Fran, his wife, and his two children. Then he wants to get back to his career as a Navy aviation officer. He loves his work, and his only concern seems to be that he'll be too far behind his contemporaries if we're stuck here for much longer. He won't have enough service to retire for three more years. He says that when that time comes, he'll weigh his options. If he does decide to retire, he may look at politics as a second career. He's a very special man who will do well in whatever he chooses.

I tell them that I really don't know what I'll do after we're free. A great deal depends on how long we stay here. I say, about half seriously, that I may be too old to command a brigade by the time we get home. If so, I'll retire and find a job. Not just any job, but something that will be a challenge, require a lot of hard work, and keep me fully occupied. I dread the thought of being one of those old colonels shuffling papers in some higher headquarters, waiting to retire. I tell Don and Sam that I already have almost thirty-one years service, so if there's no promotion, and with it additional challenges, I'll hang up the green uniform and opt for something else. Both Sam and Don are reassuring. They think I'll be promoted to brigadier general and opt to stay in the Army. I tell them the Army doesn't have as good a record as the Navy in looking out for former prisoners of war — which essentially is what we are. Another consideration, I tell them, is that if I do decide to stay and I do get promoted, there'll be those who say I was promoted only because I was a prisoner. "Let them say that if they want to. It makes no difference," Don says. We laugh at Don's very valid point.

The mid-afternoon meal here has been much better than the prison food we were fed — and nearly died eating — in Tabriz. An Iranian militant we have nicknamed

Dirty Thumb Ali is acting as cook. We have given him his nickname because of his inability to deliver a bowl of chicken noodle soup in the evening without totally immersing his dirty thumb in it. He does no better with the noon meal. A chemist could tell everything we've been given to eat in the last two weeks by analyzing the crud under Ali's thumbnail. Balanced meals and knowledge of nutrition are not among Ali's fortes. For example, today for lunch we had Ali's version of lasagna — not much meat or cheese, but plenty of noodles — and boiled potatoes. I ask Ali if he knows what protein is and he replies, "Yes, it is in the food, and Americans eat too much of it." I tell him that may be true in America, but it's certainly not true of our diet as guests of the Ayatollah. Ali does try, though, and he frequently returns to the scene of his crime, poking his head inside the door of our cell about an hour after the big meal in early afternoon and asking in a most persuasive way, "It was good, yes, and it was enough, no?"

"Yes, Ali, it was good" (our rationale here is not to discourage his efforts) "but it is never enough." Don and I have made a pact that for two people with our appetites, it'll never be enough. It has become a matter of pride and principle never to admit that we've had enough to eat. Sometimes it even produces positive results, and Ali scrapes the bottom of his cooking pan to bring us more food.

We're never quite sure why he bothers to check back to see if we enjoyed his handiwork. Sam postulates that he's checking only to count survivors. I think the militant is actually trying to learn to cook, and that he has some part of the hospitable Persian personality trait of always giving guests the very best food possible.

Ahmad makes an appearance about once a week. He says he is checking to make sure we're all right, since he is responsible for us. He also promises to brief us on what's going on, but he never does. He has made several snide comments about our stay in Tabriz, alluding to all the information we were given by Akbar. I can only assume that Reza, the security goon, tattled to Ahmad. In any case, we haven't seen Akbar in this prison. I have queried some of the less militant guards, when they were taking me to the latrine, but I haven't found a single one willing to shed any light on Akbar's whereabouts.

Although we had a series of taps on the wall to our left shortly after we arrived here, we haven't answered them. We aren't sure the occupant of that cell can be trusted, so we don't stick our necks out. We've been listening to the activity in the hall for more than three weeks, trying to determine who else is here with us. We also carefully analyze the contents of the trash bags in the common latrine when we're taken blindfolded down the hall to wash our plastic dishes and use the facility. In all, based on our trash-bag analysis and careful observation of the jumbo tubes of toothpaste stolen from the co-op and provided by our captors, we estimate that there are two dozen of us in this wing of the prison. We have positively identified most of them, including Al Golacinski, Dick Morefield, Marine Gunnery Sergeant Moeller, and Colonels Holland and Schaefer.

"Gunnie" Moeller is hard to miss. We hear him whistling "The Marine's Hymn" on his way to the latrine and also in his cell. Sporadically he also lets out a stadium roar, yelling, "Ahhhh-shit!" This causes a rumble of laughter throughout the cell block and cries of "Don'ta - espeak!" from our distraught guards.

Tonight, for the first time, Don will try to make contact with the cell to our right. We plan to wait until very late, when there are fewer guards on duty, then use the tap code to establish contact. We'll have to make sure that Don's taps are just loud enough to be heard by our neighbors without being audible to the guards. If they find out that we're communicating between our cells, we surely will be moved somewhere else and separated, if not worse.

When the time is right, Don taps lightly on the wall to attract their attention. Four light taps are almost immediately answered by two light ones. Don sends his interrogative message: five taps, then three; pause, then two, three; pause, three, five; pause, two, four; pause, four, four; pause, two, four; pause, then four, and five. "W-H-O I-S I-T?"

Without a pause, Don has his answer. It's Al Golacinski, and he has a message for us. Al begins to send his message as I listen at the door for the movements and actions of our guards. Sam is helping Don; two listeners are better than one when the taps can't be any louder than necessary.

"T-H-E S-H-A-H D. . . ." There's movement in the hall; a guard is headed toward our door. I warn Don in a whisper, and he interrupts Al's message with a series of continuous light taps to warn him of danger. We wait.

A minute stretches into ten minutes. Something about the Shah, but we can't take a chance. There is a guard right outside our door. Is he listening for the tapping to resume? Or is he just standing there smoking a cigarette? After almost half an hour, the guard finally moves back to his post. I hear his chair scraping along the concrete floor as he settles in.

Finally we get the rest of Al's message. "THE SHAH DIED IN EGYPT, 27 JULY." "I'll be damned," I say to Sam and Don. "The old boy died almost a month ago and we're still here. I wonder what's going on?"

"I don't know, but if he's really dead, our still being here is sure as hell, as you would say, a bad omen," says Don, with a puzzled look evident even in the dim candlelight.

"What else do these people want?" questions Sam in a frustrated tone.

"Keep listening, Chuck. I'll see what other

pearls of news Al has for us," says Don, moving back to the wall to continue his tapping.

Al is loaded with news, some of it significant, some of it not. He reports that John Graves, chief of the International Communications Office, was seriously injured in an accident in April when we were moved from Tehran after the rescue mission.

Al also warns us to be careful whom we communicate with, and I tell Don to let him know that we're only too well aware of that problem.

Al says the Iranians are trying to hang a paternity suit on Sergeant Moeller. He is accused of getting an Iranian woman pregnant before the seizure of the embassy. Al says the girl's brother killed her for bringing such disgrace to the family. Typical macho Iranian, I tell my cellmates.

Hamid the Liar is reportedly now a second lieutenant in the Iranian Army. That explains his absence here and Ahmad's rise to the top terrorist position.

We tell them about the rescue mission. They already had most of the information but didn't know about the eight men who lost their lives trying to rescue us.

Richard Queen reportedly has been sent home. He was very sick, possibly with multiple sclerosis. Word is that Akbar helped get him ready and was with him in the hospital here for several days before the decision was made, by Khomeini himself, to release him. They must have been afraid that he would die and they would be blamed. I pray silently for Queen's recovery. Then the irony hits me — I'm praying for one of us who is free from this terror and uncertainty, while I'm still here. But I realize I wouldn't trade places with Rich. As far as I know, I'm still fairly healthy, thank God.

About every ten days, the three of us are blindfolded and escorted to another cell where our jailers have set up a combination library and television viewing room. Before we're permitted to view videotaped reruns of old American shows, we usually are subjected to an Iranian revolutionary propaganda program. Today we're watching an interview with Father Darrell Rupiper, a Roman Catholic priest from Omaha who apparently was here during the Easter Sunday propaganda show, staged to show the world that we were being well treated. Rupiper could not possibly be less well-informed about our treatment. In answer to a direct question by the interviewer on our treatment, Rupiper launches into a three-minute condemnation of those who are more worried about the safety of the hostages than about Iran's "just grievances against the United States." Either he was completely taken in by our captors, or he genuinely supports their positions. Don, Sam, and I are vocal in our criticism of his answers to questions. Ahmad, who is sitting in the rear of the room, orders us to "shut up." Don asks to be taken back to our cell so he doesn't have to listen to the rest of Rupiper's rhetoric, and Sam and I follow suit. Ahmad, his anger rising, says we must watch the entire program in silence, or we never will be allowed to see any more TV tapes or exchange any books.

We sit grimly through the rest of the taped interview. It doesn't get any better as it progresses. In spite of Ahmad's admonishment to keep quiet, Don and I continue to vocalize our resentment.

"I'd like to trade places with this joker if he's so sure we're being well treated and the Iranians were right in what they did to us," says Don in a most belligerent tone.

"I'm not a violent man," I add, "but I'd sure like to have an opportunity to give this guy a boxing lesson."

"Shut up and watch the program," says Ahmad. "It should help you to understand how your countrymen really feel."

"If that's how they really feel, why do you burn most of our mail? What are you afraid of?" I ask. I know I shouldn't bait Ahmad, but my anger must be vented, as he is fond of saying.

"We don't burn your mail, Mr. Scott. You just don't get any."

"Yeah, sure, and you're going to get the Shah back, too. Right?" I want to know how he'll answer this one now that the Shah is dead. Will he slip and confirm the Shah's death or continue to try to deceive us?

"That is right, we will get the Shah back for trial," says Ahmad, trying to be convincing.

I decide to have a little fun with him. "Ahmad, you may be right. I've always said that you would never get the Shah back, but I have changed my mind. I think now it may be possible for you to realize your criminal dreams and get him sent here."

Ahmad's face is getting red. He doesn't know what to say. He doesn't want to tell us of the Shah's death, but he suspects that we already know. "What do you know about the Shah?"

"You people tell us nothing, Ahmad. For all I know, the old boy may be dead already. I know you never believed he was sick, but I'm sure he was very ill."

"He was not sick. If he dies, it will be the fault of your CIA."

"You want to kill him anyway. If the CIA got to him, they did you a favor."

Ahmad is at a loss for words for more than a minute. I'm convinced that he thinks I know more than I'm admitting. His face is still red and his tone of voice reveals his insecurity. "If the Shah dies in America, you will die here, because it will be a conspiracy to keep the Iranian people from having justice against the Shah."

I decide to taunt him once more and then drop the subject. "The only way you'll ever get him back here, Ahmad, is in a coffin. America will not buy your blackmail scheme."

"Then you will be here forever . . . forever!" shouts Ahmad, his voice rising to a high pitch, signalling his anger and frustration.

We watch the rest of Rupiper's interview and a rerun of "CHiPs" before we're blindfolded and returned to our cells. Ahmad personally escorts me. Halfway down the corridor, he squeezes my upper arm with all the strength he can muster and asks, "What do you know about the Shah, Mr. Scott?"

"Nothing, Ahmad, nothing."

"You are a liar, Scott . . . a liar. Tell me what you have heard."

"Thanks to you, I have heard nothing. However, I believed my government when it said the Shah had cancer. He could be dead by now. But then again, maybe not, because we're still here. If the Shah were dead we would be home by now. Right?"

"Wrong! Never mind, you may never go home." Ahmad has the final word as he pushes me back inside our cell and slams the door, almost jarring it off the heavy steel hinges.

"What did you do to needle Ahmad?" Don asks. "He was really pissed."

I tell Don about my dialogue with Ahmad on the return trip from the TV room and we all laugh. We laugh, but the Shah *is* dead and we're still here.

The Iranians have installed closed-circuit television in the latrine in an effort to prevent us from using the toilet as a message drop. They have mounted a camera high on the wall, just to the left of the door. Apparently they've discovered that we're passing messages there, but they don't know exactly how we're doing it. For long messages, where it's not practical to use the tap code, we've been hiding notes under the toilet seat, inside the paper roll, or in the float ball inside the toilet. But now, with the closed-circuit television, our message system is in jeopardy. Don, Sam, and I have been trying to figure out how to distract the guard monitoring the screen long enough to put the camera out of action. If we simply smashed it, we'd pay hell for our deed and they would just replace it. Suddenly I get an idea. . . .

"We both have to go to the toilet," I yell through the door to the guard. About thirty minutes later, a guard escorts Don and me down the hall to the latrine in chain-gang fashion — Don led by the guard, my hand on Don's shoulder, trying to walk in stride so that I don't step on his heels.

Once inside the latrine, Don immediately unbuttons his trousers, pulls them and his white boxer shorts with the red hearts down to his ankles, and "moons" the camera. It's so funny that I have trouble muffling my laughter, but I have to listen for the reaction of the guard monitoring the TV screen. Just as I had anticipated, I hear the guard yelp like a dog slapped with a rolled-up newspaper. I know he's turned his head away from the screen, because it is definitely taboo for Moslem fundamentalists, such as these guys, to look at naked flesh — male or female. Using the base of a broken chair in the latrine to help me reach the camera, I quickly apply a coat of soap to the lens. Then I jump down and rush to the sink to brush my teeth. In a matter of seconds, we hear booted feet running our way. Two guards storm in and begin to bawl out Don for his offensive display. Don explains that he had to pull his pants down to use the toilet, but the guard orders him never to do such an uncivilized, sacrilegious thing again. Don says he's sorry, but he didn't know they were "so interested in seeing us take a crap." The guards leave, shaking their heads in disgust and revulsion. On the way back to our cell, the guard tells me in Farsi to explain to Don how offensive his actions were. I agree with him and promise to enlighten Don.

We repeat the "mooning" operation several

times, but never at the same time of day; we don't want to hit the same guards twice. I have heard a couple of the guards complain that the picture on the monitor is cloudy. Finally, a guard calls for Ahmad to inspect the TV screen, protesting that he can't see a thing inside the latrine. Ahmad, who professes to be an electronics genius, inspects the TV and concludes, "There is something wrong with the television set. It will have to be replaced." The next day, we hear talk of the TV monitor being taken out. Our message system is back intact, until they discover the problem.

Ahmad enters our cell with mail. As usual, he gives Sam his letters first, then Don gets his, and finally I get mine. Always in reverse order of military rank — his way of showing us what lowly characters we are in his revolutionary eyes. Ahmad hands me a large manila envelope. It's from Betty and it has been opened by the censors for inspection. The Atlanta, Georgia, postmark is stamped "January 7, 1980." It took exactly eight months for me to receive it.

Inside the big envelope are ten crossword puzzle books — a virtual gold mine of time-passing entertainment for the three of us. I divide the books among us, and Don suggests that we all write in them very lightly with pencil so they can be erased, and eventually all three of us can do each book. Even after eight months, there remains the residual odor of Betty's perfume or hand lotion. I hold the envelope closer to my nose, enjoying the familiar scent. It's been so long. My mind races over the past year, and suddenly it dawns on me that I left my home in Stone Mountain exactly a year ago today. We have been hostages for more than ten months — ten months of our lives lost and still no end in sight. I wonder how the children are doing in school, if the thought of their father being a hostage has adversely affected their ability to concentrate on their work. I wonder what the other kids say to them about my fate. I wonder how Betty is managing: Has she given up? Is she bitter? Is she

338

resolved and determined to wait the thing out? I wonder if she has found the same peace I've found in prayer. God, how I miss my family. How I long to breathe the free air of America again, to run in Stone Mountain Park, to get up early and drive to work, to love again and be with Beth and Greg and hear their laughter. After the rescue mission and the death of the Shah, it seems there is no end to our plight. I wonder if I've changed as a result of what I've been through here. I don't think so, but I realize that I'm certainly not a good judge of change in myself. I believe I'm more caring and more capable of loving and being loved than ever before in my life, but perhaps that's a natural feeling one has in a situation such as this.

Our once- or sometimes twice-a-week trip to the shower has been deleted from the schedule for the past two weeks. Ahmad has made it a point to try to convince us that there's no shortage of kerosene, only a shortage of guards willing to tote it from outside the prison to the hot water heater in the bathroom. When I told him that I suspected they were having trouble getting kerosene to fuel the heater, he laughed. "In Iran, we have plenty of oil," he said. He was not very convincing, and I'm beginning to think that there must be some sort of trouble in the oil fields. Several of the guards have alluded to Iraq and the United States working together against Iran. I don't believe any of this, but I'm wondering if there has been an increase of border incidents between the two neighbors. Khomeini has been trying to spread this revolution by inciting the Shiite majority in Iraq to revolt against their government under Saddam Hussein. Maybe the Iraqi strongman has tired of this.

In the latrine, we frequently hear the cries and screams of men in great pain. Apparently there is a torture chamber close to the latrine, where enemies of the revolution are being flogged and tortured in other ways. Sometimes we can hear the sickening sound of a whip cracking against flesh and the anguished cries of those being beaten. At other times, we hear only screams followed by hideous moans and crying. We probably could hear these sounds from our cell except for Ahmad's classical music, which he plays on a small tape player — not for our entertainment, but to muffle the tortured cries. The music sounds nice, but knowing what it's designed to cover up leaves me with an empty feeling.

September 22, 1980

Although it is only early evening, it's dark in our cell. For more than a week, each evening at what we estimate to be about nightfall, our single light bulb has been turned off from outside our cell. Apparently the entire prison is in darkness. Guards bringing our soup and bread for the evening meal carry flashlights or candles. We're given one small candle each day by which we see to eat our supper. During the day, the light in our cell is turned on, so we assume there's no problem with the electrical generators. It's as though they're blacking out the city each evening from dusk until dawn. We wonder if the United States is threatening to bomb Iran, or if the Iraqis are now bombing Iranian cities. The guards seem to be even more jumpy than usual, and I've overheard several conversations during the past few days where the word *jang* [war] has been mentioned frequently.

We have hoarded several candles by telling each guard shift that we haven't received our daily ration. It has become sort of a game to see how many we can manage to stockpile in our cell. It's also nice to have extra light so we can play cards in the evening. We have to be careful, though, not to let the guards know we have enough candles to support our secret card games.

We're waiting for our usual supper of soup and

bread, sitting in the dark cell, talking about all the things that we would rather be doing, when suddenly the impact of exploding bombs shakes the walls of our reinforced concrete cell. Bits of paint flutter down from the ceiling, and there's a cloud of dust in the air. We're all talking at once, trying to figure out what's happening. Don's sensitive ears pick up the sound of aircraft.

"Keep the noise down!" he whispers, listening intently. We hear the unmistakable sound of a jet pulling out of a dive and increasing power to climb back to altitude.

"Those are MiGs," says Don.

The bombing continues. It sounds as though the bombs are falling about four or five miles away. Don and I both estimate the direction to be east, in the vicinity of the main commercial and military airfield at Mehrabad. Guards are running up and down the corridors of the prison, making sure all lights are out. They speak only in whispers. With the sound of the bombs, it's impossible to make out what they're saying.

Al and his people in the cell next to ours are tapping on the wall to find out what's going on, but it's too hectic and noisy to use the tap code effectively. Don confirms his earlier report of the type of aircraft. They are MiGs. He's absolutely sure of it.

A bomb explodes much closer to our prison, and the building shakes and rumbles. There's nothing we can do but listen and hope that none of them scores a direct hit on us. Air-raid sirens blare all over the city.

Then, as suddenly as it started, the bombing stops. There's relative silence for a moment. Don says the only countries with MiG aircraft close enough to bomb Tehran are the Soviet Union and Iraq. He speculates that there were not enough aircraft to indicate a Soviet strike, so it must be the Iraqis.

"Let's hear it for Saddam Hussein," I say, trying to break the tension.

"Who the hell is Saddam Hussein?" asks Sam.

"He's the president of Iraq. Looks like we need to buy some Iraqi war bonds. Maybe if these guys have a war on their hands, we'll finally get out of here," I say.

"Yeah, if we don't get killed first," adds Don.

The silence which gave us a chance to speak is shattered by the sound of cannon and heavy gun fire. Shortly after the initial explosions, we hear the Fourth-of-July-like rapid explosions of flak high in the sky. The Iranian anti-aircraft barrage continues for more than half an hour, even though we don't hear any more exploding bombs or screaming jet engines. The Iraqis apparently have headed for their home bases, but still the barrage continues. I tell Don that unless I miss my guess, it will continue until the Iranian gunners run out of ammunition. They got caught with their pants down when the air raid began, but they'll fire like hell now as long as they possibly can — even though there are no targets — to cover their shame at being surprised.

Within an hour or so, it's all over. There is quiet except for the sound of faraway sirens sounding the all clear.

Now we're sure that Iran and Iraq are at war, and we're fairly sure that the Iraqis tried to knock out the main airport. In the excitement of the bombing and the belated Iranian antiaircraft barrage answer to it, I forgot about supper. I'm hungry, and Don and Sam are, too. There's still a lot of activity in the corridor, but no sign of our evening meal. We're beginning to wonder if supper has been cancelled because of the air raid, when one of the guards enters our cell, shining his flashlight around as if to check to see if we're still here.

"Che shod?" [What is going on?] I say in my best Farsi, trying to catch him at a weak moment.

"Nothing. It is just a practice. It is just for training, that is all. . . . It is practice."

"Oh, I see. You're practicing bombing your own airport." I can't resist the opportunity to chide the guard, whom we call Space Cadet because of his constant blank look and lifeless eyes.

"Who told you they bombed our airfield?" Space Cadet is genuinely puzzled. We're not supposed to know even where we are; how could we possibly know the target of the Iraqi bombers?

"What else could they be bombing? Of course it's the airfield." I watch closely for Space Cadet's reaction. He's nervous and upset. He shines his light in my face and tells me in Farsi to tell the others that supper will be a little late tonight. I tell him we already figured that out for ourselves.

"You will be fed very soon. There is nothing to worry about. It is really nothing."

"If I were you, and my biggest city got bombed, I'd be worried. You're just lucky it's the Iraqis and not the Russians or the Americans who are doing the bombing." Again, I watch his reaction carefully.

"You are not supposed to know who did the bombing, Mr. Scott. I will not say it was Iraq; that is just your guess."

"Good guess, though, right?" Space Cadet doesn't know what to say. He hesitates before answering, "Yes, it is a good guess."

As he leaves our cell, Space Cadet realizes that he has said too much. He tries to retract his statement with another: "It is a good guess, but it is not correct."

"The airplanes were MiGs. If it was not Iraq, it must be the Russians. Are you at war with the Russians?"

"We are not fighting the Russians, Mr. Scott. You ask too many questions. I will tell you nothing."

I translate for Don and Sam, and we all enjoy a good laugh as we wait for our cup of soup and bread.

Falling asleep is not easy tonight. My mind is occupied with this latest turn of events. If Iran and Iraq are at war, Iran is going to have to mend some fences in order to get spare parts for her military forces. This could be good for us. Khomeini and his followers also have a vehicle for uniting the Iranian people — a role which I'm sure we have been playing all along — and encouraging them to forget internal problems. In sum, they no longer will need to keep us hostage if they have something to replace us as the cement that has been holding the revolution together.

However, if Iraq begins to bomb Tehran frequently, there is always the possibility that sooner or later we will be a target. I can't think of a safer place to be in an air raid, though, than inside this very formidable prison.

The bombings have stopped, but every night the Iranians send up their antiaircraft barrages. They have moved some Soviet-made 122mm antiaircraft guns to positions near the prison. When these big guns fire, the prison literally shakes on its foundation. We're spending most of our time in the dark, and time weighs heavily on us. The guards are more tense than usual, but strangely, they're not angry with us. Only Ahmad and two or three of the hard-core militants insist that the United States is behind the war with Iraq. Some of the others brief me almost daily on the progress of the war; they are anxious to discuss it. Reza tells me that the Iranian Air Force is doing well against the Iraqi army. I remind him that his country's Air Force has American airplanes and that the pilots were trained by Americans. He admits that's true. I sense that my prestige has risen among the militants as a result of the war. They frequently confide in me more information than I'm sure they are permitted, and they ask my opinion on how Iran will do militarily against Iraq. Sometimes I think many of them have forgotten the rhetoric of the early days of the takeover and would prefer to get rid of us so they could go off to war and fight the Iraqis.

Hossein and Fazollah, the two guards who were with us in Tabriz, have stopped by to talk with us frequently since the bombing. They're like children in many ways. They complain about having to guard us while their brothers are bathing themselves in combat glory against the "infidel Iraqis." They have volunteered to fight, but they've been told that their mission here is important, too. Hossein says there's nothing exciting or important about guarding hostages, taking them to the bathroom, and making sure they don't escape. This, he says, was O.K. for a few months, but now, with the war, there's more important work for men like him.

Several days later, Hossein, the aspiring warrior, enters our cell with an ear-to-ear smile lighting his young face. His eyes dance with excitement as he tells me that he finally has been given permission to join a Revolutionary Guard unit and go south to fight the invaders. I ask him if he'll receive any training before he goes.

"I have enough training already. I am ready to go now," he says proudly.

"We have been through all this before when I was with you in Tabriz. You can't fight tanks and artillery by yelling 'God is great' and firing your rifle." I almost hate to see Hossein go off to war. He's a terrorist, but he hasn't been as bad as some of the others, and he has been pretty good about giving me information.

"Are you going to say goodbye to Akbar before you leave?" I want to find out what happened to our only decent jailer, and I figure Hossein is just about my last hope. None of the others will say anything about him.

"I said goodbye to him this morning at the embassy. He is working there. He said if I saw you to tell you to be patient. He can't come to see you now, but pretty soon he will be able to see you."

"Maybe if all of you go off to war, we'll be able to walk out of here and go home."

Hossein laughs. "I don't think so. Ahmad and some of the others will stay here until you are released or shot as spies, but you will not be let go because of the war. After we beat the infidels I will come back to see you . . . if you are still here."

"And *if* you come back."

"I will come back," says a very confident

Hossein. "And when I do, I will tell you all about killing the Iraqis."

"And if you do not come back, I will say a prayer for you."

"Your prayer will not help me, but please remember always the roses from Tabriz, and remember I am not your enemy, colonel. I only hated the Shah and your government for helping him. If God wills, I will see you again."

Hossein extends his hand, and we shake hands almost like two parting friends. His going off to war poses a dilemma for me: On one hand, I hate to see an untrained, eager young man go off to a war that he is totally unprepared to fight. His youth and naiveté, coupled with his lack of experience and training, are liabilities which he'll find difficult to overcome. I don't want to see his life snuffed out. On the other hand, he is a terrorist, one of the band that has held us for almost a year, and I guess I would be justified in praying for his death. As a Christian, though, I know that I cannot seek revenge against him by asking God to take his life in combat. I'll save my special requests to God for positive things.

October 22, 1980

"You, Colonel, and you, Mr. Sharer, pack your things. You are moving," Ahmad says as he enters our cell in the middle of the night. He is not excited or upset; this must be a move they've been planning. Sam asks, "What about me?"

"You will not be moving now."

Don and I begin to pack our books and personal items in our blankets, depressed at the thought of still another move with all the uncertainty and terror it portends. Don gives last-minute instructions and words of encouragement to Sam. They have been together for more than seven months, and parting is not easy. In spite of the age and rank differences, they are close friends.

Four guards enter our cell with automatic weapons. Handcuffs are fastened to our wrists, behind our backs. The blindfolds are tightened and, as usual, a dirty blanket is draped over our heads. We're moved through the same three steel bulkheads we entered more than three months ago. Soon I feel the cold night air on my bare feet. And they're wet — it's snowing. I stand in the snow and hear the whispering of my captors. A feeling of helplessness and depression nearly overcomes me. I try not to think about my situation, but there's nothing else to occupy my mind, and my feet are freezing. Finally, I'm led up to a vehicle, pushed inside it, and seated on the floor. "Don'ta - espeak!" I sit and listen, but there's nothing to hear except the breathing of my fellow captives and the repeated orders to remain silent.

I'm struck by a feeling of *deja vu*. In my mind, I'm sitting in the station wagon of Mr. Carl Wesselhoft, an Amesbury, Massachusetts, merchant who used to give my sister Edie and me a ride to school. We would walk the two miles to his house and wait in the cold station wagon for him to drive us to Amesbury for school. We used to dread the walk on cold mornings, and we hated the wait in the frigid station wagon even more. But at least there we were free.

I'm snapped back to reality by the slamming of the door and the starting of the engine. We're on the move again.

16

EVIN PRISON
OCTOBER 22 - DECEMBER 24, 1980

Because our half-hour nocturnal ride is uphill all the way, I assume we must be north of the city. We leave the main highway and begin a series of sharp turns along winding side streets. I've worked my blindfold loose by rubbing my head against the side of the van, but the blanket over my head still obstructs my view. I lean back, raise my knees as high as possible, and try to see out from under the blanket. The guards must not be watching, because they're not saying anything. I see the vehicle lights and silhouettes of the driver and someone in the right front seat. Beyond that, there's only a black void. Since there's not much to see, and since this position, with all my weight balanced on my tail bone, is clumsy and uncomfortable, I decide to save my strength and wait until we stop before I sneak another look.

As the vehicle comes to a stop, I repeat the raised-knee routine and look past the driver and through the windshield. My heart pounds, then sinks. There's a giant steel gate directly in front of us, supported by a thirty-foot-high, smooth stone wall. I'm certain that I recognize this wall. We're waiting to enter Evin prison.

Evin is primarily a political prison, the largest in Iran. Like other Iranian prisons, it was designed and constructed for punishment, not rehabilitation. Most of the maximum-security cells are completely below ground level. Men have spent years in the grim steel-and-concrete cages without ever seeing daylight. Executions here were common under the Shah, and nothing has changed with Khomeini's regime. Before the fall of the embassy, the local newspapers

348

were replete with footage on the daily carnage here, as firing squads worked overtime in the wholesale annihilation of political opponents, minority religious groups, and petty criminal offenders. I have a sickening thought: Don and I may have been brought here for trial and execution. Sam and the other younger members of the embassy staff, who are clearly innocent of any crime against anybody, are not going to be placed on trial, so they weren't selected to move to this terrible place. I wonder how many of the others will join Don and me here. I tick off in my mind the names of those we'll be on the lookout for in the days ahead . . . if there are to be days ahead: Tom Schaefer and Lee Holland, Dave Roeder, Tom Ahern, Dick Morefield, Mike Metrinko, John Limbert, Bill Daugherty, and John Graves. If most of these senior people are here, it's an indication that the Iranians finally may be ready to go ahead with show trials. If that's the case, it surely will be the end of the line for us.

After the usual wait for our captors to get organized, I'm unloaded and escorted blindfolded to a small closetlike room, where the sounds of my guard's instructions ricochet off the walls. My blindfold is removed and the guard leaves. The cell is grim and as cold as the inside of a freezer. There's no heat and no provision for ventilation. The walls are concrete, and the door is steel. Except for a light bulb hanging from a bare wire in the center of the cell, the room is empty. The filthy walls are covered with the usual slogans written by hopeless former occupants. There is what appears to be dried blood and other body fluids on the floor in one corner of the room. I shudder, partly from the intense cold and partly from the grisliness of this place. I feel a new wave of depression. I think of other days, even in prison, when my hopes were high and I believed that somehow I would live through this ordeal and return to my family and America. But the hopes I had then seem to have faded when I entered this cell. I recall the sad words from one of Khayyám's quatrains:

The Worldly Hope men set their Hearts upon
Turns ashes — or it prospers; and anon,
   Like Snow upon the Desert's dusty Face,
Lighting a little hour or two — is gone.

     Am I to be left here alone, without another human with whom I can commiserate?

     My psychological low finally bottoms out, and I feel my mood changing. I've been alone before and I've managed pretty well. I'll do it here, too. I will not let my surroundings depress me to the point where I'm not in complete control of my thoughts. Even if we are placed on trial and executed, I will concentrate on the memories of the years that God has given me, and I'll remember that there is life after death. I will not spend the last days or the last moments of this life in sadness and despair.

     My melancholy mood is interrupted by two guards escorting Don into the cell. His blindfold is removed and he immediately begins to hassle the guards. "Damn it, it's cold as hell in here. How about getting us some blankets and a mattress? We'll freeze in here." Don is even colder than I am, judging by his shaking and his outrage.

     I translate Don's comments to the two guards as Ahmad enters our tiny cell. He says there are no blankets and no mattresses available. He promises to get some *"farda"* [tomorrow]. I tell him that tomorrow may be too late — we may be frozen by then. Ahmad laughs and tells a war story about how cold it was in the Shah's prisons, and how much he and others suffered because of the Shah and America. Our blankets from the other prison apparently are outside waiting to be inspected by the security committee. This happens every time we make a move; sometimes it's a day or two before blankets, toothbrushes, and other personal items are returned. Ahmad says that he will inspect our blankets and return them to us as soon as he has time, but it won't be tonight. I argue with him but to no avail.

In about fifteen minutes, however, Ahmad returns with one blanket for each of us. But one blanket on the cold concrete floor isn't enough. We both realize that we'll have to keep moving around to generate body heat. We take turns jogging in place to keep warm, since there's not enough oxygen in here to support both of us exercising at the same time.

After about two hours, we're both exhausted. We decide to place one blanket on the floor, lie down back to back, and place the other blanket over us. We doze fitfully through the brutally cold night.

Three days later, Ahmad delivers styrofoam mattresses and blankets. That alleviates one problem, but it doesn't do anything about another — the food. Since our arrival here, we've been fed only rice and bread. When I demand better food, he says, "You will have to be satisfied with the food you are getting. It is not possible to get anything else here." He says we will be here until we are either released or put on trial. Or, I think, until we die of scurvy.

So far, we are sure that Tom Ahern is alone in the cell to our right, and we think that Mike Moeller and Captain Paul Needham are in a slightly larger cell to our left. Judging by the trash in the latrine and the amount of toothpaste used each day, there must be about a dozen hostages here.

There are some new militants acting as guards, people we've never seen before. I talked to one young man today who informed me that he was sent here by his local mullah as an alternative to joining the Army or the Revolutionary Guards. He is as anti-Shah as the rest of them, but he appears to be less hostile toward the U.S. In spite of this, he believes that there is a good possibility of trials for some of the hostages. Some of those who guarded us before, I learn, have gone off to fight the war.

"*Salam, Agoya Sarhang Escott. Hala shoma chetora?*" [Peace, Colonel Scott. How is your health?] It's

Akbar, looking pale and even thinner than he was at Tabriz. He's wearing a military parka over an olive-drab field jacket, and his hair has been cut short by a professional barber, judging by the neatly trimmed and tapered sideburns. I use a Persian idiom which, roughly translated, means "Your place has been empty" or "You have been missed." Akbar is pleased by what I say. He smiles broadly and puts his arm on my shoulder. Although Akbar has been learning English, it's still better to speak to him in his native Farsi. He says that there have been many developments since last we saw each other, and he promises to return later in the day, when he has more time, to fill me in on all the news. I tell him that I've heard nothing since Tabriz.

"Oh my," says Akbar, "then there is much to talk about. Do you know the Shah is dead?"

"Yes, Akbar, I do know that. But not much more."

Our only benevolent captor returns, as promised, just after our supper of bread and chicken noodle soup. *"Khabara khoob va khabara bad daram"* [I have good news and bad news], says Akbar, handing each of us a bag of pistachios. I tell him to give us the bad news first. He says it wouldn't make sense without first hearing the good news.

"The *Majlis* [Parliament] will decide your fate. They will decide the conditions of your release. That's the good news."

"And the bad news?"

"I'm very sorry, but I don't know when this will be; they are too busy with other more important matters."

"Such as?" I ask with noticeable impatience.

"The war. It is taking very much of the Majlis' time and energy. It is going better for us now, but still, every day men are being killed at the front. Your situation has less priority than before the war."

"Maybe if America drops a few big ones on some of your major cities, our priority will go up again."

"No, I don't think so. If that happens, I'm afraid you will be killed by the people." Ever the optimist, Akbar adds, "I don't think it will come to that. I believe it will end for you soon, but not until after your election. Who do you think will win?"

I tell Akbar that I don't know who will win, because I haven't been allowed to receive information on what's going on at home. Right now it seems to be a dead heat, he says, according to the polls in America. Then he asks what I think Reagan will do if he wins the election. I pause for a moment, look Akbar straight in the eyes. I see no bitterness or hatred, only concern and a romantic's perennial hope that in the end, all will be well. I continue to stare at him without answering.

"What do you think Reagan will do?" Akbar is showing a rare sign of impatience. He really does want to hear my best guess.

"Boom! Boom! Boom!" I answer with my best sound effects.

"Do you really think so?" Akbar's eyes are as big as saucers. He's genuinely concerned and waiting for me to elaborate. I tell him they've been lucky that Carter has been our president, because any other American president I can recall would have lowered the military boom on them within a week or two after we were taken hostage. Carter has been more patient than they can expect Reagan to be if he wins, I continue.

The American people must be getting tired of this blackmail charade by now, and an American president will be forced to do something drastic if the situation is not resolved by January, when either Reagan takes office or Carter begins a new term, I say. I remind him that if Carter wins, he will have a new mandate from the American people, so there is no telling what he may do.

Akbar seems saddened by my prophecy. He says nothing for a minute, but he obviously is in deep thought. "I pray to God you are wrong, Colonel. I pray it will be settled and you can go home. But if Carter or Reagan uses military force, the Iranian people will resist and it will not be good for you." There is no threat in his voice. On the contrary, he seems sincerely interested in resolving the crisis without bloodshed.

I opt to change the subject; his concern and sincerity are unnerving. "Hey, Akbar, just in case we ever do get out of here, I need a favor. Do you remember the red T-shirt I had with the white eagle on it? It was stolen from me when I was moved out of the Mushroom Inn in March. Can you get me another?"

"I'll try," he says, breaking his pensive mood and grinning broadly.

Akbar says he will get us some books, too. He is in charge of the prison here, just as he was in Tabriz, but he warns that we'll have to be careful to follow all the rules, so as not to get in trouble with the hard-line security men. As long as I've got his ear, I complain that it is very cruel to keep the man in the next cell all alone — pretending I don't know that the man is Tom Ahern. He says the man has been alone for a year because he's a spy. That's pure hogwash, I say. Besides, no man should be left alone forever. I ask him how he thinks that kind of treatment will be perceived by the rest of the world if we're ever released. Akbar agrees that it would not be good, and he promises to try to arrange some system whereby the man in the next cell can have some company. I tell him that would be very considerate — and also be good for the revolution's reputation.

The hostages in the cell to our left have been moved. We think we're the only ones left in this wing of the prison, except for Tom Ahern, who is still in the cell to our right. It is difficult to raise the guards to take us to the toilet. This morning, when our bread and tea arrive, the guard walks away leaving our door open, so after a while, Don and

I decide to explore the hallway. Just as we're about to slip out the door, Akbar appears and asks where we're going. I tell him I'm tired of this place, and I'm slipping out for some decent food. Akbar laughs and says he'll leave our cell door open during the day so we can visit our neighbor. The cell block door at the end of the hall will remain secured and we'll be locked in our cells again in the evening. I thank him, and we hurry down the hall to Tom.

Although we're delighted to see him, Tom seems nervous and obviously overwhelmed by our visit. He is unusually introspective at first — a result of his eleven months alone. Like the rest of us, he has lost weight, but he didn't have any extra to lose; he looks gaunt and meek. My earlier estimate is correct: He has no information at all. He didn't even know of the Shah's death. We spend most of the day filling Tom in on what we know for sure and speculating on our situation.

As the day wears on, Tom is more relaxed and talkative. I ask him about the tapping noise we hear coming from his cell each afternoon and again in the evening. He says he does finger exercises, so he'll still be able to play the piano when he's set free. For a man who has spent almost a year alone, he is in remarkably good spirits. He was accused of spying and has been beaten and tortured; his denials obviously didn't work as well as mine. Mentally, he is as sharp as ever; he still has his sense of humor and his dignity, in spite of his long ordeal. After hearing his story, I have even more respect for him. He is a man of great moral strength and an unusual gift of faith. Not surprisingly, he says that Akbar is the only militant who has treated him decently. He has been fed the same as the rest of us, but he has had no opportunity to interact with anyone — not even the militants. Even when I was in solitary, there were guards who would visit my cell to pass the time. I realize what an advantage I've enjoyed because I speak Farsi. The three of us have supper together, after which Don and I are ordered to return to our cell to be locked in for the night.

Again this morning, the guard delivering breakfast does not lock our cell door. We continue our discussion with Tom throughout the morning and early afternoon until Akbar appears, looking emotionally distraught. His eyes are red, and it's evident that he's been crying. I ask him what's troubling him. He asks if I remember Hossein and Fazollah from our stay in Tabriz. I tell him that I remember them not only from Tabriz, but also from the early days of the Mushroom Inn.

Akbar says they were both killed at Susangerd in Kuzestan Province in an Iraqi tank-and-rocket attack, along with more than two hundred and fifty other Islamic soldiers. I ask him if any of the other guards were killed, hoping that Pig Face, Hamid the Liar, or some of the other hateful militants might have gotten theirs as well, but he says that these two are the only embassy militants killed. I sense Akbar's grief, so I pretend to be upset over this news, too. I thump my chest, in true Iranian fashion, and tell him that I'm very sorry. He says their bodies will be returned to Tehran in a day or so, and he will attend their funerals at Martyr's Cemetery.

Though we joke after Akbar's departure about my Oscar-winning performance, feigning grief over our captors' deaths, I cannot help remembering my conversations with Hossein at Tabriz. He wanted so much to be a soldier and knew so little about the profession of arms. But the thing I remember most vividly is the time he gave me the roses. How prophetic the lines from Khayyám's quatrain which he recited to me at Tabriz on that summer day. Little did I know then that Hossein and Fazollah would be taken away with the rose of yesterday. If there is a special place in heaven for soldiers who die for their country, I'm sure Hossein and Fazollah will be admitted — I respect their dedication in spite of our political differences. One man's terrorist is another man's freedom fighter, and one's gallant soldier may be another's fanatic. It depends on one's loyalties and beliefs.

Although I don't agree with Hossein's justification for the embassy attack, I do not question the sincerity of either his religious commitment or his patriotism. In the final analysis, he fought and died for his country.

President Eisenhower was right when he said, "War is man's greatest stupidity."

In the wake of Fazollah's and Hossein's deaths, Akbar has changed. He has lost his sense of humor and has reservations about some revolutionary precepts which previously he accepted as articles of faith. His customary optimism has been replaced by cynicism, and this essentially honest man has trouble hiding it. When I ask him what he would do if he had power over his destiny, and ours, he manages a faint smile and replies without hesitation, "If it were up to me, you would already be free in America, and I would be in college."

Akbar is trying to do everything possible, within the parameters of the strict rules ordered by his security people, to make our existence less unpleasant. He pokes his generous nose inside our cell and inquires, "Do you still want to move to the next cell?"

We have been trying to convince him to move us to the empty cell on our right. It's larger, and although its window has been covered by a steel plate, there's a three-inch gap on either side where fresh air enters, offering a modicum of ventilation. Even more enticing, you can see daylight. Tom's cell has a similar arrangement. I quickly answer yes, and in less than half an hour, we're moved to our new cell.

By looking through the gap between the edge of the window casement and the steel plate welded to the prison bars, we get an oblique view of the street, which apparently runs through the large prison complex. During the day, there are pedestrians and vehicles on this fairly wide and well-traveled street. The area is used for marshalling Revolutionary Guards who are preparing to move south to fight the invading Iraqis. It is no different from watching Americans go off to war. There are kisses and tears, tears and kisses. Mothers are caught up in the perplexing dilemma between the pride they feel for their sons, who are going off to do battle for "God and the Motherland," and the overwhelming fear and anxiety they experience in realizing that their sons may never return.

I try to view it all with detachment, through the narrow perspective of my prison cell, but it's too universal a scene to watch impassively. I'm reminded of my departure for Vietnam and other tours of duty which portended danger, and I sympathize with those going off to war, and with their loved ones who must remain behind to pray and hope that their sons and husbands will be spared. Amid the chatter and attempts at making light of their situation, there's an overriding air of fear and uncertainty. Each mother who embraces her son seems to sense that it may be her last chance to do so while he still breathes the life she gave him.

Finally, a mullah shouts an order, and the young men, suitcases and makeshift baggage in hand, bid farewell to parents, sisters, and wives and board the bus. As the vehicle pulls away, the mullah, acting as cheerleader for the residual group, leads them in the revolutionary slogan, *"Al-loh-Akbar"* [God is great]. In all the times I have heard this chant, this is the first time it has seemed to have an interrogative tone, a rising inflection on the end, as though it were a question rather than a declaration of faith. It's as though these people are, perhaps without even realizing it themselves, questioning: "If God is great, why must my son or my husband be a candidate for martyrdom?"

Within thirty minutes after the buses depart, the families have dispersed and there's very little activity in the area. An occasional revolutionary or prison guard passes, and less frequently a man or woman in civilian clothes, apparently going to or coming from work in the prison's administrative offices, walks through.

Don and I decide to exercise. With the window open, there's more than enough fresh air, so we take advantage of it and begin to run in place. We're distracted by a commotion outside our window.

"East!" [Halt!] Someone outside is being stopped. I quit exercising and try to see what's going on. I can't see anything — they're out of our limited viewing range — but I can hear a guard questioning another man on what he's doing in this area. The man says that he was taking a shortcut back to his home from his job on the other side of the prison compound. He says that he has always come this way. The two continue to argue, and the guard gets more and more excited and irritated.

Suddenly a shot rings out. Not thirty feet from our window, the trespasser cries out in pain and anguish, asking the guard why he shot him. The guard says he should not have been in the area. Within minutes, other guards arrive and discuss the situation with the one who fired the shot. They all agree that the guard was justified in his actions, and they leave the wounded man. He is pleading for medical help, begging someone to help him, but his cries and moans are not heeded by any of the guards or civilians who pass.

Late in the afternoon, just before dark, I hear two people talking. One asks what happened and the other replies, "He was shot by a guard. He should not have been here. Do not try to help him — you will only get in trouble with the guards." I hear them walk away.

The wounded man apparently has dragged himself to a position directly below our window. Throughout the evening and on into the night, we hear his pleas for help and his prayers for deliverance. By about midnight, his wound and the cold are too much for him. He lets out a series of pitiful moans and then is silent. We assume he's dead.

"Colonel, are you awake?" It's Akbar, entering our cell holding a small battery-operated portable radio. He has a paper bag in his other hand. He throws it onto my thin mattress and tells me it's the red T-shirt I asked him to find for me. I open the bag and thank him for the shirt. "But why so early in the morning, Akbar? You could have given this to me later."

Akbar is like a child with a happy secret he can't wait to tell a close friend. I haven't seen him in this good a mood since before he learned of Hossein's and Fazollah's deaths. He wants to share some news with me this morning when it is broadcast at six o'clock, he says. The Majlis Special Commission has sent its demands for our release to President Carter, and they have word that Carter is going to accept the conditions. Akbar is happier than I have ever seen him. "It is almost over, Colonel, it is almost over. We have won, but you have won, too. You will be going home soon." Akbar is so elated that he puts his arms around me. He's serious — he really believes that the hostage crisis is coming to an end and we're going home. I'm reluctant to believe him, but he's so sincere and so happy.

"What are these demands, Akbar?"

"America must agree never to interfere again in our internal affairs; return our money, which was frozen in America by Carter; return the Shah's fortune, stolen from the Iranian people; and cancel all debts and claims against Iran arising out of our seizure of your embassy. That's all."

"Akbar, what makes you so sure Carter will agree to these demands?"

"We have information from someone in Washington confirming Carter's willingness to agree." It's obvious that Akbar wants to believe; the romantic in him sees it as a sure thing.

But I have serious reservations about the U.S. government accepting these demands. Even if Carter wants to agree, he is still bound by the courts, and I don't think the courts will send the Pahlavi fortune to Iran to win our freedom.

That would involve a great deal of legal activity and time; it couldn't be accomplished overnight, even if the Carter administration pulled out all the stops. I have trouble understanding how our government can cancel all claims against Iran, too, and I tell Akbar how I feel.

As much as I want to go home, I realize that if all these demands are agreed to by our government — if, indeed, that's possible — it will be a clear victory for revolutionary Iran. It will mean that the United States succumbed to blackmail. Deep in my heart, I hope our country will not give in to these demands, even though it would mean freedom for us. If the basis of our release has been reduced to money, I feel safer; why would the Iranians decide to have trials and executions at this stage of the game? I'd rather see the U.S. hold out a little longer until Iran agrees to terms that will not disgrace America.

The 6:00 a.m. news broadcast is just beginning. It's the state-run radio station, and the lead story is about great victories against Iraq. I tell Akbar that if the Iraqis really are losing as many tanks and airplanes as Iran claims, the war will be over "last week." Akbar smiles and gives me a one-word answer: "Propaganda."

I watch Akbar's eyes during the fifteen-minute news summary. As the program progresses, the hope and joy he showed a few minutes ago begin to fade, replaced by a look of disappointment, betrayal, and frustration. The program concludes — there is no mention of the hostages or of any agreement between Iran and the United States.

"But I brought you your shirt with the eagle so you could wear it home. This was supposed to have been a great day for all of us. I wonder what has happened?" says Akbar rhetorically.

He is genuinely puzzled. He fully expected the crisis to be over today. He even violated his own security rules by allowing me to listen to the news. Our benevolent terrorist seems more disappointed than we are.

It is November 4, election day in America and exactly one year since we were taken hostage. With the eight-and-a-half-hour time difference, we don't expect the Iranians to get word on the outcome of the election until early tomorrow morning. Don and I discuss the election and speculate on whether or not the Iranians will tell us the results. I figure Akbar will tell us, and there's a possibility that some of the other terrorists will ask questions concerning the election which may unintentionally give us the information we seek.

For the last couple of days, Tom has not been permitted out of his cell and we've been locked in ours. Something must have happened which forced them to modify the more permissive arrangement.

An older, obnoxious-acting little weasel, who has never looked directly at a hostage, enters our cell with a retinue of guards and security people we haven't seen since the early days at the embassy. Akbar is with them. The security man looks around our cell, then tells Akbar that this is unacceptable. He says it's not secure because we can see outside, and he directs Akbar to put us back in the smaller cell without ventilation. Sensing that he understands English, I say to Don, "I wonder what apple this worm crawled out of." He understands, but he won't reply or even look at us. Akbar is hanging his head like a little boy who got caught with his hand in the cookie jar. I can tell he's angry, but he says nothing. One of the other guards informs the security chief that we have been permitted to visit with Ahern. The little weasel is beside himself with rage. He says he'll talk to Akbar alone — and this is never to be permitted again. As soon as he leaves, we're moved back to our original, more dismal cell.

Early on the morning of November 5, our bread and tea are delivered by a young guard named Mahmoud. I ask, in Farsi, about the election results. Mahmoud is surprisingly candid: "Carter lost, forty-nine to forty-two. We have changed your president. What do you think Reagan will do?" I

362

give him my sound-effects version of bombs exploding, and his reaction is the same as Akbar's. He asks if I'm serious or only trying to frighten him. I tell him that I could not be more serious. I can tell I got to him — he burns his hand on the hot tea kettle as he turns to leave our cell.

Through our tap-code communications system, eavesdropping on guard conversations, and the foul-ups in the latrine, when guards permitted people from different cells to be there at the same time, Don and I have developed a complete roster of the hostages imprisoned here. Mike Moeller and Paul Needham are in the cell to our right. Tom Ahern has been moved, but he's still in this building — we know because he answered a prearranged signal in the common-use latrine, which we had set up when we were allowed to visit him. Al Golacinski and Dick Morefield are in the cell with the window to our left. We have seen Courtney Barnes, Malcolm Kalp, Colonels Lee Holland and Tom Schaefer, and Bill Daugherty. There are twelve of us here. All are either senior people or those who consistently have given the Iranians a bad time. If they do decide to have trials, there's no question that we're the ones who will head the list. However, a guard told me the other day that we were moved here in case the U.S. tried another rescue attempt prior to the election. If any Iranians were killed in the course of an attempt to free the others, we would be shot in retaliation.

The prison diet here has been hard on Don's stomach. He makes frequent trips to the latrine — which is not good for him but is good for our information-gathering. The more we use the latrine, the better our chance to catch a glimpse of one of the others or hear them speak. Don reenters our cell after another such trip.

"Hey, guess who I just saw?" he says. "You know the other day I said I smelled perfume or hand lotion or some other female smell in the latrine? Guess who."

"Ann Swift," I reply.

"No, but you're close. I just saw Kate Koob for a second as I left the latrine. She was waiting to get in. She looks great; she must have lost seventy-five pounds or more."

"If she's here, I would think Ann is here, too. We'll have to be on the lookout. I wonder why they've been moved here. I'm sure they weren't here before."

"With these idiots, who knows?" says Don.

It's our second Thanksgiving in captivity. We have settled again into a very dull routine of exercise, reading, and waiting for meals. The routine never changes, nor does the menu. We're living on bread and rice with an occasional spoonful of the spinachlike *khoresh* poured over it. We're sure that they will not bring the TV cameras inside this dismal prison, so there's no reason for a special meal today, as far as our captors are concerned.

Don and I are feeling a bit low, sitting in the dark thinking about home, when Akbar and two of the other less hostile guards enter our cell with two lighted candles. They distribute a tray of Thanksgiving favors, obviously made by Kate and Ann — whom I caught a glimpse of yesterday coming back from the latrine. Akbar wishes us a happy Thanksgiving. I tell him it will be happy for us only when we're out of here. He doesn't answer. The favors include apples decorated with colored paper and made to look like fat turkeys, some nuts, and Persian dates. It's not much, but the idea that the girls went to the trouble is reassuring. They're two very tough and very special ladies to have put up with all this for so long. I ask Akbar who made the favors and he says, "Friends of yours." He knows that I know Kate and Ann are here, but he's not at liberty to admit it. I try not to think about my many happy Thanksgiving holidays, but it's difficult not to feel sad in this situation. I decide to have some fun with Don and perhaps cheer up both of us. "Hey, Don, how would you like to be sitting down right now in my favorite restaurant in Atlanta, where the specialty of the house is prime rib? You've just finished your first beer in a frosted mug, the melted frost is cascading down the glass, and you ask the waitress, who's serving your inch-and-a-half-thick slice of medium rare prime rib, with horseradish sauce and baked potato smothered in sour cream and butter, to do it again. She smiles and slinks away with your glass for a refill as you begin to cut into your slab of beef. . . ."

"Chuck, if I had someone else as a substitute cellmate, I'd kill you. You really know how to hurt a guy."

"Yeah, Don, but one of these days, when this is over, we'll be doing just that, and I'll never take things like good food for granted again."

"You got that right, but until then, knock off the chatter about prime rib — that's too much for me to handle." We both laugh, our spirits once again raised temporarily from the depths.

Akbar enters our cell dressed in civilian clothes. We've seen him only twice in the last two weeks, and I suspect he's not assigned to this prison anymore. He hands me a bag of pistachios and asks how we're doing. I ask him where he has been. He smiles and says he'll tell me in good time. Nothing has changed since his last visit, he says. The United States continues to resist accepting the conditions dictated by Iran for our release, and the Iranian hard-liners will not budge, either. I ask him if he sees any possibility that we'll be out of here before Christmas, and he reluctantly says he doesn't believe that will be possible. He says he has lost faith in the whole hostage affair; he never dreamed it would go on so long. To him, it seems that both sides are stalling and have little concern for him or for me. Akbar the romantic has become Akbar the realist. He says the war continues, and Iranian losses continue to mount. He is considering joining the army or the Revolutionary Guards, as he feels his place should be at the front.

I tell him that he should avoid going to the front for as long as possible. It's easy to be brave and go off to war, but his country will need men of his understanding and courage after the war is over, when Iran tries to piece together some kind of viable government. He says he appreciates my concern, but that he believes it's his duty as a follower of Islam and as an Iranian. I tell him that I admire his noble intentions, but getting himself killed will not change what's going on in his homeland.

The revolution is taking much longer than expected to develop the kind of homeland he wants, and there are things happening which he doesn't agree with, he complains. I ask him to explain. He says there's still corruption, and many petty officials and others in positions of authority are oppressing people for their own purposes, which are unrelated to Islam.

Then, suddenly, Akbar blurts out that he has taken a job with the state-run news agency, PARS, and he is here only as a visitor. He will not be allowed to visit us again. I'm stunned and angry. After holding us for more than a year, he has decided that it's too complicated and futile for him to cope with. So he just walks out and picks up the pieces of his life, while we remain here to rot in one of his prisons.

"Akbar, you and your band of terrorists started all this, and now you tell me you're tired of it. No wonder your country has been conquered by so many invaders since Cyrus the Great." My frustration is obvious in my voice. "You used to speak of commitment to your revolution — what has happened to you?"

Akbar is hurt and appears to feel guilty. "You are right, Colonel; I had hoped this would end months ago and you could go home. I even hoped we might part as friends. There is too much hatred in the world. I do not understand you in some ways, but I have learned to respect you. I guess in many ways, I admire you. You have been good to me as a human being, yet you have never compromised your principles."

My shock and anger are melting into a bizarre form of sadness. "I really don't understand you in some ways, either, Akbar, but I respect you as a sincere man who would like to be kind. I hate what your people have done, and I will always loathe people like Hamid, Ahmad, and Pig Face. . . . I guess I would kill them if I were angry enough and had the opportunity."

Akbar is in deep thought, but his expressive eyes are saying more than he'll ever be able to articulate. "I have thought many times about what I would do if I had to kill you. . . . I'm not sure I could have obeyed that order if it had ever been given. I am glad to be away from here."

"If you had been ordered by Khomeini to kill me, you would have done it. You would still do it today. The only difference now is that you know me, as I know you, so it no longer would be so impersonal. It would be more difficult, but you would do it."

"Maybe, but I am not so sure."

Akbar extends his hand, which I grasp with both of mine. He wishes me luck and says he will continue to pray for all of us and for a speedy resolution to our situation. I tell him that I also wish him luck. He asks if it would be all right if he wrote to me in America when this is over and I'm home.

"Do you still think that I ever will get home?" I ask.

"In my heart, I am sure you will live to see your family again. When you are released, if it is possible, I will come to say goodbye."

Akbar, the compassionate terrorist, turns and leaves our cell. I'm certain that his abrupt departure was an impromptu gesture to keep me from seeing his misty eyes. And for a few minutes I want to be alone, too.

PIECES OF THE GAME

Three weeks have gone by since Akbar's last visit, and there still are no signs of progress toward freedom. It's Christmas Eve, and Don and I aren't looking forward to another Christmas in prison. There has been some activity in the corridor, but it appears that we're not even going to be treated to a holiday propaganda show with decent food and TV cameras. We both feel as though we've been forgotten and may be here for the rest of our lives.

We hear tapping. There's a message coming from the cell to our left. Don answers the initial taps and gets the word from Captain Needham and Sergeant Moeller: They have been told that they're leaving this prison. Don listens against the other wall. Ahmad, or one of the other leaders, is in the cell talking to Dick and Al. He says that they have been alerted to move, too. Don and I listen to the increasing activity in the corridor, wondering if we're going to be left here while the others move. My mind races through a number of scenarios, none of which portends anything good about this latest turn of events. If we're left here while the others go, does it signal the beginning of trials? Or is there to be a Christmas release of some of the hostages? We're sure of only one thing: If we're left behind, it's a bad omen.

We hear the others escorted out of their cells. One guard tells Al and Dick that they're being moved to a much better place — a place that is not a prison. Don and I sit in the dark, depressed and confounded by our status.

The others have been gone for about an hour, when a guard enters our cell with a flashlight and asks what we're still doing here. I tell him Khomeini forgot to send me my plane ticket to America. He says we were supposed to have been moved to another place, and we should get ready to leave.

"Merry Christmas, Don."

"Same to you. At least we'll be out of here. No matter where we go, it's bound to be better than this place."

We guess it must be about midnight as we're escorted from our cell to a waiting van. Handcuffed, blindfolded, and cold, we're pushed inside the relatively warm vehicle. It's the beginning of our second Christmas as hostages.

The Price
of Freedom

17

MINISTRY OF FOREIGN AFFAIRS
GUEST HOUSE, TEHRAN
DECEMBER 25, 1980 — JANUARY 20, 1981

After no more than twenty minutes on the road, driving rapidly along a zigzag course, our driver halts in response to a sentry's command. There's whispering between the driver and someone outside, then a gate opens creakily. We're unloaded without the customary delay and taken inside a building. I feel thick carpeting under my bare feet as we move down a hallway and up a long staircase. Someone tugs the blanket away, and then my blindfold is removed, revealing a warm, pleasant, and brightly lighted room.

I squint, trying to adjust to the light. I see Don beside me and Dick Morefield and Regis Ragan on the other side of the room. Our eyes dart back and forth, but none of us speaks. Ahmad, forcing a smile, asks why we don't greet each other. Almost by command, Regis and I shake hands, and Don and Dick do the same. Regis looks pale and hollow-eyed. His long, shaggy beard emphasizes his loss of weight and generally run-down condition. I haven't seen him since early March, almost ten months ago. At that time, he had been pretty well worked over by the interrogators and was living in constant fear of more questioning. He also was bothered by a severe skin rash, which evidently has not improved. Mentally, though, he seems as agile and alert as ever. As our tentativeness subsides, our initial handshake turns into a warm bear hug.

Ahmad and his guards seem to be enjoying our little reunion; they're smiling broadly in the background as Dick and I also greet each other. Ahmad asks if we're hun-

373

gry. In unison, Don and I tell him we're always hungry. He instructs one of his guards to bring us cheese and bread. Ahmad says that we'll be staying here at least over the holidays. Then he adds as we walks out the door, "You will be having very important visitors very soon."

Dick says that he and Al, his cellmate at Evin prison, were moved here about two hours ago. Al was separated from him and apparently is in another room. We figure the Iranians shuttled us over here a few at a time for security reasons. Ragan was moved here about a week ago, directly from Khomeiteh prison. He was not in our group at Evin at all. He says the food here is better than any he has had in the last thirteen months. So is the room — it's like a large Holiday Inn double with a private bath. Regis says the water is even hot most of the time, and that he has showered every day since he arrived. Don and I check out the facilities. There are built-in bookshelves and cabinets along one wall; the tiled bathroom is clean and inviting. Glass sliding doors open onto a balcony, but heavy steel bars have been welded in place to prevent our escape. Heavy draperies, in a gaudy, dark blue material, cover the glass doors. Regis says there are guards outside, and the drapes must be kept closed at all times. The standard wooden door at the entrance to our room has been replaced by a makeshift steel one. All the standard motel furniture has been removed, except for a large table and four straight-backed chairs. Regis has a styrofoam mattress, but there are no other beds or mattresses.

We carefully check the entire room for electronic listening devices — after the closed-circuit TV in the toilet at Khomeiteh prison, I wouldn't put anything past Ahmad and his people — but find nothing.

Then we discuss why we've been moved to this relative paradise, and we all agree that it's strictly staging for a holiday propaganda show. It's our second Christmas in captivity, and the Iranians are trying again to convince the world that we're being well treated. We also speculate on how long we'll stay here. Dick says it will depend on the progress of negotiations. Judging from Ahmad's solicitous attitude, we suspect the negotiations must look promising. In any case, all of this is a good sign.

As we prepare to stretch out on the floor to sleep, Ahmad reappears with our blankets and personal articles. He says he'll get mattresses for us in the morning. If he's expecting visitors, we'll probably get them as promised. He also will be on his good behavior until the visitors are gone.

In spite of my fatigue, I have trouble sleeping. I hear Don snoring and Dick and Regis rolling over, bothered by the sound which I've become accustomed to in eight months as Don's cellmate. But it's not Don's snoring that's keeping me awake; it's the fact that it is Christmas, the second one we have spent as prisoners. How many more will there be? I realize that the next twenty-six days may be the most critical of my life. We have been hearing about negotiations since early November. If there's no agreement before Carter leaves office, it'll mean that the new administration will have to start all over again. If President Reagan tries to bully our release or simply refuses to negotiate with the Iranians, they could put some of us on trial to try to rekindle American interest in the crisis. If the Iranians really want to end the stalemate, they must realize that this is their best chance.

As I get drowsy, my mind takes me to another world. I'm listening to Christmas music as I throw the Yule log on the fire and sip cognac. It's cold outside, but the house is warm and peaceful. Beth and Greg have gone to bed, after opening their gifts, and Betty and I are listening to a medley of songs commemorating the birth of our Savior. *"It came upon a midnight clear. . . ."* Then I hear my favorite, "Oh, Holy Night." But this time I actually *am* hearing it — not just dreaming it. Someone out in the hall is playing a recording of Christmas music. I lean forward, my arms over my knees, and listen.

Oh, holy night, the stars are brightly shining;
It is the night of the dear Savior's birth.
Long lay the world. . . .

"Dear God," I pray quietly, "if it be Thy will, bring peace to my loved ones this night. And give wisdom to the leaders here and at home, so that we may know again the peace and liberty of our land which You have so richly blessed." Perhaps it's this night, perhaps it's the music or just my feeling of closeness to God when I pray spontaneously, but I feel at peace with all men. I feel unbelievably good for a man who has been a hostage for so long. The music has stopped, but in my mind it continues to echo.

"Wake up, my friends, you are going to celebrate Christmas." As I sensed, Ahmad is on his best behavior. The usual snarl is missing from his voice, and he's calling us his "friends." He says we are to dress quickly, and he'll return to take us to church services. He leaves, but before we're dressed, he returns with new shirts for each of us — taken from the small store at the embassy. I'm given a medium-sized, red knit sport shirt with a blue collar and trim. I try it on, thinking it'll be too small, but the fit is perfect. I used to wear a large, but my weight still must be about thirty-five pounds below normal.

Ahmad returns in about an hour, all milk and honey. He tells us to put our blindfolds on and line up, one behind the other, chain-gang style. After a short march, we're told to remove our blindfolds. We're in a large room with bright green walls and heavy drapes covering the windows. A priest I recognize as Yohanan Issaye, the Chaldean Catholic Bishop of Tehran, greets each one of us. He appears nervous and apparently is concerned about his own safety. TV cameras and bright strobe lights are pointed directly at us. I see two small, sickly-looking Christmas trees and the usual revolutionary propaganda posters, extolling the great virtue of Khomeini and his teachings and condemning the United States as the "Great Satan." The room is alive with the usual gallery of militant spectators, smiling and acting as though they've done something special for us. The bishop asks us to sit with him behind a long table. The Papal Nuncio in Tehran, Monsignor Annibale Bugnini, walks out of the shadows. He greets us, too. He's wearing the traditional black clothing of a priest and the Roman collar. The Chaldean bishop is wearing a full-length white robe with a red skull cap. He begins to read from the Bible. His English is spotty at best, and his nervousness makes his words all but unintelligible. His hands are shaking as he struggles with the text of the Christmas story according to St. Matthew. Finally he can't go on, so he asks me to read the scripture for him. I take the Bible from him and read the rest of the story of the birth of Christ, as the TV cameras capture the entire sad spectacle on videotape.

After the reading, the bishop asks if we would like to take communion. Don and I tell him we're not Catholic. He says it doesn't matter and asks if we've been baptised. When we tell him we have, he asks us individually if we believe in God. I tell him I do, and he blesses me, giving me absolution. I take communion with the others. The members of the gallery are silent and intent, as though they understand the significance of this sacrament and either respect or fear it. The bishop, his hands still trembling, embraces each of us, makes the sign of the cross, and says he will continue to pray for our safety. We're given gifts, wrapped in blue and white flowered tissue paper, some apples, nuts, and Hershey chocolate bars. Then Ahmad says that it's time for us to go so others also may celebrate. They apparently are going to parade all the hostages in front of the camera one more time.

Late in the afternoon, we're told that we will have additional visitors: senior diplomats from Algeria. In less than thirty minutes, our Christmas show resumes with the entrance of several Algerian diplomats in business suits.

I recognize the Algerian Ambassador to Iran, Abdul Karim Gheraieb, and Muhammad Bel Hossein, from the Algerian Foreign Ministry. Bel Hossein officially informs us of the negotiations in progress between his country and Iran and his country and the United States. He makes it clear that there are no direct discussions between Iran and the U.S., and that Algeria is acting as intermediary. He says they'll be returning to Washington later in the day to convey the latest Iranian position to our government. Even his carefully selected, noncommittal words give us hope. He asks if we have any questions, so I ask him if he thinks that there's any possibility we'll be released before Reagan takes office on January 20. He says his team is working very hard to settle the remaining issues between Iran and the United States as soon as possible, but he doesn't want to mislead us or give us false hopes by implying that he thinks an early agreement is probable. I ask him to assign a probability figure to the chances of our being out of here within one month. He hedges, in true diplomatic fashion, saying it's all too complex and involved for him to come up with a probability. I tell him I understand all this, but I still would like his best guess. Reluctantly, he says the probability of our getting out of here while Carter is still in office is less than fifty-fifty. The Algerian ambassador interjects that they're doing their best to speed the negotiations along, because they realize complications and delays could result from the change of administrations in Washington.

Ahmad tries to hurry the diplomats along, but Bel Hossein raises his hand in protest; there's something else he wants to say to us, and he's not going to let this militant who has no diplomatic status or position hurry him. I sense that he's a very tough and determined man, and I'm glad he is working with his colleagues from Algeria to resolve our crisis. He says he'll return in about an hour to pick up any letters we want to write. He makes it a point to let us know that he personally will take them to America and they will not be subject to censorship by our captors. The smile is gone from Ahmad's face, but he says nothing. I feel a real affinity for these men who are helping my country, and a very special respect for Bel Hossein.

I write a short letter to Betty and the children, wishing them a happy holiday season and enjoining them to keep the faith as we begin a new year. I also write a short note to my mother and my sisters, Edith and Mary. True to his word, Bel Hossein returns in less than an hour and collects them.

At about four o'clock in the afternoon, we're served a turkey dinner. It obviously has been prepared by someone with extensive knowledge of traditional American holiday menus, if not any great expertise in cooking them. I get a medium-sized drumstick, again cooked medium rare — great for steak, but not for turkey. I eat it anyway, along with mashed potatoes, gravy, peas and carrots, and a helping of tossed salad.

After dinner, Ahmad brings packages for Dick and Don from their wives. He says there were no gifts from home for Regis or me; we assume that our gifts were delayed in the mail. But he does give us several gifts addressed to "American Hostage in Iran." One is an outlandish-looking yellow warmup shirt with a hood. Another is a set of springs with hand grips for exercising the upper part of the body. And then the jackpot: a small, fairly heavy package containing a *1981 World Almanac and Book of Facts*. I've been reading these every year since I was a boy in grammar school. Ahmad and four other militants stand around and watch us open our gifts, seemingly very interested in this American holiday tradition. The younger militants want to handle the gifts, and they ask questions about Don's and Dick's families. They're about as excited as we are. I fidget with the wrapping paper, nervously waiting for Ahmad to take the almanac away from me; he must know that these books contain a chronology of major events for the previous year, but he makes no move. I push the almanac aside, as though I'm not very interested in it. I can hardly wait for the militants to go so I can confirm the bits and pieces of information that we've been able to gather during the long thirteen months of isolation and total news blackout.

As soon as they leave, I turn to page 897, the beginning of the chronology of the year's events from November 1, 1979, to November 1, 1980. It's all here: the takeover of the embassy, the fall of the Bazargan government, the formation of the Islamic Republic, the escape of six embassy staffers with the help of the Canadians, the aborted rescue mission, the Soviet invasion of Afghanistan, Rich Queen's release, the Iranian war with Iraq, and everything else right up to the end of October, 1980. I think of Akbar as I read and reread these events. Everything he told me was accurate, or at least as accurate as one could expect it to be when viewed by an Iranian militant. But the chronology ends in mid-October; there's nothing on current negotiations. We all read the almanac and discuss the contents, speculating on what will happen next. I advise all of my cellmates to read everything they're interested in before Ahmad realizes how much information is contained in this book. I'm sure he will take it away when he does.

Three days after Christmas, Ahmad enters our room and demands that the almanac be returned. I give it to him, complaining that I haven't had an opportunity to read it yet. Of course he doesn't believe me, but it's too late. As the militants always say, "It does not matter."

Our days have become routine once more. Dick Morefield is an accomplished bridge player, and he gives the rest of us lessons every evening after supper. We play for several hours each night. In the mornings after breakfast, we move everything to the center of the room and run for an hour or more. Then we read until the afternoon meal at about two. After lunch, we play poker for three or four hours, using dominoes for chips. Each day we redistribute the chips equally and begin a new game. One would think we were playing for high stakes, judging by the seriousness of the bidding and the play.

We limit our discussions of our circumstances to certain periods of the day, when each of us openly reveals things which may be bothering him. There's a splendid spirit of cooperation and mutual support among us. If I had had a choice, I could not have picked a better group of people to be with under these circumstances. Don and I are old friends by now — closer than two brothers could ever expect to be. I understand him, his moods, his strengths and weaknesses, and he knows more about me than anyone I've ever known. Dick is a solid, easygoing man with a good intellect and a strong personality. I find his assessment of our situation mature and logical. Regis Ragan is a tough, bright, dedicated man with an unusual gift of faith. I'd do anything for any of them, and I know they would for me.

Our treatment by our captors has changed dramatically for the better. We're being well fed, compared to our long months on the high-carbohydrate, low-protein diet. About twice a week, we're given a hard-boiled egg to supplement our bread and tea in the morning. The mid-afternoon meals have been exceptionally good — spaghetti and meat sauce (heated), hamburgers, lasagna, or even a freezer-burned steak once in a while. In the evening, we have the standard soup and bread, but it's usually supplemented with leftovers from the earlier meal or with cheese and fresh oranges or apples.

Ahmad sends his guards around almost every day to get a list of things we need. We call it our "dream list." I always start my list with the number one and write the word *azade* [freedom] in Farsi next to it. So far, that request has not been honored, but the guards understand what I'm saying, and when we go over the list with them, some say,

"Not yet, Colonel, but maybe soon." Others say nothing, but in this way, we seem to get a pulse on the progress of negotiations. We list toothpaste, crackers, and other items on our daily list, and are provided about half of the items we request. Little Ali, the guard who visited me frequently in the cold interrogation room in the Mushroom Inn, seems to do the best job of filling our requests. I listed pretzels the other day, and he asked me to describe a pretzel to him. I knew there were cases of pretzels in the embassy cooperative, so I gave him a description of the box. Little Ali came through. After we ate the pretzels, though, we discovered both dead and living worms in the bottom of the box.

We take a hot shower almost every day after we exercise. I feel that I may be gaining back some of the weight I lost, and most of the time my spirits are higher than they've been since our imprisonment. Then there are those times when I realize that if we don't get out of here before Reagan takes the oath of office, we may be moved back to a prison.

Outside our window each morning, we hear laughter during recess at a nearby girls' school. In addition to play, the recesses are used for teaching revolutionary slogans. We hear these children screaming on cue, "Death to America! Death to Saddam Hussein!" and, in the last few days, "Death to Reagan!" If it is the policy of the government of Iran to instill that kind of hatred in children, then I wonder if they're serious about negotiating our release, or if they're playing the traditional Middle East game of bazaar bartering — hoping the other side will sweeten the pot and, when they do, raising the ante. It seems strange, but time is passing very slowly here, in spite of the additional companionship and the better treatment and living conditions. I guess it's because of the haunting realization that this time is so very critical, and any change in our treatment or our location now could signal an end to the crisis, in which case we all could be tried and executed or sentenced to long prison terms.

About once a week, we're moved to another room to view videotapes of old Super Bowl games. I'm not much of a football fan, but the others enjoy them very much. I watch them because it's an opportunity to see something of America and mentally escape from here for a little while.

January 19, 1981

Something is up . . . we can sense it. There is a lot of activity in the halls, and we wonder if we're going to be moved before Reagan takes office tomorrow because the Iranians are afraid of immediate military action. Shortly before breakfast, two guards come for me. I'm taken to another room on the same floor as our motellike cell. Ahmad is sitting at a table. He tells me to sit down.

"Colonel, do you know you may be put on trial as a war criminal because of your crimes in Vietnam?"

"Yes, Ahmad, we have been over all this a hundred times. When is my trial?" My tone is nonchalant, but I fear a serious answer.

"It depends on you. Right now you are a candidate for release."

"When?" My pulse quickens and I wonder if this is another of Ahmad's cruel games.

"Today, if you will do exactly as you are told to do and not give the doctors who are going to examine you, or the lady who will interview you on TV, a difficult time. If you do not cooperate, then you will go on trial."

I can tell Ahmad is trying to intimidate me. I know if there is to be a release, it's out of his hands. So I decide to jostle him one more time.

"Well, then, I guess I'm not going home."

His face reddens instantly. "You are a son of a bitch, Scott. We should have shot you long ago. I am trying to be nice to you. I am offering you a chance to go home."

"What do I have to do?"

"Just be nice and do not complain of your treatment here or say anything bad about us."

"You want me to lie; is that it?"

"If that is what it takes, yes. Do you want to be free or not?"

"Yes, I sure as hell do."

"Then I will recommend you as a candidate for release."

Ahmad acts as though he's having his last chance to lean on me, and he's still trying to impress me with his authority. I'm elated, so I decide not to rock the boat anymore. "Thanks, Ahmad, I appreciate your recommending me, as you say, as a candidate for release."

"You are welcome. It has not been so bad, has it?"

"No, Ahmad, I've enjoyed every minute of it. Thanks for making it all possible," I answer sarcastically.

"You will be taken back to your room now. Remember what I said — you must be nice."

"If it means getting out of here, I can be very nice."

As I enter our cell, Ragan is taken out. He returns in about thirty minutes. He gave Ahmad a hard time, refusing to be interviewed on TV, so Ahmad's goons punched him in the ribs and pushed him around — nothing that would leave any marks, but one last show of power. Regis is furious, but we tell him to cool it, that this may be the real thing, and there's no sense in getting himself in trouble at this late stage. Don and Dick, in turn, are taken to their meeting with Ahmad. Then we all excitedly discuss this latest turn of events.

Within an hour, the guards are back for me again. I'm taken downstairs to a room that has been set up for cursory physical examinations. The doctors are Algerian, and there also are Iranian nurses checking blood pressure, pulse, and other vital signs. The nurses are dressed in uniforms with bandanas covering their heads and most of their faces. I address an Algerian doctor in Arabic, asking him if it's finally going to end. He says it will be over soon. An Iranian militant cautions us to speak only in English. I wink at the doctor as I leave his station, and he gives me a thumbs-up.

Later in the afternoon, I'm led downstairs to a room that has been set up for TV interviews. A female Iranian militant in a black chador — we call her Black Mary — goes over the questions that I'll be asked in front of the camera. She says if there is a question I will not answer, or will not answer in a way that's acceptable to the Iranians, I must tell her now, before the actual interview begins. I tell her generally how I'll answer her questions.

The interview begins. She asks if I've turned against the Iranian people because of what has happened to me. I tell her that I've had a long and friendly association with the Iranian people, and the actions of terrorists have not changed the way I feel. My affinity for the people of Iran remains undaunted . . . in spite of my illegal detention for more than a year. That's not the answer I gave in our rehearsal. She is nonplussed, but she continues with her list of questions and I continue to deviate from the practiced replies.

When the interview is over, Black Mary is livid, although she maintained her composure very well for the cameras. She says I'm a liar and shouldn't be permitted to go home. I tell her I'm sorry I offended her, but I thought I should tell the truth.

When I'm returned to my cell, there's a copy of *Kayhan*, the local English-language newspaper, the first we've seen in fourteen months. The headline, in English, speaks of "the great Satan being brought to his knees by the will of the Iranian people." According to *Kayhan*, an agreement has been signed by both parties and we're to be released. Iran claims to have won a great victory over imperialism and the United States. Ahmad stops by our cell later in the afternoon and says nonchalantly that we may be going home tonight.

We wait in anticipation of the event for which we've prayed and hoped for so long. We're all talking at once, and the level of excitement is too high for us to relax, much less try to sleep.

Minutes and hours pass slowly; still there is no indication of a move. Exhausted from the excitement and anticipation, we decide to try to sleep. I hear Don snoring within fifteen minutes after we turn off the light, but I can't sleep. I've waited too long for this event. It must be about 3:00 A.M., and we still haven't moved. There are only a couple of hours left, because I'm sure they will not move us to the airport during daylight. Has something fallen through the cracks?

I'm first to awaken. I can see daylight through a tiny opening at the top of the drapes. Something happened — it didn't work out. We're still here. It is January 20. My whole body feels a flood of depression and helplessness that I know will destroy me if I don't get it under control. I think about the time difference between here and Washington. It's about midnight in Washington. The day of President Reagan's inauguration is just beginning. There's still time, but what the hell are these people waiting for? I mentally estimate the impact of the time difference on events here. When Reagan takes office, it will be 8:30 in the evening here. It will be dark. Are these dramatic, scheming people going to wait until after Reagan is in office before releasing us? Are they going to try to give Carter one last kick in the pants before they end this?

I've packed all my letters from home, and the ones from Americans I've never met, in a shoe box, on instructions from our captors. They say we can take nothing with us except our mail and the clothing we're wearing; our personal clothing and other items that we haven't seen since

386

the embassy attack will be sent to us later. I'm sure this is a lie, because I have seen some of my slacks and sweaters worn by our captors throughout our imprisonment. But those things are not important, anyway.

The day drags by. There's no further word on our release or anything else. Ahmad hasn't made an appearance all day. The only good sign we've had, and we're always alert for good signs, is that the usually fairly good midday meal was not served. Instead, we were given bread and cheese, as though they hadn't planned on our still being here.

At about 5:30, Ahmad appears and says we're leaving. Contrary to earlier statements, he confiscates our boxes of letters and says he'll send them to us. We're blindfolded and taken to a waiting commercial bus. We're told to be quiet and not to move around at all. I hear others being loaded, and I hear a few words in English from Bill Daugherty and Kate Koob. The bus must be filled, because now they're seating hostages on the floor in the center aisle. Finally we hear the engine start and the bus begins to move. God, is this a dream, or are we really headed to the airport?

The traffic is heavy — horns are honking under the hands of typically impatient Iranian drivers, anxious to get home after the day's work. We're going downhill most of the way, a good sign that we may be headed for the airport. Then we level out and there's less strain on the bus's engine. It seems that we're getting out of the heavier traffic and moving along a fairly good road. Then I hear jet engines warming up in the background over the noise of the bus. We're here.

We stop for a checkpoint and then move on. As we stop again, I hear a demonstration in progress all around our bus. The chants haven't changed: "Death to America! Death to Reagan! Death to the hostages!"

After thirty minutes of nervously sitting on the bus, the order is given to remove our blindfolds. It's like no reunion you've ever seen. We stumble over each other, laughing and crying at the same time. Hostages seek out friends whom they haven't seen in more than a year. There are hugs and kisses between tough, grown men, normally not given to this kind of emotional outburst. The Iranians tell us to sit down and be quiet, but their orders are useless. Finally they give up and just watch our outburst of warmth and excitement.

The noise inside the bus competes with the noisy demonstrators outside, making it almost impossible for the orders and instructions from our captors to be heard. Finally, the bus door is opened and we're told to move out single file. I catch a glimpse of a waiting Algerian jet. There are men in civilian clothes standing in the door at the top of the ramp, waiting for us to board. Around the aircraft, Algerian security men with automatic weapons at the ready peer intently into the crowd of demonstrators, who have come to vent their hatred of America one last time.

The single file of weary hostages begins the walk through the tunnel of shouting and menacing Iranians, from the bus to the jet airplane. Some of the hostages in the front are punched and poked by the volatile demonstrators as they move cautiously toward the plane.

Then it's my turn to walk the gauntlet. It has been a long ordeal, and I decide to march this final distance as a soldier. I pull my shoulders back, look beyond my tormentors toward the waiting Algerian diplomats, my eyes straight to the front, my head held high, and march between the lines of taunting rabble. Out of the corner of my eye, I see young Iranians moving back slightly to permit me to pass. *"On Sarbaz ast!"* [That one is a soldier!], I hear one of the Iranians caution his fellows. Not one of the militants forming the tunnel touches me or gets in the way as I proudly march toward my destination. I climb toward the ramp, my heart racing in realization of this precious moment, and board the aircraft. Ambassador Gheraieb welcomes me aboard. Muhammad Bel Hossein says to me in Arabic, "I told you it would be soon."

The others board and we sit and wait. The noise level is beyond belief as we continue to greet each other and compare notes on our four hundred and forty-four days as hostages.

"Let's get this bird in the air!" I hardly realize I've spoken until I hear my own voice. I'm concerned that some opposition group may try to destroy our aircraft before we can get off the ground. I know that we won't be safe until we take off and fly beyond Iranian air space.

Three beautiful Algerian stewardesses move up and down the aisle, checking our seat belts. They're smiling and friendly, looking so very lovely in their smart uniforms. I turn to Tom Schaefer, who is seated behind me, and tell him that I think I'm falling in love. He says he already has — three times. There's a chorus of "Amens," as some of the others overhear my comment and Tom's. We've all fallen in love, at least three times, and we're not even off the ground. We all laugh, conscious of our long period without the things that make life pleasurable.

It is five minutes past nine in the evening as we finally hear the engines revving for takeoff. My mind races to Washington. It is thirty-five minutes after noon on the East Coast. We should have a new president by now.

We're off the ground. There are cheers from all the hostages — no, it dawns on me, we now are "ex-hostages." God, that sounds so good. As we climb to cruising altitude and head north, I know we're the happiest people on the face of this earth.

My thoughts are of home and freedom as I await the signal that officially will end our ordeal — word that we are out of Iranian air space.

18

IN THE SKY ABOVE TURKEY
JANUARY 20, 1981

"Ladies and gentlemen, we have just cleared Iranian airspace. Welcome back to freedom!"

With these words, the Iranian hostage crisis is history. We are free! After four hundred and forty-four days of constant terror, darkness, isolation, and seemingly endless uncertainty, we're finally going home.

Thank You, God. Thank you, America. It's finally over. Over!

I try to isolate my feelings and put them into words: Relief. Joy. Appreciation. A deep sense of pride in being an American. Humility. Reverence. And an eerie feeling of resurrection. Yes, that's it — I feel as though I've been born again. What a wonderful, sublimely beautiful feeling.

Above the chatter and merrymaking of my fellow ex-hostages, I hear corks popping from chilled bottles of vintage French champagne. Our three lovely Algerian stewardesses are moving happily up and down the aisle, pouring the bubbly beverage of celebration into our waiting glasses. It's a carnival atmosphere, as it has been since we soared skyward from Tehran's Mehrabad International Airport an hour and a half ago.

In my comfortable airline seat, ready to take my first sip of champagne, I recall an agreement that Don and I made several days ago, when our release began to appear possible. It seems so silly now. We agreed not to have a drink until we were reunited with our families. Rising from my plush seat, I look for Don. We spot each other simultaneously. Don also has a glass of champagne.

"What do you say, Don? Should we disregard our earlier chatter and have a drink?"

Don's reply is short and final. "Come on, Chuck, you should know by now that my word is no good. Here's looking at you."

We both laugh as we sip our first drink in a long, long time.

Bruce Laingen proposes a toast to the Algerians, who worked so tirelessly to make our dream of freedom a reality. Then we toast the United States of America and the American people. Bruce, who spent all but the last few days of our captivity at the Iranian Ministry of Foreign Affairs, says our government never forgot us, and that the American people prayed for us and kept us constantly in their hearts. I wonder if the American people really cared about us, or if Bruce's words are just another example of his diplomatic prowess.

After the toasts, the noise levels off to a stadium roar, and I have a few moments to look around at my compatriots. I didn't realize how much this ordeal had taken out of me until I looked at them. They're a haggard, pale, sloppy-looking band of survivors, and I know I'm a mirror image of them. I haven't seen most of them in more than a year. I can't get over how much they've aged. I guess I have, too, but I really don't know . . . or care. My deepest thoughts are not of my physical appearance, or of anything as mundane as getting a haircut or trying to spruce up my clothing; I'm just glad to be here. Fourteen months ago, I wrote myself off for dead as a psychological defense against the terror and boredom of my hostage existence. That ordeal is only a bad dream now, as I anticipate my return to freedom.

Ann Swift, seated in front of me, turns and asks if I used to own a Rolex GMT Master. I figure she's going to make a joke of my losing one of my prized possessions. It would be right in character. I tell her my watch was taken from me early on, and that I expect never to see it again. She smiles and says that Kate Koob was given a watch several months ago by one of our captors, and she thinks it might be mine. I unfasten my seat belt and look for Kate Koob. She's seated three rows behind me.

"Hi, Kate, I understand you have a Rolex watch."

Kate smiles as she holds her left arm up, unfastens the watch, and passes it up to me. The bezel is badly faded, and the crystal is scratched from years of wear. It's my watch — no question about it. I thank her for giving it to me, and then I thank her for taking good care of it. We all laugh. How ironic: My only personal possession to survive fourteen and a half months with our light-fingered jailers is the one item which I would have most preferred to have returned. From now on, it'll be my good-luck charm.

I feel a sense of pride in being with this group. I think about Kate and Ann, two of the toughest, most wonderful women I've ever known. I see Tom Ahern, Bill Daugherty, Billy Gallegos, Bob Ode, Sam Gillette, Don, Al, and all the others who have made it through this traumatic year without losing their sense of humor or their dignity. There are at least ten small groups engaged in animated discussions of the ordeal we've experienced, where we're going, what we can expect there. And there is excited talk of America and the final return to our loved ones.

Bruce calls for quiet and we comply, after a fashion. He says we'll be landing first in Athens, Greece; then in Algiers, where we will be turned over to the U.S. government; then on to West Germany and a few days in a military hospital at Wiesbaden. Then we'll fly to an unannounced destination in the States for a reunion with our families, before we go to Washington for a special ceremony at the White House. We all cheer, but there are questions about the duration of the hospital stay. Some want to go home as quickly as jets can fly them. Personally, I'm resigned to spending a few days in the hospital before I return to Atlanta. I realize that I may not be in as good a shape as I think I am. Besides . . . if there's one thing I have learned during the past year, it's to be patient. There is so much catching up to do. The time passes quickly, and before I realize it the pilot announces that we soon will be landing in Athens.

On arrival, we're required to remain aboard the aircraft. Although it's late, there are people everywhere with welcome signs in English — the entire American community in Athens has turned out in the middle of the night to greet us. We're not even home yet, and there are cheering crowds welcoming us.

I recall the elderly woman protester who hit me with her purse when I returned from combat duty in Vietnam. The Vietnam War was unpopular and divisive, but as a professional soldier, I understood what was going on and learned to live with it. Perhaps that homecoming made me cynical. I don't really expect to be welcomed home with ruffles and flourishes this time, either, but I do hope people will not look down on us because we surrendered the embassy. We had no choice, and I honestly believe that we made the best of a very bad situation. Despite this Athens greeting, I'm not sure how we'll be received by the American people. In fact, I'm not even sure how I'll be greeted by my own family.

We're airborne again, this time destined for Algiers. I'm tired, but there's no time to sleep with all the excitement. It's going to be a long night, but one I know I'll remember and cherish always.

Charlie Jones, the only black American who was not released early in the crisis, walks down the aisle greeting friends. One of the Marines yells at him, "Hey, Charlie, how does it feel to be white?" Charlie roars with laughter and the rest of us join in. He is a very special person: He never let the Iranians get to him with their racially oriented propaganda.

As we land at the Algiers airport and taxi toward the main passenger terminal, I see large crowds again. Camera flashes are popping everywhere. We get last-minute instructions to let the two ladies and Bruce Laingen deplane first. Then it's first come, first off. Don Sharer and I have donned the red T-shirts with American eagles that were handed out the first Christmas. I remember Akbar's finding me another shirt after mine was taken during the second mock execution. I think of Akbar at this moment, and I wonder how he's doing. With the war and all the political intrigues in his country, how long will he survive without being shot by either the Iraqis or some opposition faction? I wish him well.

These red T-shirts, Don and I agreed, were to be our "uniform" if we ever returned to freedom. Praise God, we pulled it off, and (with a little help from Akbar) we're wearing them now! We want the world to see that we're still proud to be Americans. I fall in behind Vic Tomseth, the senior political officer who was with Bruce at the Foreign Ministry throughout most of our ordeal. Malcolm Kalp, who was accused of being a spy and consequently spent more than a year in solitary, is behind me as we descend the ramp to the tarmac amid a panoply of flashing lights, American and Algerian flags, and excited greetings from well-wishers.

We're escorted inside the terminal to a large reception room. I see Deputy Secretary of State Warren Christopher in the receiving line. There are bright TV lights and cameras everywhere. It's exciting, but my thoughts are not here. I'm already home, wondering what it will be like to wander around the house again, drink an early-morning cup of coffee, and go outside any time I want to get the morning paper.

Christopher looks almost as tired as we do, but

he's neatly dressed and well groomed. He speaks, praising the successful Algerian efforts in securing the agreement for our release. Then he officially announces his acceptance of us, on behalf of the United States, from the Algerians. It all sounds tremendous to me, but I feel like an expensive piece of property which has just been transferred from one owner to another. He promises that we'll receive a tremendous welcome when we return to America, and he says the American people have prayed for us throughout our imprisonment. He adds that we are considered heroes at home. I still wonder about that. I hear the words, but I guess they don't really sink into my happy but tired brain.

I have orange juice and cookies, then decide to have a cup of coffee. This is all too exciting and interesting to sleep through, and I know the coffee will help keep me awake. It's delicious — my first cup in more than a year. It's beginning to register: I'm really free and on the way home.

I feel composed and at ease, in spite of the excitement. We're asked to move outside to our aircraft for the trip to Germany. Two beautiful United States Air Force C-9 medical evacuation jets, brightly painted with "United States of America" markings and a huge Red Cross on the tail, await us. The flight and medical crews greet us warmly. They're as excited as we are, having waited for this mission for more than a year.

They seem to have thought of everything — I never have been treated so royally on any flight. We're served a delicious steak dinner, and each of us is presented a brand-new Air Force arctic parka. The head nurse, Major Toni Garner, shows me a stainless-steel bracelet with "Colonel Chuck Scott — Free the Hostages" engraved on it. It's a hostage bracelet. She says they're very much in vogue in America, but I wonder if she's just being polite. I haven't seen anything like this since the Vietnam era. Toni's eyes dance as she tries to prepare me for my return to America. "Wait until you get home; they're going to go wild when all of you return." I think she's overestimating the magnitude of our welcome.

I notice that the tempo of activity has subsided; it's relatively quiet for the first time since we left Tehran. I decide to close my eyes and join the others in trying to get some rest before we land at Rhein Main Airport.

Bill Daugherty nudges me awake and says we'll be landing in a few minutes.

It's about an hour before daylight as we deplane. The heavy parkas feel good in the cold night air of West Germany. I notice that we're on the military side of the airfield. The "Gateway to Europe" sign on the main building, below the tower, is unchanged since my last visit here, but there are giant new signs everywhere: "Welcome back to freedom," and "Welcome back home." There are smiling faces painted over the letter *o* on most of the signs. We board buses for the twenty-five-mile trip to the hospital at Wiesbaden. Although the weather is bitterly cold and dark, crowds of normally unemotional Germans line our route ten deep. They wave American and German flags, and many hold signs welcoming us. Seeing these happy people sharing in the joy of our release is almost too much for me.

As we approach the Wiesbaden Kaserne, where the hospital is located, there are crowds and welcome signs everywhere. When we enter the gate and pull up in front of the hospital, I see a huge hand-painted sign draped from the second floor porch: "WELCOME TO THE FREEDOM HOTEL."

Inside the hospital, I'm assigned a semi-private room with Colonel Lee Holland, the Army attaché. I haven't seen him since we were moved out of the Mushroom Inn for passing information to the other hostages in March. I'm sent to an Air Force flight surgeon, who gives me the most thorough physical examination I've ever had. Then I'm assigned what the Department of State calls "a dedicated psychiatrist," an Army lieutenant colonel. We're required to complete a battery of psychological tests — four hours of multiple-choice questions. It's hard to answer many of the questions; it's been a long time since any of us made any decisions at all. Some of the younger ex-hostages seem to have even more difficulty concentrating on the test. I persist in spite of my trouble, figuring that if I didn't let the Iranians break me with physical abuse and isolation, I'm certainly not going to allow a bearded State Department psychiatrist to grind me down at this stage of the game.

During the day, we're visited by VIPs from all over Germany. We're presented with books and other gifts from the mayors of major German cities, and we enjoy excellent food in the hospital dining hall. Word is that lobsters are being flown in from Boston for our meal tomorrow evening. From the hospital commander to the lowest-ranking airman, our welfare and comfort is a top-priority mission.

On this first night of freedom, we also will be visited by former president Jimmy Carter and former Secretary of State Cyrus Vance.

It's a tense and emotion-filled meeting. I wonder how we'll react to the presence of our former Commander-in-Chief — the man who admitted the Shah to the United States, thereby setting the stage for the outpouring of Iranian hostility that led to our imprisonment. Many of the embassy staff blame Carter for the whole thing. I did, too, at first, but time heals many wounds. I have sensed President Carter's dilemma this past year from my prison cell, and I know, realistically, that there was little he could do to achieve our release once the embassy fell. I think he has demonstrated great courage and patience in working for our eventual freedom. It may have even cost him his political career. As a professional soldier, I must show proper respect to my Commander-in-Chief. But I wonder how the others will act, and what he'll say to us at this awkward moment.

We're assembled in a large room, awaiting the former president's arrival.

I can feel the tension as Carter is announced and enters the room. He moves directly to the front and faces our U-shaped gathering. We remain silent and reserved. The president begins to speak.

"It's a great honor for me, on behalf of the American people and our new President Reagan, to welcome you back to freedom." The president says that he knows that we haven't been kept informed of the feelings of the American people or the efforts to win our release, but that more prayers have been offered for our health and safety in the past four hundred and forty-four days than at any time in the history of our country. He congratulates us on the way we conducted ourselves during the ordeal, and informs us that we're considered heroes by the people at home. He also mentions the courage shown by our families, and he accepts full responsibility for all the decisions made by our government.

Many of our group have said they will not shake hands with President Carter. I wonder, as I look around the room, if they still feel the same way after hearing him bare his soul. I don't, but the point is academic anyway — there is no hand-shaking. After a few moments of clumsy silence, Carter and Bruce Laingen embrace like two long-lost friends, and the rest of us follow suit.

When my turn comes to meet President Carter, he greets me by name. We're both too choked up to talk. We embrace warmly and all the frustration, anxiety, and hatred of the past fourteen and a half months are drained from me, replaced by a feeling of mutual respect that comes only when two people have survived an ordeal together. In a very real sense, our nation and our president were held hostage along with the fifty-two of us. Considering the hostility he must have expected, Carter's visit took considerable courage.

Twenty direct overseas telephones have been set

up in an empty room for us to call our families in America. They've been busy since the moment of our arrival. Finally, I get my turn to call home.

My talk to Betty, Beth, and Greg is lighthearted — small talk for the most part. I try to remember important things I've promised myself for months that I would not forget if I lived to make this call, but they don't seem as important now. I tell Betty that I already know about the ceremony at the White House when we return, but as soon as it's over, I want to slip back to my home unnoticed. I ask her to bring my civilian clothes for me when she meets me either in Washington or at West Point, where the families are to be reunited.

Betty can't believe I'm so ill-informed. She laughs and says the people of Georgia will not let me sneak back home. They're planning a press conference and a giant welcome-home ceremony. Throughout the conversation, however, I sense that there's something she's not telling me. I ask if she and the children are really O.K., and she assures me they're fine. Our little dachshund, Heidi, is also in good health. I ask other questions, but all her answers are positive. Still, I perceive that all is not well at home. Maybe it's just the tension of this first call. I hope that's all.

My doctor says I'm generally in good health, and the "dedicated psychiatrist" has submitted a written evaluation on my mental state in which he says that I'm probably about as sane now as when I accepted the assignment to Iran. I'm not sure I find that comforting at all.

We say goodbye to Toni and the rest of the wonderful hospital staff and prepare to leave. I have a new uniform, compliments of the U.S. Army, and two hundred dollars in my pocket — advance pay which we all received. After a physical, temporary dental work to patch damage suffered during my interrogation, a haircut, and plenty of good food, I feel human again.

We board a beautiful Air Force plane, christened Freedom One, and take off for Stewart Air Force Base. I'm composed and feeling great.

We stop for about two hours in Shannon, Ireland, where we're greeted by the Prime Minister and members of the Irish Parliament and shop in the duty-free shops at the Shannon Airport. The shops have been closed to all other customers. I don't buy anything, because I'm too engrossed in conversation with the friendly Irish politicians. Finally, we're off the ground again, en route to the United States.

It's the most memorable flight of my life, even more exciting and memorable than my return from Vietnam. As we approach the coast of the United States, the pilot connects his FAA control radio to the internal aircraft communications system, so we can hear his instructions from the control tower.

"Freedom One, this is Bangor FAA control. You have just entered American airspace. Welcome home to freedom. On behalf of all Americans, we congratulate you on a job well done."

My eyes mist as the cheers of the ex-hostages fill the cabin of Freedom One. I'm proud. I'm happy. I'm home.

I look for Betty and the children in the crowd of anxious relatives. I spot her and make it through the crowd to where she's standing. We kiss and embrace for a long time before I ask her about Beth and Greg. She decided to have them wait in Washington, so we could have some time alone.

The cheering crowds that lined our route from Stewart Air Force Base to West Point create images of patriotism and love in my heart that never shall be erased. Betty is with me as I enter the Cadet Chapel at West Point for a special service of thanksgiving for our deliverance, and a memorial service for the eight servicemen who gave their lives last April at Tabas, in the Iranian desert, in the attempt to rescue us. The chapel is crowded for the joyful but solemn service. I say a prayer for those brave men who volunteered to take part in the rescue attempt. They understood the risks involved, yet they persisted anyway. They are the heroes of this crisis — there's no question about it. I sit with my head bowed and my eyes closed. After about five minutes, I gaze up at the sanctuary of this beautiful chapel, with its splendid pews and ornate stained-glass windows. It's a clear, cold day; the sun's rays beam through the windows behind the pulpit, bathing the chapel in a serene glow of natural light. And then at this emotional moment, I see three simple words inscribed in the stained glass above the pulpit — three words that mean everything to me; three words that give meaning and purpose to all we have endured; the same three words that were on my lips, giving me strength and endurance and a sense of purpose, during the most harrowing moments of my military service, and especially during the past fourteen months.

Duty. Honor. Country.

Tears well in my eyes, blurring my vision. I reflect on these words and on the America we have come home to. It's no longer the bitterly divided America of the Vietnam era. There's a new sense of patriotism, a revitalization of the American spirit of unity. I don't know how long this renaissance of patriotism will endure, but it's tremendously uplifting and inspiring to me. It's the fulfillment of a dream born during the Vietnam War, when the old woman attacked me with her purse. I prayed then that I would live to see an America as united as the one I grew up in during World War II, an America where love of country and plain, old-fashioned patriotism would be in vogue. I don't know what has happened to cause this change in our country, but I do know that it surely will improve the image of America abroad. It will serve as a warning to our adversaries that they're no longer dealing with the divided America of the Vietnam era. I'm elated by the changes I've seen in less than twenty-four hours on American soil. And if, in some small way, the ordeal in Iran contributed to this change in America, then it all was worth it.

EPILOGUE

ATLANTA, GEORGIA
NOVEMBER 4, 1983

Exactly four years ago, the Tehran embassy attack sent shock waves around the world. For all of us who lived through that experience, November 4 always will be a day for sober reflection and prayers of thanksgiving. After being updated on events outside our cloistered cells during those perilous four hundred and forty-four days, I realized, even more than I did during the crisis, the precariousness of our situation. It was a miracle that we finally were released alive.

I offer my personal gratitude to those who worked so hard to make our dream of freedom a reality: President Jimmy Carter, Deputy Secretary of State Warren Christopher, the Algerian government, the American news media, and the courageous men who volunteered for the ill-fated rescue mission in April, 1980. All played significant roles in resolving the crisis.

But the lion's share of the credit for our safe return from bondage — in a land where political murder is in vogue, if not endemic — must go to the American people. I never will forget their sustained determination and interest throughout our long ordeal. Amid all the frustration and anger, Americans showed great patience and a stoic commitment to our safe return.

When we returned home, I was inspired by the great spiritual strength of America. It wasn't something new; I just hadn't realized it before Iran. In the thousands of letters I received during those first months home, one theme was almost universal: Americans of all religious denominations prayed for us and believed that our safe return was God's answer to their prayers. In my heart, I know they were right. I could feel the strength of those prayers, even during the most harrowing moments of my captivity.

After meeting with President Reagan, attending the welcome ceremony at the White House, and being thrilled by all the fanfare in Washington, I opted to skip the ticker-tape parade in New York and return to my home in Georgia. My welcome here was a tremendous outpouring of love, emotion, and patriotism. I was not prepared for the many honors or the deep affection that came my way. I repeated over and over again, I was not a hero. I was only a victim — a man in the wrong place at the wrong time — but my utterances had little impact as the celebration continued. I believe that I looked at it all very realistically: I wasn't being honored; the American people were using their returned hostages as symbols to express their resurrected love for America and all that she represents. That perspective helped me to make the transition to normalcy when the outpouring of admiration had subsided, and I was once again just another member of my community.

I am asked frequently if the former hostages keep in touch. Many people seem to think we have an ex-hostage club, where we meet periodically to discuss "old times." Nothing could be more off the mark. While we always will share a bond of mutual respect and admiration, we each have gone our separate ways.

Commander Don Sharer, my cellmate, has been promoted to Captain. After serving as a squadron commander on an aircraft carrier, he is now the ship's operations officer. He's doing very well. We always will keep in touch.

Sam Gillette is a college student in Pennsylvania. He has married and will be commissioned in the Navy after graduation.

L. Bruce Laingen, our Chargé who spent all but

the last three weeks of the crisis at the Iranian Ministry of Foreign Affairs, under a form of house arrest, is now the Deputy Commandant of the National Defense University in Washington.

Both Kate Koob and Ann Swift are in school in Washington, preparing for another assignment abroad.

Al Golacinski is with the White House Security Service. Tom Ahern is working at the State Department in Washington, along with Bill Daugherty and many of the others. Colonel Lee Holland is commander of a small Army post in Virginia. Colonel Tom Schaefer recently retired from the U.S. Air Force and lives in Tacoma, Washington. We chat from time to time.

Sergeant Major Regis Ragan is working at the Army War College in Pennsylvania. We also keep in touch.

Joe Subic is no longer in the military services. He was the only hostage not decorated for his conduct in Iran.

Except for what I read in an occasional news article, I have lost touch with the others.

Hossein (The Tooth) Sheikholislam, who was a leader of the initial assault on our embassy, is now in a key position in the Iranian Foreign Ministry.

Hojat al-Islam Ali Hussein Khamene'i, the Tehran prayer leader and Deputy Minister of Defense who visited me in Tabriz, is now the president of the Islamic Republic of Iran.

I have heard unofficially through friends that General Sayas finally got his green card and now lives in the United States.

Luigi is the cook for the Danish ambassador to Italy.

Akbar wrote to me in July of 1981. He asked about Don Sharer and the others and said he wanted to send me a letter of congratulations on the occasion of my return to freedom, but he was "a little bit afraid and hesitated." He

said it was still hard for him to bear the loss of his friends
Fazollah and Hossein, who were killed in the war with Iraq.
He wrote that he had been at the war front for a short time
and that "every day a large number of people were being
killed and injured." I answered his letter, enjoining him to
stay as far from the fighting as possible. I told him that one
day his country will need men of his courage and
understanding.

On the personal side, I retired from the Army
within a few months of my return. I had more than thirty-one
and a half years in uniform. After the Iran experience, I
knew that I wouldn't be content in a routine assignment, and
I had vowed never to be an old colonel waiting for mandatory retirement.

In spite of the honors and recognition that high-
lighted my homecoming, my first year back was not without
heartbreak and disappointment. Betty and I agreed to a
divorce. It was the most difficult decision I have ever had to
make. We had grown apart. It wouldn't be fair to say anything else — that part of my life always will be very personal. In retrospect, the ordeal in Iran must have been God's
way of preparing me for the loneliness and despair I lived
through during the breakup of our marriage.

Just when I needed her most, I met Kathy, to
whom this book is dedicated. Without her faith, love, encouragement, and strength, this book never would have been
written. We happily celebrated our first wedding anniversary last month.

Sunrises and sunsets have never been more
beautiful, and I'm still mesmerized by the line where the
trees meet the sky. My time as a hostage was a time for
gathering strength. I learned many things about myself and
about the indomitable human spirit. I'm still very proud of
my America and her great people.

History is always the best indicator of the future. After Khomeini is gone and the frenzied Iranian hatred

of America loses some of its momentum, men like Akbar and myself may have an opportunity to sit face to face to discuss a new relationship between our two countries. Iran is strategically important to the Free World, and I never have believed in burning my bridges behind me.

Meanwhile, my faith in God is stronger than ever, and I look to the future with my customary romantic optimism.